W9-CFL-109

THE CLASSICAL CD LISTENER'S GUIDE

by Howard J. Blumenthal

To: Jim

From:

Billboard Books
An imprint of Watson-Guptill Publications/New York

For my wife and children, who put their lives on hold so I could listen to music.

Senior Editor: Bob Nirkind
Managing Editor (Logical Extension, Ltd.): Sharon Blumenthal
Design: Howard J. Blumenthal
Jacket Design: Barbour Design

First published in 1998 by Billboard Books, an imprint of Watson-Guptill Publications, a division of BPI Communications, Inc., 1515 Broadway, New York, NY 10036

Library of Congress Cataloging-in-Publication Data

Library of Congress Cataloging-in-Publication Data for this titlecan be obtained from the Library of Congress.
ISBN 0-8230-7676-8
                        97-40493
                        CIP
                        MN
Manufactured in the United States of America
First printing, 1998

1 2 3 4 5 6 7 8 9 / 06 05 04 03 02 01 00 99 98

Introduction

The term "classical music" has been stretched thin—it's an umbrella term that covers about 800 years of mostly European musical history. The focus of this book is more limited; its begins in the mid-1600s with Vivaldi and Purcell, emphasizes the 1800s (when most of the best-known classical music was created), and provides a reasonable view of 20th century music, and classical music created in the U.S. Composers like Amy Beach and William Grant Still get the space they deserve.

For purely mercantile reasons, a relatively small group of famous works get the majority of attention from record companies and retailers. You'll find just about every important classical work described here with a recommendation for a particular recording. And, you'll find a suggestion for further listening, called a "LINK." Some links are CDs by the same composer, while others are alternative recordings of the same symphony or chamber work. Some links are simply suggestions for further recordings in a similar style.

With hundreds and hundreds of classical composers to choose from, subjective decisions were inevitable. Why Walter Piston but not Roger Sessions? Why Alfred Schnittke but not Erich Korngold? There is no universal answer besides the author's need to fit a whole lot of great music into about 200 pages. Most notable composers are represented in a main entry or a link. A handful of notable performers also get their own pages, too. (And don't just skip past the biographies; many of these life stories out-do anything in today's tabloids!)

Arranged alphabetically by composer, this book should be a useful companion for record store visits. Each composer's entry includes reviews of recordings written by the author; everything here is the opinion of one person who took the time to listen.

I sincerely hope you find this book useful. Writing this book has been a pleasure.

Howard J. Blumenthal
November, 1998

Listening setup:

Loudspeakers: Thiel 3.6
CD player: Meridian 508.20
Pre-amplifier: Balanced Audio Technology VK-3i
Amplifier: Balanced Audio Technology VK-200
Loudspeaker cables: Cardas Golden Cross
Interconnect Cables: Cardas Golden Cross

Acknowledgments

I'm grateful to the many record company publicists who helped in every conceivable way, and also to friends who encouraged me and offered their own opinions in order to guide me. These people include:

- Ron Goldberg
- Giora Chamizer
- Oliver Goodenough
- Charles Nordlander
- Laurence Vittes - NAXOS
- The Staff of Record Archive, Rochester, NY
- Dan Kessler - London Records
- Lisa Krorr - Atlantic Records
- Brian Drutman- PolyGram Classics
- Carol Della Penna- PolyGram Classics
- Glen Petry - PolyGram Classics
- Gerfried Horst - Deutsche Grammophon Gesellschaft
- Philicia Gilbert- Polygram, BMG
- Dan Marx - Denon
- Gary Lipton - Qualiton
- Juan Gomez - Harmonia Mundi
- Sarah Folger - Harmonia Mundi
- Forrest Faubion - Allegro
- David Farneth - Kurt Weill Foundation
- Giel Bessels - Philips Music Group
- Karel Husa
- Rudi Simpson - Delos

- Arthur Moorhead - Atlantic Records
- Roger Evans - Angel/EMI
- Tina Pelikan - ECM/BMG
- Susan Schiffer - SONY Classical
- Amy Kolker - SONY Classical
- Esther Won - SONY Classical
- Tony Scafide - KOCH
- Jeanne McCafferty - Berlin Classics
- Kelly Hong - PolyGram Classics
- Irene Malacos - Atlantic Classics & Delos
- Karin Heurling - Svensk Musik
- Anthony J. Day
- Sir Malcolm Arnold, CBE
- Debbie Ferraro-Smith - Nonesuch
- Paul Tai - New World
- Jennifer Percibale - (formerly) EMI
- Lynn Joiner - Northeastern
- Melanne Mueller - BMG
- Peter Elliot - Nimbus
- Jessica Corbin- BMG
- Philip Cassese - Arabesque
- Joseph Dalton- CRI
- Valerie Thorson - Telarc
- Vicki Rickman - Telarc

I'm also thankful to Apple Computer for the invention of the Newton; about 1/3 of this book was written on the road, using that remarkable product's handwriting recognition.

John Adams

New Englander John Adams, born in 1947, combines minimalism, popular culture, folk, and religious themes in very original ways. He's the son of a saxophone player who encouraged exposure to many types of music, including classical, jazz, and pop. A graduate of Harvard, Adams experienced the changes of the 1960s in a direct and visceral way. After studying with John Cage, he went to San Francisco and immersed himself in radically new musical ideas with Terry Riley, Philip Glass, Steve Reich, and others who were experimenting with musical form, content, instrumentation, and acoustics. The 1970s were spent composing mostly instrumental works. Adams slowly gained popularity with audiences who were curious about new, serious music. By the 1980s, the effort was paying off as forward-thinking opera companies staged his *Nixon in China* and *The Death of Klinghoffer*. Both works were based on contemporary political and social issues; they expanded the definition of opera.

Violin Concerto; Shaker Loops – Gidon Kremer (violin), London Sym. Orch. / Kent Nagano; Orch. of St. Luke's / John Adams   Nonesuch 79360

Shaker Loops evolved over six years, from 1977 until 1983. It started as a minimalist string quartet, then thickened to embrace emotion as well as oscillation, and was eventually orchestrated for strings. Frequently performed and heard on the *Barfly* soundtrack, its nervous frenzy and imitations of tape loops are interesting mainly to see where Adams began. With Kremer as soloist, 1993's Violin Concerto is wholly different. Its first movement is lyrical, somewhat dissonant, and only vaguely related to repeated rhythm patterns. The second movement is slow and introspective, with ambient accompaniment. The peppy third movement successfully combines the rhythmic concepts of minimalism with modern romance. It's fascinating.

LINK➤ *Jean Barraqué – Oevres complètes*   *CPO 999-569*
Barraqué (1928–1973) defines modern classical music by challenging assumptions relating to noise vs. music, the use of time and space, and coherency. There's a romantic underpinning to his work, notably parts of ". . .au delà du hasard," but there's also tumult. Not well known in the U.S.

Harmonium – SF Sym. Orch. / Edo de Waart   ECM New Series 21277

Harmonium, according to Adams, "began with a simple, totally formed mental image: that of a single tone emerging out of a vast, empty space, and by means of a gentle unfolding, evolving into a rich, pulsating fabric of sound." The composer's words minimize the work's impact. Oscillating choral pulses are surrounded by majestic fanfares and climactic associations of orchestra and chorus. The music features superbly contoured peaks and peaceful valleys. That's the first part, based on poet John Donne's "Negative Love." The second, based on two Emily Dickinson poems, is characterized by somber, hymnlike music. This is in sharp contrast with the unbridled orchestral sex and violence of "Wild Night." Debuted in 1981.

LINK➤ *Lou Harrison – Piano Concerto, Suite for Violin, Piano & Small Orchestra – Keith Jarrett (piano), Lucy Stolzman (violin), New Japan Phil. Orch. / Naoto Otomo*
New World 366
Harrison was a generation before Adams, a talented innovator who based his outlook on the teachings of Henry Cowell and non-Western music. This, and the connection to Adams, can be heard in the very accessible violin-piano suite. Suberb use of instrument sounds.

Harmonielehre – City of Birmingham Sym. Orch. / Simon Rattle
EMI 55051

Harmonielehre, which borrows its title from a 1911 Schoenberg tonal harmony textbook, is one of the best symphonies in recent years. Composed in 1985, it breaks barriers. There is, for example, a tremendous orchestral cry of very apparent pain during "Part II: The Anfortas Wound." (It's a kick in the creative groin, in fact.) Minimalist cycling weaves in and out of Mahlerian symphonics during Part III. This is a remarkable, important work that demands attention. Compared with it, the kinetic "Short Ride in a Fast Machine" seems a novelty, but it's a serious modern celebration. "The Chairman Dances" imaginatively presents surreal themes later employed in *Nixon in China*.

LINK➤ *Robert Ashley – Improvement*　　　　　　　　　　**Nonesuch 79289**
Mostly a verbal theatrical experience, the clever transposition of words and phrases results in a musical experience. The traditional notion of music sometimes plays a part, but a hypnotizing use of sound in storytelling possesses its own special appeal.

Nixon in China – Orch. of St. Luke's / Edo de Waart　　　Nonesuch 79177
Director Peter Sellars brought Adams together with poet Alice Goodman to collaborate on an opera based upon contemporary history. They riff on personalities and caricatures, take liberties to poke fun, and somehow connect the dots to create a coherent, even captivating look at the events of 1972. The chorus greets the president with frenzied choral cycling, reaching a crescendo with "the people are the heroes now." Nixon fumbles as he sings of the event's importance as news. His wife, Pat, makes speeches during a sight-seeing aria. Henry Kissinger becomes part of a Chinese ballet. Mrs. Mao Tse-Tung sings a bel canto aria. Follow the libretto; it all makes musical sense. From 1987.

LINK➤ *Tan Dun – Symphony 1997: Heaven Earth Mankind – Yo-Yo Ma (cello), Yips Children's Choir, Imperial Bells Ensemble of China, Hong Kong Phil. Orch. / Tan Dun*
SONY Classical 63368
A celebration of Hong Kong's return to China unifying "the eternal and the external," this large-scale work combines Chinese and Western classical music in an engaging, joyous, coherent, often exciting whole. The combination of children's voices and ancient bells is especially striking.

Chamber Symphony, Grand Pianola Music – London Sinfonietta
Elektra 79219
It's not every composer who'd connect Schoenberg and soundtracks from hyperkinetic 1950s cartoons. Adams not only heard similarities, he made them work in his 1993 *Chamber Symphony*. The cross-fertilization is most clearly heard in the second movement ("Aria with Walking Bass") and in the random dancing and skating of the third movement ("Roadrunner"). Rewritten many times, *Grand Pianola Music* is often subtle. It's a minimalist pastoral landscape of winds and strings; sweet, wordless, vocal harmonies; and the delicacy of two grand pianos (plus a grazing tuba). As the piece progresses, it becomes a relentlessly modern blend of Chopin, Lizst, glib melodies, urban brawl, interstate speed racing, and aggressive minimalism.

LINK➤ *The American Innovator – Alan Feinberg (piano)*　　　　**Argo 436-925**
Adams in context. His short piece, Piano Gates, *is one of 17 by iconoclastic American modernists. Here's an ideal place to first experience Milton Babbitt, Henry Cowell, John Cage, Ralph Shapey, John Harbison, even Thelonious Monk. Feinberg is a clever, careful pianist.*

Isaac Albéniz

A prodigy, Albéniz learned the fundamentals of piano before he was a year old, and first performed publicly at age 4. Recognizing a good thing, his father put him on stage to earn some extra cash. By 1867, at age 7, his mother had taken the boy from their home in Caprodon, Spain, to Paris for studies. Despite praise for his talent, Albéniz was turned down because he was too young. Over the next few years, he ran away from home, performed in vaudeville, and stowed away on an Argentina-bound ship; he ended up in the U.S., working as a brothel pianist. Restless travel remained a constant, but Albéniz did settle down long enough to befriend or study with Liszt, Debussy, d'Indy, Dukas, and ultimately, Felipe Pedrill, who encouraged him to become a distinctively Spanish composer. A century later, Albéniz is remembered as exactly that. He died in 1909.

Iberia (Piano) – Alicia de Larrocha (piano)   London 417-887
This 2-CD set is the definitive statement of Albéniz's much-admired piano music. It's well recorded, and it contains *Iberia* in its entirety. De Larrocha is an amazingly articulate pianist who makes even the most difficult passages flow. Most importantly, she is able to evoke many of the same colors as the full orchestra, and in tones no less vivid. De Larrocha makes it easy to become lost in the bright colors, decorative patterns, and impressionist views of a Holy Week procession in Seville ("El Corpus Christi en Sevilla") and the Port of Santa Maria's Andalusian dances ("Triana") and Granada's Moorish district ("El Albacín"). *Iberia* was composed in parts between 1906 and 1909; the orchestrations followed.

LINK▶ *Enrique Granados – Goyescas – Alicia de Larrocha (piano)*   London 448-191
Where Albéniz was aggressive and vivid, the Spanish composer Granados was subtle and elegant, looking to Goya and Madrid for inspiration. Try also Reiner's orchestral version, which also includes Albéniz's Iberia, *and excerpts from Falla's* El Amor Brujo *(RCA 62586).*

Iberia (Complete) – Cincinnati Sym. Orch. /
Jesús López-Cobos   Telarc 80470

Although it's better known in suite form, *Iberia* deserves to be heard in its full 82-minute version. It's a travel essay told in four musical books, each with three sections. Albéniz offers an illustrated tour of Spain, complete with musical interpretations of the characters of various cities and towns. After a brief introduction, Albéniz visits Cádiz, where sunshine dances on the water and flamenco's spirit is born. Next is the joyful kaliedoscope of Madrid, with its street-life, classic architecture, churches, and bullfights. His exploration of gypsy life in Granada is intentionally abstract and complex—Albéniz rarely opts for the stereotypical answer. Medieval Jérez offers yet another view of Spain.

LINK▶ *Isaac Albéniz – Iberia Suite – The Philharmonia / Yan Pascal Tortelier*
                                                          Chandos 8904
This suite includes less than half of Iberia, *but it's a satisfying piece that's nicely performed here with spectacular engineering. The other benefit to this 1990 CD is Manuel de Falla's ballet score for* The Three-Cornered Hat, *a farcical love story set in a Spanish village.*

Hugo Alfvén

A beloved Swedish composer, Alfvén was born in 1872 in Stockholm. His father died in 1881, and his mother supported the family by running a grocery store. Alfvén spent summers with relatives on Stockholm's archipelago islands. During the 1880s, he studied with Johan Lindberg both at the conservatory and privately. The early 1890s were dominated by violin performances; the later 1890s saw the emergence of a major national composer. Alfvén's Symphony No. 2, completed in 1899, was the breakthrough; the next decade brought travel and and renown as a conductor. In 1904, Alfvén started what would become a half-century with the Siljan Choir (then called the Leksand). In 1910, he became conductor of Uppsala's male choir (known as OD, for Orphei Dränger); Alfvén continued until 1947. From 1916's *Sveriges Flagga*, celebrating Sweden's first flag day, to 1954's first stereophonic recording, Alfvén has been one of Sweden's finest. He died in 1960.

Sym. No. 2, Midsommarvaka–Stockholm Phil. Orch. / Neeme Järvi BIS 385

Alfven's Swedish Rhapsody No. 1, *Midsommarvaka* (or *Midsummer Vigil*), is a 13-minute celebration of Swedish folk music from 1903. It follows a particular program: a spirited bass tries to get a folk song going; the fiddlers join in, and the dance blossoms. Shortly after, a fight provides two lovers with a chance to disappear into the bright night light. When dawn breaks, they dance again just before the piece ends. Varied, entertaining, and delightful, the music makes fine use of orchestral color. Alfvén's Second Symphony, from 1899, paints with a broader brush, but plays on similar inspiration. With some fine melodies and a warm connection to folk traditions, it's a very pleasant surprise.

LINK► *Various Composers – Ports of Call – Minnesota Orch. / Eiji Oue*   **Reference 80**
Don't be put off by a collection of seven snappy tunes from seven different cultures. An exuberant performance, great engineering, and interesting repertoire make this CD valuable. Alfvén's Midsummer Vigil *and Alexander Borodin's* In the Steppes of Central Asia *get especially good readings.*

En Skärgårdssägen; Symphony No. 4 –
Stockholm Phil. Orch. / Neeme Järvi   BIS 505

The first piece is also called *A Legend of the Skerries*. It debuted in 1905, a kind of rough draft for 1919's Symphony No. 4 (*Från Havsbandet*). Translated, the title is "From the Outermost Skerries." A skerry is a rocky island; there are many in the archipelago near Stockholm, and Alfvén often sailed among them for inspiration. He transforms the way light plays upon these islands into sheer romance; the mood is set as a soprano sings a fresh and inviting siren song in the symphony. The music feels like the sea; it lies calm, starts to rock, and then bursts into storminess. Like the ocean, the music bewitches, soothes, and demands respect.

LINK► *Hugo Alfvén – Swedish Rhapsodies – Iceland Sym. Orch. / Petri Sakari*
Chandos 9313
In addition to the well-known Midsummer Vigil (Rhapsody No. 1), *Sakari presents the vivid, evocative* Upsala-rapsodi (Rhapsody No. 2), *plus the* Dalarapsodi (Rhapsody No. 3), *some incidental music from a play about Gustav Adolf II. For a good sampling of Alfvén's choral music, try* OD Sings Alfvén *(BIS 633).*

William Alwyn

A British composer better known in his own country than in the U.S., Alwyn may be familiar to film buffs for his soundtrack to Disney's *Swiss Family Robinson* (one of over 60 soundtracks to his credit). Born in 1905, Alwyn attended the Royal Academy of Music; remarkably, at age 21, he was appointed Professor of Composition. His first important work, Five Preludes for Orchestra, debuted at the Proms (Promenade Concerts) in 1927. Most of Alwyn's symphonies were introduced by two of Britain's finest conductors, Sir Thomas Beecham and Sir Thomas Barbirolli. In 1960, Alwyn moved to the village of Blythburgh on England's east coast. Inspired by the Blyth River landscape visible from his home, he created a great many fine pastels and oil paintings (these can be seen on various Chandos albums). Alwyn also wrote poetry, an autobiography for children, two operas, and other musical works. He died in 1985.

Symphony No. 4 – London Sym. Orch. / Richard Hickox   Chandos 8902
An ideal stereo test recording, Alwyn's Fourth Symphony, from 1948, begins with quiet winds repeating a simple melody. In the background, weightier strings come in; within thirty seconds, clouds have gathered. The melody bravely continues, drenched by the majestic passage of a storm; it's refreshing, bracing, and kind. The resulting watercolor warms the heart. Alwyn has much to say and communicates these ideas in an engaging way. He wastes no time, moving from one prismatic view to the next. The result is imaginative and often thrilling. Alwyn has his own ideas about structure, too; he changes structure with each symphony. Completing the CD are his vibrant and quite original *Elizabethan Dances*.

LINK➤ *E.J. Moeran – Symphony in G minor – Ulster Orch. / Vernon Handley*
Chandos 8577
Completed in 1937, this symphony persuasively portrays Moeran's feelings for his Irish ancestry in the first movement and his love for the British countryside in the second. Although Sibelius was an influence, Moeran is very much a part of the British symphonic school. Outstanding sonics.

Autumn Legend – Rachel Masters (harp), Nicholas Daniel (cor anglais), Stephen Tees (viola); City of London Sinfonia / Richard Hickox   Chandos 9065
Chandos deserves special commendation for recording and releasing so much of the 20th-century British repertoire, and for its consistently outstanding sonics. On 1954's *Autumn Sonata*, the cor anglais (English horn) warmly glows as a solo instrument; this opportunity is not provided by many other composers. Alwyn creates his magic as the cor anglais winds through a pastoral landscape and weaves its way through the heavier weight of the strings to emerge with a fresh statement. His *Lyrica Angelica*, also from 1954, was used by U.S. figure skater Michelle Kwan during the 1998 Winter Olympics. It's refined, relaxing, and ultimately jubilant. The wholly wonderful *Pastoral Fantasia*, from 1939, features the viola.

LINK➤ *Grace Williams – Symphony No. 2 – BBC Welsh Sym. Orch. / Vernon Handley*
Lyrita 327
Williams (1906–1977) was a student of Ralph Vaughan Williams, and her music carries both the lyricism and clear pronouncements of her teacher. She has a darker side, too, expressed in the Ballads for Orchestra *included here. Also try* Carillons for Oboe and Other Works *(Lyrita 323).*

Malcolm Arnold

Best known for such film scores as *Bridge Over the River Kwai*, Sir Malcolm Arnold has been one of Britain's most prolific 20th-century composers. A native of Northampton, young Arnold was so taken with Louis Armstrong's playing that he became a professional trumpeter for the London Philharmonic in early 1941. He was 20 years old and just beginning a composition career, prompted by training at the Royal College of Music. Arnold remained with the Philharmonic for two years before becoming a principal player. After serving in WW II, he worked for the BBC, then returned to the Philharmonic. Arnold has scored over 80 films; it's a money-making proposition that helps to support his many classical compositions (including 9 symphonies, 20 concertos, various overtures and dances, 5 ballets, and many vocal works). The 1970s and 1980s brought a splendid array of awards; Arnold was knighted in 1993.

English, Cornish and Scottish Dances ("Arnold on Brass") –
Grimethorpe Colliery Band   Conifer 16848
These performances have heart. There is something special about the glory of an English brass band, a spirit captured in the 1996 motion picture *Brassed Off*. The band heard in that picture is the same band featured here. The principal contents of this 1993 CD are several dance suites. Arnold knew his brass sonorities well; when he designed the mournful trombone solo for the English Dances in 1950, he captured the sadness of loss. Similarly, the hymnal quality of his third Cornish Dance, the way it gains confidence in its noble purpose and engenders a crowdful of goodwill can't help but raise goosebumps. The fourth Scottish Dance is the liveliest of all.

LINK➤ *Malcolm Arnold – Scottish, Irish, Cornish, English Dances – The Philharmonia /*
Bryden Thomson   *Chandos 8867*
Full-scale orchestral treatments of the dances, still heavy on the horns but augmented by strings, add a certain British formality to these proceedings. Taken on their own, though, they're wonderful. Excellent sound, too.

Flute Concerto, Oboe Concerto, Sinfoniettas – Edward Beckett (flute),
Malcolm Messiter (oboe); London Fest. Orch. / Ross Pople   Hyperion 66332
It's easy and fun to follow the oboe's melody line through the rolling hills of Arnold's carefree chamber work. This sunny spring day allows the soloist to sound as if he's improvising. The challenging second movement is very fast and has many changes; it even sounds a bit like free jazz. In contrast, the third movement turns formal. Arnold's flute concerto, composed a year earlier in 1953, is generally freed from the formal, frilly treatment typically associated with that instrument. Instead, this is an assertive string piece led by a flute that sings and struts its melodies and adornments with the utmost modernism. Similarily, the pair of sinfoniettas update older ideas. Superb engineering.

LINK➤ *Benjamin Frankel – String Quartets – Nomos Quartet*   *cpo 999-420*
Like Arnold, Frankel earned his living with film scores and also wrote exquisite chamber music and symphonies. He's very inventive, modern, and a major find for many. CPO has released six Frankel discs, notably his symphonies (Nos. 1& 5: 999-240; Nos. 2 & 3: 999-241; Nos. 4 & 6: 999-242).

Symphonies Nos. 3, 4 – London Sym. Orch. / Richard Hickox Chandos 9290

Symphony No. 3, from 1957, bravely progresses through a dark terrain that reflects an aspect of Arnold's personality. While maintaining a stiff upper lip, Arnold constantly introduces new ideas and variations on the main theme, always providing dash, rushes of new emotions, and rich (often brassy) patches. The second movement's desolate beauty suggests a gloomy North Sea afternoon with a bracing breeze. Symphony No. 4, from 1960, was composed after Notting-Hill's race riots. Bernstein-style percussion outbursts suggest street fighting, and various instruments simulate a Jamaican steel band. Arnold's juxtaposition of contemporary sounds with British complacency is brilliant, as is his interpretation of avant-garde music in the second movement and the sultry Caribbean homeland evoked in the third.

LINK➤ *E.J. Moeran – Violin Concerto – Lydia Mordkovitch (violin), Ulster Orch. / Vernon Handley* **Chandos 8807**

First performed in 1942, Moeran's violin concerto evokes the feelings of his natural surroundings; few composers were so sensitive to, and affected by, their physical setting. The piece goes down easy with plenty of intense turns for Mordkovitch to show her talent. Fine recording, too.

Symphony No. 6 – Royal Philh. Orch. / Vernon Handley Conifer 15005

The stabbing thrusts of jazz great Charlie Parker's saxophone provided Arnold with inspiration for his sixth symphony, completed in 1967. As the throbbing subsides, the strings develop their own tense direction. Various factions announce their presence, collide, and explode. Arnold's theatrical sense was skillfully developed over dozens of film soundtracks. Here, he chooses climaxes with perfect timing. In the second movement, Arnold buries faddish pop music in an orchestral storm, then resolves with a wide-open finale. But that's not all. The disc continues with a ballet suite from Arnold's ironic *Sweeney Todd* score and the ribald *Tam O'Shanter* Overture recalling Robert Burns's drunken carouser. The music even features the sounds of off-kilter Scottish dancing.

LINK➤ *Malcolm Arnold – Symphony No. 5 & Symphony No. 6 – London Sym. Orch. / Richard Hickox* **Chandos 9385**

The popular Fifth Symphony, from 1961 dominates the CD. Tragedy's tension informs the first movement, but Arnold's experimentation with serialism and unexpected instrumentation begin a refreshingly modern work, which features a fiery third movement and a disturbing anticlimax.

Film Music: Suites – London Sym. Orch. / Richard Hickox Chandos 9100

Although most film music could hardly be accepted in concert halls, Arnold's best film suites are as appropriate as Grieg's *Peer Gynt* (a suite based on incidental music for a stage play). Arnold's excellent communication skills were well suited to soundtracks—he composed over one hundred of them. Certainly the most uplifting of his soundtracks is *The Bridge Over the River Kwai*, in which he quotes at length from *Colonel Bogey's March*, written in 1914 by Kenneth J. Alford. The best of the CD's four suites is probably 1958's *The Inn of the Seventh Happiness* because of its determined personality at the start and the way Arnold carries it through to a brave finale. Recommended.

LINK➤ *Paul McCartney – Standing Stone – London Sym. Orch. / Lawrence Foster* **EMI 56484**

While some classical composers have crossed over into popular music, the "rules" don't generally allow movement in the other direction. Stronger in melodic patches than structure, McCartney seems to be learning his new craft and taking it quite seriously. He shows promise.

Johann Sebastian Bach

Bach was a hard-working Lutheran who wrote for God, was most often employed by a church school, and was not considered particularly special during his lifetime. He was born in northern Germany in 1685, one of many generations of Bach musicians. His appetite for musical education was voracious, and there are many stories of his walking long distances to hear noted musicians. After several years of work as an organist, Bach became the conductor of Duke Wilhelm Ernst of Weimer's private orchestra. Throughout this period—his mid-20s to mid-30s—Bach wrote many of his best organ pieces. In 1717, he left to compose for Prince Leopold of Anhalt in Cöthen; in 1723, Bach became the cantor of Thomasschule (St. Thomas school). There, he taught and wrote music for four churches; he remained in that position until his death in 1749. Bach's work was forgotten until an 1820s revival; today, he is revered.

Works for Organ: Volumes 1-7 – Kevin Bowyer (organ)
Nimbus 5280, 5289, 5290, 5377, 5400, 5423, 5457/8

Start with Vol. 1 (5280) for the dramatic Toccata and Fugue in D minor from 1710. This is a piece whose opening phrases will instantly sound familiar, whose music scampers all over the church then wells up in thunderous blasts of raw energy. The same disc includes Fantasia and Fugue in G minor, first performed a decade later; it's more controlled and subtly complex, with an extended flight of dark fantasy at the start, followed by a delightfully intricate fugue. Throughout the series, Bowyer's control is impressive, for this is often complicated work, and he consistently balances bombastics with clear-thinking mathematical forms. The Macussen organ in St. Hans Kirke (St. John's Church) in Odense, Denmark, is radiant and impeccably recorded; it sounds glorious on a top-notch stereo system. (Play it loudly!) The alternation of organ and chorus, a Lutheran mainstay, is best heard on *Das Orgelbüchlein* (A Little Organ Book) from the 2-CD Vol. 7 (5457/8); it is perhaps the finest recording in the series. On Vol. 3 (5290), Trio Sonata II in C minor has an entirely different feeling: it is light, whimsical, and quick in its first and third movements, while the second movement is slower and gloomy. The waterfall of sound that begins Toccata in G minor on Vol. 4 (5377) provides access to a rich landscape with many intricate details and a winning rhythm. It's one of the most instantly accessible pieces in Bach's organ catalog. Bowyer's 1990 recordings are by no means the only choice; Marie-Claire Alain's CD series for Erato is fresh, recent, and wonderful.

LINK➤ *A Celebration – Marie-Claire Alain (organ)*   Erato 15343
A 5-CD spectacular featuring virtually every significant work in the organ repertoire. From 1963 through 1993, Alain recorded a wide range of work, from Bach's idol Buxtehude to mainstreamers such as Lizst and Mozart, to 20th-century composers such as Milhaud and Polenc.

Cello Suites – Mstislav Rostropovich (cello)
EMI 55363

The six cello suites, most likely composed around 1720, are concerned mostly with textures and colors, not melodies. Rostropovich excels, with passion, in bringing these tones and underlying feelings to life; it is this essence that makes his 2-CD set the outstanding choice. (Pablo Casals's recordings from the late 1930s, available on EMI [66215], have the passion and precision, but lack sonic fidelity.) The first suite is luminescent and optimistic, youthful and exuberant. The second is gloomy and introspective. Words don't begin to describe the cumulative wonder, and casual listening reveals little more. This is music for a quiet Sunday afternoon; close your eyes and feel the music.

LINK➤ *Johann Sebastian Bach (& others) – Cello Suites (& other works) – Thomas Demenga (cello) & others*　　　　　*ECM New Series (Various)*
The first four suites are presented on individual CDs, mated with a work from a contemporary composer: Suite 1 with Sandór Veress (ECM New Series 1477), Suite 2 with B.A. Zimmermann (1571), Suite 3 with Elliott Carter (1391), and Suite 4 with Heinz Hollinger (1340). Good idea, well executed.

Brandenburg Concertos Nos. 1-6 – Boston Baroque/
Martin Pearlman　　　　　Telarc 80412

Inspired by the music of contemporary Italian composers like Vivaldi, and written for the Margrave of Brandenburg (who, most likely, never bothered to open the manuscript), these six works present a peak in Baroque composition. The music is cleverly arranged so that sections of the small orchestra sometimes answer one another, establish themes that others repeat, and then combine for a singular effect. In the first concerto, Bach introduces horns (previously relegated to special effects and hunting calls) as a principal part of the orchestra. (Listen carefully and note that some of this music was reworked from the earlier *Hunt* Cantata (BWV 108.) The second concerto begins with a buoyant mixture of violin, recorder, oboe, and trumpet; the piece generally favors soloists, notably a high trumpet solo (and a difficult one at that). The character of the third concerto is entirely different, emphasizing strings in a perfect balance between the high, middle, and low registers of the violin section; once again, part of the concerto is borrowed from an earlier cantata (BWV 174). The solo harpsichord in the fifth concerto was an entirely new idea—a keyboard had never been used as the solo instrument in a concerto before. The deeper resonances of the sixth concerto are brought about through violas and cellos; the piece is performed without violins. All told, these are among the greatest works in the classical repertoire. The Boston Baroque plays beautifully, and as usual with Telarc, the recordings bring out the shimmering highs and the gutsy bass. A 2-CD set, highly recommended.

LINK➤ *The Baroque Experience – The Academy of Ancient Music / Christopher Hogwood*
　　　　　L'Oiseau-Lyre 433-523
A 5-CD survey of Baroque music demonstrates the enormity of Bach's accomplishments in comparison with notables from the same era, including Vivaldi, Telemann, Pachelbel, and Corelli. A more scholarly approach lacking the sizzle of the Boston Baroque performances.

Violin Concertos Nos. 1, 2 & Double Concerto –
Arthur Grumiaux, others
Philips 420-700

By 1720, after several years of transcribing Italian concertos for solo instruments, Bach tried his hand at composing a violin concerto, then a very new form. These 1970s recordings remain the best choices. Grumiaux (violin) is joined by Herman Krebers (violin) and Heinz Hollinger (oboe), plus assorted soloists and the New Philharmonia Orchestra. The delicacy of Grumiaux's work is haunting, particularly in the second section (Andante) of the first concerto. The second concerto is spirited and shows considerable advancement past the original Italian format. The Double Concerto (for two violins in the lead role) is a well-known piece: it is full, rich, and played with verve, with some handsome, sensitive patches.

LINK► *Antonio Vivaldi – Violin Concertos – Miriana Sirbu, I Musici* *Philips 442-145*
Vivaldi's concertos are straightforward and possess few of the complexities associated with Bach's violin concertos. Sirbu's violin presents an enthusiastic argument for their long-term popularity.

Violin Sonatas & Partitas – Itzhak Perlman (violin)
EMI 49483

To truly understand what's happening here, start with one of the most difficult pieces in the violinist's repertoire: the fifth movement of Partita No. 2—the nearly impossible Ciaccona, a 15-minute test of virtuosity and dramatic interpretation aced by Perlman in a stellar performance. With your ears now well trained, go back to the beginning of Sonata No. 1 and thrill to Perlman's deft polyphonic manipulations and his unerring knack for expressiveness, especially during the most complex passages. The sonatas are a workout, but give them time and you'll be amazed. The partitas, based partly on folk dances, are easier. Per Bach's intention, the two forms alternate here. Can sound squeaky on a mediocre stereo system.

LINK► *Johannes Brahms – Violin Sonatas –*
Itzhak Perlman (violin) & Vladimir Ashkenazy (piano) *EMI 47403*
These sonatas were written more than 150 years after Bach helped to invent the form. They're sweet, melodic, and very easy to enjoy. Bach wrote for the Lutheran church; Brahms wrote these for salon society—two different worlds.

Cantata No. 140: Wachet auf; Cantata No. 147: Herz und Mund –
Monteverdi Chorus, soloists / John Eliot Gardiner
Deutsche Grammophon 431-809

Each Sunday's Lutheran Mass involved several hours of music, and part of Bach's job at Thomasschule was to write cantatas for these liturgies. Bach composed hundreds of these multipart works, combining vocalists, chorus, organ, and often a small orchestra. Gardiner is an expert interpreter of this type of work, placing a sharp emphasis on instumental excellence as well as vocal performance (often, on the cantatas, one is favored). This CD is the place to start on the cantatas and might well begin a very large collection. Cantata No. 147, *Herz und Mund*, contains the familiar "Jesu, Joy of Man's Desiring" theme used later by Bach and other composers. Cantata No. 140, *Wachet auf*, is gorgeous.

LINK► *Johann Sebastian Bach – Cantatas 1 - Christ Lag in Todesbanden, etc. –*
Bach Collegium Japan / Masaaki Suzuki *BIS 751*
A new series, made by a top-notch Japanese ensemble and beautifully recorded. The series begins with the well-known Cantata No. 4, Christ Lag in Todesbanden, *and includes two other cantatas.*

English Suites – Andras Schiff (piano)   London 421-640

Bach probably didn't call these solo piano suites "English" (though they may have been created for an English patron). Completed around 1725, they're sophisticated, easy to enjoy, and an ideal introduction to the composer. There are six suites; each begins with a prelude and is followed by a series of movements patterned after dances (Allemande, from Germany; Courante, from France; Sarabande, from Spain; and so on). The ethnic connection is diffuse, if apparent at all. What emerges from this 2-CD set are highly structured Baroque works of considerable invention, characterized by a joyous freedom and flow. Schiff is a fine interpreter, but Glenn Gould's iconoclastic renditions (CBS 42268) are not to be missed.

LINK➤ *Johann Sebastian Bach – French Suites – Angela Hewitt (piano)*
Hyperion 67121/2
On these equally important works, Hewitt's 1995 recording equals or tops Schiff's (London 433-313) and offers a compelling contrast with Gould (CBS 42267). For a completely different sound, try Ton Koopman's harpsichord version (Erato 94805).

St. Matthew Passion – John Eliot Gardiner   Archiv 427-648

Bach composed five Passions, and of these two survive. *St. Matthew Passion* is the grand master-piece—presented with a double chorus and double orchestra, it's the zenith of sacred art. Christ's final days are described through scripture; additional material, mostly for the chorus, was written by Picander, Bach's frequent lyricist. Anthony Rolfe Johnson provides the voice of St. Matthew; Andreas Schmidt performs Jesus Christ in the recitatives (vocal solos); the chorus and other soloists fill in the story and enhance the sacred power. Gardiner's considerable scholarship results in music that lives and breathes; this is not a museum piece, but a celebration of life and love. A 3-CD set with complete lyrics; magnificently recorded.

LINK➤ *Johann Sebastian Bach – Mass in B minor –*
Collegium Musicum 90 / Richard Hickox   *Chandos 0533/4*
This complete Mass is also considered to be one of Bach's best works. It's not composed as a single work, but instead is pasted together from smaller elements. Still, the music is resplendent, and Hickox's work is superb. The version by Herreweghe (Harmonia Mundi 901614.15) is also thrilling for both its performance and its sonics. The Gardiner version (Archiv 415-514) is quite good, too.

Six Partitas – Angela Hewitt (piano)   Hyperion 67191/2

Possibly the finest Bach keyboard recording available today. Hewitt's approach is transcendent, the recording is perfect, and the pieces themselves, composed by a mature Bach in 1731, combine the nobility of the *English* and *French* Suites with the freshness of a folk dance. Start with the very popular Partita No. 1, accessible from the start, and possessing an exciting ending in its final movement, the Gigue. Partita No. 4 is more complex and ambitious; it's particularly notable for a delightful fugue toward the beginning, the Allemande's intimate finery, and the lively formality of the Courante. Partita No. 5 is perhaps the most joyous and certainly the most technically challenging. Highest possible recommendation for this 2-CD set.

LINK➤ *Wolfgang Amadeus Mozart – 4 Piano Sonatas – Mitsuko Uchida (piano)*
Philips 420-186
Few classical CDs and fewer piano recordings reach the level of Hewitt's work, but Uchida is certainly in her league. Of the many Mozart sonatas recorded by Uchida, this is one of the very finest. Uchida's version of Sonata in B flat is wholly mesmerizing.

Goldberg Variations – Glenn Gould (piano)
CBS Masterworks 52619

Gould established himself as a recording artist with his debut recording of these pieces in 1955, and recorded new interpretations in 1982 (among his last recordings). Gould follows his own tempos, taking some very briskly, and yet articulates Bach's ideas with consistent clarity and flowing musicality. The result is always riveting (a conversation between two geniuses), even when Gould is heard softly vocalizing. Technically, these pieces are the "Aria & 30 Variations," apparently provided around 1742 to a young harpsichordist, Johann Gottlieb Goldberg, working for Count Keyserlingk of Dresden. Like many Bach piano pieces, they are both mathematically ingenious and soulful.

LINK➤ *J.S. Bach – Goldberg Variations – Christophe Rousset (harpsichord)*
Oiseau-Lyre 444-866

Although Glenn Gould has made this work his own and has popularized it as a piano piece (complete with his own idiosyncracies), the harpsichord's tonality and feeling is probably closer to what Bach had in mind. This performance is the best available.

The Well-Tempered Clavier (Books I & II) – Andras Schiff (piano)
London 414-388, 417-236

A clavier is an ancestor of our piano (with major and minor keys); "well-tempered" indicates tuning with equality across all notes, so almost every note is slightly off-key. Each piece is written in a different key; since there are 24 major and minor keys, the result is 24 preludes and fugues. Bach completed *Book I* by 1722. *Book II*, completed by 1744, adds far more sophistication and texture. These pieces offer a textbook lesson on the associations between keys and emotions. They also demonstrate Bach's finest thinking on the subject of fugues (his obsession for decades). Schiff is a superior Bach performer; this is among his finest work. Outstanding recording quality. A delightful starting place.

LINK➤ *(Book) – Gödel, Escher, Bach: An Eternal Golden Braid – Douglas R. Hofstadter*
Vintage Books ISBN 0-394-74502

This is a book, not a CD, but it's an essential companion to Bach's music. In a long series of clever essays and illustrations, Hofstadter links Bach's musical mathematics with M.C. Escher's pretzel logic, makes fugues fun, and connects it all to computer science.

The Art of the Fugue – Davitt Moroney (harpischord)
Harmonia Mundi 1169/70

A fugue presents a melody in one, then several voices. Bach composed them with precision, grace, humor, and God's touch. In the 1740s, Bach started work on this new series of fugues and canons (expanding on *Well-Tempered Clavier* ideas). He was fascinated by underlying mathematical patterns. Some of this music is unfinished, the order is a mystery, and no one knows on which instrument(s) the work was to be played. Educated guesses suggest harpsichord, and Moroney's precise, swinging 2-CD set offers the best on record.

LINK➤ *Johann Sebastian Bach – The Art of the Fugue –*
Cologne Musica Antiqua /Richard Goebel   *Archiv 413-642*

A 3-CD set presenting The Art of the Fugue *with a larger ensemble (also on period instruments) along with another later work,* A Musical Offering, *and ten canons. For a contemporary reading, try Sir Neville Marriner's version of* A Musical Offering *(Philips 442 556).*

Samuel Barber

Privileged doctor's son Samuel Osborne Barber II was born in West Chester, PA, in 1910. His aunt, Louise Homer, was a famous opera singer, and his uncle was the renowned composer Sidney Homer. Because of their influence, the 14-year-old Barber was accepted at Philadelphia's newly formed Curtis Institute. (The young man possessed a fine singing voice; composing would come later.) At Curtis, Barber and Gian Carlo Menotti became fast friends; they later co-owned a country home for two decades. In 1935, Barber won the Prix de Rome, permitting two years of study in Italy, away from the conservatism of Philadelphia. In 1938, Arturo Toscanini performed Barber's *Adagio for Strings*, and Barber diligently expanded a franchise for romantic American music. Many awards followed, including two Pulitzer Prizes. After the failure of his *Antony and Cleopatra*, written to open the new Metropolitan Opera, Barber slowly sank into obscurity. He died in 1981.

Adagio for Strings, Essays for Orchestra, others –
St. Louis Sym. Orch. / Leonard Slatkin   EMI 49463

A splendid collection of Barber's best-known orchestral pieces, made in 1988. Barber wrote the Overture to *The School for Scandal* as a Curtis Institute graduation project in 1932. His most famous work, *Adagio for Strings*, was completed in 1936. Typical of Barber's composing style, the Adagio begins quietly, develops slowly, and steadily adds power as it moves forward and builds to a fierce climax. Barber's first two *Essays for Orchestra* come from 1938 and 1942; his more significant Third Essay was composed in 1978. All three works are coherent, abstract romances with lovely passages and bits of typically Barberian tension. Excellent Slatkin performances. Handsome engineering, too.

LINK► *Quartets by Wirén, Tchaikovsky, Wood, Barber – Lindsay String Quartet ASV 825*
The second movement of Barber's 1936 quartet, which stands as one of his finest pieces, was orchestrated for Toscanini and became Adagio for Strings. *Here it's included with quartets by 20th-century composers Dag Wirén, Hugh Wood, and Poland's André Tchaikovsky.*

Symphony No. 1, Piano Concerto – St. Louis Sym. Orch. / Leonard Slatkin
Chandos 8958

Compact at 22 minutes, Barber's first is considered a single-movement work. It actually has five movements though, with the same motifs used throughout. As the first movement's gentility gives way to pure industrial energy and a percussive climax, the lyrical second movement takes shape with a lone oboe solo. By the finale, the orchestra has built up a major head of steam—one that' erupts with real power. John Browning is the soloist on the impossibly difficult Piano Concerto, just as he was when the piece debuted in 1962. It's formal piece with periodic jazzy or modern interludes. Browning has more fun alongside pianist Slatkin as they perform the four-hand piano pieces called *Souvenirs*.

LINK► *Samuel Barber – Symphony No. 2 – Detroit Sym. Orch. / Neeme Järvi*
Chandos 9169
A product of WW II, parts of Barber's Second Symphony were inspired by the sensation of flying, as related by U.S. Air Force pilots at a Texas base. It's followed by Barber's well-known Adagio for Strings *and by a symphony by 18th-century violinist George Frederick Bristow.*

Violin Concerto – Gil Shaman (violin); London Sym. Orch. / André Previn
Deutsche Grammophon 439-866

Those seeking Barber's violin, cello, and *Capricorn* concertos should consider the work of leading Barber interpreter Leonard Slatkin (RCA 68283) with the Saint Louis Symphony Orchestra. The first movement explores two distinct melodies; both are handsome and modern. The second movement, which provides ample and plaintive solo space for Shaman, leads to a very difficult third. Here, the soloist must play very rapidly for extended periods without a break. It's all rhythm and energy, but Shaman's up to the task. Also included is a beautiful Shaman performance of Erich Wolfgang Korngold's Violin Concerto. Stunning fidelity.

LINK➤ *Randall Thompson – Symphonies Nos. 2 & 3 –*
New Zealand Sym. Orch. / Andrew Schenck   ***Koch 7074***
A gleaming sample from a modern American symphonist whose work should be heard in U.S. concert halls, but isn't. (This CD comes from New Zealand.) Hanson's Rochester Philharmonic debuted it in 1932; it's romantic, fresh and melodic, with muscle in all the right places. Worth hearing.

Vanessa – Eleanor Steber, Nicolai Gedda, others;
Met. Opera Orch. / Dimitri Mitropoulous   RCA 7899

Vanessa lives in a country house, waiting for her lover Anatol to return after 20 years' absence. A young man, Anatol, returns; he's the man's son, and he carries with him the news of his father's death. Vanessa falls in love with the younger Anatol. However, on the night of his return, Anatol had seduced Vanessa's cousin, Erika. Erika becomes pregnant, and when Vanessa and Anatol leave for Paris as a married couple, she is left waiting. This 1958 stereo recording features the original cast, notable for the dark soprano of Steber's Vanessa, the giddy charm of Nicolai Gedda as Anatol, and Mitropoulous's aggressively detailed orchestrations. Sung in English, with some affectations.

LINK➤ *Sallie Chissum Remembers Billy the Kid –*
Barbara Bonney (soprano), André Previn (piano)   ***London 455-511***
Bonney is related to William Bonney, a.k.a. Billy the Kid. She commissioned Previn to write a song about Sallie Chisum, the prostitute who knew both Billy and Pat Garrett. Bonney also does a marvelous job with Barber's Hermit Songs, *and with Copland's* Twelve Poems of Emily Dickinson.

Songs of the Old – Cheryl Studer (soprano), Thomas Hampson (baritone),
John Browning (piano)   Deutsche Grammophon 435-867

Accompanied by Browning's piano, two opera stars take turns singing Barber's refined art songs. "Of That So Sweet Imprisonment" and "In the Dark Pinewood" are songs based on poetry by James Joyce, while "The Secrets of the Old" is based on a W.B. Yeats work. The formal, European character of these songs is at first an obstacle, then a classic aspect of their undeniable beauty. Barber's Hermit Songs, sung by Studer, were based on informal poems written in the notes of 8th- to 13th-century Irish texts. Hampson's best song, "Dover Beach," is based on Matthew Arnold's despondent poem; it's accompanied by the Emerson Quartet. A 2-CD set covering works written from 1925 to 1972.

LINK➤ *Dawn Upshaw – Knoxville: Summer of 1915*   ***Nonesuch 79187***
Barber wrote this evocation of times gone by on commission from American soprano Eleanor Steber; the text comes from an article by James Agee, and the music is a melodic pleasure. Also includes John Harbison's Mirabai Songs, *plus some Stravinsky and Menotti. Beautiful!*

Bela Bartók

Born in 1881 in Nagyszentmilkos, Hungary (modern-day Sinnicolau, Romania), Bartók was a sickly child, the son of a woman who tried to make ends meet by teaching piano at nearby schools. He was composing original material before his tenth birthday, and as a teenager he attended Budapest's Academy of Music. Bartók graduated in 1903; the following year, he became enthralled with rural folk music. Bartók and his friend (and fellow composer) Zoltán Kodály ventured into the countryside, where they collected music. (In time, the two traveled as far as North Africa.) To earn a living, Bartók taught piano at the academy for 27 years, beginning in 1907. He worked as a composer and as a locally known pianist. Concerned about the Nazi takeover of Europe, he moved to the U.S. in 1939. He taught at Columbia University in NYC and lived very modestly until his death from leukemia in 1945.

Bluebeard's Castle – Siegmund Nimsgern, Tatiana Troyanos; BBC Sym. Orch. / Pierre Boulez   SONY Classical 64110

In composing his only opera, Bartók adapted Charles Perrault's fairy tale into a psychodrama. The fairy tale allows Duke Bluebeard's wife to open every door in his castle, except one. Behind that locked door are the severed heads of his former wives. Bartók builds his one-act, two-character opera by allowing wife Judith (Troyanos) to open seven doors. Each door reveals a horror. A torture chamber lies behind the first door, for example. Even when there is beauty, as there is behind the fourth door, there is blood on the roses. Door number seven seals Judith's fate. This dark 1918 work operates at a symbolic level and demands intelligent musicianship, provided here in ample portions.

LINK► *Zoltán Kodály – Háry János Suite, Concerto – Budapest Phil. Orch.;*
Hungarian State Orch. / János Ferencsik   *Hungaroton 12190*
Bartók and Zodály were friends who changed the course of Hungarian music. Háry János, from 1927, is a suite from a lighthearted opera about a soldier (the suite begins with a giant orchestral sneeze and maintains its whimsy). Concerto for Orchestra, from 1939, is filled with delightful melodies and wonder. A great CD.

6 String Quartets – Emerson Quartet
Deutsche Grammophon 423-657

Bartók's quartets are the backbone of his musical legacy and a cornerstone in Hungary's musical heritage. Bartók also pioneered 20th-century chamber music by forcing effects that resulted in unusual tones, textures, and percussion. He instructed violinists, for example, to play at the extremes of their strings and bows, and even to pluck strings so hard that they rebounded off the fingerboard. Energized by Bartók's absorbtion in Hungarian folk music, his quartets only vaguely resemble formal 19th-century successes in the form. Quartet No. 1, from 1909, eulogizes a love affair. It begins slowly, periodically dips into something resembling a dirge, and gradually brightens. The third movement combines a Hungarian folk sensibility with some strenuous reaches into the depths of instrumental capabiltities. Quartet No. 2, written in 1917, grows from a bleak, postwar frustration. The confident, original Bartók, however, molds a sweet melodic flow by piecing together angular sounds and feelings. Here's an example of the Emerson Quartet's considerable interpretative skill at work: improperly played, this piece turns into pointless modernist mush. The musicians here get the tension right and in so doing, uncover the beauty. Inevitably, dissonance gives way to fury, and Bartók's rage is palpable. Quartet No. 3, from 1927, is even less conventional. Instrument sounds are harsh and discomfiting; they growl and shout, avoid melody, and blast away, then converse among themselves in a seemingly scattered way. The final section ties everything together with a fierce performance. By 1928's Quartet No. 4, tonality was just a memory; as in No. 3, there are special effects galore and odd clusters of sounds patched together in very interesting ways. Parts of the second movement sound like a 1970s experiment with electronic music or like the random buzzing of bees. Unlike less talented adventurers, Bartók really knew what he was doing; every minute of this music remains intriguing and appealing some 70 years later. By comparison, Quartet No. 5, from 1934, and 1939's Quartet No. 6 are easier to appreciate. While retaining his mutinous edge, Bartók reinstates the pleasantries of proper quartet music. As a result, these quartets are more accessible and in some ways, Bartók's most interesting work in the genre. This is a journey worth taking. The Emerson Quartet proves an extremely capable guide; fortunately, all of Bartók's unusual ideas are clearly heard in a sparkling digital recording.

LINK► *Béla Bartok – Bartók & Janácek String Quartets – Tokyo String Quartet*
RCA 68286

RCA adds a third CD to accommodate Janácek's two string quartets. Both composers relied on folk influences and worked out some love issues through chamber music. Ultimately, Bartók's gutsy tactics make his music work; the Tokyo Quartet smoothes out his rough edges.

Concertos – Stephen Kovacevich (piano), London Sym. Orch. or BBC Sym. Orch./ Sir Colin Davis; Henryk Szeryng (violin), Royal Concertgebouw Orch. / Bernard Haitink   Philips 438-812

Speed and agility mark the first movement of Piano Concerto No. 1, from 1926; Bartók zips from a jazzy feel to the incessant pounding of piano keys. Next is a whirling folk dance that gives way to what feels like marching band music. Bartók jumps from one idea to the next without giving the listener time to think. The second movement slows down, but sparks fly as the piano and percussion instruments sometimes strike each other like two swords in conflict. Drums and pumping piano open the industrial-strength third movement, with near comical remarks from winds and brass. It's not unlike a silent film soundtrack. Kovacevich and Davis continue to follow Bartók's brutalizing instructions in a resounding version of the Second Piano Concerto (1931); ideas are presented in loud fragments with powerfully sharp edges, but never so harshly that they can't be brought back around with a clever horn arrangement or piano hijinks. In contrast, Violin Concerto No. 2 (1939) is a noble, often tranquil, and sometimes formal excursion with a Hungarian folk music foundation. The most important work on this bargain-priced, fine-sounding 2-CD set is 1943's Concerto for Orchestra, performed by Bernard Haitink's formidable Concertgebouw Orchestra. Bartók explained the structure of this piece as "a gradual transition from the sternness of the first movement and the lugubrious death song of the third to the life assertion of the finale." Brilliant themes, vividly and loudly sung by huge sections, and winning solos for one or two instruments seem to celebrate the orchestra's versatility.

LINK► *György Kurtág – Musik für Streichinstrumente – Keller Quartet*
ECM New Series 21598

A consistently intriguing collection of chamber pieces that presents waves of sound whose basis is buried somewhere among Bach, Bartók, and Debussy, with some Hungarian folk sensibility in the mix. Most of the music was composed from 1988 to 1991. Recommended.

The Miraculous Mandarin – London Sym. Orch. / Claudio Abbado
Deutsche Grammophon 445-501

A grotesque magazine story becomes a harsh 1919 ballet. A prostitute lures men up to her apartment, where three gang members wait. Two worthless victims arrive, dance, and leave. Then a rich Chinese official arrives. By dancing, the prostitue dissolves the Mandarin's reservations; overwhelmed, he chases her. The thugs rob him and also smother him, stab him, hang him, and—he doesn't die! It's only when the prostitute shows the Mandarin tenderness that he bleeds and succumbs to death. The story is easy to follow, and Bartók's music is turbulent, explicit, powerful, and, in its own black way, cynically humorous. Excellent, aggressive Abbado; great recording. Bartók's *Two Portraits* and Janácek's *Sinfonietta* complete the CD.

LINK➤ *Béla Bartók – The Wooden Prince – Chicago Sym. Orch. /Pierre Boulez*
Deutsche Grammophon 435-863

Here's another bizarre story: a princess falls in love with a wooden prince, who comes to life and scorns her before they finally end up together. Making lavish use of orchestral colors and unorthodox scoring, Bartók finished the ballet in 1917. A superlative 1992 recording of a very handsome work.

Concerto for Orchestra; Music for Strings, Percussion and Celesta –
Chicago Sym. Orch. / Fritz Reiner   RCA 61504

Fibonacci numbers provided the structure for the first movement of 1936's *Music for Strings, Percussion and Celesta*. They're the integers in the infinite progression that defines the spiral of a Nautilis shell, a pinecone, or the seeds on flowerheads. Greek artists much admired the natural world's perfect proportions. Progression is the key creative concept; Bartók's work progresses from early dissonance to ultimate balance and beauty. This music bears analysis at the microscopic level. Inversion and opposition abound, yet it's most listenable, particularly the dances in the final movement. All told, the composition is a work of genius. Reiner's dramatic 1955 Living Stereo recording of Concerto for Orchestra is authoritative and deeply involving.

LINK➤ *György Ligeti – Concertos for Cello, Violin, Piano – Pierre-Laurent Aimard (piano), Jean-Guihen Queyras (cello), Saschko Gawriloff (violin); Ensemble InterContemporain / Pierre Boulez*
Deutsche Grammophon 439-808

Known for his a cappella piece Lux Aeterna *(used in Stanley Kubrick's* 2001: A Space Odyssey*), the Transylvanian Ligeti is at times a harsh modernist, a minimalist, a folk interpreter, and an iconoclast, with touches of romanticism. These three concertos provide only a glimpse of his wide range of ideas. A surprisingly accessible disc.*

Amy Beach

Amy Marcy Cheney was born in Henniker, NH, in 1867. A child prodigy who started composing and improvising before age 4, Cheney gave her first professional recital with a Boston orchestra. By age 18, she was a soloist with the Boston Symphony Orchestra. That same year, she married noted doctor Henry Harris Aubrey Beach. Mrs. H.H.A. Beach, as she was now known, agreed to her husband's request, and all but stopped public performances (except for an annual recital). Instead, for the next 25 years, she concentrated on writing music. She became one of the nation's finest, and best-known, composers. (She published over 150 compositions.) After the 1910 death of her husband, Beach resumed her performing career. From 1921 until 1941, she often worked at the MacDowell Colony, an artists' retreat in Peterborough, NH. Beach died in her New York apartment in 1944, leaving her royalties to the colony.

Symphony in E minor ("Gaelic") – Detroit Sym. Orch. / Neeme Järvi
Chandos 8958

Beach's only symphony is nicknamed "Gaelic" because it was influenced by Irish folk melodies (she dismissed Dvorak's promotion of Native American influences as naive; although she was American, her heritage was Irish). Beach's symphony has four movements. Ideas for the first come from one of her songs ("Dark Is the Night"); she skillfully balances turbulence with mystery and hope. The second suggests Brahms with a sweetly flowing chamber-style melody. Beach turns to a pair of Irish melodies for the third , making them her own with imagination and verve. The final movement is surprising—a splendid march gives way to lavish, passionate closure. Included on the CD are Barber's *School for Scandal* Overture and his First Symphony.

LINK➤ *And the Band Played On: Music Played on the Titanic – I Salonisti* **London 83822**
Classy chamber music to soothe rich people's souls. A sentimental slice of music popular around 1912. A warm mix of classics from Schubert, Mascagni, and Tchaikovsky, plus lighter fare from Irving Berlin, Percy Grainger, and Scott Joplin. And, at the end, "Nearer My God to Thee."

Violin-Piano Sonata – Arturo Delmoni (violin), Yuri Funahashi (piano)
John Marks Records 2

A breathtaking reproduction of the violin that puts most other recordings to shame, Delmoni's violin tugs at the heart, causing the world to melt away. Simply extraordinary. Richly lyrical, Beach's piano sonata is lovingly performed. As the first movement moves from a darkly mysterious mood, the violinist fiddles and drifts along a rainy New England autumn day. Few violin pieces are so articulate. The second movement is carefree; it's springtime, there's plenty to do, and the violin and piano dance in perpetual motion. The piano and then the violin present a long, sad song, but the brooding (and clever counterpoint) gives way to freedom, peace, confidence, and optimism. Brahms's First Sonata ("Rain") is also beautiful.

LINK➤ *(Solo violin works) – Arturo Delmoni (violin)*
John Marks Records 14
A phenomenal recording made in a monastery chapel features three exquisite works. Eugène Ysaÿe's second sonata is quite difficult, but Delmoni's energy and technical skill makes it smooth and easy. Fritz Kreisler's Recitativo and Scherzo and J.S. Bach's Partita No. 2 complete a fabulous disc.

Piano Quintet – Martin Roscoe (piano), Endellion Quartet   ASV 932

Elegant, well proportioned, and effective, Beach's piano quintet is among her finest works. The piece runs just under 30 minutes, so it's paired with two chamber compositions by the 20th-century British composer Rebecca Clarke. (Records consisting entirely of Beach music are uncommon.) The quintet is set up in three movements. In the first movement, the piano plays an interesting role: it carries the mood while a fluid violin line carries most of the melody. The music is quite formal and serious, especially in the expressive second movement. Ideas coalesce in the third movement, where piano and violin dance together and sometimes intensify to a tightly wound couple. An underappreciated piece of music.

LINK➤ *The American Romantic – Alan Feinberg (piano)*   *Argo 430-330*
Pianist Feinberg explores three aspects of American romanticism. Dreaming *and* Ballade, *two pieces by Amy Beach, begin the recital. Louis Moreau Gottschalk follows with three more, notably* La Chute des feuilles *(Falling Leaves). Composer Robert Helps contributes homages to Fauré, Rachmaninoff, and Ravel.*

Cabildo – Ransom Wilson (conductor)   Delos 3170

An American evolution of European opera, this story of pirate Pierre Lafitte is set in Cabildo, the old Spanish governor's palace in New Orleans. The opera starts in the present day with a group of typically American tourists (who happen to sing as an opera chorus). A tourist falls asleep to dream of 1814, and Pierre's dance with his Lady Valerie. She dies, but returns as a ghost to help Pierre escape and ultimately save New Orleans from the British in the War of 1812. The music is spirited and original, handsome and evocative of the period. A commendable CD is completed with six short pieces (including "Dark of the Night").

LINK➤ *Scott Joplin – Treemonisha – Houston Grand Opera / Gunther Schuller*
Deutsche Grammophon 435-709
Joplin's finest work was not performed in his lifetime. Treemonisha *is an engaging, uplifting story celebrating the possibilities of black improvement through education. The producers of Joplin's time despised it, feeling black composers such as Joplin shouldn't attempt grand opera. A beautiful performance not to be missed.*

(Piano works) – Virginia Eskin (piano)   Koch 7345

Beach spent some time in the famed MacDowell artist's colony in Peterborough, NH. Amid encouragement from other female artists (a new breed at the time), Beach so enjoyed the solitude, she wrote two pieces based on bird song. To be more specific, she copied the song of the hermit thrush in musical notation, and this provided two of her most famous piano compositions. *Four Sketches* is an impressionist view of autumn, phantoms, dreaming, and fireflies. *Valse Caprice,* an early work, is a rather difficult piano piece, performed by one of Beach's finest advocates, Virginia Eskin. It's very much of the era, an evocation of turn-of-the-century America. A good Beach introduction.

LINK➤ *Edward MacDowell – Piano Music, Vol. 1 – James Barbagallo (piano)*
Marco Polo 8.223631
Composed around 1900 and sounding very much of their time, these short piano pieces are like small fairy tales—extremely well-constructed fantasies. Woodland Sketches, *from 1896, is arguably the best, although the songlike portraits of salamanders and a haunted house from* Fireside Tales *are satisfying, too.*

Ludwig van Beethoven

Born in Bonn, Germany, Beethoven lived most of his life in Vienna, Austria. He was one of music's most creative, prolific souls, but his personal life was extremely difficult. Beethoven's alcoholic father saw in his son a budding Mozart. He taught Ludwig to play and beat him when he didn't live up to expectations. By age 14, in 1784, Beethoven was a working musician; his fees supported his family. By his early twenties, Beethoven was a respected soloist and composer. Harboring resentments of rich benefactors, he also developed filthy living habits, a tendency to impregnate and disavow women, a notoriously foul mouth, a habit of playing the piano so hard he broke strings, and a generally obnoxious demeanor. By the time Beethoven was in his 30s, deafness had added to his fury. Still, he continued to compose (the period from 1812 to 1817, was a slow yet productive one). Beethoven died in 1826 after a cold developed into pneumonia.

Violin Sonatas Nos. 1–10 – Gidon Kremer (violin), Martha Argerich (piano)
Deutsche Grammophon 447-058

Although these works are called violin sonatas, they were originally composed to emphasize the piano; the violin provided accompaniment. Pianist Argerich and violinist Kremer sound like they're having a grand time with wide emotional palette here; they can express playful and somber moods equally well. Often, new ideas begin as intimately performed miniatures that grow into louder, large-scale expressions of complete themes. This style of melodic development makes for consistently intriguing listening—and drama. This 3-CD set contains some famous work, notably Sonata No. 5 (*Spring*) and Sonata No. 7 (*Kreutzer*), but it's more fun to follow the unfamiliar themes as they unfold. Handsome recording, but the violin sounds too big at times.

LINK➤ *Giuseppe Tartini – The Devil's Sonata – Andrew Manze (violin)*
Harmonia Mundi 907213

In 1765, the normally rational Tartini was visited by Satan, who performed "a sonata so unusual and so beautiful . . . with such mastery and intelligence, on a level I had never before conceived . . . possible!" He wrote down what he remembered and composed this piece around those memories. Manze is extraordinary.

Violin Concerto – Gidon Kremer (violin),
Chamber Orch. of Europe / Nikolaus Harnoncourt   Teldec 74881

For the first few minutes of this 1806 concerto, the tympani dominates. Then Kremer's violin comes in for the first solo. Both performer and composer shine, for the remainder of this movement is a showcase for the complex emotive lines so unique to Beethoven—and so completely supported by a no-holds-barred giant orchestra (the contrast between delicacy and big energy is a key concept here). The second movement initially belongs to Harnoncourt, whose exquisite control and patience unfolds a theme, which becomes a dialogue with soloist Kremer. The best part is the final movement, with its familiar melody, musical trickery, and big finish. A crystal-clear recording makes the most of Kremer's artistry.

LINK➤ *Isaac Stern: A Life in Music – Isaac Stern (violin)*   **SONY Classical 67193**

An 11-CD set featuring one of the century's greatest violinists. This is an inspired, and inspiring, investment whose many high points include Beethoven and Brahms concertos, and a wealth of standard repertoire by Mozart, Bach, Vivaldi, Bruch, Tchaikovsky, and so on.

Piano Concertos Nos. 1–5 –
Maurizio Pollini(piano), Claudio Abbado / Berlin Phil.

Deutsche Grammophon 439-770
Although Murray Perahia and Bernard Haitink's Royal Concertgebouw deliver a fine mid-1980s performance (Sony Classical 44575), the crown goes to this 3-CD set from 1994 because it sounds better. The concertos were not published in the same order they were written. Start with Piano Concerto No. 2, composed (and revised several times) mostly in the first half of the 1790s. (Beethoven actually wrote a piano concerto in 1784, but it didn't survive.) Acknowledging a debt to Mozart's mastery of the form, Beethoven presses ahead with urgency and begins to reinvent it. The "second" concerto is extremely varied—a stormy patch segues into a beautifully serene passage; multiple themes are thoroughly developed, seemingly discarded, and then brought back with either simplicity or great majesty. Pollini demonstrates awesome versatility as he alters mood, color, and dynamics, sometimes within seconds. Piano Concerto No. 3, from 1803, is more closely related to Beethoven's early symphonies (which he wrote in the early 1800s) than to Mozart's ideas. (Incidentally, many of these dates are not precise; Beethoven composed part of this work in the late 1790s, added to it around 1800, and continued this way until the work was published in 1803.) By now, Beethoven is exploring conflicts. The piano overpowers the orchestra at times in the first movement. This is enormously challenging material—serious and complicated. The second movement provides relief; consistent with the form, it's slow and dreamy, but the dignified presentation strongly suggests the bold resolution of conflict. Throughout both movements, melodies and dramatic touches will be very familiar. The third movement is a brilliant resolution—a celebration. Piano Concerto No. 5, from 1809, is thrilling in its titanic splendor, but it's also filled with delicate melodic expressions. It's a test of skill for all involved, including the recording engineer who must balance blasts of orchestral power with microtones associated with solo piano (or small groups of strings). Consistent with proper form, the slow second movement relaxes the pace, and Pollini's solo performance is lovely (Beethoven helps out with a handsome bed of violins). The final section, a rondo, begins with a nod to the original concept of the concerto—to replicate a series of European dances. At this point in Beethoven's musical development, the actual dances are in shadow, surrounded by far livelier ideas. This is music for the ages.

LINK➤ *Ludwig van Beethoven – Triple Concerto –*
Beaux Arts Trio, Kurt Masur / Gewandhausorchester Leipzig   **Philips 438-005**
The Concerto in C, Op. 56 for Piano, Violin and Cello, with Orchestra often sounds like a symphony, but lacks focus and climax. Opening themes, in a storm of cellos and basses, are intriguing, and this is a very convincing 1992 performance, as is an older one from 1969 by Oistrakh, Rostropovich, Richter, and von Karajan (EMI 6474).

Classical CD Listener's Guide   *21*

Symphonies Nos. 1-9 – Staatskapelle Dresden / Sir Colin Davis
Philips 446-067

This supreme accomplishment is unavailable in the U.S. but it's easy to justify the special effort required to purchase it from a specialty mail order or a Web retailer. The 1994 recording is excellent, and the performances are smart and invigorating but slightly conservative, emphasizing clarity of expression over bombast. The 6-CD set also includes the *Egmont* and *Lenore* Overtures. The first eight symphonies were composed from 1800 until 1812; the ninth is a decade newer. Symphony No. 1 follows eighteenth-century heroes like Haydn, emphasizing dance, humor, and grace. Symphony No. 2 is more original, from the eruptions breaking through pretty string arrangements to rapid changes in temperament. Sometimes working with gigantic proportions, Beethoven accumulates energy, releases it, and then works even the delicate themes into mounting storms—this must have been completely incomprehensible to an 1802 audience! His Symphony No. 3 (*Eroica*) is a masterpiece that starts with a jolt, and then twists and turns a basic theme throughout the first movement, further perfecting his gather-and-release approach to cinematic storytelling. Symphony No. 5 is greater still—it's one of Beethoven's most popular works and one of the defining works of mankind's music. Beethoven rarely did the same thing twice. Symphony No. 6 (*Pastoral*) is a soundtrack for a stroll through the countryside; inevitably, there's a thunderstorm (with lots of special effects), followed by sunny skies. The final three symphonies are also masterpieces: Symphony No. 7 is triumphant in its mighty rhythms, Symphony No. 8 follows some ideas explored in Symphony No. 2, and Symphony No. 9, with its quotation from "Ode to Joy," is an appeal to God.

LINK➤ *Ludwig van Beethoven – 9 Symphonies – Arturo Toscanini*   **RCA 60324**
Here's the other end of the spectrum—Beethoven as a roller coaster ride, jam-packed with thrilling fast tempos and gargantuan finales. These radio-quality recordings from the early 1950s capture the excitement, but not the nuance. Still, it's a not-to-be-missed 5-CD set.

Symphonies Nos. 2, 5 –
Chamber Orch. of Europe / Nikolaus Harnoncourt   Teldec 75712

This is exciting! In the early 1990s, Harnoncourt confronted listeners with an aggressive, emotional take on Beethoven's symphonies—and made them sound new, exciting, and irresistible. Symphony No. 5 is his showcase, supported by a remarkable engineering job. Harnoncourt's strategy magnifies the importance of trombones, piccolo, and double bassoon, and the military imagery that accompanies Beethoven's addition of these instruments to the symphony orchestra. Somehow that same strategy makes the lightness of the work's slower second movement more expansive. The payoff, in the final movement, is enormous. As for Symphony No. 2, the work has rarely been afforded sufficient attention; Harnoncourt's brilliant choices regarding emphasis of smaller instrument sounds bring the piece to life.

LINK➤ *Ludwig van Beethoven – 9 Symphonies –*
Chamber Orchestra of Europe / Nikolaus Harnoncourt   **Teldec 46452**
This 5-CD box presents a refreshing, coherent approach to all of Beethoven's symphonies, each of which is brilliantly recorded. As a direct follow-up to the above CD, try the coupling of Symphony No. 6 and Symphony No. 8 (Teldec 75709) or the slightly fast, but totally electrifying, Symphony No. 9 (75713).

The Complete Sonatas – Richard Goode (piano)   Nonesuch 79328

By most counts, Beethoven composed 32 piano sonatas. The first 23 were written between 1795 and 1805; the rest were created every few years through 1822. Many have been popular for nearly two centuries. Start right in with Piano Sonata No. 1. The familiar Allegro opening is introduced by a formality associated with a courtly dance, but alters the size and pace of the piano's presentation so many times that the dance becomes little more than a seedbed for newer ideas. The same sonata ends with an especially dramatic Prestissimo, designed to show off the pianist Beethoven's technical skill and bravura. Among the other well-known pieces, there's Sonata No. 8 (Pathetique), with the complicated emotional demands of its first movement; the often-played Sonata No. 14 (*Moonlight*), with its velvet-covered chords that evoke the night; the complex virtuoso turns of Sonata No. 23 (*Appassionata*); and the huge undertaking known as Sonata No. 29 (*Hammerklavier*), where Bach's fugues are clearly heard as influences (interesting to hear Bach's ideas filtered through Beethoven's enthusiasm). The style and texture of these pieces is extremely varied; Beethoven used his sonatas as a kind of creative sketchbook, a smaller-scale workspace where he could grow on his own without the need for other musicians. Richard Goode has emerged as a leading Beethoven (and Mozart) interpreter. His creative decisions allow more than ten hours of solo music to flow without causing the listener to tire or to question his choices. This is yet another boxed set (10 CDs) that belongs in every collection.

LINK▶ Ludwig van Beethoven – Piano Sonatas – Alfred Brendel (piano)   Philips 412-575
The long-term champion, although Daniel Barenboim provides serious modern competition (EMI 62863). The previous generation revered Wilhelm Kempf (Deutsche Grammophon 447-966). For moments of absolute magic, Brendel often leaves Goode behind.

The Quartets – Quatour Végh   Valois 4400

Beethoven's 16 string quartets were written in three groups; many of the Late Quartets are masterpieces, and others are spectacular in their own right. Once again, with an artist of Beethoven's stature and infinite genius, the excursion through decades of exciting composition is wonderfully rewarding. From 1798 until 1800, Beethoven wrote the set of six quartets that make up Opus 18 on a commission from the wealthy Austrian Prince Lobkowitz. The quartets are generally formal and somewhat similar to works by Haydn (who also wrote for Lobkowitz) and sometimes to Mozart. Beethoven, however, typically moves the basic formulas into a thicker, more emotional space, and the Végh Quartet responds by applying the appropriate weight (these pieces can be overplayed for the drama, destroying Beethoven's keen balances). The engineer also deserves recognition for achieving clarity and equilibrium. Three pieces composed in 1805 and 1806 are known as the Rasumovsky Quartets in honor of the Russian ambassador (and amateur violinist) who paid Beethoven to write them. The third of these quartets, the Eroica, takes some time to develop, but ultimately revises then-current thinking about the form and content of a quartet. Still, the best was yet to come. The Late Quartets, written mostly in 1824 and 1825, are richly emotional statements only vaguely resembling formal quartets (the first three of these were commissioned by Prince Galitzin of Russia). This is especially true of Opus 130 (the later opus numbers contain only one quartet) built within six movements (instead of the traditional three or four) and including the Grosse Fugue, a devishly difficult work that Beethoven subsequently, and reluctantly, replaced with a rondo that was easier to play.

LINK➤ *Ludwig van Beethoven – The String Quartets – Emerson String Quartet*
Deutsche Grammophon 447-052
Beautifully recorded 1996 box (7 CDs) demonstrates a more aggressive, more filigreed approach to the quartets. The added muscle makes the late quartets even more appealing as theatrical ventures, but the Végh versions are easier to bear for extended listening sessions.

Symphony No. 9 – Berlin Phil. Orch. / Herbert von Karajan
Deutsche Grammophon 415-832

Among the many fine recordings of the Choral Symphony, this 1976 release most successfully captures the connection between man, God, and the universe. Karajan's approach is furious and fiery, certainly in the volcanic second movement, and especially in the blazing finale, where expert solo voices and the Vienna Singverein (a large chorus) are transformed into a singular force. From the moment the cellos establish Beethoven's quotation from Schiller's "Ode to Joy," to tenor Peter Schreir's splendid solo, to instrument-like vocal arrangements (with little space for breaths), to the instrumental bridges, to the overwhelming power of the chorus, this is a stunning work of art. Analog recording does the job.

LINK➤ *Ludwig van Beethoven – Symphony No. 5 – Vienna Phil. / Carlos Kleiber*
Deutsche Grammophon 447-400
Another truly great recording from the mid-1970s. Other esteemed single recordings include Günter Wand's early 1990s Symphony No. 3 (RCA 60755) and Symphonies Nos. 5 and 6 (61930), Bruno Walter's late 1950s Symphonies Nos. 4 and 6 (Sony Classical 64462), and Claudio Abbado's Symphonies Nos. 7 and 8 (DG 423-364).

Missa Solemnis – Orchestre Révolutionnaire et Romantique,
Monteverdi Choir / John Eliot Gardiner   **Archiv 429-779**

Unlike other great Masses, which tell Christ's story and sanctify God's message, Beethoven's *Missa Solemnis* explores individual faith. And unlike most Masses, which attempt to satisfy churchgoers, Beethoven sets up a major creative challenge: to combine symphonic majesty with the ultimate simplicity of sacred music. Gardiner excels, where others often stumble, in divining religious ecstacy, getting the most out of abused vocalists (Beethoven treated them like instruments), and gliding the massive choral passages (which dominate the first two movements) so that they glisten alongside the orchestrations. Awe-inspiring moments include the opening Kyrie, the fugues that end the Gloria, and the final prayer for peace, interrupted by military madness. Requires careful listening.

LINK➤ *Clemens non Papa – Missa Pastores quidnam vidistis –*
Tallis Scholars / Peter Phillips   *Gimell 13*
The Tallis Scholars preceded the current interest in ancient music and chant. And they're better than everybody else. Their attention to detail, their ability to evoke a time and place, and the pure beauty of their voices should encourage sampling of their work. This Flemish piece from the Renaissance is a good place to begin.

Vincenzo Bellini

Bellini wrote his operas slowly (no more than one per year), taking time to develop the perfect combination of emotion, melody, and lyric—a heartfelt approach to storytelling unlike the more formulaic working style associated with his contemporaries Rossini and Donizetti. Bellini was born in Sicily in 1801; he attended music school in Naples, subsidized by the duke and duchess of San Martino. He was a good pupil, and started writing student operas around 1820. Bellini's renown grew, first in Naples and then throughout Italy. By 1827, he was one of the country's top composers and a principal creator of the bel canto style—a romantic approach demanding enormous vocal capacity and range. While living outside Paris, Bellini's health declined; he was exhausted by the effort required to create *I Puritani* and suffered from a serious liver ailment and an intestinal inflamation. Bellini died at age 34 in Puteaux, France, in 1835.

La Sonnambula (The Sleepwalker) – Luba Orgonasova, Raúl Giménez, others; Netherlands Radio Chamber Orch. / Alberto Zedda   NAXOS 8.660042

A melodrama with sweet, pretty songs, *La Sonnambula* moves rather slowly, but it includes several outstanding moments, and a bang-up finale. It's the story of Anima, who moves through a Swiss town walking and talking in her sleep; mostly, she talks about love, and because her words come from the subconscious, they're especially credible. Most of the best work is in the second act, notably Orgonasova's performance of "Reggimi, o bouna madre," and the quartet featuring Elvino (tenor Raúl Giménez). Although the performance is a bit provincial, it comes together nicely. For those more interested in star turns, try Joan Sutherland (somewhat fussy, but in fine voice) and Luciano Pavarotti on Bonygne's 1980 version (London 417-424).

LINK► *Vincenzo Bellini – Il Puritani (The Puritans) – Sutherland, Pavarotti; Royal Opera House Orch. / Richard Bonynge/*   *London 417-588*
Bellini's final opera, with both Sutherland and Pavarotti in excellent form, circa 1974. Highly recommended, but don't miss Maria Callas's classic 1953 performance (with a shakier supporting cast and a recording that isn't as good).

Norma – Maria Callas; La Scala Orch. / Tullio Serafin
EMI 56271

Don't let the 1954 mono recording slow you down; this is one of Maria Callas's finest performances of one of Italy's best operas. Bellini's melodies are vividly emotional, but never overbearing; they require a wicked combination of power, perfect vocal timbre, and tragic acting, all of which Callas mastered. The voices command center stage, and they are magnificent. The purity and lack of affectation in Callas's soprano demands rapt attention. And when she sings "Mira O Norma (See, Oh Norma)" in the third act, she soars (her partner in this duet is also splendid; she's Ebe Stignani, an aging opera heroine). Serafin's style and theatrics are excellent. Highly recommended. Composed in 1831.

LINK► *Amilcare Ponchielli – La Gioconda (The Joyful Girl) – Maria Callas; La Scala Orch. / Antonio Votto*   *EMI 49518*
From 1959, one of Callas's more inspiring performances (with a technical flaw here and there). Her intensity, especially on "Suicidio!" is without equal, although the Caballé version (London 414-349) is a worthy second choice. Excellent support and direction from Votto.

Alban Berg

Born into a Viennese family in 1885, Berg showed promise as a teenaged composer, but financial realities encouraged him to begin a career as a government clerk. Berg's musical education, however, continued; in 1904, he began a relationship with Arnold Schoenberg. Over the next decade, Berg came to embrace Schoenberg's radical ideas, both in his operas (*Wozzeck, Lulu*) and in his chamber pieces (a 1913 performance of his songs resulted in an audience riot). Berg continued composing through military service in WW I and a break in relations with his friend and teacher Schoenberg. Berg died of blood poisoning in 1935, and after a decade of relative silence (due in part to a Nazi "degenerate" label attached to his music), his work gained acceptance in a postwar world. Berg's compositions have proven to be the most accessible of the so-called Second Viennese School.

Wozzeck – Franz Grundheber, Hildegard Behrens, others;
Weiner Phil. / Claudio Abbado   Deutsche Grammophon 423-587

Wozzeck is a soldier whose personal devastation becomes a metaphor for the crumbling of German life in the 1930s. (In fact, it's based on a play written by Georg Bücher 70 years earlier.) Wozzeck is abused by his senior officers, cuckolded by his wife, and hated by the crowd after he murders her. Every adult is guilty; the innocent child in the final scene faces a dismal future of physical and emotional abuse. Lyrics are delivered in a singing-speaking combination called "sprechgesan," sometimes elevating into a violent passion. The music is aggressively grating and unbeautiful, but Berg's use of motifs and an overall unifying structure is admirable. From 1923.

LINK▶ *Krzysztof Penderecki – Anaklasis, Threnody, others. –*
London Sym. Orch.; Polish National Radio SO / Penderecki   *EMI 65077*

Making Berg seem like a light sitcom, Penderecki's fierce nightmare brings the listener face to face with horror in Threnody for the Victims of Hiroshima. *This brief piece is the reason to purchase the CD; the other pieces tend to be slow-moving experiments in sound shaping.*

Neue Viennese School: Second Viennese School—LaSalle Quartet
Deutsche Grammophon 419-994

One of the finest recordings of Berg's complete *Lyric Suite for String Quartet* is part of a significant 4-CD box filled with chamber works by Berg's cohorts, Arnold Schoenberg and Anton Webern. First, the *Lyric Suite*. It's a work comprised of six movements, and it only vaguely resembles traditional European chamber music. Composed on the 12-tone scale, the first movement seems nearly traditional at the outset; it's an airy chat between violins and cello. The mood becomes increasingly discordant, but maintains a familiar, comforting coherence. Musical relationships between instrument sounds, climaxes, and melody lines are handled in a more or less "normal" way. Given the time and energy to follow Berg's paths, the piece proves to be forward-thinking and brilliant. The second movement pursues a more solitary feeling, but evolves into a pleasant, if surreal, dance. The third movement begins with unrelated trails of practice sounds and plucking; it slowly comes together, painting an abstraction with broad strokes. And so it goes—this relentlessly modern music is always intriguing and surprisingly accessible for the patient listener. In truth, more than half of this set belongs to Schoenberg, and the majority of the 340-page liner notes are devoted to his music (complete with excerpts from scores). And if Berg is the more accessible, Schoenberg is a far more adept communicator, a confident force whose several pieces here provide new insight regarding his influence over a generation of forward-thinking composers.

LINK► *Schoenberg - Berg - Webern – Berlin Phil. / Herbert von Karajan*
Deutsche Grammophon 427-424

The ideal orchestral mate to the LaSalle Quartet offering, this 3-CD set contains many of the important pieces from the "Second Viennese School," performed with great conviction and fury by Karajan. Berg's Lyric Suite, *Schoenberg's* Pelleas und Melisande, *and Webern's* Passacaglia for Orchestra *are among many distinguished selections.*

Lulu – Teresa Stratas, others; Orchestré dl'Opera de Paris / Pierre Boulez
Deutsche Grammophon 415-489

Stratas is an expert at creating deranged females, and Lulu is one of the best. This 1935 opera, completed by Friedrich Cerha after Berg's death, follows Lulu from a snake metaphor, to cheating wife, to murderer, to prostitute. Her destructive personality was created by German playwright Frank Wedekind, and Berg does little to beautify the proceedings. Stratas is probably best during her intense and terrified last song, "Wer Ist Das?" ("Who's This One?"), an ominous duet with Jack the Ripper, who kills her. Songs are performed in a style that straddles speaking and singing, and time spent listening will reveal structural excellence, deft weaving of motifs, and some striking musical ideas.

LINK► *Ervín Schulhoff – Flammen (Flames) –*
Kurt Westi, Iris Vermillion, Symphonie-Orchester Berlin / John Mauceri   **London 444-630**

A well-known composer between the wars, Schulhoff was imprisoned by the Nazis and died in a concentration camp. The passions of the 1920s—jazz, dancing, sex—were part of his music. Here, he tells the Don Juan story by combining modern sizzle, fire and brimstone, and old-fashioned romance. It's exciting music.

Violin Concerto – Thomas Zehetmair (violin);
Deutsche Kammerphilharmonie / Heinz Holliger   Teldec 97449

Berg's 1935 violin concerto sets out gently, a solo fiddle trying out a few notes here and there, establishing a direction. Muted horns show the way. As the blossom unfolds, other instruments thicken the texture. The young voice becomes steadier, now leading other strings in a series of tense variations. It shimmers on its own, then becomes grim. The second movement blends Eastern European folk dancing with 12-tone harshness; the two seem to cooperate. Big and symphonic, the third movement finds a violinist strong against gigantic forces. The fourth movement is true to the work's subtitle, "To the Memory of an Angel." With a Janácek and Hartman violin concerto.

LINK► *Piano Works of the New Viennese School – Yuji Takahashi (piano)*   **Denon 1060**

A literate, meticulous performance of piano pieces by Schoenberg, Webern, and Berg, this is probably the best place to start on their excursions through the twelve-tone system. The liner notes are brief, but comprehensive. A 2-CD set.

Hector Berlioz

Berlioz was a doctor's son; he grew up near Grenoble, France. Although he showed little talent as a child, he wanted to become a musician. In 1821, his father sent him to medical school in Paris, but Berlioz dropped out, and enrolled in the Paris Conservatory to study composition. In 1827, Berlioz saw Irish actress Harriet Smithson in a performance of Shakespeare's *Hamlet.* Infatuated with Smithson, he badgered (and terrified) her for six years until she became his wife. (A dreadful marriage; no surprise.) Meanwhile, Berlioz established himself as a composer and a conductor. His penchant for large-scale compositions peaked with 1855's *L'Imperiale,* performed by an orchestra, military band, 1,200-voice chorus , and five secondary conductors who were electrically connected to maintain a consistent beat. Almost all of Berlioz's compositions were gigantic; over time, they were performed less and less. Berlioz died, miserable, in 1869.

Symphonie Fantastique – Cleveland Orch. & Chorus / Pierre Boulez
Deutsche Grammophon 453-432

Throughout this 1830 symphonic fantasy, a single theme is repeated. In Berlioz's mind, this *idée fixe* represents Harriet Smithson; he wrote this symphony for her. The work is deranged, but well organized into five distinct scenes (it's also the first major symphony to tell a story.) "Reveries, Passions" describes love at first sight, and then a dizzying vortex of jealousy, furious anger, and finally, tenderness. In "A Ball," he observes his intended everywhere. "A Scene in the Country" calms him. Racked with insecurity, he takes opium for the "March to the Scaffold," underdoses, hallucinates, and conjures the hysterical "Dream of a Witches' Sabbath" for the death of both lovers. Stunning performance, masterful recording. Fabulous!

LINK➤ *Oliver Knussen – Flourish with Fireworks, other pieces –*
London Sinfonietta / Oliver Knussen   Deutsche Grammophon 449-572
Well-known for 1980s fantasies like the opera version of Maurice Sendak's Where the Wild Things Are, *Knussen proves himself a master of orchestral color, timing, and drama with the title work, the dreamy ". . .Upon One Note," and a clever Purcell fantasia. A gem.*

Harold in Italy – London Sym. Orch. / Sir Colin Davis   Philips 416-431

Two stories inform this music. One has Paganini commissioning it, looking at the sheet music, and hating it because there were no virtuoso turns; he later begged forgiveness (on his knees) when he heard it performed. The other is about inspiration: after walking in Italy, Berlioz composed something between a viola concerto and a symphony about what he saw. (He felt a bit like Byron's sad dreamer, "Childe Harolde," hence the title.) By 1834, Berlioz had advanced his *idée fixe* concept to include variations, and this complex work, brimming with orchestral storms and wonderful solos by Nouko Imai (viola), is mastered by Davis's 1975 recording.

LINK➤ *Hector Berlioz – Harold in Italy –*
Orchestre Révolutionnaire et Romantique / John Eliot Gardiner   Philips 446-676
A positively thrilling period performance, largely because Gardiner is unfraid to make the most of the extreme contrasts that are so central to this piece. Even if you're not a big fan of period instruments, this rendition should not be overlooked.

Les nuits d'été – Dame Jane Baker, Sir John Barbirolli / New Philharmonia Orch. EMI 69544

By the mid-1850s, the Germans had great song cycles, but the French didn't. Using Théophile Gautier's poems, Berlioz gracefully composed six songs, united by languishing imagery of exquisite depression and lustrous beauty. Barbioli provides tender accompaniment to mezzo-soprano Baker's clear, warm, wonderful voice. They shine, particularly on the lament called "Sur les lagunes (On the lagoons)" and "Absence." In razor-sharp English, the lyrics seem overblown, but sung in French, they're evocative: "The flower of my life is closed," "Upon the yew a pale dove, mournful and alone," and so on. No problem with the 1968 recording. Excerpts from *Les Troyens* complete the disc.

LINK▶ *Franz Schubert – An 1826 Schubertiad – Christine Schäfer, John Mark Ainsley, Richard Jackson, Graham Johnson* **Hyperion 33026**
A re-creation of an 1826 party, thrown by Schubert's friends, to hear his music. Pianist Johnson's series (he's recording every known Schubert song) is excellent. A good place to start on classical "songs."

La Damnation de Faust – Susan Graham, Thomas Moser, José Van Dam, Orch. and Chorus of Opera de Lyon / Kent Nagano Erato 10692

Berlioz called his version of Goethe's devil story a "dramatic legend" or "concert opera," intended to be sung, not staged. It's sung beautifully here by soloists and a splendid chorus. Aided by a top-notch recording, Nagano's expert mood-setting brings the whole story to life. He's often at center stage, slashing away on "Hungarian March," lyrical on "Dance of the Sylphs," and terrifying as Faust and Méphistophélés "Ride to the Abyss." Song by song, Berlioz is remarkable: a lovely romantic piece for Faust's lover Marguerite (Susan Graham), consistently brilliant melodies for the clever Méphistophélés (José Van Dam), and character pieces for Faust (Thomas Moser). Berlioz and Nagano share exquisite taste. A 2-CD set from 1994.

LINK▶ *Arrigo Boito – Mephistopheles – Samuel Ramey, Vincenzo La Scola, others; La Scala Orch./ Riccardo Muti* **RCA 68284**
Boito lacked Berlioz's natural songwriting talent, but he wrote a demonstration piece for an operatic devil. Ramey masters the role.. Superb 1996 recording; good storytelling, too.

Les Troyens (The Trojans) – Jon Vickers, Josephine Veasey, others, Covent Garden Opera House Orch. / Sir Colin Davis Philips 416-432

A sprawling epic long enough to occupy 4 CDs, Berlioz's masterwork is unreasonable for nearly any opera company, even split into *La Prise de Troie* (The Taking of Troy) and *Les Troyens à Carthage* (The Trojans at Carthage). Berlioz wrote his own libretto, basing it on Virgil's stories of the Greek triumph over Troy, Aeneas's plan to found a new Troy, and an ultimate vision that would become Rome. Berlioz loved these stories and told them well, through brilliant orchestral colors, and showcase songs (which Jon Vickers, as Aeneas, performs extremely well). A major achievement for Colin Davis, nurtured by a 1969 recording that still sounds new. Stupendous! (But beware—it's very time-consuming.)

LINK▶ *Michael Tippett – King Priam – Norman Bailey, Heather Harper, others; London Sinfonietta / David Atherton* **Chandos 9406/7**
The stories of the Trojans, King Priam, and Dido and Aeneas, have been mined by other opera composers. Tippett's 1962 version shocked the opera world because it was rough, intentionally awkward, and fearless. Atherton and his singers manage a remarkable perfomance of a difficult piece.

Leonard Bernstein

Growing up in the early 1960s: JFK was president, and Leonard Bernstein was classical music. Bernstein became famous because he was on television. He was an energetic, photogenic man who made sense of the classics and conducted like an Olympic athlete. Bernstein was born in Massachusetts in 1918, attended Harvard University and the Curtis Institute, and assisted Serge Koussevitzky at Tanglewood and Arthur Rodzinski at the New York Philharmonic. Bernstein won renown in 1943 when he conducted the orchestra in Bruno Walters's place (Walters was ill). In 1958, Bernstein became the New York Philharmonic's first U.S.-born conductor. In the interim, he composed for Broadway, setting a new standard with 1958's *West Side Story*. Beginning in the 1960s, he also presented television's *Young People's Concerts*, wrote books, composed film scores, lectured, and conducted top European orchestras. In short, Leonard Bernstein became the American face of classical music. He worked until shortly before his death in 1990.

A Portrait: The Theater Works, Vol. 1 — SONY Classical 47154

This exciting side trip begins with *Fancy Free*, a ballet choreographed by Bernstein collaborator Jerome Robbins. Evocative of 1944 wartime NYC, it told of three sailors on a 24-hour shore leave, prowling for love. This work led to Bernstein's 1944 Broadway debut, *On the Town*, whose original cast album begins this 3-CD set. Musically, it's an important precursor to *West Side Story*, represented here by ten *Symphonic Dances* lovingly presented by the New York Philharmonic. Bernstein's grand-scale film score for Elia Kazan's *On the Waterfront* is another NYC thriller, but its *Symphonic Suite*, included here, modernizes classicism. Ditto for the *Candide* overture, and the complete opera *Trouble in Tahiti*. Just terrific!

LINK➤ *Leonard Bernstein – On the Town – Frederica von Stade, Tyne Daly, Samuel Ramey, Thomas Hampson, others; London SO / Michael Tilson Thomas*
Deutsche Grammophon 437-516
The best recording of Bernstein's first Broadway musical reveals considerable sophistication ("Not Out of Bed Yet"), and many songs, such as Ramey's "Gabey's Comin'," are marvelous. Much humor stands up (Tyne Daly singing "Come Up to My Place" works), but some overreaches.

West Side Story (Original Broadway Cast) –
Carol Lawrence, Larry Kert, others — Columbia 60724

West Side Story is Leonard Bernstein's masterpiece, but there is no perfect recording of his 1957 Broadway street opera. The original cast album offers the best combination of acting, effective storytelling, and pleasant singing voices; it sounds "right." The 1960 film soundtrack (Sony 48211) is okay, but Broadway's Carol Lawrence outperforms Marni Nixon (who sang Maria for Natalie Wood). Bernstein's version with opera singers (Deutsche Grammophon 415-254) contains more of the score (and too much badly acted dialogue). Kiri Te Kanawa plays Maria and José Carreras does Tony. Songs like "Maria," "Tonight," "I Feel Pretty," and especially "Somewhere" contribute to a score that ranks high on any list of 20th-century music. The remastered 1998 re-issue also contains Bernstein's *Symphonic Dances from West Side Story*.

LINK➤ *Leonard Bernstein – West Side Story – Oscar Peterson Trio* — **Verve 821-575**
Bernstein's musical inspired many jazz stars (and still does), and there have been many jazz renditions of "Somewhere" and other songs. Make no mistake—this version is jazz, not a Broadway rehash. Peterson's trio understands Bernstein's music and takes it further than Bernstein did himself.

A Portrait: Orchestral Works   SONY Classical 47162

Bernstein composed his Symphony No. 1 ("Jeremiah") in 1942, at age 24. It's filled with youthful outbursts, many interesting—but rarely developed—ideas, energetic brass excursions, and a rough connection to the Babylonian destruction of Jerusalem. This is all rather dramatically resolved by a soprano lamentation and a musical setting of sacred Hebrew text in the third movement. Symphony No. 2 ("Age of Anxiety") was inspired by W.H. Auden's poem; like 1971's *Mass*, it passes through many styles, taking the best from romantic and 20th-century music. Unencumbered by later expectations, Bernstein freely explores human existence through two sets of handsome, well-considered thematic variations. Some are winsome and introspective; others are impressive in their storm and struggle. This is a six-movement symphony based on four lonely people in a NYC bar. By the fourth movement, everyone is quite drunk (the orchestration cleverly describes their condition), and it becomes clear that the anxiety in the work's title is an inner struggle. Bernstein's third symphony is a "Kaddish," a Jewish prayer for the dead. It was written in remembrance of John F. Kennedy. Bernstein's wife, Felicia Montealegre, speaks through much of it with gnashing earnestness. The symphonic orchestrations are reduced to background and incidental status. Chicester Psalms, from 1965, illuminates some of Symphony No. 3's ideas with a full-scale chorus and an orchestra unafraid to present very modern, sometimes jazz-style accompaniment. The music is very optimistic, energizing, and performed with great vigor. A quiet, rarely heard piece from 1954 is one of the set's jewels. It's called *Serenade for Solo Violin, String Orchestra, Harp and Percussion*, and was inspired by Plato's "Symposium," which discussed aspects of love. Unerringly classical in design, but with sonorities that would again be heard in *West Side Story*, it's a joy. The best piece on this set is also the shortest—under 8 minutes. Composed for Woody Herman, 1949's *Prelude, Fugue and Riffs* very successfully merges swing jazz with classical form; it's one of Bernstein's best pieces. The prelude blasts its freewheeling rhythm, but Bernstein's clever take on the rigid fugue form is the piece's heart. By the final section, the riffs sound like 52nd Street jazz, yet they're orchestrated, not improvised. Bernstein's adaptation of jazz for orchestra is well beyond Gershwin's best ideas. For this and for so many reasons, this 3-CD set deserves more attention than it has received.

LINK▶ *Benny Goodman – Collector's Edition: Compositions & Collaborations*
                                                                  CBS Masterworks 42227
Clarinetist Goodman performs on several jazzier classical pieces: Bernstein's Prelude, Fugue and Riffs *(same recording), Aaron Copland's excellent* Concerto for Clarinet, *Igor Stravinsky's* Ebony Concerto, *plus works by Morton Gould and Béla Bartók. Excellent!*

Candide – Jerry Hadley, June Anderson, others;
London Sym. Orch. / Leonard Bernstein   Deutsche Grammophon 429-734

What a great overture! Bernstein captures the sweep of opera and operetta in a delightfully melodic review based, in large part, upon the Panglossian theme, "Best of All Possible Worlds." The arrangements are breathtaking, and Bernstein's at the peak of his conducting powers. Voltaire's 1759 book provided the inspiration, characters, and storyline, but it's Jerry Hadley's smashing performance as Candide that brings this satire to glorious life. Credit Richard Wilbur for the tongue-in-cheek lyrics, and also Lillian Hellman, Dorothy Parker, and Stephen Sondheim. Many musical homages and many good songs, such as "Glitter and Be Gay" and "Oh, Happy We," dot this outstanding 1989 recording.

Classical CD Listener's Guide   *31*

LINK► *Various Composers – Golden Days – Jerry Hadley (tenor); American Theatre Orch.*
/ Paul Gemignani   **RCA 62681**

*Hadley visits the early days of Broadway (when operetta was a close kin) and has a plenty of fun with
material by Sigmund Romberg, Victor Herbert, and Rudolf Friml. "The Streets of New York" and
"When I Grow Too Old to Dream" are among many stylish highlights.*

Mass – Leonard Bernstein   SONY Classical 63089

When Bernstein's *Mass* opened the Kennedy Center in Washington,
D.C., in 1971, most listeners didn't think much of his show-biz
approach to religious celebration. Bernstein finds a snappy rhythm
in the phrase "Kyrie eleison (Lord have mercy)" and makes it work
for a street chorus, that uses a sweet-voiced rock singer to confess in
vernacular terms ("Get this load off my chest!"). A formal, classical
soprano song and a cutesy Broadway musical number simulating a
preacher's sermon are included among some highly original, and mostly appealing work. Pre-
tentious patches aside—and there are no shortage of these—Bernstein's attempt at something
truly new and different is worth a listen. It gets an earnest, well-intentioned performance, too.

LINK► *Michael Daugherty – Metropolis Symphony –*
Baltimore Sym. Orch. /David Zinman   **Argo 452-103**

*This 1993 score, which employs rock, jazz, funk and avant-garde styles, celebrates "the mythology of
Superman." Movements draw their energy from the diabolical "Lex" (Luthor), the mischevious
"Mxyzptlk," the exploding "Krypton," and of course, Lois Lane. It's really fun.*

Leonard Bernstein's New York – Soloists; Orch. of St. Luke's / Eric Stern
Nonesuch 79400

With "(New York's a) Lonely Town," Dawn Upshaw sets the tone for the wonder of Leonard
Bernstein during Manhattan's golden era. One can easily picture her walking along along a
darkened Sixth Avenue, pre-skyscraper brownstones lining the sad streets, her teary eyes glim-
mering in the street lights. On *Wonderful Town*'s "What a Waste," Richard Muenz laments the
way NYC devours talent. Mandy Patinkin is the busy New Yorker who sings "(Oh well, we'll
catch up) Some Other Time." Upshaw and Muenz create the finest version of *West Side Story*'s
"One Hand, One Heart" ever recorded. Despite Bernstein's earnest efforts at art songs, his
Broadway work was the best of his career.

LINK► *Leonard Bernstein – Songfest, Symphony No. 1 –*
Saint Louis Sym. Orch. / Leonard Slatkin   **RCA 61581**

*Songfest, from 1977, is a song cycle of American poems. It's formal, vast, and impassively serious.
Bernstein's 1988 cycle, Arias and Barcarolles, studies a marriage through really silly lyrics (on occasion,
Bernstein's attempts at artfulness can be truly embarrassing);* A Quiet Place Suite *and* West Side
Story*'s "Symphonic Dances" complete an otherwise fine CD (DG 439-926).*

Georges Bizet

Georges Bizet loved bonbons. He also enjoyed chocolates, petits fours, and other sweet indulgences. Born in Paris, France, in 1838, Bizet was a prodigiously talented child who was a Paris Conservatory student at the age of 9. A young man with tremendous promise, Bizet had a bad temper, a tendency to roll up into a psychosomatic ball when things went badly, and shaky judgment. Bizet won the Prix de Rome in 1857 and then meandered from one project to the next, rarely finishing any of them. He married the daughter of Conservatory teacher Jacques Haléy in 1869 (Halévy had also composed a popular French opera, *La Juive*). Bizet then focused all of his energies on a seedy street-life tale called *Carmen*, and when its March 3, 1875, premiere went badly ("a definite and hopeless flop"), he became ill. On June 3, Bizet died from a heart attack at age 36. Shortly thereafter, *Carmen* became one of opera's greatest hits.

L'Arlesienne Suite – Montreal Sym. Orch. / Charles Dutoit   London 417-839
Bizet had a gift for writing basic, elemental music. These two suites (*L'Arlesienne* and *Carmen*) require neither study nor liner notes—only the willingness to sit back and listen. They are completely satisfying, brilliantly performed, and wonderfully recorded. *L'Arlesienne* was a tragedy for stage written by Alphonse Daudet; Bizet composed the incidental music. The warmth of the Arles sunshine, the bright colors of the flowers, and the smell of the air were all captured by Bizet and presented with lavish orchestrations. An underlying air of nationalist pride and a feeling for the music and sound of Provençe enhance the suite's appeal. And of course, Dutoit's rendition of the suite from *Carmen* is a treat.

LINK➤ *Claude-Michel Schönberg – Les Misérables (Original Cast)*   *Relativity 8410*
Although the Tenth Anniversary Concert version (Relativity 1559) is larger-scale, recorded with the Royal Philharmonic Orchestra at Royal Albert Hall, the original 1985 cast album tells Victor Hugo's story with great heart. Many moments of pure magic.

Carmen – Julia Migenes Johnson, others;
Orch. National de France / Lorin Maazel   Erato 45207

There is so much here that's familiar: vivid melodies, fresh street smarts, and endless charm combine to make *Carmen* the perfect introduction to opera. Included among the many hightlights are: the unforgettable overture; the street urchins who imitate the Spanish soldiers in "Avec la garde montante" (The new guard comes, hurrah!); Carmen's "Habanera" (a melody that's been featured in dozens of cartoons), which Migenes Johnson sings in such a tempting way; the "Toréador en garde" (another Looney Tunes favorite); and the wondrous baritone aria so skillfully handled by Ruggiero Raimondi as Escamillo. Preferable by large measure to any competitor, this is straight-ahead music, not fussy or overblown. Kudos to Migenes Johnson for an invigorating performance.

LINK➤ *Manuel de Falla – El Amor Brujo (Love the Magician) – Nancy Fabiola Herrera, Jordi Galofré, others; I Cameristi / Diego Dini-Ciacci*   *NAXOS 8.553499*
This 1915 Spanish opera is the real thing. The instrumentation is consistently invigorating, and recorded to emphasize the brass's richness and the percussion's punch. "Danza del Fin del Día" (Dance at the End of the Day) later became known as the Ritual Fire Dance. *An engaging, enthusiastic vocal performance, too.*

Johannes Brahms

Born in Hamburg, Germany, in 1833, Brahms easily impressed teachers with his perfect pitch and talent for piano. As a teenager, he earned money playing in taverns and, probably, bordellos. (Brahms never married and had a tough time maintaining relationships with women.) In his early 20s, Brahms befriended William and Clara Schumann and lived in their Düsseldorf home. When William died in 1856, Brahms comforted Clara. By 1860, Brahms started serious work as a composer. Soon his choral work, *A German Requiem,* brought fame. He moved to Vienna, summered in Baden-Baden (where Clara had a house), and for three decades wrote vast amounts of music, mostly larger works. During the 1890s, Brahms focused on chamber and solo compositions. Clara Schumann died in 1896. An avid cigar smoker, Brahms developed stomach cancer; he died the following year. For much of his life, Brahms took great pride in his German heritage and his collection of rare music manuscripts.

Piano Concerto 1 – Stephen Kovacevich (piano); London Phil. / Wolfgang Sawallisch — EMI 54578

Now this is a concerto! The traumatic first movement begins as if a score from a gigantic horror movie, then settles down to make room for frantic strings and winds, before Kovacevich's piano paces nervously, and finally finds its own (much calmer) theme. Then the whole mood changes to a long, proud piano solo; in time, the orchestra picks up the more optimistic idea. Sawallisch and Kovacevich coordinate their efforts for fine dramatic effect; the intensity comes and goes rapidly here, and when it's big, it's huge. The second movement is much more relaxed, but the insanity returns for the third. A pair of songs complete the 1992 disc. Recommended.

LINK▶ *Johannes Brahms – Piano Concertos Nos. 1 & 2 – Emil Gilels (piano), Berlin Phil. Orch. / Eugen Jochum* — **Deutsche Grammophon 447-446**
Now a part of the DG Originals re-release program, this 2-CD set was originally released in the early 1970s. Gilels and Jochum achieve enormous heights, and the Berlin Philharmonic takes these difficult compositions in stride. The sound is quite good, too.

Ein Deutsches Requiem (A German Requiem) – Monteverdi Choir, Orchestre Révolutionnaire et Romantique / John Eliot Gardiner — Philips 432-140

A study of early music, Bach, and Handel all guided a work that Brahms had considered for a decade before composing this requiem in 1868. In the wrong hands, recordings of this piece can sound turgid (and boring) or fussy with overcooked operatic voices. The first movement is darkened to medieval embers because no strings are used; the second is illuminated with the radiance of choral voices and uplifting melodies. Several movements are led by a single voice, accompanied by choir and orchestra. The overall message is hope for reunion after death; it is neither mournful nor overtly reverent, but cleansing. Gardiner's music is often ravishing; the strident chorus fills the soul with cheer.

LINK► *Various Composers – Century Classics I: 1000-1400 –*
Sequentia, Deller Consort, others **DHM 77600**
More than an inspired marketing idea, this series presents early music by century. The first volume accumulates 400 years and features Hildegard von Bingen, Perotinus Magnus, and others. Try also 1400-1500 (76012) for Missa Barcelona and John Dunstable.

Hungarian Dances –
Budapest Sym. Orch. / István Bogár NAXOS 8.55011

Featured here are 21 dances, mostly 2 or 3 minutes long, delivered with gusto and native beauty in Budapest. The music's snappy, the melodies mostly come from gypsy folk tunes, and both orchestra and recording are top-notch. Brahms tips his hand here; much of his symphonic work comes from melodies like these. Brahms composed these dances for two pianos, others (including Dvorak) wrote most of the orchestrations. These fast tempos, expressive melodies, catchy rhythm patterns, and quick climaxes were strip-mined for cartoon soundtracks. The stereotype describes about half the dances (in fact, the earlier, more authentic ones). Those with higher numbers are moodier; these are mostly original Brahms concoctions.

LINK► *Arthur Fiedler: The Collection – Boston Pops Orch. / Arthur Fiedler* **RCA 68011**
Arthur Fiedler made classical music fun. These fine-sounding Living Stereo recordings, made from 1954 until 1962, capture his enthusiasm and his broad repertoire. From Victor Herbert's March of the Toys to Liszt's Hungarian Dances, this 3-CD set is one smile after another.

Violin Concerto in D – Joshua Bell (violin); Cleveland Orch. /
Christoph von Dohnányi London 444-811

Among worthy competitors, Bell and Dohnányi stand out because their 1994 recording is sufficiently clear to truly hear Brahms's varied tonal palette (evidenced by the winds in the first movement, for example). Brahms wrote the 1878 piece for a showman violinist, and Bell takes full advantage of the opportunity. It's easy to lose oneself in Bell's romantic lyricism, particularly in the dappled second movement where he stands before the orchestra and solos the melody. As this theme blossoms in the third movement's full orchestral treatment, Bell makes elegant, technically perfect music (that only occasionally lacks passion), but allows Dohnányi the spotlight. A very fine version of Schumann's *Violin Concerto* occupies nearly half the disc.

LINK► *Johannes Brahms – Violin Concerto in D –*
Itzhak Perlman (violin), Carlo Maria Giulini **EMI 47166**
Here's the antithesis of Bell: deeply heartfelt playing, nuances revealing the gypsy soul, and rampant joy (particularly in Perlman's third movement). Unfortunately, Perlman's focus in the first movement is a tad off, and the 1977 recording lacks the ultimate resolution of Bell and Dohnányi's work.

Piano Concerto 2 – Emil Gilels (piano); Chicago Sym. Orch. / Fritz Reiner RCA 60536

Written 20 years after Piano Concerto No. 1, and with the experience of several symphonies, Brahms's approach here is more sympathetic, less bombastic. The centerpiece is clearly the piano, and Gilels's spirited approach makes this recording a pleasure. The second movement is most important for its glistening theme and the way it's passed between piano, cello, and orchestra. The excitement—and there's plenty of it—is well paced, less random, and cleverly constructed. Reiner's boundless energy is kept in check, victoriously piercing through with precision and thunder. The recording is 40 years old; despite minor drawbacks, it more than does the job. Eugene Ormandy's Philadelphia Orchestra completes the CD with a 1969 performance of Haydn Variations.

LINK➤ *(Video) – The Art of Conducting* **Teldec 4509-95038-3**
Arturo Toscanini. Bruno Walter. Richard Strauss. Leopold Stokowski. A surprising number of the century's top conductors are presented, in all their glory, on this VHS tape. And despite the age of some of these performances, the soundtrack is remarkably satisfying. Don't miss this!

Symphonies Nos. 1-4 – Berlin Phil. / Claudio Abbado
Deutsche Grammophon 435-683

At their best, Brahms's symphonies are hearty and full of fire, requiring a conductor who does not fade from the monumental approach. Abbado follows in the line of Fritz Reiner and Leonard Bernstein, injecting life into Brahms's most energetic works and compassion in the slower sections. This 4-CD set, from 1991, is well recorded, and adds several additional pieces, notably the *Alto* Rhapsody (the discs are also available individually as 431-790, 427-643, 429-765, and 435-349). Brahms struggled with Symphony No. 1, completed in 1876 and very much influenced by Beethoven; the first movement seems cautious and somewhat noncommital, but the last is towering. The infernal swelling, the deep chasms and heroic relief, the toe-tapping homage to "Ode to Joy" and Beethoven's work, the enormous mountain peaks and the titanic finale suggest a "throw everything in" show-biz closer. The more sensibly constructed and far less frantic Symphony No. 2 was composed by a man who no longer feared the form. The initial theme is clearly established and consistent with Brahms's melodic talent; the third movement's play on formal dance and chamber music is a delight. Symphony No. 3 is wholly different, composed six years later and considerably more subtle. It begins big and brazen, tightly concentrated and authoritative. Then it loosens up a bit to allow the winds to explore a theme, but rarely without the full force of the orchestra close at hand. This is Brahms's best symphony, but it takes a bit of listening for the ideas to sink in. It's also Abbado's best performance, though the rest are close behind. The Hungarian dances are buried deep within, and the angst has largely dissipated; this is a work of large ideas and huge orchestral melodies. The second movement maintains the density, but the handsome horns and winds lead to a rhapsodic fantasy. The final movement is a brilliant roller coaster ride—excitement without the gloomies. Symphony No. 4, from 1885, starts big and grows to gargantuan dimensions. The room shakes when the third movement begins, but Brahms was smart enough to periodically back off with a pretty theme and delicate instrumentation before unleashing the next wave of his musical thrill ride.

LINK➤ *Johannes Brahms – Symphonies –Berlin Phil. / N. Harnoncourt* **Teldec 13136**
While maintaining most of Abbado's visceral pleasures, the scholarly Harnoncourt bases his wonderfully musical renditions on research of early documents that revealed how Brahms intended these symphonies to be performed. The 1997 recordings are compelling and refreshingly clear.

Double Concerto – Isaac Stern (violin), Yo-Yo Ma (cello); Chi. Sym. Orch. / C. Abbado SONY Classical 42387

A work of extremes—violinist Isaac Stern's mature fluid technique and newcomer Yo-Yo Ma's dark intensity. This is "big" music; the entire orchestra follows a melody established on Stern's violin, and plays rhythms following Ma's cello patterns, creating a vortex that would make Beethoven proud, and generating giant finales. Yet there are those lacey moments when Stern is alone with his violin, creating magic. The third movement draws much from gypsy dances, allowing Stern to have some fun fiddling alone before the whole orchestra joins in. Piano Quartet from 1855 is the (excellent) counterweight; Stern and Ma are joined by Emanuel Ax (piano) and Jaime Laredo (viola).

LINK► *Charles Stanford – Sym. 3 ("Irish") – Ulster Orch. / V. Handley*　　　　**Chandos 8545**
Stanford (1852–1924) was a friend of Brahms, who clearly influenced him here. Stanford was also the teacher who ignited a generation of top British composers. Irish folk music inspires the lovely quieter passages and some peppier ones; larger-scale pyrotechnics are inspired by the military.

Violin Sonatas – Itzhak Perlman (violin), Vladimir Ashkenazy (piano)
EMI 47403

Perhaps the secret is Perlman's connection to Eastern European fiddling. Or Ashkenazy's poetry on the keyboard. Or Brahms's love for Hungarian folk melodies. Few classical pieces touch the heart the way Brahms's Violin Sonatas do. The graceful tenderness of Violin Sonata No. 1's first movement lapses into the grief of endless raindrops in the last; the composer remembers his young friend Robert Schumann. It was written in 1878. Violin Sonata No. 2 begins with a winsome conversation between violin and piano, and remains sunny throughout (it was composed on holiday). With more contrast between light and dark, and an ebb and flow reminiscent of his symphonies, Violin Sonata No. 3, from 1888, runs deepest.

LINK► *Johannes Brahms – (Piano music) – Stephen Bishop Kovacevich (piano)*
Philips (Various)
Brahms's piano music often provides the same emotional experience as the Violin Sonatas. Three well-recorded, well-played CDs survey the material: Philips 411-103, which includes ballads; 411-137, filled with fantasias and Brahms's late Klavierstücke; *and 420-750, mostly rhapsodies and waltzes.*

Clarinet Quintet – Thea King (clarinet); Gabrieli Quartet　　　Hyperion 66107

Brahms's 1891 Clarinet Quintet is one of the world's finest chamber pieces, beautifully performed and nicely recorded on this 1983 disc. Beyond its memorable melodies and tricked-out interplay between clarinet and cello, with the mahogony tones that result, the piece possesses a lightness and inner peace rare in Brahms's work, an effortless statement of wisdom. The second movement is pure elation, with Thea King's clarinet floating among angelic sounds; there is sweet sadness here. The fourth movement is intricate and varied, smart but demanding attention for its many ideas. Clarinet Trio, from the same year, proves even more intriguing because its gentle nature masks unresolved turbulence. It's complicated, underrated, and should be heard.

LINK► *Johannes Brahms – String Quartets – Alban Berg Quartett*　　　　**EMI 54829**
Three noble quartets fill this 2-CD set. This outstanding chamber music comes from the same deep and awesome well as the symphonies (also composed in the mid-1870s). The Alban Quartett gets the drama but maintains the delicacy. Very good recording, too.

Benjamin Britten

Britten has been the model 20th-century British composer: a modernist who defines the term with dignity. Born in 1913 in Lowestoft, Suffolk, Britten was skilfully reading scores and creating original works before he turned 10 years old; by 16, he was a prolific young composer. Britten studied with Frank Bridge and John Ireland—two legendary names in British classical music—and got a job writing music for Post Office department documentaries. While there, he met poet W.H. Auden, who became a friend and frequent collaborator. Britten left England in 1939, lived in the U.S. several years, and returned home in 1942 to work on a new opera, *Peter Grimes*. He subsequently formed the English Opera Group and the highly regarded Aldeburgh Festival. So began a series of operas, many introduced by longtime friend tenor Peter Pears. After developing heart problems in the late 1960s, Britten was forced to slow down. He died in 1976.

Peter Grimes – Peter Pears, others; Orch. of Covent Garden Opera House / Benjamin Britten   London 414-577

Britten's 1945 work breathed life into England's moribund opera world. In the prologue, Grimes is being tried for the death at sea of his apprentice. When a second boy in his care accidentally dies, Grimes goes insane. The story is really about the town's mistreatment and lack of compassion for Grimes, who is not an admirable character. Some of the music is quite lovely, especially a duet ("The truth . . . the pity . . . and the truth") by Grimes and his lady, Ellen (Peter Pears and Claire Watson, both sounding splendid). Grimes's mad scene is especially frightening: "Steady, don't take fright, boy!" Orchestrations are atonal and dramatic. No misgivings about this 1958 recording.

LINK➤ *Percy Grainger – (Songs) – Monteverdi Choir, English Country Orch. / John Eliot Gardiner*   *Philips 446-657*
Britten and Grainger were two well-known collectors of British folk songs. Grainger provides subtle structure and exquisite settings to the songs in this collection, especially "I'm Seventeen Come Sunday" and "Brigg Fair." A wide range of styles, all ably executed with the benefit of clear, rich sound.

The Young Person's Guide to the Orchestra, Sinfonia da Requiem – City of Birmingham Sym. Orch. / Sir Simon Rattle   EMI 55394

Originally composed for an educational film soundtrack, Britten based 1946's *Young Person's Guide to the Orchestra* on Purcell's themes. Thirteen variations are performed by small groups: Variation D, for example, is carried by bassoons; Variation H features double basses; and Variation L spotlights trombones and bass tubas. Serious in tone, majestic but slow moving, it requires an adult's patience. *Suite on English Folk Tunes*, from 1974, is more spirited, with section titles like "The Bitter Withy" and "Hankin Booby." *Sinfonia da Requiem*, completed in 1940, is a symphonic memorial to Britten's parents. Its first movement recalls Mahler; the second movement dances with death; and the third settles into a life-affirming peace. Superb Rattle.

LINK➤ *Percy Grainger – In a Nutshell – City of Birmingham Sym. Orch. / Sir Simon Rattle*   *EMI 56412*
Compare this version with Richard Hickox's CD of the same title (Chandos 9493). Both are superb anthologies of the distinguished, accessible British composer's work. Here, the joy of discovery adds snap and crackle. The best piece: The Warriors.

The Prince of Pagodas – London Sinfonietta / Oliver Knussen — Virgin Classics 59578

This fantasy ballet's story began in the 1930s, when Canadian composer Colin McPhee periodically lived in Bali. McPhee wrote some pieces based on gamelan music, and Britten debuted them in England in 1944. Twelve years later, working on a commission from the Sadler's Wells Ballet in London, Britten found himself exhausted and unable to make his deadline. He visited Bali to rest, and the result fills much of Act Two: it's Balinese music set to orchestra. The music evokes exotic rhythms and Western instruments mimic gamelan with a soothing, otherwordly quality. The first act's musical portraits of Middle Kingdom kings and princesses is a more traditional highlight. Overall, a magnificent, underappreciated score.

LINK➤ Colin McPhee – Tabuh-Tabuhan – Eastman-Rochester Orch. / Howard Hanson — Mercury 434-310
This recording's quality belies its 1956 studio date. McPhee's repeated patterns on xylophone (adapted from Javanese and Balinese music), seem to be a prequel to Philip Glass. Plus, substantial works by Virgil Thomson (Symphony on a Hymn Tune) *and Roger Sessions* (The Black Maskers).

A Midsummer Night's Dream – Alfred Deller, Peter Pears, others; London Sym. Orch. / Benjamin Britten — London 425-663

All of Britten's operas from the 1940s and 1950s are worth owning; generally, the recordings of choice are the ones conducted by Britten, as these feature many of Britain's top singers. The wish list should include 1947's *The Rape of Lucretia* and *Albert Herring*, 1951's *Billy Budd* (revised 1960), and 1954's *Turn of the Screw*, as well as the church parable *Curlew River* (1964). For this 1960 opera, Britten abridges Shakespeare and provides extremely original themes for the main characters. It's probably the most accessible of Britten's operas. There's an appealing dark side here as well, which Britten brings out through lavish low-register instrumentation.

LINK➤ Benjamin Britten – Curlew River – Peter Pears, John Shirley-Quick, others; English Opera Group / Benjamin Britten — London 421-858
Not an opera but a "church parable," this 1964 musical drama derives from the austere minimalism of the Japanese Noh storytelling tradition. Britten applies an unusual blend of Western and Eastern musical palettes. All voices are male, which is consistent with Noh.

War Requiem – Soloists; London Sym. Orch. / R. Hickox — Chandos 8983/4

Landmark 2-CD recording of a severe 1961 protest. Britten despised war, and his alternation of a Latin Mass and Wilfred Owen's antiwar poetry are a potent combination; they're made even more haunting with the inclusion of a boy's choir. The work proceeds slowly and with pure reverence; the solo voices, however, strike wholeheartedly with such lyrics as "What passing-bells for these who die as cattle?" and "(Death) has spat at us with bullets and coughed schrapnel." The orchestra's heart-shaking percussion strikes, military horns and merciless battles are clearly heard, as are the extraordinary soloists Hearther Harper, Philip Langridge, Martyn Hill, and John Shirley-Quirk. Superb choruses, too. A definitive *Sinfonia da Requiem* is also included.

LINK➤ William Walton – Troilus and Cressida – Judith Howarth (soprano), Arthur Davies (tenor), others; English Northern Philharmonia / Richard Hickox — Chandos 9370
Based on Chaucer's telling of the Trojan tale, this spectacular performance (on 2 CDs) emphasizes characterizations brought forth in a revisionist English bel canto tradition. It's not perfect, but moments such as Cressida's "Slowly it all comes back to me" are extraordinary.

Anton Bruckner

Born in Ansfelden, Austria, Bruckner moved to a monastery in St. Florian at the age of 13, following his father's death in 1837. There, he sang in the choir and studied music. For the next 27 years, Bruckner performed as a church organist and taught in Linz and St. Florian. In 1865, a blaze of creative inspiration struck when he attended a performance of Richard Wagner's opera *Tristan und Isolde*. Bruckner had already been composing, but Wagner's music showed him the light. A frenzy of symphonies led to an inevitable nervous breakdown. Through the late 1880s, Bruckner composed in surges lasting several years; he revised his works, often many times, in order to make his music more acceptable. Along the way, Bruckner fell in love with several teenage girls and suffered from an intense insecurity about his art. He died in Vienna in 1896; his body lies beneath the organ at St. Florian.

Symphony No. 4 (Romantic) – Philadelphia Orch. / Wolfgang Sawallisch   EMI 55119

A dreadfully insecure man who frequently changed his work to please others, Bruckner reworked his Fourth Symphony more than five times. Somehow, the work retains a coherent charm. The first movement establishes its theme through haunting horns, and builds a powerful head of steam through variations before returning to the horns for emphasis. One revision added the "hunting horns" scherzo, perhaps Bruckner's best-known piece of music; this horn theme is repeatedly employed. Ultimately, this is a musical landscape painting whose subject matter is the Austrian countryside. Each dramatic swell quickly subsides, relaxes, and is transformed into a leisurely amble. Sawallisch and the Philadelphia Orchestra brilliantly re-create Bruckner's pastoral romance.

LINK▶ *Anton Bruckner – Symphonies Nos. 3 & 4 – Vienna Phil. / Karl Böhm*
London 448-098
This bargain-priced 2-CD set leads with one of the best recordings of Bruckner's Third Symphony on record. It's as if the Vienna Philharmonic had some inside information on Bruckner's intentions. The sonics are remarkable, especially given a 1970 record date.

Symphony No. 5 – London Phil. / Franz Welser-Möst   EMI 55125

Perhaps more than any other composer, Bruckner utilized brass instruments to establish and manipulate major themes. He blasts through several well-considered ideas in the slow opening movement, then introduces strings with no less bluster. The tension is palpable. At times, the plucking of the strings sounds like a Hitchcock movie theme. Bruckner draws the audience into an unfolding masterpiece, a shifting mood begging for resolution that doesn't come until the finale. And what a finale! Bruckner's well-organized fugue communicates chaos; his horns suggest religious ecstasy, and the entire tower of ideas magnificently takes shape as a coherent whole. A work of genius, performed and recorded in a most excellent manner.

LINK▶ *Kalevi Aho – Symphony No. 10 (Rejoicing of the Deep Waters) –*
Lahti Sym. Orch. / Osmo Vänskä   BIS 856
Since 1992, Aho has been composer-in-residence at Lahti, a city 60 miles north of Helsinki, Finland. This 1997 symphony debuted on radio and television. It's an exhilarating work with fantastic highs and lows, extremist theater, and contrasts as great as Finland. Worth discovering.

Symphony No. 6 – Bavarian State Orch. / Wolfgang Sawallisch   Orfeo 24821

Too often overlooked, Bruckner's Sixth Symphony is probably the best entry point to the man's work. The first movement gets down to business with a glorious military theme; the introspective winds and strings are juxtaposed with particular skill, and ideas are articulated in a very straightforward, comprehensible way. The Adagio, or second movement, is sentimental and thought-provoking, and makes fine use of the winds to carry an interesting theme. The darkening clouds of the Scherzo are unusually well balanced with the folk dance quality of the third movement's primary theme (the cascades are very charming). The fourth movement draws everything together for an inspiring finale. An excellent performance and an unusually fine recording.

LINK➤ *Anton Bruckner – Symphony No. 1 –*
Chicago Sym. Orch. / Sir Georg Solti   **London 448-898**
Solti's demonstration-quality 1996 recording of the neglected First Symphony finds a meandering first movement that culminates in a delightfully warm melody. There's also a calming middle section and a finale that's full of surprises, including a "wall of silence."

Symphony No. 7 –
City of Birmingham Sym. Orch. / Sir Simon Rattle   EMI 56425

The first few minutes of this 71-minute symphony suggest its scope. The cellos intensely develop the long opening theme, then release it to the winds and other strings. The mood is proud and strong, but becomes restless as Bruckner passes it around the orchestra, almost as if asking for opinions from the various instruments. A confident restatement ends the movement. The second movement, an elegy to Bruckner's hero Wagner, is slower still; the depth of this 1997 recording keeps the essential lower tones clear and full. The fourth takes the opening ideas and brings them to a full boil. Rattle does the finale justice by finding just the right sonorities.

LINK➤ *Bernard Herrmann – Vertigo – Scottish Nat. Orch. / Joel McNeely*
Varèse Sarabande 5600
The rich effectiveness of Herrmann's film soundtracks is partly drawn from a classical starting point. The demonic menace of the opening "Prelude" and the musical inevitability of the death scene represent some of Herrmann's (and Alfred Hitchcock's) best work for the big screen.

Symphony No. 8 –
Vienna Phil. / Herbert von Karajan   Deutsche Grammophon 427-611

Longer still at 88 minutes, the Eighth Symphony is thunderous at the start, but soon finds a major melodic theme that is applied throughout. Although the tenderness of the first movement finds expression in a single wind instrument or a horn bravely working through a theme, Bruckner strives for gigantic climaxes. Each climax is followed by a quiet release. The passive moments, however, are always smothered by predatory orchestrations or a threatening effect. While the third movement, an Adagio, is truly contemplative, the aggressor returns with military precision and pomp in the fourth. This is the ultimate Bruckner and the sort of the music that made Karajan famous. A good, but not great, recording.

LINK➤ *Robert Simpson – Symphonies Nos. 1, 8 –*
Royal Phil. Orch. / Vernon Handley   **Hyperion 66890**
Born in 1921, Simpson is one of the century's most aggressive, capable, brilliant symphonists. Far better known in Britain than in the U.S., it's worth tracking down his Symphonies Nos. 3 and 5 (Hyperion 66728) and also Symphonies Nos. 2 and 4 (66505). Stunning, imaginative music.

Elliott Carter

Born in NYC in 1908, Carter received early encouragement from Charles Ives, who at the time was his family's friend and insurance agent. Carter attended Harvard and studied English before switching his focus to music. (Walter Piston was among his teachers.) Against his parents' wishes, Carter studied music in Paris during the 1930s; his teacher was the formidable Nadia Boulanger. By the early 1940s, Carter was teaching Greek, mathematics, music, philosophy, and physics; the underlying beauty of these subjects resonates throughout his compositions. His music attracted attention beginning in the 1940s. Carter's Piano Sonata, from 1946, Cello Sonata, from 1948, and 1951's String Quartet No. 1 were works that balanced structure and chaos while utilizing unorthodox approaches to time. His String Quartet No. 2, from 1959, won the Pulitzer Prize. Carter has continued on his own path, teaching at most major East Coast universities and gaining a kind of iconic status among younger innovators.

String Quartets Nos. 1-4 – Juilliard String Quartet   SONY Classical 47229
One of the most important figures in twentieth-century music, Carter remains inscrutable for many. Often, his music does not obey the "rules" of time, and while this is ultimately a strength, new listeners naturally find his rhythms discomfiting. He also shuns traditional notions of space for individual instrument's statements, sometimes offering multiple thoughts simultaneously. And while he has a gift for romantic composition, it's balanced by an interest in confrontation. His Second Quartet assigns a kind of personality to each instrument, then allows precision, romance, aggression, and lyricism to converse and sometimes attack one another. It's captivating. The Third Quartet is set up as a parallel pair of duets, performed at the same time. It's fantastically complex.

LINK▶ Edgar Varèse – Arcana, Amériques, Ionisation, other works –
Ensemble Intercontemporain, NY Philharmonic / Pierre Boulez   SONY Classical 45844
Varèse was a musical pioneer whose impact is greater now than when his best work was composed. Here's a good sampling of his organized arrangement of sounds; for more (notably Ecuatorial *and* Hyperprism*), try the companion SONY Classical 68334, which begins with a Carter symphony.*

Chamber Music for Winds – Ensemble Contrasts   CPO 999-453
In these absolutely brilliant examples of modern chamber composition, Carter recapitulates the traditional, then drives off on his own. The best way to enjoy this music is to simply select any of the wind instruments and follow its line as it winds through and around the other instrument sounds. Intellectually stimulating and extraordinarily well played, this recital includes 1948's *Woodwind Quintet* (dedicated to Nadia Boulanger), and the gripping *Eight Etudes and a Fantasy*, from 1949-50, scored for flute, oboe, clarinet and bassoon. The changes in pitch, dynamics, time, and color in these studies produce fascinating results. *Espirit rude / esprit doux*, a flute-clarinet duet honoring Pierre Boulez, is another Carter manipulation of time.

LINK▶ Donald Martino – A Set for Clarinet, Quodlibets for Flute, other works –
Michael Webster (clarinet), Samuel Baron (flute), others   CRI 693
Martino (born 1931) developed his own twelve-tone system, amply explored here and viscerally not so different from the music of jazz innovator Charlie Parker. The clarinet set, once outrageous, is now standard repertoire. The flute piece mostly feels like classical-jazz improvisation. With several more chamber pieces.

George Chadwick

A contemporary of Dvořák, whose impact on American classical music was profound, George Whitefield Chadwick is one of America's great forgotten composers. He was born in Lowell, MA, the son of an insurance man who lacked enthusiasm for music. Fortunately, business trips to Boston provided time for lessons at the New England Conservatory, and long quiet evenings at the Lowell office provided ample time for practice. In 1876, at age 22, Chadwick left home to teach at Olivet College in Michigan. He saved his money and paid for an 18-month stay at the Leipzig Conservatory; within a year, he was a successful composer. Chadwick returned to a teaching job at the New England Conservatory and became its director in 1897. Over the years, he proved to be a prolific composer of chamber works, symphonies, and choral music. Chadwick died in Boston in 1931; only now is his music being rediscovered.

Melpomene Overture, Symphonic Sketches –
Czech State Orch. / José Serebrier   Reference Recordings 64
Completed in 1887, *Melpomene Overture* became Chadwick's most popular work. He named it for the muse of tragedy and comedy; there are lighthearted, tongue-in-cheek approaches to symphonic drama throughout. Considered one of the first important symphonic pieces from America, it suggests the directions that Copland, Rodgers, and Gershwin will follow a few decades later: hearth, home, and the bold aggression of big dreams. The four *Symphonic Sketches* (composed mostly during 1895 and 1896) are more obviously American, particularly the bandstand celebration Chadwick called "Jubilee." This, too, unfolds into patriotic walk down Main Street. "Hobgoblin," from a decade later, is a musical portrait of a mischievous supernatural child—a typical American boy.

LINK➤ *Richard Rodgers – Carousel –*
Katrina Murphy, Joanna Riding, others / Martin Yates   *First Night 6042*
Although Rodgers and Hammerstein were centered in musical theater, the distance to opera isn't all that far with Carousel. *Larger-than-life themes, colorful iconic characters, and marvelous aria-like songs that reinvent the medium (Billy's "Soliloquy") make this a very special experience.*

Symphony No. 3 – Detroit Sym. Orch. / Neeme Järvi   Chandos 9253
Chadwick blossomed at a time when Dvořák was America's musical leader. The latter encouraged composers to find their roots among black heritage and Native American song. Chadwick, who won $300 for this 1894 symphony in a competition judged by Dvořák, knew better. He heard America's true voice, and he knew how to make it sing. Here, Chadwick finds Brahms a useful mentor, but there's an earnest flavor in the harmonies, a propulsive sense of progress and tension in the slow movement, and a peppy optimism in the third that could only be American. The finale has just the right energy. Four Samuel Barber pieces complete the CD.

LINK➤ *George Chadwick – String Quartets – Portland String Quartet*
Northeastern 235, 234, 236
Three individual CDs present some impressive chamber music by America's most underrated composer. The first two quartets (236) are best, followed by the third, which is paired with Chadwick's piano quintet (235) and his fine fourth and fifth quartets (234). They're as strong as his symphonic compositions.

Frederic Chopin

Chopin's father, Nicholas, came to Poland from France; his mother was of a noble Polish heritage. Chopin was born near Warsaw in 1810 and had developed a reputation for fine work before he was even a teenager. In 1830, while traveling to London, he stopped in Paris, and lived there for the next 19 years. Chopin's first recitals in 1831 attracted little attention, but well-connected Polish friends in Paris introduced the pianist to Baron Rothschild's salon. Now associated with the wealthy, Chopin became a successful piano teacher and composer (he performed infrequently, mostly in private concerts). In 1838, Chopin also met and became romantically involved with the free-thinking female writer Aurore Dudevant, who wrote under the pen name George Sand. Many of Chopin's best works were composed at Dudevant's Chateau de Nohant, near Reims. Their relationship lasted until 1848. Chopin, who had long suffered from poor health, went to England, became quite sick, and died of tuberculosis in 1849.

Ballades – Murray Perahia (piano)
SONY Classical 64399

Chopin's ballades—which aren't actually ballades by strict musical definition—are just over 30 minutes long, so the remainder of the disc is filled with excellent mazurkas, waltzes, and piano studies (études). By any measure, this is one of the very finest Chopin discs available. Each ballade is distinct. Ballad No. 1 was completed in Paris in 1835. Its cultivated form makes great use of silences and sparse phrases, embroidery and the occasional virtuoso race across the keys. Ballad No. 3, from 1841, feels nostalgic (and familiar from *Our Gang* comedies); it's gentle, pretty, and especially melodic. Ballad No. 4, from 1842, offers variations both delicate and powerful on a dreamy melodic theme.

**LINK▶ *Charles-Valentin Alkan – Symphonie Opus 39, Overture, Two Études –
Bernard Ringeissen (piano)***   **Marco Polo 8.223285**
Alkan was a top pianist and composer for piano in the era of Chopin, but his name faded. This fine recording should reinstate at least some of his reputation; his sense of drama and his delicacy often overshadow the work of Chopin and even Liszt. Highly recommended.

The Mazurkas – Artur Rubenstein (piano)   RCA 5614

At a ball, the formal-yet-folksy dance called the mazurka begins with a procession. Couples pair up to show off their skills, both together and separately, sometimes for an hour or more, before returning to the closing procession. Chopin didn't write dances; he evoked the images of dancers. And he wrote plenty of them—enough to fill a 2-CD set. The folksy bowing and curtsying are evident in the first part of Opus 7; the dancer's pride centers the final part of Opus 24; the end of Opus 33 contrasts a dancer's dream state with his or her obvious athletic skill. Rubenstein is marvelous; 1966 engineering is competitive with today's standards.

LINK▶ *Frederic Chopin – Mazurkas – Vladimir Ashkenazy (piano)*   **London 448-086**
This 2-CD set collects recordings from 1977–85. Ashkenazy's interpretations flow easily and with great affection and tenderness; his freshness, periodic formality and bravura, and clear enjoyment of this music places this (and all of his Chopin recordings) near the top of any list.

Nocturnes Nos. 1-19 – Artur Rubenstein (piano)
RCA 5613

Rubenstein's mid-1960s recordings continue to dominate the top Chopin slots (these were made in Rome). Although ornate visual images associated with this music sit rather stiffly in some forgotten Paris salon, Rubenstein etches fine crystal and authentic romance in the elegant calm. Within this format, Chopin manages at least some range. Opus 62, for example, starts with translucent dignity and daintily meanders for six or seven minutes, but in its second section, the clouds roll in to block not only the eternal sunshine, but also to drop hailstones onto the perfect garden. These are but occasional interruptions. The garden repairs itself in nanoseconds. High society protects its own. Outsiders sometimes yawn.

LINK➤ *John Field – Nocturnes – John O'Conor (piano)*   ***Telarc 80199***
Field (1782–1837) developed the nocturne, Chopin later perfected and popularized the form. O'Conor's peformance of Field's Piano Concertos Nos. 2 and 3 are better still; Charles Mackerras is the conductor (Telarc 80370). Both are highly recommended.

7 Polonaises – Artur Rubenstein (piano)
RCA 5615

Artur Rubenstein's entire series of Chopin piano pieces has long been a favorite in the catalog: no other pianist so completely combines sheer artistry, musicality, virtuosity, and sympathy with Chopin's intentions. And so these rather formal Polish dances take on a wholly delightful, quite varied character, heard clearly from the stage of Carñegie Hall in 1964. The famous A major "Military" is precisely the right choice for introducing a great general atop the stairs at a fancy ball. The A-flat "Heroic" is the other well-known Polonaise (from old movies and the film *Three Amigos*); it's performed with proper dignity and stirring virtuosity here. Conversely, the C Minor is cautious and foreboding.

LINK➤ *Frederic Chopin – Polonaises & Impromptus –*
Garrick Ohlsson (piano)   ***Arabesque 6642***
Chopin wrote his first polonaise at age 8 in 1817 and his last in 1846. All 16 polonaises are included on this well-played 2-CD set (which also includes four impromptus). The sound quality is very fine.

Waltzes – Garrick Ohlsson (piano)   **Arabesque 6669**

Chopin's waltzes tend toward formality and are often intricate and complex. Listen as one of the leading Chopin interpreters of the 1990s conquers the impossibilities of the Waltz in E Minor. Or imagine—as Chopin did when he wrote the spinning opening to Opus 64 ("The Minute Waltz") George Sand's little dog chasing its tail. In fact, this often-heard opus is a series of panels suggesting life with Sand; the third movement recalls a happier time, valiantly attempting composure. As with the mazurkas, Chopin uses the waltz form as a basic structure, but offers dancers no consistent rhythm for dancing. This is parlor music, some of the most intriguing in Chopin's large catalog.

LINK➤ *Louis Moreau Gottschalk – (Piano works) – Philip Martin (piano)*   **Hyperion 66459**
Gottschalk lived only from 1829 until 1869, but he made his mark as an important American voice in romantic piano composition. Martin, in a series of three CDs, provides a full-blooded rendition of the composer's many short pieces; try also Vol. 2 (66697) and Vol. 3 (66915).

Sonata No. 3 – Evgeny Kissin (piano)   RCA 62542

Kissin makes the piano sing on this extraordinarily poetic rendition of Sonata No. 3 (he's equally good on another Chopin recital [RCA 60445]). Chopin wrote this sonata in 1844, concerned about romanticism, the beauty of classical proportions, and the challenge of a larger-scale work (it's just shy of 30 minutes in length). He produced a rich work of art, one whose themes are for the ages. The skill with which Chopin eases from one musical idea to the next and integrates everything into a singular conception is inspiring, and it is from this structure that Kissin manages a world-class performance. And then he turns around to master a dozen mazurkas.

LINK➤ *Frederic Chopin – Sonatas Nos. 2 & 3 – Artur Rubenstein (piano)*   **RCA 5616**

Sonata No. 2 should be part of every collection (if for nothing more than the funeral march that every child seems to know). Rubenstein's amazing interpretation makes exquisite use of time and space, and digs deep. On Sonata No. 3, Rubenstein probably wins, but let's give young Kissin the break.

Piano Concertos Nos. 1 & 2 – Martino Tirimo (piano),
Philharmonia Orch. / Fedor Gluschenko   Conifer Classics (BMG) 51247

Chopin finished both these piano concertos in the early 1830s. Although he was a piano man, he makes fine use of the contrasting colors and temperaments of the strings and winds in Piano Concerto No. 1's first movement, a sweeping affair that takes time to rest and reflect before leaping to the next idea. Both romantic second movements are lavish, introspective, and extremely pleasant. In both works, the orchestra breaks for large-scale, frilly piano solos; in each, the piano eventually dominates, reducing the orchestra to (powerful) accompaniment. When Chopin truly writes for orchestra (there are scattered passages throughout), he's excellent—but he didn't do it often. Solid 1994 British recording.

LINK➤ *Alexander Scriabin – Complete Piano Sonatas –*
Marc-André Hamelin (piano)   *Hyperion 67131/2*

This 2-CD set traces Scriabin's development from a spokesman for Russian emotions (a funeral march in Sonata No. 1 is especially effective) to an increasing interest in the mysteries of the universe (Nos. 4 and 5). Hamelin makes this complicated music seem so easy.

Piano Concerto No. 2; 24 Preludes – Maria João Pires (piano)
(with Royal Phil. Orch. / André Previn)   Deutsche Grammophon 437-817

Pires excels with Chopin. Half of this 1994 disc is filled with a beautiful performance and a spectacular recording of Piano Concerto No. 2; her solo piano truly stands out. Chopin wrote his 24 preludes during a dismal vacation in Majorca in 1838. In fact, these preludes don't lead to anything except themselves; they're more properly called miniatures. Each one runs only a minute or two, and each is open to a very unique interpretation. Prelude No. 7, a popular recital piece, is happiness drifting away. Prelude No. 4 and Prelude No. 6 were played at Chopin's funeral. Prelude No. 9 is bold, and Prelude No. 13 perhaps addresses a faraway passion. Superb recording.

LINK➤ *Frederic Chopin – Études – Vladimir Ashkenazy (piano)*   *London 414-127*

Like the preludes, each of the piano studies is very brief. Opus 10 contains six, and Opus 25 contains a dozen. Each study is based on a particular piano technique, such as an arpeggio, but Chopin simply uses these concepts as starting places for magnificent piano compositions.

Aaron Copland

Born in 1900, Aaron Copland grew up in Brooklyn, the son of poor immigrant parents from Lithuania. In 1921, he spent most of his money to study with Nadia Boulanger in Paris, then returned to the U.S., where he supported himself by lecturing, working for music societies, and playing piano in a New York hotel. By the early 1930s, despite encouragement from Serge Koussevitsky, Copland had not made much progress with his composing. His career took off with a series of extremely original American ballet scores written in the late 1930s. By 1944, Copland's collaboration with Martha Graham on *Appalachian Spring* secured his fame. He also worked with jazz great Benny Goodman and on eight movie scores, including *Of Mice and Men* and 1950's *The Heiress*, which won an Oscar. An educated man and gifted teacher, Copland wrote several fine books about music. He composed and conducted through the 1970s. Copland died after a long struggle with Alzheimer's disease in 1990.

The Copland Collection: Early Orchestral Works
(1922-1935)   SONYClassical 47232

In these three sets, Sony Classical presents most of Copland's best music performed by the composer and some kindred spirits. *Dance Symphony* was a student project that started in 1922 as Grohg, a "vampire ballet"; Copland subsequently added several dances, a new introduction, and a new title. *Symphony for Organ and Orchestra*, written in 1925, is performed here by longtime friend Leonard Bernstein with E. Power Biggs on organ. This 1967 version is a more conservative reworking of the symphonic form; some cunning solos and a jazzy scherzo suggest things to come. *Music for the Theater*, also from 1925, is another attempt to work jazz into the classical forum. Two years later, Serge Koussevitzky debuted Copland's Piano Concerto—a shocking piece because of the way it demonstrated what American symphonic music could be. The work has two principal themes; one recalls a spiritual and the other is snappy and very 1920s. Copland's own piano leads the way, and it is at various times discordant, honky-tonky, and stiffly classical. This magnificent piece of work is accessible, fun, and significant. The more serious Symphonic Ode from 1929 suggests Mahler in its intensity, but Copland's fresh snap of optimism and his gift for melody and tonal alterations make this grand statement his own. Some similar comments might apply to *Statements for Orchestra*, completed in 1935. Copland conducted the more serious works with the London Symphony Orchestra; most of the other pieces in this 2-CD set were performed by the New York Philharmonic, led by Leonard Bernstein. The 1960s sound is uniformly excellent.

LINK➤ Ferde Grofé – Grand Canyon Suite –
Cincinnati Pops Orch. / Erich Kunzel   Telarc 80086
You have to love a CD with a warning sticker that reads: "Caution!: Digital Thunderstorm." This splendid slice of Americana is lovingly performed—it's as fine as anything by Copland—and the recording is demo quality. A good rendition of Gershwin's Catfish Row *begins the 1987 CD.*

The Copland Collection: Orchestral & Ballet Works (1936–1948)   SONY Classical 46559

This is the crowd pleaser. On this 3-CD set, you'll find just about all of Copland's famous ballets and orchestral suites. Built from authentic Mexican folk music and other careful research, 1936's *El Salón México* makes ample use of the orchestra to imagine the sights, sounds, colors, heat, swirl, and city life of Mexico City. It was first conducted by Carlos Chávez; here, it is one of several works conducted by the composer. The year 1939 brought a ballet suite based on *Billy the Kid*, a score Copland wrote on commission for Lincoln Kirstein a year earlier. Once again, Copland leans on existing tunes such as "Git Along, Little Dogies" and "The Old Chisholm Trail" for flavor and context. Composing a symphonic work based on the life of an American folk hero was a relatively new idea; this one has endured because Copland did the job so well. His 4-minute portrait of John Henry is no less effective. Copland created the popular *Fanfare for the Common Man* in 1942; it is perhaps the finest musical portrait of America's noble heritage. It's often paired with his *Lincoln Portrait*, narrated here by Henry Fonda. Copland revisited the America's western frontier for *Rodeo*, a 1942 Wild West bonanza that includes at least two pieces known by every schoolchild: "Buckaroo Holiday" and "Hoedown." Copland's matter-of-fact style of putting together a melody and scoring for maximum emotional impact is equaled only by film composer John Williams. Then, there's the remarkable *Appalachian Spring*, or more accurately, Copland's 1945 suite from the ballet he composed for Martha Graham. Bittersweet and defiantly American, it is his finest work. Perhaps more than any other classical composer, Copland was a very careful listener and an extremely skillful synthesizer. His 1941 trip to Havana led him to a dance hall, where he heard a fairly formal Cuban form called danzón; a few years later, this memory led to a stylized orchestral piece called *Danzón Cubano*. This overwhelming Copland festival continues with his jazzy Clarinet Concerto (commissioned by Benny Goodman, who performs here), and his Symphony No. 3, from 1946. Life affirming and plainspoken, it combines Copland's serious tendencies (echoes of Mahler) with his own very appealing sense of melody and thematic development. It's another of Copland's finest projects.

LINK▶ *Carlos Chávez – Sinfonia India, Sinfonia de Antigona, Sinfonia Romantica – Stadium Sym. Orch. of NY / Carlos Chávez*   *Everest 9041*
The career of Chávez in many ways paralleled the career of Aaron Copland. Chávez's promotion of native Mexican themes, his brilliant orchestrations and advanced compositional technique, and his involvement in education resulted in spectacular music. He's long overdue for a definitive modern recording.

Charles Fierro – Piano Fantasy (and other solo works)   Delos 1013

Fierro performs four key Copland piano pieces, each from a different era. *Passacaglia*, from 1922, is dedicated to Copland's Parisian piano teacher Nadia Boulanger. It's a rigorously formal theme followed by eight stiff variations, some delicate, others anxious, but none suggesting future direction. *Piano Variations*, written in 1930, is totally different; it's severe, sometimes dissonant, music that relies on odd angles and strange sensations of space and time. The longest work (nearly a half-hour) is 1957's *Piano Fantasy*. With a complex and varied masterwork, Copland takes his place alongside Liszt as one of the finest piano composers. *Night Thoughts* was composed in 1972 as a test piece for competition participants.

LINK➤ *Aaron Copland – The Complete Music for Solo Piano – Leo Smit (piano)*
SONY Classical 66345

The combination of superior engineering and a more compelling performance favor Fierro, but this 2-CD set includes more music. Specifically, there's the original piano version of Down a Country Lane, *1941's challenging Piano Sonata, and perhaps a dozen other pieces.*

The Copland Collection: Late Orchestral Works (1948–1971)
SONY Classical 47236

The year 1948 brought the last of the great Copland orchestral suites; it's a setting of music composed for a motion picture, *The Red Pony*. (It's hard to imagine a more compatible pairing of storyteller and composer than John Steinbeck and Aaron Copland.) Copland also waxes poetic on 1962's *Down a Country Lane*, and returns to Mexico for *Three Latin-American Sketches*, his last orchestral composition. *Music for a Great City* was supposed to be called *Music for New York*, but it was commissioned by the London Symphony, and so Copland submitted to its wishes. Constructed on the foundation of his eighth (and final) film score (1961's *Something Wild*), this music pounds the New York pavements, shakes with its jackhammers, and is permeated with the crazed expressions of its gray-suited advertising men and street people. The despair and brutality are palpable, but only in sections. Like the city itself, Copland does not retain a singular mood for long. But make no mistake—this is louder, more gripping, and more dangerous than standard orchestral repertoire. *Inscape*, Copland's most challenging piece, is a 12-tone serialist work whose off-center tonality and massive chord blocks sometimes bother the ear. Copland makes the most of an edgy palette, pushing and slashing hard in directions that some listeners will not enjoy at all, and yet he somehow manages statements that are close kin to his more accessible compositions. Leonard Bernstein does an extraordinary job with this very difficult work, as he does with *Connotations*, a precursor. Everything else is conducted by Copland.

LINK➤ *Joseph Schwanter – Velocities, Concerto for Percussion and Orchestra, New Morning for the World – Evelyn Glennie (percussion & solo marimba); National Sym. Orch. / Leonard Slatkin*
RCA 68692

For Slatkin's first recording with the National Symphony, he chose an all-Schwanter program: a monumental memorial to Martin Luther King, Jr., as effective and evocative as Copland's Lincoln Portrait, *spoken here by Vernon E. Jordan, Jr.; and a demanding, original percussion concerto. A breath of fresh air.*

John Corigliano

A respected late 20th-century composer, Corigliano was born in NYC in 1938. His father was the long-time concertmaster at the New York Philharmonic, and his mother was a pianist of some renown. Educated at the Manhattan School of Music and Columbia University (his teachers included Otto Luening), Corigliano gradually attracted serious attention in the early 1960s with several works played at Tanglewood; Spoleto, Italy; and elsewhere. He also served as music director for the eclectic NYC radio station WBAI, and served as assistant musical director for television's *Young People's Concerts*. Corigliano has composed numerous works, but two have attracted considerable attention. They are his Symphony No. 1, created in response to the AIDS epidemic, and *The Ghosts of Versailles*, the first new opera commissioned by the Metropolitan Opera in more than 20 years. In 1991, Corigliano joined the faculty of NYC's Julliard School, teaching composition. He continues to compose.

Concerto for Piano and Orchestra –
Barry Douglas (piano); St. Louis SO/Leonard Slatkin RCA 68100
A solidly inviting introduction to Corigliano's world, this 1967 work was commissioned by the San Antonio Symphony. Corigliano begins with an angular fanfare, pleasant cacophony, and a strong percussion wholeheartedly supported by melodic banging on the piano and xylophone. Then, the mood changes—it smoothes out, expands, and transforms itself from icy fragments to floating particles and waves in space. In time, this builds into a romantic climax. Two aggressive themes develop, eventually winding into one another. The second movement is brief and tense; the third movement sets up the fourth, which recapitulates the symphony's ideas for a vivid climax. A modern, entertaining, and intriguing work. With three more pieces.

LINK► *John Corigliano – Concerto for Clarinet and Orchestra –*
Stanley Drucker (clarinet); NY Phil. / Zubin Mehta ***New World 309***
Excellent 1977 concerto—performed with outstanding vigor and imagination by Drucker—brings modernist ideas about percussion, orchestral dynamics, and energy together in a most accessible way. The second movement is an elegy, and the third is an "Antiphonal Toccata." Very good.

Of Rage and Remembrance, Symphony No. 1 –
National SO / Leonard Slatkin RCA 68450
Several glimpses suggest the power of Corigliano's frustration and anger with AIDS: the ferocious intensity of the first movement's strings, the slow painful tarantella of the second, the excesssive pounding that ends the third movement ("Giulio's Song"), and the eerie epilogue. The cello material in the third movement also forms the basis of a chorus work, *Of Rage and Remembrance*; both are rooted in a 1962 tape of an improvisation between Corigliano and a cello-playing friend, recently deceased. This 1990 symphony is not depressing; it is truthful, compelling work that's likely to resonate for most contemporary listeners. Barenboim's premiere recording (Erato 45601) is equally fine.

LINK► *Aaron Jay Kernis – Second Symphony –*
City of Birmingham Sym. Orch. / Hugo Wolff ***Argo 448-900***
Born in 1960, Kernis is among the best of contemporary composers. The first movement ("Alarm") of his second symphony is searing: blasting contrasts of orchestral power, followed by a plea for peace and harmony ("Air/Ground"). The wartime metaphor plays out with "Barricade," the final movement.

Claude Debussy

Born outside Paris in 1862, Debussy's early interest in music was supported by an aunt, who paid for piano lessons. By the time he was a teenager, Debussy was an excellent pianist and a very difficult student (he questioned everything). Debussy won the Prix de Rome in 1884, hated the formal experience, and returned to Paris, where he eventually found his direction as a composer after hearing Gamelan music from Java. In Debussy's extraordinarily unique world view, this path led to what some called the musical equivalent of French Impressionist painting. For the remainder of the 1880s and into the early 1890s, Debussy was a starving artist living in Montmartre. With a growing catalog of original works, his reputation increased; his 1902 opera *Pelléas et Mélisande* made him famous. Debussy was subsequently awarded the Légion d'honneur and became a respected advisor to the Paris Conservatory. Cancer plagued him for several years before his death in 1918.

String Quartet: G minor – Hagen Quartet   Deutsche Grammophon 437-836

With its emphasis on tonal colors, Debussy's 1893 quartet differs from most chamber music. It's vibrant, but quite abstract. There's a comforting warmth in the darker shades, a vivid, even insistent pressure provided by the violins and viola, and a tension that unfolds through the first movement. The pointillism of the jaunty second movement, in which strings are often plucked before they're bowed, settles into a quite peaceful, thoughtful place. The development of the studied and serious fourth movement ties up a very handsome package. Ravel's String Quartet in F major was clearly inspired by Debussy's work. Webern's 1905 "Streichquartett" is also similar. Airtight performances from the Hagen Quartet; world-class engineering.

LINK▶ *Claude Debussy – Chamber Music – Athena Ensemble*   ***Chandos 8385***
Six chamber pieces, most heard infrequently, all delightful. The harp is well suited to Debussy's style, and 1916's Sonata for Flute, Viola and Harp is enchanting. These later chamber works include a violin sonata, a cello sonata, and the lovely Syrinx *for Solo Flute.*

Images, Prélude à L'après-midi d'un faune, Nocturnes, La mer, Jeux–
Royal Concertgebouw Orchestra / Bernard Haitink   Philips 438-742

This bargain-priced 2-CD set provides excellent performances of Debussy's finest orchestral works. *Prélude à "L'après-midi d'un faune"* (Prelude to *The Afternoon of a Faun*) was originally intended to be a complete musical treatment of a poem by Debussy's friend Stéphane Mallarmé, but Debussy never composed anything more than the winsome prelude. It was one of his first orchestral works, completed in 1894, expert in its muted use of tonal colors to evoke a gentle, vital, woodsy, altogether perfect day. *La mer*, an attempt to capture the ocean; is more ambitious. Debussy struggled with the idea, and decided to write it in the mountains of Burgundy (he wanted no distraction from the sea). During its two-year gestation, Debussy left his wife for a noted Parisian banker's wife, caused a major scandal, fathered a child with his new lady, and lost his place in Paris society. It is not an altogether calm piece of music. Not particularly melodic, it's more like incidental music for sea gazing, often calming, sometimes rumbly. Two other major pieces, *Images* and *Nocturnes*, are more completely described in their Dutoit renditions. In addition, there's a wonderful clarinet rhapsody in the *Faune* style, an ethereal set of harp dances, and Debussy's fine ballet piece, *Jeux*. Haitink is excellent throughout, and these recordings, from the 1970s, are up to contemporary standards. A bonus track, from 1959, features Eduard van Beinum leading the Concertgebouw in 1959 on *Berceuse héroïque*.

LINK➤ *Claude Debussy – La Mer, Jeux, Le Martyre de saint Sébastien, Prélude à l'Apres-midi d'un faune – Orchestre Symphonique de Montréal / Charles Dutoit*   London 430-240
There are two strong reasons to buy this disc, despite the duplications: Timothy Hutchins's flute and Dutoit's temperament, which offer a more comely Faune, *and Debussy's refined* Sébastien *incidental music. Very good digital sound, but Haitink's predigital 1976* La mer *often sounds better.*

Pelléas et Mélisande – Colette Alliot-Lugaz, Didier Henry, others; Orchestre Symphonique de Montréal / Charles Dutoit   London 430-502

Debussy specifically set out to write an opera based not on action, but on feelings. Given the time to listen to this lovely recording in the relaxed quiet of one's own comfortable armchair, Debussy's subtle treatment of the operatic form proves delightful. Dutoit and his cast make it so, but others have been equally successful. The story is based on poetry by Maurice Maeterlinck, who hated this opera. Golaud gets lost in the forest, finds Mélisande, marries her, invites his brother Pelléas to meet his bride, encourages them to spend time together, and (no surprise here), they fall in love. Golaud kills Pelléas, and the pregnant Mélisande dies in her bed.

LINK➤ *Arnold Schoenberg – Pelleas und Melisande – Chicago Sym. Orch. / Pierre Boulez*   Erato 45827
This large-scale symphonic piece challenges Debussy's version of the sad love story with considerably more powerful German romanticism. It's dramatically different from the forward-thinking Varia-tions for Orchestra *which begins this CD.*

Images, Arabesques – Zoltan Kocsis (piano)   Philips 422-404

Among nine solo piano pieces here, the two volumes of *Images* (Livre 1 and 2) are especially distinguished. The first book, completed in 1905, begins with "Reflets dans l'eau," a dignified, optimistic reflection composed with 18th-century sensibilities. The second movement, "Hommage à Rameu," again proceeds with affectation and the utmost care, but proves beauti-ful in pianist Kocsis's attentive execution. A hypnotic "Cloches à travers les feilles" second book, from 1907, and the exotic (and reasonably well known) Arabesque No. 1 are distinctive for their haunting melodic development. There are plenty of decorative flourishes here, ultraserious formality, and excursions into dreamland. "Hommage à Haydn" is one of the set's many deli-cate miniatures.

LINK➤ *Ernest Chausson – Poeme, Piano Trio, Andante and Allegro – Chilingirian Quartet, others*   Hyperion 67028
Allow yourself to be immersed in the poetic, gentle, sensual world of Chausson. His music is a pastel rainshower on a summer pond: light, airy, sweet. The Andante and Allegro are performed, ever so tastefully by just two instruments: the clarinet (Charles Neidich) and piano (Pascal Devoyon).

Images, Nocturnes – Orchestre symphonique de Montréal / Charles Dutoit   London 425-502

Debussy's Nocturnes appear in twilight with languishing phrases, subtle instrumentation, and the poetry of slow movement. This moody three-movement suite is notable for the cor anglais solo in *Nuages* and the choral sirens in *Sirènes*. Three unrelated pieces make up the *Images pour ochestre*. Debussy's study of Spanish culture and music were the basis for 1908's *Ibéria*. Rondes de printemps, from 1909, is livelier; it's based on French folk music. The graceful *Gigues*, from 1912, is based on an English folk song; its center is an oboe d'amore, blended with a harp. Very, very subtle. Dutoit is a very careful watercolorist.

LINK➤ *Sky Music – Yolanda Kondonassis (harp)*   *Telarc 80418*
Harp records don't come around too often these days. This one deserves special attention because it gets the impressionism right (Debussy, Fauré, and the lesser-known Carlos Salzedo), but features longer, more ambitious pieces by Alan Hovanhess and Ned Rorem.

Preludes, Books 1-2 – Walter Gieseking (piano)   EMI 61004

Although Krystian Zimerman's 1991 renditions (Deutsche Grammophon 435-773) and Paul Jacobs's 1978 set (Nonesuch 73031) are commendable, Gieseking's early 1950s performance stands out as the indisputable first choice. No other recent musican has been so naturally at ease with Debussy's piano compositions, particularly these 36 miniatures. The works themselves sound like improvisations with feather-thin structure. "Le fille aux cheveux de lin" (The Girl with the Flaxen Hair) and "Minstrels" (about black-face performers), with its show-biz flair, are among many highlights in *Book 1* (from 1910). In *Book 2* (from 1914), "Feux d'artifice" is a flashy keyboard demonstation, and "La puerto del vino" dances in a Mediterranean port city, albeit quite properly.

LINK➤ *Claude Debussy – Complete Works for Piano – Walter Gieseking (piano)*
EMI 65855
Gieseking's Preludes are included here, along with the Études, Images, and the Suite bergamasque *(which includes* Claire de lune*). Another highlight: Children's Corner, piano pieces written for Debussy's four-year-old daughter. An extraordinary, must-have collection.*

12 Etudes (12 Studies) –
Mitsuko Uchida (piano)   Philips 422-412

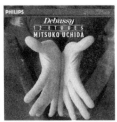

A child's piano exercise, suggesting utter simplicity, opens this series of twelve piano studies. In an instant, this simplicity evaporates, and Uchida is caught in the midst of complicated, challenging work. The first six studies are sophisticated harmonic explorations, and the final six deal with texture and feeling, familiar themes reconsidered by a mature composer in 1915. With many of these works, such as "Pour les Quartres," and especially "Pour les sonorités opposées," Debussy sets the course for twentieth-century music's unorthodox use of time and space. The latter's use of counterpoint influenced several modern composers. As she has on so many Mozart performances, Uchida creates definitive modern renditions of these works.

LINK➤ *Water Music of the Impressionists – Carol Rosenberger (piano)*   *Delos 3006*
A shimmering seascape, summer at a turn-of-the-century French resort. The connection with water, and a watercolor treatment, is apt. Rosenberger's repertoire is weighted toward Ravel and Debussy. There's a contribution in a similar vein from American Charles Tomlinson Griffes. World-class engineering (as is often found in Delos recordings).

Léo Delibes

Léo Delibes worked his way up through the opera world by assisting Berlioz, Bizet, and Gounod. Although he made a substantial impact with opera, his work for the ballet is his legacy. Delibes was born in St. Germaine-du-Val, Sarthe, France, in 1836. His first teacher was his mother; at age 12, he entered the Paris Conservatory. By the 1850s, Delibes was working as on organist, but progress toward any truly personal success was slow. After years as a chorus singer and choral director, Delibes made his mark with a series of popular operettas. Now secure, his 1866 debut as a ballet composer (with *La Source*) was a success, so he focused his attention on ballet for the next decade or so, with *Coppélia*, and later, *Sylvia* defining the modern symphonic ballet. Still, Delibes remained connected to opera; his 1883 opera, *Lakmé*, remains popular. Delibes died in Paris in 1891.

Coppélia – Orchestre de l'Opéra de Lyon / Kent Nagano   Erato 91730

This 2-CD set contains some of the most famous ballet music ever written. Beyond the familiarity of various themes (from cartoons and elsewhere), the feeling of movement that Nagano provides is both charming and almost visual. The scenario is based on an E.T.A. Hoffman short story called "The Sandman," which was also the basis for Offenbach's *Tales of Hoffman*. In Delibes's 1870 ballet, Coppélia is a doll who comes to life; she was created by, and is controlled by, Coppélius. The story turns on his protection of the lovely creature and its interaction with the real world. The score is filled with engaging dances, notably Act One's mazurka and czárdás.

LINK➤ *Leo Delibes – Coppélia, Sylvia – Minneapolis Sym. / Antal Dorati;*
London Sym. Orch. / Anatole Fistoulari   **Mercury 434-313**
A low-priced 3-CD set featuring not only a fine performance of Coppélia *(from 1957 by Dorati), but also Delibes's other well-known ballet,* Sylvia. *The latter was first produced in 1876 and is based on Renaissance spectacle. Fine Mercury Living Presence sound.*

Lakmé – Joan Sutherland, others; Orchestre National de l'Opéra de Monte-Carlo / Richard Bonynge   London 425-485

This 1883 opera is set in 1850s India, where the Brahmin princess Lakmé completely entrances Gérald, an English army officer. The bad news: he's wandering around sacred land, and Lakmé's father wants to kill him for this trespass. Lakmé's siren song draws Gérald into a trap laid by her father; and by the end of Act Two, Gérald has been stabbed. In Act Three, Lakmé nurses him back to health; she kills herself when Gérald decides to leave. Don't stay for the story. Stay instead to hear Joan Sutherland sing "Bell Song" and her "Flower Duet" with Gérald. Sutherland sings beautifully and never becomes tiresome. A budget-priced 2-CD set.

LINK➤ *Tan Dun – Ghost Opera – Wu Man (pipa); Kronos Quartet*   **Nonesuch 79445**
Authentic music from a different part of the East, employing Bach, Shakespeare, plus various gongs, Tibetan bells, water bowls, a string quartet, and a variety of unusual instruments. This coherent 1994 drama juxtaposes ideas from East, West, and the spiritual world.

Frederick Delius

Delius's father was a successful German wool merchant who sent his 20-year-old son to Florida to manage his orange plantation in 1882. Entranced by the a capella harmonies of the plantation's black workers, Delius took some very effective lessons in music theory from local organist Thomas Ward. Then it was back to Europe and his father. By 1885, Delius was a full-time student at Leipzig Conservatory. He befriended Edvard Grieg, then moved to Paris and spent several Bohemian years among artists and writers. He married a painter, Jelka Rosen, in 1897. Around the turn of the century, Delius found his voice. He became well known after Thomas Beecham conducted his music. Ill-health, brought on by syphilis, ravaged his body, but Eric Fenby was able to piece together his musical ideas. By 1929, when Beecham presented his first Delius festival, the composer lay dying. He died in 1934.

Beecham Conducts Delius – Royal Phil. Orch. / Sir Thomas Beecham   EMI 47509

Here is English orchestral music at its very best. Masterful compositions, exquisite recordings, and invigorating performances make this 2-CD set essential. Start with 1908's *Brigg Fair*, with its questioning wind solo and deep orchestral foundation. Listen and enjoy the twinkling of flutes, a pace and structure resembling a wandering minstrel, and the pretty strings that meander through a perfect village. *Over the Hills and Far Away*, from several years earlier, engages a dream with the slightest feathers of an orchestra's sound. The deep relaxation is slowly overtaken by brassy whirls of near military seriousness before returning to another inviting dreamscape. Over many years, Beecham adjusted Delius's expression marks, never changing a note, but radically altering (many would say, improving) the composer's creative work. Miniatures are the stuff of Delius's reputation, and many are included here. There's an evocative "Sleigh Ride," complete with sleigh bells and an appealing, if sometimes elusive, wintertime melody. Two other seasons inspired his more famous miniature works. Typically presented together, 1911's *On Hearing the First Cuckoo in Spring* and 1912's *Summer Night on the River* evoke the seasons through inventive use of winds and strings, often as solo instruments or small clusters to articulate particular moods. There is much more here— a total of 14 pieces, including the popular *Florida Suite* and *Songs of Sunset*, which is set for chorus and soloists. These pieces were recorded in 1958, 1960, and 1963; reservations about their fidelity are wholly unfounded.

LINK▶ *Frederick Delius – Violin Concerto – Tasmin Little (violin), Welsh Nat. Opera Orch. / Sir Charles Mackerras   Argo 433-704*
Ms. Little presents Delius's idiomatic music with delicacy and verve; in short, she's terrific! There are plenty of other pieces here, as well, including two Dance Rhapsodies, Cuckoo/Spring, *and* Summer Night. *Don't miss Little and Mackerras, plus Rafeael Wallfisch on the* Double Concerto *(EMI 2185).*

Florida Suite, North Country Sketches –
Ulster Orchestra / Vernon Handley   Chandos 8413
North Country Sketches, written in 1923, are organized by season. (Nature was a primary influence in the Delius's writing.) Images of orange and yellow leaves whirling, brown leaves crunching beneath the feet, and bracing air are brought to life in "Autumn," the first sketch. Childhood memories of long walks through the Yorkshire Moors near his home invigorate the last movement, "The March of Spring." The superb *Florida Suite*, from 1889, contains the gently flowing "By the River" theme, a blazing sunset, and an extremely vivid evocation called "At Night." Delius's clarity of vision and presentation are stunning, and this wonderful recording brings his mastery to life.

LINK➤ *Bridge, Bantock & Butterworth –*
Bournemouth Sinfonietta / Norman del Mar   *Chandos 8373*
Lovely music by three wonderful (but not famous) British composers. Frank Bridge's Suite for String Orchestra *is a springtime delight, and his tone poem entitled* Summer *is no less evocative. Granville Bantock's* The Pierrot of the Minute *and George Butterworth's* The Banks of Green Willow *complete a very special CD. Extraordinary sonics.*

A Village Romeo & Juliet – Helen Field, Arthur Davies, others;
Austrian Radio Symphony / Sir Charles Mackerras   Argo 430-275
Sali, a boy, and Vreli, a girl, play together in their fathers' fields. As they grow up, their fathers become enemies. While defending Vreli, Sali strikes her father and causes him to be placed in an asylum. The couple enjoy a brief period of happiness until the return of the Dark Fiddler (sung by Samuel Ramey), whose predictions have plagued their lives together. The result: the lovers take a river ride and drown together. The leads present their roles well, but Mackerras's handling of the instrumental score sets this piece apart from most other opera recordings. He maintains all that is special about Delius's orchestral colors, textures, twists, and musical turns.

LINK➤ *The Vagabond and Other English Songs –*
Bryn Terfel (bass-baritone); Malcolm Martineau (piano)   Deutsche Grammophon 445-946
Opera singer Terfel came into his own in the 1990s, making a big critical and commercial impact with this deeply felt collection of songs by Vaughan Williams, Butterworth, Finzi, and Ireland. He single-handedly raises the British song to the level of a German lied.

Sea Drift, Songs of Farewell, Songs of Sunset –
Sally Burgess, Bryn Terfel; Bournemouth SO / Richard Hickox   Chandos 9214
Vocal music may not be everyone's cup of tea, but the tenderness of these three pieces may sway even the iron-hearted. *Sea Drift* was written in 1904 with lyrics from a Walt Whitman poem. It starts with a lengthy, handsome orchestral base; the chorus then blends in, and baritone Terfel emerges as the lead. 1907's melancholic *Songs of Sunset* has lyrics by Ernest Dowson; it's propelled not by sadness, but by the gradual unfolding of affection and admiration. Burgess and Terfel sing together beautifully ("Cease smiling, dear!"), and the chorus is delightful. Delius based 1929's sad *Songs of Farewell* on Whitman; it's magnificently performed and recorded.

LINK➤ *Gerald Finzi – Dies natalis, Imitations of Immortality –*
John Mark Ainsley (tenor); Corydon Orch. / Matthew Best   *Hyperion 66876*
Finzi (1901–1956) found his strength in a spiritual connection with nature. This vocal performance is his most emotional, profound, and sacred. It's based on meditations on the birth of Christ, written by a seventeeth-century writer.

Gaetano Donizetti

The son of a Bergamo weaver, Donizetti was born in Italy in 1797. His father was against the idea of a career in music, but reluctantly allowed Donizetti to attend music school. Opera became the boy's passion, and by 18, he'd composed a substantial work, *Enrico di Borgogna*. At first Donizetti mimicked the work of his hero, Rossini; he then found his own voice, often developing operas based on great characters and stories from literature and history, such as Anne Boleyn, Mary Stuart, and Lucretia Borgia. Over the course of 30 years, Donizetti wrote more than 70 operas; when he wasn't writing, he was producing or directing operas for the stage throughout Europe. A happily married man, his life began to change in 1837, when his wife died. Weakened by physical and mental problems, Donizetti died in Bergamo in 1848 from the combined effects of syphilis, paralysis, and a stroke.

L'elisir d'amore (The Elixir of Love) – Joan Sutherland, Luciano Pavarotti; English Chamber Orch. / Richard Bonynge   London 414-461

One of Donzetti's most appealing overtures opens this 1832 opera, and it's soon followed by the first of many tenor showpieces, the famous "Quanto è bella" (How lovely she is); the other enormous tenor number is a Caruso favorite, "Una furtiva lagrima" (A furtive tear). Pavarotti and Sutherland are almost entirely free of affectations, and deliver the performances of their recorded careers. This is a relentlessly fine composition; the overture's promise blossoms into a fantastic number of excellent melodies, performed as if in a dream. The best songs progressively stack ideas and excitement so high that the performers are assured the loudest bravos. Excellent Bonynge, good 1969 recording.

LINK▶ *Gaetano Donizetti – La Fille du Régiment (The Daughter of the Regiment) – Joan Sutherland, Luciano Pavarotti; Covent Garden Orch. / Richard Bonynge   London 414-520*
In 1967, the crew first got together to record Donizetti's 1839 story of military brat Marie who wants a soldier she can't have (until the finale, that is). Good recording, lots of winning interaction between Pavarotti and Sutherland, and a spectacular tenor aria, "Ah mes amis." Highest recommendation.

Lucia de Lammermoor – Cheryl Studer, Placido Domingo; London Sym. Orch. / Ion Marin   Deutsche Grammophon 435-309

Set in craggy Scotland at the end of the 16th century, Sir Walter Scott's *The Bride of Lammermoor* is essentially a Romeo and Juliet tale involving Protestant Lucy Ashton (Cheryl Studer; all sweetness and light), who loves a man on the wrong side of a family feud, the Catholic Edgar of Ravenswood (Placido Domingo). Highlighting a string of fine songs (mostly solos and duets), there's Lucy's "mad scene," and Edgar's "Wolf's Crag." Marin's conducting is in control, and the sonics are of the highest quality. Still, the pure power and emotion of Maria Callas's Lucy (EMI 63631 or 69980) or Enrico Caruso's Edgar (harder to find) shouldn't be missed. Composed in 1835.

LINK▶ *G. Donizetti – Don Pasquale – Renato Bruson, Eva Mei, others; Munich Radio Orch. / Roberto Abbado   RCA 61924*
There's a light, comedic flair to Abbado's approach, one that's carried forth by the singers as well. This 1842 opera zips back and forth between physical comedy and sentimentality, and the richness of the score never lets the listener down. Competes with many other fine renditions.

Antonin Dvořák

An orchestral, choral, and chamber music composer of the highest order, Antonin Dvořák was born in a sleepy Bohemian village north of Prague in 1841. Following in his father's footsteps, young Dvořák apprenticed to become a butcher. An uncle intervened, encouraged the teenager's obvious musical talents, and financed a proper music education in Prague. Dvořák spent most of the 1860s studying, performing in orchestras and cafés, and composing. It wasn't until the 1870s that Dvořák found his own voice; when he did, the profusion of decidedly Bohemian influences helped make him famous. During the 1880s, Dvořák was one of England's most popular choral composers. In 1893, he became director of New York City's National Conservatory, earning a fantastic salary that only added to his prestige. Dvořák later returned to Prague, where he became head of that city's conservatory. He died a national hero in 1904.

Slavonic Dances (Op. 46 & 72) –
Cleveland Orch. / George Szell   SONY Classical 48161
Although Dvořák doesn't quote directly from folk dances, he certainly re-creates the character of a people: the old farmer's ruddy skin; the rosy glow of young men and women dancing; and colorful skirts, shawls, and braids whirling under a sunny sky. This is extremely picturesque music, magnificently played in an energetic, vivid recording from the early 1960s. In 1878, Dvořák published Opus 46, consisting of 8 dances, including a Ukranian dumka (No. 2), Bohemian polka (No. 3), and two sousedskás (Nos. 4 and 6). He followed with 1886's Opus 72, containing 8 more dances. The odzemek or shepherd's dance (No. 1) and the Serbo-Croat kolo (No. 7) are particularly smart and invigorating.

LINK➤ *Samuel Coleridge-Taylor – 24 Negro Melodies –*
Frances Walker (piano)   *Orion 7806*
From the liner notes, written by the British composer (whose father was African): "What Brahms has done for the Hungarian folk music, Dvořák for the Bohemian...I have tried to do for these Negro Melodies." Earnest, classical compositions based on work songs, spirituals, and dances. A bit weird.

Symphony No. 6 – Czech Phil. Orch. / Jiří Belohlávek   Chandos 9170
Dvořák's 1880 Symphony No. 6 separated him from the pack of central European composers. Dvořák mimicked Brahms's Second Symphony (from 1877), earnestly creating a comparable work for his own culture. Indeed, the first movement includes several patches that resemble Brahms, such as big cascades, sentimental violins, and honest substance. As the liner notes point out, Brahms also learned from the younger Dvořák's earlier works, so the similarites are not suprising. Dvořák's skill in writing for flute and winds allows a winsome delicacy throughout the second movement, and the furiant, a Czech dance, distinguishes the third. Dvořák also whips up an impressive storm for the finale. Very nicely performed and engineered. With *Holoubek*, a symphonic poem.

LINK➤ *Antonin Dvořák – Symphonies Nos. 5 and 7 –*
Slovak Phil. Orch. / Stephen Gunzenhauser   *NAXOS 8.550270*
Gunzenhauser recorded all of Dvořák's symphonies in the late 1980s. These are solid, meaningful performances. A slight edge in exuberance and recording quality gives first choice designation to competitors. Those on a budget need not think twice about this series.

Symphony No. 7 – Royal Scottish Orchestra / Neeme Järvi Chandos 8501

This is Dvořák's finest hour. Several forces conspired to inspire this superb symphony. First, in the background, was Brahms's third symphony, which provided structure. Next, an opera assignment that didn't work out encouraged scale. Additionally, Dvořák was up to the challenge of composing for the London Philharmonic Society without sacrificing nationalism. Serious but never ponderous, this symphony works on several levels. The first movement is stately, with pastel transitions to vibrant, sophisticated ideas based in folk traditions. A graceful second movement hides some intriguing dissonance and counterpoint; it leads to the vivacious dancing of the third (with dual rhythms in competition). The fourth movement knits the symphony's themes into a tension-filled finale.

LINK➤ *Antonin Dvořák – The Complete Symphonies –*
Royal Scottish Orch. / Neeme Järvi Chandos 9011-13

Too often remembered only for his Ninth Symphony (New World), Dvořák deserves more attention for his final four, and for the fifth, too. Järvi makes a compelling case for all nine symphonies, and he's helped by superb Chandos engineering. A 6-CD set, usually sold for the price of five.

The Piano Trios – Trio Fontenay Teldec 76458

The Piano Trio in E minor (*Dumky*) is pensive, somewhat melancholy, and restless. It is a way of thinking that Dvořák apparently found comfortable, and was well suited to his personality. The name is also the plural form of dumka, a Slavic dance style that originated in Ukraine. Each of the six *dumka* that comprise this trio explores facets of sadness, delicacy, nostalgia, warm feelings, and drifting memories. On certain days, there is no better tonic. Among Dvořák's many fine works, this 1891 trio has always been one of the most popular. It's found here amongst three other piano works, all intelligent compositions performed with dignity, grace, and sincere emotion. A 2-CD set.

LINK➤ *Antonin Dvořák – Stabat Mater – New Jersey Sym. Orch. / Zdenek Macal*
Delos 3161

Macal recorded a top-notch series of Dvořák symphony discs for Koss Classics. Here, in Dolby Surround, he presents Dvořák's best-known choral work, which is excellent and certainly on a par with his orchestral compositions. Both sound and performance are extraordinary.

Symphonies Nos. 8, 9 ("From the New World") –
Berlin Phil. Orch. / Rafael Kubelik Deutsche Grammophon 447-412

Kubelik's 1966 recording of Symphony No. 8 is a shining example of Deutsche Grammophon's miraculous engineering. Few recordings have so successfully captured the weight and resonance of the violins and violas as well as the microtones of the winds. Dvořák did most of this creative work in a single happy month at his country cottage, writing mainly to please himself. After a boisterous first movement, he settles into the musical equivalent of a landscape painting, lively with village rhythms and ripe with natural exuberance. The folk character runs through the breezy third movement, and the fourth is a series of clever, often rapid variations carried off with swirling energy by strings and flutes. Symphony No. 8 is usually (and unfairly) obscured by 1893's Ninth Symphony. Dvořák wrote this symphony in New York. He had been brought to the U.S. to teach American composers how to integrate indigenous folk music. He did a lot of writing and lecturing, and encouraged some students. Things didn't always work out as planned, however. The only Native American music Dvořák heard, for example, was show business fluff at Buffalo Bill's Wild West Show. He did simmer bits of American spirituals into a mostly European soup, however, and was influenced by Longfellow's "Song of Hiawatha."

Classical CD Listener's Guide 59

Undeniably, there are moments—the end of the first movement, for example, and probably the start of the second—when Dvorák is every bit as American as Copland or Ives. Mostly, though, this is a pleasant, well-intentioned work that falls far short of his marvelous Eighth Symphony.

LINK➤ *John Williams – The Five Sacred Trees –*
Judith LeClair (bassoon); London Sym. Orch. / John Williams **SONY 62729**
Famous for his movie soundtracks, Williams excels in classical composition. This bassoon concerto studies the mythology of five trees and establishes a fundamental connection with nature. Other pieces include the Japanese work, Tree Line, *by Toru Takemitsu, and Tobias Picker's* Old and Lost Rivers.

String Quartet No. 12 ("American") –
Hagen Quartet   Deutsche Grammophon 419-601
Dvorák spent his first summer in the U.S. in the comfortable Czech community of Spillville, IA. Within a month of his arrival, he wrote his most enduring piece of chamber music—arguably the piece that made the most use of American spirituals and Indian rhythms. Regardless of its influences, the first movement takes off with a jaunty folk dance style, first on viola and then on violin. The second movement follows an arc: it begins and ends quietly, but along the way there's an emotional song carried by violin and cello. The last movement begins with rhythmic drumlike patterns and works through a hymnlike sequence. Kodály's Second Quartet completes an expert recital.

LINK➤ *Edgar Meyer – String Quintet –*
Edgar Meyer (double bass); Emerson String Quartet **Deutsche Grammophon 453-506**
Finding a voice Dvorák imagined a century ago, pop bassist Meyer builds on his successful Appalachian Waltz *outing (with Yo-Yo Ma) and creates a distinctive, folk-based, minimalist report on American heart and soul. By comparison, a Ned Rorem quartet included here seems hopelessly dated.*

Concerto for Cello & Orchestra – Yo-Yo Ma (cello),
NY Phil. / Kurt Masur   SONY Classical 67173
Victor Herbert was Dvorák's academic colleague in NYC. An accomplished popular composer, Herbert taught and played cello. In 1894, Herbert debuted his Second Cello Concerto with the New York Philharmonic; he was the soloist. Despite depressing reviews—the cello was regarded as an inappropriate solo instrument—the piece rekindled Dvorák's interest in balancing the dark, thin cello sound with the orchestra's opulence. At the time, Dvorák was seriously homesick, and this feeling provided his emotional voice. Cello and orchestra converse; their discourse involves brilliant themes and glowing memories. Slow and steady, deep and heartwarming, Dvorák's cello concerto is a beautiful piece. The contrast with Herbert's narrower talent is striking. Among Ma's best.

LINK➤ *Victor Herbert – L'Encore –*
Eastman-Dryden Orchestra / Donald Hunsberger **Arabesque 6547**
Beginning with a suite from the well-known Babes in Toyland, *this collection of popular stage music from the early years of this century is invigorating, nostalgic and fun. It's easily his best score, though 1900's* Punchinello *and 1914's* When You're Away *are also special.*

Edward Elgar

Despite the upper-crust stature of his music, Edward Elgar grew up poor. His father operated a small music shop in Worcester, England, and earned extra money as a piano tuner. Beginning at age 12, in 1869, Elgar sometimes replaced his father as church organist; as a teenager, he taught himself piano and violin so that he could play in local chamber groups. By 1879, he was teaching locally; he was also the headmaster of a lunatic asylum, where he experimented with a small orchestra. Elgar married well; his wife, Caroline Alice Roberts, provided the resources and inspiration necessary for his leap into national and international renown. Elgar was famous for his choral works, military marches, symphonic works, and for his bracing rejuvenation of British music. All these accomplishments led to a knighthood in 1904. Until 1920, Elgar's creative output was prodigious; then his wife died, and he slowed down. He died in Worcester in 1934.

Enigma Variations – Baltimore Sym. Orch. / David Zinman   Telarc 80192

In October 1898, Elgar was restless, discouraged, and absentmindedly tinkering with his piano. His wife, Alice, called his attention to a particular tune, and Elgar extemporized friends' reactions to the piece for fun. These became *Enigma Variations*, which are labeled with the initials of friends. ("W.N." stands for neighbor Winifred Norbury, for example.) These miniatures manage only a scarce relationship with the opening theme; most are instrumental songs emphasizing a specific musical idea. For example, "R.P.A." (the young poet Richard Penrose Arnold) finds oboes mimicking his laughter amidst a friendly smile of a string melody. Most are fairly formal with dramatic touches. *Cockaigne*, a concert overture from 1900, depicts images of London. Wonderful performance, fabulous recording.

LINK➤ *Edward Elgar – Enigma Variations –*
Royal Phil. Orch. / André Previn   **Philips 416-813**
An equally fine rendition of Enigma Variations *is paired with 5 military marches known collectively as* Pomp and Circumstance. *The first march, "Land of Hope and Glory," contains the famous graduation theme (and much more); the fourth, too, is impressive, but all are quite good.*

Symphony No. 1 – London Phil. Orch. / Leonard Slatkin   RCA 60380

Style, grace, and excitement mark one of the better 20th-century symphonies. The first movement glides through lush meadows of violins and winds, wells up in seemingly uncontrollable outbursts of youthful energy (Elgar was 50 years old when he wrote his First Symphony), and then returns to an extended pastoral setting. The second movement constantly shifts and turns with enthusiastic new melodies. Elgar makes fine use of his winds, and the lower string registers to generate warmth. From this darkened seedbed, the third movement grows its fresh new ideas. The final movement explores before settling into the obligatory bravado. Slatkin's orchestra is eloquent and extremely attentive to Elgar's tiniest details. A handsome recording.

LINK➤ *Hans Pfitzner – Symphonies Op. 44 & 46 –*
Bamberg Sym. Orch. / Werner Andreas Albert   **cpo 999-080**
Known as the Kleine *(Small) Symphony and the Symphony for Large Orchestra, this pairing is a fine representation of Pfitzner's work. Composed in 1939 and 1940, they feel like a series of dignified romantic scenes, more like chamber music than symphonies. Still, they are very satisfying.*

Violin Concerto – Nigel Kennedy (violin);
London Phil. Orch. / Vernon Handley   EMI 63795

Never a simple composer, Elgar makes remarkable demands of the violinist and the orchestra, requiring very rapid changes in mood and technique. Hidden beneath the second movement's velvety romance, for example, is a delightful, delicate song expressed in an almost casual way by the soloist. Very gradually, the orchestra embroiders the theme; within moments, violinist Kennedy is drawing his bow in a more strenuous fashion, and yet he must sustain the paper-thin tone required to convey romance. The orchestra becomes larger, and Elgar balances the forces so that the violin's import is undiminished. Kennedy's skillful, artful recording of this 1910 classic has dominated the catalog since 1984. Refined engineering, too.

LINK▶ *Gerald Finzi – Clarinet Concerto –*
Emma Johnson (clarinet); Royal Phil. Orch. / Sir Charles Groves   *ASV 787*

With spectacular dynamic range and fascinating lines to keep the listener entranced, Johnson and Groves prove to be among Finzi's most attentive interpreters. While shopping for this exquisite CD, try also Finzi's Cello Concerto, performed by Raphael Wallfisch (Chandos 8471).

Cello Concerto; Sea Pictures –
Jacqueline DuPré (cello), Dame Janet Baker (soprano),
London SO / Sir John Barbirolli   EMI 47329

No composer has plumbed the depths of the cello as successfully as Elgar. The cavernous darkness of this 1919 concerto directly reflected Elgar's mood and England's immediately after the Great War. The elegy does not remain entirely gloomy, however. As with so many of Elgar's statements, lower registers are fertile ground for winsome melodies played by higher strings and winds. DuPré gives the performance of her life—no cellist has ever sounded so fine on record—and Barbirolli's noble accompaniment is quite special. Remarkably, this spectacular 1965 recording also includes five of Elgar's finest songs, beautifully sung by Dame Janet Baker. A treasure, with stunning sonics.

LINK▶ *Les Introuvables de Jacqueline du Pré*   *EMI 68132*

"You cannot explain genius," explains producer Suvi Raj Grubb, as he applies the term to the radiant music created by one of the century's great cellists. There are so many treasures on these six CDs, moments when the musician and instrument are one. Very, very special.

Symphony No. 2 – BBC Sym. Orch. / Andrew Davis   Teldec 74888

This is one of Elgar's more subtle compositions, with a first movement that gently flows from one idea to the next, rendering a series of watercolor variations. The second movement can become ponderous, but it's here that Davis distinguishes his art by digging down to the proud heart of the piece. The third movement's rondo has a spritely air that's rather like a country walk on a breezy spring day. Consistent with the piece's relentless dignity, it never really lets loose, and even becomes involved in its own nervous introspection. By building on the second movement's soul, the final movement brings all of the symphony's ideas together beautifully. A Serenade completes the disc.

LINK▶ *Elgar – The Dream of Gerontius – London Sym. Orch. / R.Hickox*   *Chandos 8641/2*

Regardless of Elgar's label, this is an oratorio, a contemplation on the soul of Gerontius from life to death. Elgar's accretion of influences, from Wagner to Gregorian chant, caused mixed reactions in 1900, but today, this piece is a radiant, soul-fulfilling classic.

Gabriel Fauré

Conservative and quiet, Fauré was one of France's beloved composers. Born in the French Pyrenees in 1845, he was one of a large family and received little attention. A neighbor urged his father to enroll the young Fauré in a Paris music school; his talent won him tuition at the new École Neidermeyer. In 1861 he met lifelong friend Camille Saint-Saëns, who was then a teacher. For the next few decades, Fauré made his way from one organ job to the next; he eventually reached one of the best in France, at La Madeleine, in 1896. The same year, Fauré became the composition teacher at the Paris Conservatory; his students included Maurice Ravel and Nadia Boulanger. In 1905 Fauré became the Conservatory's director. Over the years, his reputation as a composer grew. Fauré continued to write music in his last few years even though he had become deaf. He died in Paris in 1924.

Piano Quartets Nos. 1 & 2 – Domus   Hyperion 66166

Fauré composed his first quartet in a disconsolate state of mind, and its emotional outpouring reflected his feelings. Fauré had been engaged to the beautiful Marianne Viardot, whose family was part of Paris's opera circle. Fauré's future was seemingly secure, but his dreams vanished with the love affair. Devastated, Fauré turned to chamber music. Quartet No. 1's first movement compares two themes, as if considering the circumstances from every possible angle. The second is delicate and lovely, yet lively. Then, darkness falls; the third is sheer melancholy, not so distant from Fauré's *Requiem*. Themes are recapitulated in the fourth movement and brought to an impressive ending. The Second Quartet is equally impressive.

LINK▶ Gabriel Fauré – Piano Quintets – Domus   *Hyperion 66766*
For the many who are susceptible to the tender passions of Fauré's chamber music, the series continues with the addition of violinist Anthony Marwood to the Domus string quartet. A perfect balance of heart-tugging stringed instruments and a life-affirming piano line. Superb.

Requiem – Oxford Camerata   NAXOS 8.550765

Comforting to the soul, Fauré's *Requiem*, written in 1880 and revised several times thereafter, is the musical equivalent of an old stone church in a quiet European city. This is music for the ages; sacred voices fill the void with images of God and all His goodness. An inspiring combination of carefully selected instrumentation and ravishing choir, the Mass is performed here in its original arrangement, with a solo violin, four violas, four cellos, and an organ. Two more Fauré pieces, both in a similar genre, are also on the CD: 1906's *Messe Basse* (Low Mass) and 1865's *Cantique de Jean Racine*. Works by Louis Vierne and de Séverac complete a superior recording.

LINK▶ Ragnar Grippe – Requiem –
Madeleine Kristoffersson (soprano); Ragnar Grippe (synthesizers)   *BIS 820*
The 1996 version of a requiem has no orchestra, only a Synclavier, several Roland keyboards, and related hardware, plus the voice of an angel. Stylistically, Grippe dashes from ethereal New Age to classic Renaissance liturgy to the occasional percussion sequencing.

César Franck

Belgian-born Franck was a young musical genius, but his outlook and creative output were decidedly different from his contemporaries. Franck was born in 1822; his family moved to Paris in the early 1830s so he could study with the best teachers. He toured as a virtuoso pianist. In time, Franck took on students and settled into a quiet Paris lifestyle that combined teaching, playing organ at various city churches, and composing. His original work was respected neither by the public nor by other French composers. (In particular, both Saint-Saens and Gounod thought it dreadfully incompetent.) Franck's music was subtle, thoughtful, and somewhat impressionistic, influencing later composers like Debussy. In 1858, Franck took a permanent position as organist at St. Cothilde's Church; he became a Paris Conservatory organ professor in 1872—a very happy experience thanks to the students who adored him. Somewhat absent-minded while walking the Paris streets, Franck died after being hit by a bus in 1890.

Symphonie – Pierre Monteux / Chi. Sym.   RCA 61967

This landmark recording comes from 1961; here, it's paired with Franck's Pièce Heroïque, and Vincent d'Indy's Istar: Symphonic Variations (from 1945). The Symphonie is Franck on a grand scale, sometimes employing fat sonics in the style of Wagner and frequently referring to his background as an organist for large patches of color. Monteux approaches the work with enthusiasm and respect (too often, conductors ruin this work with adornment). Huge swells of melody, brilliant resolutions, and perfect instrumentation decisions are found throughout. The charming cor anglais (English horn) and judicious use of orchestra sections distinguish a refined second movement. In formal style, the third movement recapitulates ideas established earlier. Good (not great) sound quality.

LINK➤ *César Franck – Great Organ Works – Marie-Claire Alain (organ)*   **Erato 12706**
A 2-CD set (import only) from one of the great contemporary organists. There are very strong similarities between Franck's organ compositions and his Symphonie—big blocks of sound predominate. Even in the popular Prelude, Fugue and Variations, *his brush is wide and thick.*

Violin Sonata in A – Arturo Delmoni (violin), Meg Bachman Vas (piano)
John Marks Records 8

Franck's violin sonata is among classical music's treasures, and Delmoni's treatment is thrilling. The combination of his free-flowing musicality and an audiophile recording (typical of the tiny John Marks Records) truly sets this CD apart. Pianist Vas is deliberate and focused, a marked contrast to Rogé's wispier touch (see below). Franck wrote his warmly melodic sonata as a wedding present for his Belgian friend violinist Eugène Ysaÿe, who debuted the work in 1887. There are four movements; the third's dreamy fantasia is Delmoni's showcase, and the drifting melody of the fourth shows Franck's elegant compositional technique. The CD also contains Fauré's Sonata 1 for Violin and Piano—an appropriate pairing, beautifully presented.

LINK➤ *Cesar Franck – Symphonic Variations, Sonata in A, Piano Quintet –*
Pascal Rogé (piano); London Festival Orch. / Ross Pople   **ASV 769**
Rogé's impressionist touch is always a delight, particularly in combination with Pople's cello on their version of the violin sonata. The Piano Quintet is one of Franck's best works, and the Symphonic Variations, *with their transforming themes, is another. Fine performance and recording.*

George Gershwin

A product of the Jewish ghetto known as Manhattan's Lower East Side, Gershwin lived in a tenement and grew up poor. It was a piano purchased for his older brother Ira that forever changed his life. Gershwin was born in 1898; as a teenager, he worked as a song plugger in NYC's Tin Pan Alley. By 1919, he was writing hit tunes and soon after, smash Broadway shows (brother Ira wrote the lyrics). Despite his skyrocketing success, Gershwin wanted to compose serious music. Bandleader Paul Whiteman had similar aspirations. Together, they debuted *Rhapsody in Blue* in 1924. Suddenly, Gershwin was accepted as the U.S. equivalent of a serious classical composer. More compositions in a similar vein followed. The Gershwin brothers made their fortune in Hollywood, but George's uniquely American opera, *Porgy & Bess*, received mixed reviews. Gershwin died a young man in 1938 from a brain tumor.

An American in Paris, Rhapsody in Blue – Leonard Bernstein (piano); N.Y. Phil. Orch. / Leonard Bernstein   SONY Classical 47529

The all-American enthusiasm that Bernstein brings to Gershwin is not to be missed. Close your eyes and enjoy the pure experience of 1928's *An American in Paris* without Gene Kelly's visualizations. Experience Gershwin's vivid colors; his unabashed pleasure in every pretty face, his joy in hearing even small French cars honk their horns, or seeing lovers strolling the Seine's promenade with Notre Dame Cathedral looming above. *Rhapsody in Blue*, from 1924, is a stunning piece of music. Consider its fetching clarinet, its repeated theme played proudly and loudly by the full orchestra, its jazz piano, shades of blues, and sped-up recaps. It's a true American original. With Bernstein's *Candide* overture.

LINK► *George Gershwin – Rhapsodies – L.A. Phil. Orch. / Michael Tilson Thomas*
                                                                    SONY Classical 39699
An especially fine version of Rhapsody in Blue *leads off a disc filled with Gershwin concert music not often heard. Preludes for Piano, from 1926, and 1932's* Second Rhapsody for Orchestra with Piano *are included, as is Gershwin's delightful miniature* Promenade.

Piano Rolls, Vol. 1 – George Gershwin (piano)   Nonesuch 79287

Piano rolls cut by George Gershwin are brought back to life through contemporary technology. It's a little weird, akin to hearing Gershwin's ghost, but the music is so captivating that the awkward feeling soon passes. "Sweet and Lowdown" is a peppy little number from 1926 that Gershwin wrote for his Broadway show *Tip-Toes*. There's a lively rendition of "Swanee" that shows the song can stand without Al Jolson's vocal. The two most significant pieces are a 16-minute 1933 rendition of *An American in Paris* and a mid-1920s version of *Rhapsody in Blue*. Both are very exciting, perhaps more so here because although the performance is old, the fidelity is very clear and sounds new.

LINK► *Scott Joplin – Rags – Joshua Rifkin (piano)*   *Nonesuch 79449*
This CD contains most of the music from all three of Rifkin's popular LPs from the 1970s—including music heard on the soundtrack of The Sting. *Joplin applied classical rigor to his rags, and Rifkin performs them with refreshing accuracy. Consistently entertaining.*

Rhapsody in Blue, Piano Concerto in F – Peter Donohue (piano); London Sinfonietta, City of Birmingham Sym. Orch. / Simon Rattle   EMI 54280

Too often overshadowed by other, more accessible and dynamic works, Gershwin's Piano Concerto in F is itself a formidable work. When played aggressively, as Donohue does here, its smashing climaxes and romantic angst can't help but stir an audience's emotions. With sweeping orchestrations, several enormously clever passages, and a loose, modern definition of serious music, it's a pleasure. Donohoe goes to town, unaccompanied, on a set of 18 briefs of Gershwin's best pop songs; each one is about a minute long. As a further enticement, Rattle and Donohoe present one of the finest recent versions of *Rhapsody in Blue* on record. Terrific recording. Highly recommended.

LINK▶ *Portraits in Blue – Marcus Roberts (piano)*   **SONY Classical 68488**
With members of two NYC orchestras, jazz pianist Roberts explores the improvisational possibilities in Rhapsody in Blue *and Gershwin's "I Got Rhythm." The gem here is a serious work called* Yamekraw *by 1920s jazz pianist James P. Johnson, orchestrated by William Grant Still.*

I Got Rhythm: Music of George Gershwin   Smithsonian Collection 107

The first 2 CDs are devoted to Gershwin's enormous catalog of popular songs, including many from movies and Broadway musicals. Often, they're performed by their originators or suitable substitutes from the 1930s and 1940s. Gene Kelly makes magic of "S'Wonderful" in MGM's *An American in Paris,* and popular singer Lee Wiley sings "Someone to Watch Over Me." CD3 contains Gershwin's best-known classical works, notably a 1927 recording of *Rhapsody in Blue* by Paul Whiteman with Gershwin as pianist. Several preludes, also performed by the composer, are here as well. CD4 is filled with jazz renditions of Gershwin works performed by big bands or sung by Billie Holiday, Miles Davis, and others. Spectacular!

LINK▶ *Ella Fitzgerald Sings the George & Ira Gershwin Song Book*   **Verve 539-759**
When it comes to definitive interpretations of George's music and Ira's lyrics, Ella Fitzgerald is the gold standard. This (20-bit remastered) 4-CD set includes over 70 songs. Some of the many notables: "Our Love Is Here to Stay," "Someone to Watch over Me," and "The Man I Love."

Porgy and Bess – Willard White, Cynthia Haymon, Damon Evans; Glyndeborne Chorus; London Phil. Orch. / Sir Simon Rattle   EMI 49568

A show-biz overture gives way to Jassbo Brown's honky-tonk piano, as Catfish Row residents begin singing along. As the crowd clears, Clara (Harolyn Blackwell) sets the steamy Southern scene with "Summertime," a fisherman's wife rocking her baby to sleep. Her husband, Jake, grabs the baby and angrily sings "A Woman Is a Sometime Thing." The local crap game turns violent, bringing the crippled Porgy together with Bess. The unlikely combination of South Carolina writer DuBose Heyward, Broadway lyricist Ira Gershwin, and his versatile composer brother created a 1935 opera whose characters, songs, and orchestral score are without equal. An enthralling three-hour performance, on three CDs, captured on a flawless recording.

LINK▶ *Porgy & Bess – Miles Davis*   **Columbia 40647**
With its jazzy underpinnings, most of Gershwin's catalog has been popular with jazz musicians for decades. Here, Davis's group creates a vivid rendition of "Summertime," and "There's a Boat That's Leavin' Soon." Davis's tone is magical. One of his best.

Gilbert & Sullivan

W. S. Gilbert was the son of a naval officer. Born in London in 1837, he spent his childhood traveling through Europe. Gilbert started his career in the early 1860s, contributing drawings and articles to *Fun*, a new humor journal. Within about five years, Gilbert was becoming well known as a writer of stage burlesques. Sir Arthur Sullivan was the talented son of a London bandleader, a prodigy who won a Mendelssohn prize and studied at the Royal Academy of Music and later, the Leipzig Conservatory. By the time he met Gilbert in 1871, Sullivan was a prestigious composer and conductor. Their comic opera collaboration lasted about two decades, into the 1890s; producer D'Oyly Carte deserves credit for their success as well (and for maintaining peace in the collaborators' stormy relationship). Sullivan died in 1900, a lonely man devastated by the morphine he required for pain relief. A heart attack took Gilbert's life in 1911.

H.M.S. Pinafore (or The Lass that Loved a Sailor)–
Soloists; Nat'l Welsh Opera Orch. & Chorus /
Sir Charles Mackerras   Telarc 80374

From 1878, Gilbert and Sullivan's best-known operetta was their first major hit. Poking good-hearted satirical fun at the British Navy and class distinctions then prevalent in British life, few musicals have so successfully united music and lyrics. The characters are distinctive: the enormous Little Buttercup, whose song is so absurdly well suited to her character; the proud and hardy Captain of the Pinafore who is "hardly ever" sick at sea; and Sir Joseph, the ruler of the Queen's navy, who travels with his sisters and his cousins and his aunts. While no recording can quite compete with the humor of a competent stage production, this 1994 recording's clarity and style come admirably close.

LINK➤ *Arthur Sullivan – Symphony in E ("Irish") –*
Royal Liverpool Phil. Orch. / Sir Charles Groves   ***EMI 64406***
A romantic symphony performed in 1968, this is one of the few works on CD by composer Arthur Sullivan unrelated to his collaboration with W. S. Gilbert. Finding it in the U.S. may be tricky; you may need to contact a U.K. importer or search on the Web.

The Pirates of Penzance (or The Slave of Duty) – Soloists;
Nat'l Welsh Opera Orch. & Chorus / Sir Charles Mackerras   Telarc 80353
The attitude of this 1879 operetta is captured in the Pirate King's statement "I don't think much of our profession, but contrasted with respectability, it is comparatively honest." He is the story's noble center, a marked contrast to the "very model of a modern major general," whose foolishness picks up from a similar character in *H.M.S. Pinafore*. Many individual songs suggest that this work is filled with stronger musical stuff than its predecessors. Two examples are "Come Friends Who Plough the Sea" (which became "Hail, Hail, the Gang's All Here" in the U.S.) and Mabel's "Poor Wandering One." An evenhanded performance of an absurdly funny script, this is G&S at their best.

LINK➤ *(Film) – Pirates of Penzance*   ***MCA Bookservice 6300182762***
In the early 1980s, Joseph Papp staged The Pirates of Penzance *in NYC's Central Park with Kevin Kline and Linda Ronstadt in starring roles. The original performance was recorded for TV (but not released for home video). Here's the second-best choice, a rollicking film version.*

The Mikado (or The Town of Titipu) –
Soloists; Soloists; Nat'l Welsh Opera Orch. & Chorus / Sir Charles Mackerras   **Telarc 80284**

Recommended with reservations, this fine performance of G&S's 1885 pseudo-Japanese operetta was compressed onto a single CD by eliminating the overture and other music. What's left includes terrific versions of "Behold the Lord High Executioner," "Three Little Maids from School Are We," "Willow-tit-Willow," and other favorites. The story involves two couples whose spouses are flipped under oddball circumstances. The real joy, however, is in Sullivan's adaptation of Japanese themes and imagery; the best of these is "Miya-Sama," which precedes the Mikado, or King. A close second is Gilbert's subversive presentation of the mightily corruptible Pooh-Bah. Mackerras's 1992 G&S debut for Telarc.

LINK➤ *Stephen Sondheim – Pacific Overtures*   *TER 1152*
The history of Japan has fascinated many composers; in the mid-1970s, Sondheim and librettist John Weidman put together the story of Commodore Perry's arrival, and the resulting modernization. Sondheim's score is extraordinarily clever in its use of Japanese musical ideas.

Ruddigore (or The Witch's Curse) – Soloists; Glyndeborne Festival Chorus; Pro Arte Orch. / Sir Malcolm Sargent   EMI 64412

From 1887, *Ruddigore* pokes fun at the English melodrama. This time, the target is middle-aged spinsterhood. Dame Hannah is drained of any remaining romance as her theme is presented by a disconcerting cello. Mad Margaret is subjected to both a parody of Lucia di Lammermoor's infamous "mad scene" and bridesmaids who are far too anxious to do their jobs. The combination of overcooked romantic music and Sullivan's splendor works well enough, but *Ruddigore's* somewhat old-fashioned storyline and lack of memorable melodies keep it on the lesser-knowns list, just a step or two ahead of *The Sorcerer* and *Patience*. (And shame on EMI for printing liner notes without lyrics!)

LINK➤ *Gilbert & Sullivan – Iolanthe – Soloists; Glyndeborne Festival Chorus, Pro Arte Orch. / Sir Malcolm Sargent*   *EMI 64400*
Pronounced eye-oh-LAN-thee, the sophisicated music in this 1892 collaboration is among Sullivan's best, particularly as the themes apply to individual characters. The performance is spritely and engaging, and the 1959 recording is pleasantly clear.

The Yeoman of the Guard & Trial by Jury – C. Mackerras   Telarc 809404

After *Ruddigore* closed, Gilbert and Sullivan were casting about for a new idea and coming up dry. Then Gilbert spotted a poster with a beefeater, sparking the comic possibilities of the Tower of London. So began the pair's eleventh collaboration, a convoluted love story endowed with a more serious musical score and finer characters than ever before. Musical highlights from this 1888 operetta include the folk song "I Have a Song to Sing-o" (covered by Peter, Paul & Mary decades later), and "When Our Gallant Norman Foes," by Tower housekeeper Dame Carruthers. *Trial by Jury*, from 1875, was Gilbert and Sullivan's first successful collaboration and a send-up of the British legal system; it completes the 2-CD set.

LINK➤ *Cole Porter – Anything Goes – John McGlinn*   *EMI 49848*
Porter's Broadway scores contain wonderfully witty language, and sublime music. It's set on an ocean liner, as good a place as any for a comedy of manners. Criswell is excellent; her voice is central to many 1980s and 1990s studio recreations. Fine engineering, too.

Philip Glass

Glass was born in 1937; his immigrant father owned a Baltimore record store, and one of Glass's early jobs was selling rock 'n' roll records. As a teenager, Glass became proficient on flute and violin; these skills permitted early enrollment in the University of Chicago. Glass next studied at NYC's Juilliard School with Steve Reich; he completed his modern composer's education with Darius Milhaud and Nadia Boulanger. Glass's course began to change after a mid-1960s meeting with Ravi Shankar, which led to travels in Asia and Africa. Glass found his stride in NYC's downtown arts community of the late 1960s. At first he composed and performed rather loud instrumental works. He next explored opera with Robert Wilson; their *Einstein at the Beach* was performed at NYC's Metropolitan Opera in 1976. Glass has become well known for film soundtracks, as well as technically advanced instrumental productions, ballet scores, more operas, and other commercially viable modernist works.

The Photographer – Philip Glass   CBS 37849

Released in 1983, the sequential stop-motion photography of Eadweard Muybridge could not be better suited to the unique creative approach taken by Glass. Where Muybridge considered objects in motion by inspecting steps along the way, Glass composes music through an additive process, sequencing small ideas, then cycling them repeatedly. The magical effect, as the otherworldly chorus points out, reveals some pictures never seen before. The first act's chorus eventually gives way to a keyboard, and then to violinist Paul Zukovsky, as themes give way to variations. The confident and urgent second act changes the tempo and mood, but the melodies remain the same, lapsing into heavenly realization. One of Glass's best.

LINK► *(Book) – Animals in Motion – Eadweard Muybridge*   *Dover (Various)*
Many of Muybridge's photographic sequences are available in book form from Dover, and can be found in a well-stocked library or bookstore. Visually fascinating, they connect directly with Glass's music. Try also The Human Figure in Motion *and* Male and Female Figure in Motion: 60 Classic Sequences.

Koyaanisqatsi – (Original soundtrack)   Antilles 814-042

A contemporary composer's catalog is likely to include not only orchestral and chamber works and operas, but also film soundtracks. Glass's film scores include *Mishima, The Thin Blue Line,* and *A Brief History of Time.* Subtitled *A World Out of Balance,* this 1983 score was the only sound heard in the theater; there is no spoken dialogue. As footage of modern life and alternative possibilities stream past the audience, Glass's intense, highly repetitive choruses (on the title track), electronica, and dark-toned string instruments (on "Pruit Igoe") are extremely effective in establishing mood. Glass pushes much, much harder here than on later works—the desired result is total immersion, nearing hypnosis. He succeeds.

LINK► *Philip Glass – Dancepieces – Philip Glass Ensemble*   *CBS 39539*
The inherent movement in Glass's compositions makes his vision ideal for dance. "In the Upper Room," composed for Twyla Tharp, shimmers with energy but goes down easy. "Glasspieces," choreographed by Jerome Robbins in 1983, sometimes recalls John Adams.

Einstein on the Beach –
Soloists; Philip Glass Ensemble, Michael Reisman   CBS 38875

Just under five hours long in live performance and just over three here, this metaphoric analysis of Albert Einstein's life begins with a chant of numbers and ends with an atomic bomb blast. A 1976 collaboration with theatrical innovator Robert Wilson, the work is built of numerous bizarre components, including some spoken speeches, chants, and excerpts from news radio broadcasts. These are placed beside, beneath, or within an extended violin solo (as in "Mr. Bojangles"), for example. Much of this is the sonic equivalent of a huge postmodern painting built with blowups of random print items and repeated color geometry. Adored by NYC's arts community and likely to be discarded by nonbelievers. A 3-CD set.

LINK➤ *Ralph Shapey – American Masters – Various performers*   *CRI 690*

Although Glass and Adams have become well-known contemporary composers, a generation of others, including Ralph Shapey and Charles Wuorinen toiled in relative obscurity. This uncompromising collection shows off Shapey's originality and disregard for mass appeal.

Satyagraha – NYC Opera & Chorus / Christopher Keene   CBS 39672

The term Satyagraha was coined by Gandhi, whose nonviolent philosophy of passive resistance provided Glass with this 1980 opera's subject matter. As in other Glass works, musical ideas are developed as mosaics whose larger structure unfolds over time. Instrumentation (and overdubs) combines strings and winds common to the U.S. and India; voices, some positively beautiful, are scored within the sonic landscape. The acts are mentored in turn by Gandhi, Leo Tolstoy, trusted scholar and poet Rabindranath Tagore, and Martin Luther King. The story deals with Gandhi's protest against the Black Act in South Africa; the success of his efforts secured freedom for the many Indians who lived in South Africa during the early 1900s.

LINK➤ *Karlheinz Stockhausen – Stimmung – Singcircle*   *Hyperion 66115*

Stockhausen is a connection between iconoclasts like Messian and Schoenberg, and modern composers like Glass. Stockhausen, like John Cage, was as concerned about the underlying theories of sound and emotion as he was about music. This 1968 piece, inspired by Maya and Aztec culture, is a good starting place.

La Belle et la Bête –
The Philip Glass Ensemble / Michael Riesman   Nonesuch 79347

By 1995, Glass had composed over a dozen operas covering a wide range of topics. This one revisits a longtime admiration for French filmmaker Jean Cocteau and also reveals some interesting connections between Glass's musical ideas and those of French composers like Milhaud and Debussy. The opera rescores Cocteau's version of "Beauty and the Beast," as Glass dances between his usual repeating patterns and more traditionally dramatic film scoring. Glass does an excellent job in capturing a cagey love-starved beast and in evoking the magical character of the castle; his combination of extreme technical precision, unexpected musical events, and deeply personal musical characterizations is enormously original and distinctive. On two CDs.

LINK➤ *Philip Glass – Low Symphony –*
Brooklyn Phil. / Dennis Russell Davies   *Point Music 438-150*

Based on songs and instrumentals composed by Brian Eno and David Bowie, this 1992 recording is a pleasant convergence of ambient music, dashes of classical tradition, and Glass's spin-cycle approach to composing. The orchestrations are lush; a good intro to Glass.

Henryk Górecki

Górecki was born in 1933 in Czernica, Poland, near the industrial center of Katowice. He attended Katowice's music academy and took an interest in serialism and other musical forms despised by Poland's Communist leadership. Although Górecki started working as a composer in 1955, teaching provided his income. Górecki's First Symphony was written in 1959. The Polish countryside, in particular the Tatra Mountains so revered for the local folk music traditions, was the inspiration for his Second Symphony in 1972. Górecki lived near Oswiecim (better known by its German name, Auschwitz); visits to this tragic reminder of the Holocaust encouraged Górecki to compose music that told of Poland's history. A very successful recording of Górecki's Third Symphony changed his life, allowing a small city music teacher to buy a house in the country. The recording has sold over 350,000 CDs—a stunning number in the classical market.

Symphony No. 3 – Dawn Upshaw (soprano);
London Sinfonietta / David Zinman   Nonesuch 79282
Why this particular symphony captured the heart of so many listeners is difficult to explain. It shares some of the appeal of medieval chant recordings in that the music develops in extremely subtle fashion; Dawn Upshaw's floating soprano solo, mirrored by the orchestra, is the setting for Holy Cross Lament, a 15th-century Polish prayer. In some ways, the music vaguely recalls Terry Riley and Karl Stockhausen, and in others, it's a stony old city church. With an extremely fine recording, the exploration illuminates long-darkened passageways. A somewhat minimalist instrumentation oscillates as Upshaw returns for a final prayer, apparently sung from a jail cell lit by a single ray of hope.

LINK▶ *Veljo Tormis – Forgotten Peoples –*
Estonian Phil. Chamber Choir / Tonu Kaljuste   *ECM New Series 21459*
A combination of folk music, chant, and wonderful harmonies associated with the likes of the Bulgarian women's choir, here are six song suites from the Karelians, Livonians, and others who live near the area of northern Russia near Finland. A superlative recording.

Kleines Requiem fur eine Polka, others –
London Sinfonietta / David Zinman   Nonesuch 79362
A nearly transparent piano pattern played repeatedly is eventually joined by a sad and lonely violin, and then by other instruments. It's as if one very old man wandered Katowice's wizened streets, joined by another and another. Nobody has very much to say, but everybody has plenty on their minds. So it is with 1993's *Kleines Requiem fur Eine Polka* ("Small Requiem for a Bit of Poland"). In comparison, the bright extroversion of 1980's *Harpsichord Concerto* hardly seems possible. Listen carefully, and the infamous repeated patterns appear, played more rapidly than usual. Working beside an emotional alto flute, Dawn Upshaw returns on this 1995 album for the slow-paced *Good Night.*

LINK▶ *Giya Kancheli – Light Sorrow; Mourned by the Wind –*
I Fiamminghi (The Orchestra of Flanders) / Rudolf Werthen   *Telarc 80455*
Kancheli's quieter moments are studies in stillness, but he's also a big fan of the gigantic dynamic leap. Just when you're soothed by a quiet cello, a frighteningly loud piano chord will knock you out of your seat. Very beautiful moments, handsome textures, nice recording.

Charles Gounod

A profoundly religious man who found women irresistible, Gounod was born in Paris in 1818. His parents owned a lithograph business; his mother taught music and his father painted, and their son learned both talents. Still, Gounod did not pursue music wholeheartedly until age 18. Three years later, he won the Prix de Rome and became fascinated with 16th-century music and the work of Palestrina. Gounod studied for the preisthood, but music, women, and a robust love of life led to a decision to compose opera instead. He wrote a mild hit (*Sappho*) in 1850, but 1856's *Faust* made him famous. At the same time, Gounod became skillful as a choral director; this career served him well during the 1870s, when he lived in England, and formed Gounod Choir (which eventually became the Royal Choral Society). Gounod's later years, devoted to sacred music, were relatively unproductive. He died in Paris in 1893.

Faust – Jerry Hadley, Cecilia Gasdia, Samuel Ramey, others; Chorus & Orch. of Welsh National Opera / Carlos Rizzi   Teldec 90872

Gounod reduced Goethe's *Faust* legend to a relatively simple story. Faust (Jerry Hadley) wants to be young again, to have sex with young women. He trades his soul to Méphistophélès (Samuel Ramey), who provides Marguérite for Faust's enjoyment. Marguérite becomes pregnant, Méphistophélès prevents her from reaching the altar, and she murders the baby. Marguérite reaches heaven; Faust does not. This recording is Hadley's showcase; "Salut! demeure chaste et pure (how pure, how chaste)" is silky smooth and sensitive. His duet with bass Ramey, "A moi les plaisirs (Oh give me again [a maiden's caress])" is classic. With endless flowing melodies, it's easy to understand why Faust has always been so popular.

LINK➤ Charles Gounod – Caruso Sings Faust – Enrico Caruso   RCA 61244
Seven songs from Gounod's Faust *begin a disc of French opera songs; others include work from Bizet, Massenet, and Saint-Saëns. Several such CDs are available; also recommended is* Caruso Sings Verismo Arias *(61243), which contains his legendary "Vesti la giubba" from* Pagliacci.

Roméo et Juliette – Placido Domingo, Ruth Ann Swenson; Münchner Rundfunkorchester / Leonard Slatkin   RCA 68440

In 1867, Gounod once again proved himself to be one of the most capable and talented opera composers. This 1995 recording, crisp and lively, delivers on Gounod's promise of a good story with appropriately dramatic tunes. The plot has all of the familiar Shakespearean touchstones immortalized in song: Roméo sings "Ah, lève-toi, soleil" (Ah, arise sun) beneath Juliette's balcony; Roméo and Juliette come to Friar Lawrence's cell to be married; in fine operatic tradition, both lovers die in the finale. Domingo and Swenson are way too old to play teenagers, but they sing well enough to be forgiven. Slatkin's control, taste, and pace are flawless. Many scenes match Bernstein's version, *West Side Story*.

LINK➤ Jules Massenet – Werther – Jerry Hadley, Anne Sofie von Otter, Dawn Upshaw, others; Orchestre de l'Opéra de Lyon / Kent Nagano   Erato 17790
Werther is a poet who falls in love with the engaged Charlotte. As the story progresses, Werther becomes increasingly frustrated because he cannot have her (she wants him, too). Eventually, he kills himself. Standard plot. Very fine performances and a thrilling score make it great.

Edvard Grieg

Grieg was born in Bergen, Norway, in 1843. His Scottish grandfather had emigrated and changed the family name from Greig to Grieg. After taking piano lessons from his mother, the talented young musician captured the imagination of Ole Bull, a violinist with a love for Norwegian folk music. Bull encouraged Grieg's parents to send their son to the Leipzig Conservatory; this was a mostly unhappy adventure that resulted in Grieg's chronic health problems. By 1863, Grieg was spending time in Copenhagen with composer Niels Gade, who encouraged his interest in composing distinctively Scandinavian music. Grieg also befriended Rikard Nordraak, the composer of Norway's national anthem. Nordraak helped expose him to Norwegian folk music. In 1869, Grieg established the Norwegian Academy of Music. Next came *Peer Gynt*, and a government decision to support him, so that he could concentrate on his art. Grieg died at his country home in Troldhaugen in 1907.

Violin Sonatas – Lydia & Elena Mordkovitch (violin; piano)   Chandos 9184
Fabulous engineering brings the talented mother and daugther team directly into one's listening space. Violin Sonata No. 1demonstrates a young Grieg's instinct for simple flowing melodies and dashes of up-tempo emphasis. His simulation of the native hardanger fiddle in the second movement is very affecting. The Violin Sonata No. 2 came two years later. It's quite different: more searching, a bit edgy, and somewhat moody. Grieg is more closely simulating folk music here, but he's also experimenting with alternative structures. These ideas blossomed with the completed Violin Sonata No. 3 in 1890. It's more dramatic, demanding and darker than the earlier sonatas, as well as being quite a bit more modern, too.

LINK➤ *Edvard Grieg – Violin Sonatas Nos. 1-3 –*
Henning Kraggerud (violin), Helge Kjekshus (piano)   *NAXOS 8.553904*
Less conspicuous, prettier, and glossier than the Mordkovitch affair, this CD suggests a more honest approach to the music. The sound coaxed from the violin is intentionally rougher. Kraggerud is extremely effective, particularly in the Third Sonata. A worthy alternative.

Lyric Pieces – Andrei Gavrilov (piano)   Deutsche Grammophon 449-721
Although you might select this 1993 CD for its sound, you should know that Gavrilov's performance essentially mimics a classic 1975 version by Emil Gilels (Deutsche Grammophon, 449-721). Both allow Grieg's personal and musical development to unfold through a lengthy series of miniatures; the earlier ones are folksy while the later ones consider newer musical ideas. Grieg also incorporated ideas and influences from other composers. Schumann might be heard in "Butterfly," for example, and Tchaikovsky's spirit lies inside "Nocturne." Grieg's "Wedding Day at Toldhaugen" became well known in its orchestrated form. In general, these pieces are easily enjoyed, but not always as melodic or as light-footed as Grieg's orchestral work.

LINK➤ *Edvard Grieg – Piano Music, Vols. 8, 9, 10 –*
Einar Steen-Nøkleberg (piano)   *NAXOS 8.553394, 5, 6*
These three bargain CDs contain all of the Lyric Pieces, not just the two dozen excerpts found on the Deutsche Grammophon collections. They're very well played and nicely recorded. They're also part of a wonderful 10-volume series of Grieg's piano music by Steen-Nøkleberg.

Concerto for Piano and Orchestra – Murray Perahia (piano); Symphonie-Orchester des Bayerischen Rundfunks / Sir Colin Davis   SONY Classical 44899

A definitive reading of one of classical music's best-known, most stereotypical themes. You'll recognize the noble piece from the start, and after getting past its overexposure on late night TV commercials, you might marvel at Perahia's creative flow. Grieg's exuberant small melodies are handsomely woven into a glistening first movement, warmly glowing with the resonance of violins. Gorgeous piano melodies dominate the final movement. The disc is shared with Schumann's concerto, which inspired Grieg and encouraged him to write a concerto filled with lengthy piano solos periodically supported by the strings. Grieg's concerto was revised many times after its debut in 1868; the final version was released in 1907.

LINK➤ *Robert Schumann – Piano Quintets – Kodály Quartet; Jenö Jandó (piano)*
NAXOS 8.550406
A pair of classically beautiful quintets, one by Schumann (Opus 44) and the other by Brahms (Opus 34). Both are familiar, frequently performed, and should be a part of every classical music collection. The performances are close to the heart, and the sound is fine.

Peer Gynt Suites Nos. 1 & 2; Holberg Suite – Academy of St. Martin in the Fields / Neville Marriner   Hänssler Classic 98.995

A vivid and articulate presentation of Grieg's creativity, this 1996 recording is a pleasure. Marriner starts with *Holberg Suite*, a bicentennial celebration of Scandinavian playwright Ludvig Holberg. The young Grieg's fresh, joyful string arrangements are graceful, even ravishing. The eight selections in the two *Peer Gynt* suites—incidental music for an 1876 Ibsen play that made Grieg famous—are all familiar and beautifully performed. "Morning" and "Anitra's Dance" are highlights; Marriner does a good job with the stormy "Homecoming," too. The sadness of "Two Elegiac Melodies" shows a more emotional side of Grieg. Orchestrations of two selections from *Lyric Pieces* (more often heard for piano) complete an excellent CD.

LINK➤ *E. Grieg – Peer Gynt – Lon. Sym. Orch. / Per Dreier   Unicorn-Kanchana 2003-4*
Grieg's complete music for Peer Gynt. *The addition of singing voices is a revelation. The eruptive version of "In the Hall of the Mountain King" makes Karajan's bombast seem timid. Still, if it's instrumental fireworks you want, buy Karajan's Deutsche Grammophon recording (439-010).*

Haugtussa (& other songs) – Anne Sofie von Otter (mezzo-soprano), Bengt Forsberg (piano)   Deutsche Grammophon 437-521

Among Grieg's many accomplishments, his writing for female voices stands out. (His wife was his inspiration.) Because Grieg's musical approach tends to be straightforward, the meaning of nearly every song is clear despite the language barrier. Anne Sofie von Otter is decidedly unfussy in her style; she delivers the *Haugtussa* song cycle with an appropriate characterization as a herdswoman. Many of Grieg's best-known songs are included here; all are marvelously sung. The breadth of Grieg's range was very wide: Hans Christian Andersen wrote the lyrics for "I love but thee," but Grieg is equally effective working with the despondency of Goethe on "The time of roses." Splendid accompaniment, fine sound.

LINK➤ *Wings in the Night: Swedish Songs –*
Annie Sofie von Otter   **Deutsche Grammophon 449-189**
A 1996 followup by the same pair of performers, this time featuring songs by Hugo Alfvén, Wilhelm Stemhammar, and the romantic Wilhelm Peterson-Berger. Harkens back to Jenny Lind ("The Swedish Nightingale"), who made P.T. Barnum's career and then married him.

George Frederic Handel

Handel was born in 1685 (the same year as J.S. Bach) in Halle, a village in northern Germany. His father worked as a barber-surgeon at the prince's court, where musicians recognized the youngster's talents (his father wanted his son to become a lawyer, not a musician). By age 18, Handel was an accomplished organist who was interested in writing opera. He traveled first to Italy to learn the craft, and eventually settled in England. Throughout the 1720s and 1730s, Handel was one of England's best-known opera composers. He also invested in an opera company and made a fortune. Unfortunately, a second investment was a disaster, nearly causing bankruptcy (and time in a debtor's prison). Handel suffered a nervous breakdown, but he came back. This time, he popularized the oratorio (a Bible story told on a grand scale by chorus and orchestra), and regained fame and fortune. Handel was buried in Westminster Abbey following his death in 1759.

Water Music – Academy of St. Martin-in-the-Fields / Marriner   EMI 49810
It's July 17, 1717. Imagine King George I's royal party on the Thames River. On the king's barge, members of the court and guests are dining and dancing. Nearby, there's a barge filled with 50 musicians led by the esteemed Handel. The music currently played in three discrete suites was not originally heard that way. Instead, there were fanfares for the king's grand entrance, as well as dance music and music to aid digestion. In short, this is real-life soundtrack music with many memorable themes. In lesser hands, this can become orchestral mush, but in Marriner's, each instrument's sound is carefully sculpted, and small groups vividly describe the purpose of each composition. The recording quality is excellent.

LINK▶ *Heinrich von Biber – Violin Sonatas – Romanesca: Andrew Manze (baroque violin); Nigel North (lute, theorbo); John Toll (harpischord. organ)*   *Harmonia Mundi 907134.35*
Eight sonatas from the late 1680s played with the passion of rock 'n' roll. Biber is unpredictable; he makes lavish use of the widest possible dynamic range and alters space and time to his liking. The music sometimes sounds more like Philip Glass than Bach or Handel. A very popular 2-CD set.

Organ Concertos – Ton Koopman (organ), Amsterdam Bar. Orch.   Erato 91932
Composed as music to keep the audience entertained inbetween oratorio performances, Handel's organ concertos have a pleasant ease and achieve a winning balance between soloist and orchestra. The organ leads the way; the orchestra follows, underscores, and recapitulates. Although the concertos are rather formal, Handel leaves some space for interpretation (and, in his day, improvisation). Handel composed and performed these concertos when he was in England during the mid-1730s. The spirited zest of the Allegro section of Opus 1 is representative, as is the more expansive slow Larghetto that begins Opus 5. There are six concertos in all. NAXOS has a good low-priced alternative by Simon Lindley (8.553835).

LINK▶ *Christophe Gluck – Iphigénie en Tauride – Diana Montague, John Aler, others; Monteverdi Chorus; Lyon Opera Orch. / John Eliot Gardiner*   *Philips 416-148*
Gluck was Haydn's rough contemporary, an important figure in the early development of opera. For sheer entertainment (and a magnificent performance), start here. Or, take the more traditional approach with Orfeo ed Euridice; the Gardiner version is also preferable (Philips 434-093).

Concerti Grossi – I Musici de Montréal / Yuli Turovsky   Chandos 9004/5/6

These 12 baroque grand concertos were composed in October 1739 because Handel needed the money that sheet music sales could generate. The scheme worked. Along the way, Handel also created some of his best music—and plenty of it (3 CDs worth). Each of these 12 concertos is unique, but all are generally based on dynamic contrasts between soloists and small orchestra. Concerto No. 1, for example, begins with a formal, pastoral setting, but the pace picks up with the romping second section, a somber third, then a fugue, and finally an upbeat recap. (Note: This grouping is called Opus 6; the Concerti Grossi Opus 3 was written years before.) Amazing recording; spirited ensemble.

**LINK► Arcangelo Corelli – Six Concerti Grossi –
English Consort / Trevor Pinnock**   *Archiv 431-706*
Not only did Corelli (1653–1713) devise the concerto grosso (and the Baroque trio and solo sonata forms), he was also a major force in the development of the orchestra as a singular unit. And, he was one of the first virtuoso violinists. No surprise that this music is fresh, clever, original, and dynamic.

Messiah – Royal Phil. Orch. & Chorus /
Sir Thomas Beecham   RCA 61266

The "Hallelujah" Chorus is the sacred equivalent of fireworks, and nobody ignites this oratorio like Beecham. Forget that this was recorded in 1959—the sound is blazingly clear, and the operatic voices (including tenor Jon Vickers and bass Giorgio Tozzi) fill the house with sound. Handel wrote the music for this patchwork of scriptures about Christ's birth in about three weeks in 1741. It's packaged in three parts: the first is prophecy and setup, the second is the birth story, and the third is commentary. It's sung not by individual characters, but by members of the community. Prefer your *Messiah* with less bombast? Try Robert Shaw's smooth, extremely musical version (Telarc 80093).

**LINK► George Frederic Handel – Samson – Tear, J. Baker, Lott, others;
English Chamber Orch. / Raymond Leppard**   *Erato 45994*
Composed a year later, this straightforward oratorio more closely resembles an opera's structure. Includes "Let the Bright Seraphim," a well-known aria, magnificently sung by Felicity Lott.

Music for the Royal Fireworks –
Cleveland Symphonic Winds / Frederick Fennell   Telarc 80038

One of Telarc's first recordings (from 1978) remains one of the best. The pomp of 1748's peace celebration in London's Green Park provided the appropriate setting for Handel's bold statement—a story told with 101 brass cannons, 40 trumpets, 20 horns, 16 oboes and bassoons, 8 pairs of kettledrums, and a few dozen more incidental instruments. Fennell's somewhat smaller ensemble (totalling three dozen instruments, mostly winds and horns) manages a handsome performance that ranges from regal formality to the inspiring chaos of fanfares. Holst's First and Second Suites are winning examples of 20th-century British brass band music (see Holst). Bach's Fantasia in G Major completes an excellent package.

**LINK► Georg Philipp Telemann – Overture-Suites –
Vienna Concentus Musicus / Nikolas Harnoncourt**   *Teldec - Das Alte Werk 93772*
A prolific contemporary of Bach and Handel, Telemann was regarded, in their time, as the greatest talent. His output and recorded legacy is enormous. One might start here, or with violin concertos (Chandos 519 and 512) or his Magnificat in C (CPO 999-109). Plenty more is available.

Roy Harris

One of America's great lesser-known composers, Harris is revered by those who favor the development of American classical music and is unknown to other listeners. Harris was born outside of Chandler, OK, in 1898; his family moved to California, where Harris studied at the University of California. He also drove a dairy truck, became competent on the clarinet and piano, and remained uninterested in composing until age 26. Encouraged by Aaron Copland, Harris traveled to Paris and learned from Nadia Boulanger; by the 1930s, he was one of the most promising composers in the effort to establish a distinctively American classical school. Harris befriended Leonard Bernstein, a Harvard graduate half his age. Bernstein became a major promoter of Harris's music, especially in Europe. With over 200 works to his credit and an impressive number of disciples, Harris's impact on this country's music deserves more attention.

Symphony No. 3 – New York Phil. Orch. /
Leonard Bernstein   Deutsche Grammophon 419-780

Hailed as one of America's greatest symphonies, and yet not often heard in live performance, Harris's Third Symphony rewards patient listening with handsome melodies, vivid orchestral colors, and honest emotion. Listen once again to visualize hardworking farmers, dust storms, and corn growing high in glorious sunshine.You'll discover the cab driver who makes just enough to feed his family, the tiny railroad town, and the train heading into the city. Harris communicates subtly with toiling horns and busy strings. Amidst the understatement, there is one resounding Copland-style pronouncement. The anchor of this symphony, it occurs midway and carries the traveler home. U.S. composer William Schuman contributes his Third Symphony to complete the CD.

LINK▶ *William Schumann – New England Triptych, other works –*
Seattle Sym. / Gerard Schwarz   ***Delos 3115***
Former president of the Juilliard School and Lincoln Center, Schumann will be remembered for 1939's American Festival Overture and his adaptation of William Billings's American Revolution music as New England Triptych. Plus, his orchestral arrangement of Ives's Variations on "America."

Sym. No. 6 ("Gettysburg") – Pacific Sym. Orch. / Keith Clark   Delos 3140

Taking his rightful place next to Barber (*Capricorn Concerto, Essay for Orchestra*) and Copland (*Saga of the Prairies*), Harris articulates in music all that Lincoln said in words. Composed in 1944 on commission from the NBC-Blue Radio Network, the first movement ("Awakening") patiently accumulates admiration as frail textures become bold and brief melodic fragments become fully developed themes. The second movement, called "Conflict," moves from a funeral march to a military march; Harris skewers "When the Caissons Go Rolling Along." The third movement, "Dedication," remembers the dead with crystalline eloquence. The fourth movement, "Affirmation," promises that "these dead shall not have died in vain."

LINK▶ *Ellen Taaffe Zwilich – Symphony No. 1 –*
Indianapolis Sym. Orch. / John Nelson   ***New World 336***
Winner of the 1983 Pulitzer Prize, Zwilich found the precisely the right balance of old, romantic ideas about thematic development and melody and newer ones about variations and orchestral textures. Complex harmonies add considerable depth to the work.

Franz Joseph Haydn

Haydn was born to a working-class family in Rohrau, Austria. At age 8, in 1740, he joined St. Stephen's choir and then taught himself music theory by concentrated study. He started composing and got a musical director job with an Austrian count in 1759. Two years later, he began to compose for Prince Anton Esterhazy, who had heard Haydn's work at the count's estate. The prince died a year later, but his brother, Nicholas, loved music and kept Haydn employed for three decades. Working with tremendous creative freedom, with an orchestra and a 400-seat hall at his disposal, Haydn became one of Europe's best-known composers. When Prince Nicholas died in 1790, the family continued to support Haydn, but no longer required his full-time services. Haydn lived in Vienna, but worked several years in England, where his fame and fortune grew. Haydn died in 1809.

Mass in Time of War, Nelson Mass –
Norman Scribner Choir, Westminster Choir
NY Phil. / Leonard Bernstein   SONY Classical 47563

Full of life and passion, Bernstein was a powerful Haydn interpreter. On these two late Masses, Haydn treated voices as a magnificent section in the orchestra. *Mass in Time of War* (*Missa in tempore belli*), composed in 1796, is a huge outpouring of military and sacred power dominated by the thunderous combination of full orchestra and chorus (with occasional somber solos of a more delicate nature). The *Lord Nelson Mass*, from 1798, was probably named for Nelson's visit to London. It's a gigantic, sweeping celebration by orchestra, chorus, and particularly soprano Judith Blegen. A 2-CD set recorded in 1963 (*Lord Nelson Mass*) and 1973 (*Mass in Time of War*); dynamic range is a bit constrained.

LINK▶ *The Historic Broadcasts 1923-1987 – NY Phil.*   **NY Philharmonic 9701**

A very popular 10-CD set, this box is part of an increasingly popular trend: orchestras mining their broadcast archives for historical collections. Magic abounds: David Oistrakh playing Shostakovich's First Violin Concerto, Artur Rubenstein's Chopin, Bernstein conducting Copland, the list goes on. Generally good sound, too.

Piano Trios – Beaux Arts Trio   Philips 454-098

These 43 trios, on nine CDs, are a major commitment (even at a budget price); this is 10 1/2 hours of music! As chamber music goes, however, it's difficult to find a more uplifting, interesting series by a single composer. What's more, these works cover a period from 1767—when piano trios were a new idea—to around 1790, when the use of a piano (in place of a harpsichord or clavichord) smoothed the sound and permitted untold sophistication. This is music in perfect balance. Begin with the Trio in F (37), set up in three exquisitely crafted themes reminiscent of elegant dances. The varied weight of the line drawn by a single violin (played by Isidore Cohen) is art in itself. When played with the added depth and resonance of the cello's voice (played by Bernard Greenhouse), and against a secondary concept spoken by Manham Pressler on piano, the violin's lines interweave with awesome emotion. Certainly this is not music for casual listening, nor is it intended for more than perhaps an hour at a sitting. It is music for a quiet afternoon or evening, when time permits contemplation. Remarkably, each of these pieces is quite different from the rest. The popular Trio in G (25) concludes with the fast, flashy "Gypsy" rondos, one of the tastiest dances in this collection. The wistful "Andante Cantible" opening of Trio in E flat (31) is one of Haydn's prettier melodies and a delicate counterweight to the piece's carefree "Allegro" second half. Handsome recording, too.

LINK➤ *Girolamo Frescobaldi –*
Partite & Toccate – Pierre Hantaï (harpischord)   *Auvidis 8585*
Leaping backward to a time when harpsichords were much in vogue (the first quarter of the seventeenth century), Hantaï dazzles listeners with a phenomenally passionate, athletic, remarkably musical demonstration of what a harpsichord can do. This CD has won endless awards. It's quite special.

String Quartets (Opus 76) –
Kodaly Quartet   NAXOS 8.550314, 8.550315

The six quartets included in Opus 76 were delivered to Count Joseph Erödy in 1797; Haydn had already written about 60 quartets over a period of more than 35 years. These are particularly good examples of his later, more intellectually stimulating work. The third quartet, String Quartet in D minor, Op. 76, No. 3, is one of a great many fine examples of Haydn's quartet compositions; its opening, an "Allegro," playfully varies the beginning theme. Next is a formal slow section and the very different sound of the "Menuetto," emphasizing chords, not counterpoint, and played by two pairs of instruments. Compare this with the exuberant "Sunrise" of the fourth quartet, which slowly takes shape as the morning mist clears, a piece whose viola voice dominates and provides a new day with heart. This quartet's second movement is abstract, almost impressionistic, benefitting from Haydn's newfound interest in the somber dramatic possibilities of a very slow tempo. After a formal minuet, the final piece returns to the themes established in the opening, at first quite world-weary; gradually, as the two violins and the viola sing to one another (very quickly!), the piece is replenished with enthusiasm for the day and a snappy ending. (Haydn's instincts for cuing audiences to applaud are unmatched in classical music.) The sixth quartet is quite difficult to play, but makes for particularly interesting listening. The Kodály Quartet gets very high marks for expressiveness and depth, and the Naxos recording is fine. (No hesitations about any of the many Kodály recordings of Haydn quartets on Naxos—and there are a great many of them!)

LINK➤ *Luigi Boccherini – Cello Concerto in B flat –*
Ludovit Kanta (cello); Capella Istropolitana / Peter Breiner   *NAXOS 8.550059*
One of so many examples of Naxos offering a very fine performance at an absurdly low price, Boccherini's concerto is paired with two Haydn cello concertos. Cello virtuoso Boccherini was a Haydn contemporary. Try also his Flute Quintets *(Naxos 8.553739).*

The Paris Symphonies (82-87) –
Philharmonia Hungarica / Antál Dorati
London 448-194

No longer bound by an exclusive contract with the Prince of Esterházy, Haydn freelanced and eventually made a deal with Paris's Concert de la Loge Olympique for six symphonies, which he delivered in 1785 and 1786. With a large orchestra (more than 50 musicians) at his disposal for the first time, Haydn expanded the definition of a symphony, writing works with tremendous range. The best known, Symphony No. 86, starts slowly, then develops a series of swells of increasing intensity. It calms down again only to break loose with thunder, then settles down, then breaks into a very fast dance—all this within the first 90 seconds! It's a thrilling display of orchestral fireworks, masterfully charged and moderated by Antal Dorati, whose 1971 recordings have been the standard for over two decades. There are six symphonies on this (budget-priced) 2-CD set. Symphony No. 82 (nicknamed "The Bear") shows its muscles earlier by establishing its themes, and setting them among long and lovely violin lines. This symphony's finale is a gathering storm, demonstrating a brilliant use of instrumental colors and textures to portray feelings. (The higher tones of the violins and the rumbling portention of the basses is especially effective here.) The melodies recall rustic folk traditions, but the portrayal is large-scale, contemporary, and powerful. In short, Haydn really knew how to put on a show, and these symphonies, brilliantly led by Dorati, ought to be in every collection. The showmanship is complete; even the endings of each of these big dramatic works slash away, then terminate in a very theatrical silence. Great fun!

LINK➤ *Franz Joseph Haydn – Symphonies –*
Philharmonia Hungarica / Antál Dorati
London 448-531

One of the great achievements in classical recording history, this 33-CD box (bargain priced, on a per-CD basis) contains 104 symphonies. With superb composition, excellent performances, and very fine engineering (from 1969-73), this is a fabulous investment.

The London Symphonies (Nos. 93-104) –
Royal Concertgebouw Orchestra / Sir Colin Davis
Philips 442-614, 442-611

It's December 1790. Prince Esterházy is dead, and Haydn is free to accept an offer from English impressario Johann Peter Salomon to work in England with a much larger orchestra. He rises to the occasion; by 1795, Haydn had written a dozen new symphonies (his last ones, as it turned out). They're his best. Start with Symphony No. 94; for the delights of the swirling dances in the first movement, the familiar slow sing-song of the second (punctuated by a sudden loud note, which gives symphony its nickname, "The Surprise"). All of this music is likely to sound familiar, particularly the big finish with its dancing violins and thumping bass. Haydn's imposition of one song played by the violins and another played by the lower strings is brilliant; the way they come together is even more so. Symphony No. 101 ("The Clock") is another of the many well-known symphonies on this pair of 2-CD sets (why this is not a 4-CD box is an unsolved mystery). The piece opens with a combination of mystical darkness and sobriety, then horns establish the principal themes with regal sunshine. With the horns and strings engaged in lively chatter, the enormous force of the entire orchestra breezes through. Once again, it's the range of sound within a given section that provides enormous energy and excitement. The tick-tock rhythm of the third movement gives the work its nickname, but the string melody above that rhythm, and its punctuation with winds, provides the deeper charm. And so it goes for a dozen symphonies, all unique and dazzling, all essential listening, and all very well played.

LINK► *Franz Joseph Haydn – Symphonies Nos. 88, 92, 94 –*
Vienna Phil. Orch. / Leonard Bernstein　　　　　*Deutsche Grammophon 445-554*
Although his repertoire was enormously varied, it's a particular joy to hear Bernstein take hold of a Haydn symphony. Among many pleasures here, two of the Oxford *Symphonies (88 and 92) offer a wonderful opportunity to hear Bernstein in his glory.*

Three Favorite Concertos – Yo-Yo Ma (cello),
Wynton Marsalis (trumpet), Cho-Liang Lin (violin)
CBS Masterworks 39310

This single CD recaps the Haydn works from three popular concerto discs. A young Wynton Marsalis made headlines with his lively reading of Haydn's somewhat prim and proper Trumpet Concerto, his first significant classical recording. It was composed in 1796, just a few years after the introduction of the first modern trumpet. The Cello Concerto, a repertoire standard, comes from (roughly) 1783. Like Marsalis, Yo-Yo Ma is fresh and energetic, serious and thoroughly musical. Cho-Liang Lin's Violin Concerto completes the package, and once again, the performance is engaging and youthful. These performances were made on different dates with different orchestras; Neville Marriner's work on the Violin Concerto is outstanding.

LINK► *Franz Joseph Haydn – Trumpet Concertos – Håkan Hardenberger;*
Academy of St. Martin-in-the-Fields / Sir Neville Marriner　　　*Philips 420-203*
Marriner outshines Raymond Leppard on the Marsalis disc, and Hardenberger delivers a careful performance that, technically speaking, is probably superior to Marsalis's work. This disc also contains trumpet concertos by three lesser knowns: Hummel, Hertel, and Stamitz.

Die Schöpfung (The Creation) – Stuttgart Bach Collegium;
Gächinger Kantorei Stuttgart / Helmuth Rilling　　Hanssler Classic 98-938

There are many fine recordings of this oratorio, but Rilling's 1993 version is especially well recorded and lovingly performed. This is the story of Earth's creation, from the start of Genesis through the Garden of Eden. It begins with the orchestral version of the big bang (not that Haydn would have thought that way), then continues with reverential, nearly heavenly singers. By carefully sculpting the balance between instruments and voices, Rilling makes fine use of his soloists, Christine Schäfer (soprano), Michael Schade (tenor), and Andreas Schmidt (bass), whose phrasing and intonation are excellent. The three play roles derived from Milton's *Paradise Lost*, on which this libretto is (loosely) based. A 2-CD set.

LINK► *George Dyson – The Canterbury Pilgrims –*
London Sym. Orch. & Chorus / Richard Hickox　　　　　*Chandos 9531*
One of the finest recordings of 1997, this magnificent retelling of Chaucer's Canterbury Tales *invigorates the British choral tradition. A big hit in the 1930s and 1940s, this is the work's premiere recording. The performances are excellent, as is the sound quality. A 2-CD set.*

Paul Hindemith

When Hindemith's parents refused him a musical education, he left home for nearby Frank-furt, Germany; as a young teenager, he supported himself by fiddling in cafes for tips. Hindemith enrolled in Frankfurt's conservatory and got a job playing violin for the Frankfurt Opera Or-chestra. He served in WW I, cofounded the Amar Quartet to perform contemporary music, and took over the opera's orchestra in 1919 at age 24. Through the 1920s, Hindemith made his name as a radical composer. His operas were laced with sexuality, and his music was akin to that of Stravinsky and Bartók. Hindemith was also a train fanatic—his office at Berlin's best music school featured an elaborate model railroad, whose trains ran on a timetable. In time, Hindemith's music calmed down; still, it was banned by the Nazis. After WW II, Hindemith regained his stature. He continued composing and conducting until the 1960s. Hindemith died in Frank-furt in 1963 following a stroke.

Kammermusik Nos. 1-7 –
Royal Concertgebouw Orch. / Riccardo Chailly   London 433-816

Although the term "kammermusik" literally translates as "chamber music," these pieces were composed for small orchestra. The first, from 1921, is a suite for a dozen instruments. The first two movements are jaunty and dissonant; the third is pastoral and contemplative, performed by three wind instruments and a glockenspiel accenting with a single repeated note; the fourth movement is anarchy that passes through scales in eleven major keys before a silent movie road race of a finale, complete with xylophone and siren. Kammermusik No. 2, from 1925, is a modern piano concerto that intentionally recalls Bach and baroque composition; the first move-ment seems as much a math lesson as a musical construction. Its close kin is the miniature cello concerto, Kammermusik No. 3, with its distinctive melodic theme that's repeated, upsided, transformed, and otherwise explored by the cello, winds, and other instruments. And that's just the point of this music: to update the progressive mathematical ideas of Bach and to cast them in a 20th-century setting. By design, Kammermusik No. 4 is ponderous and complicated by design; the solo violin works intricate patterns over a complex cauldron of percussion, rhythm, and meandering horns; the instrumentation includes only the lower strings, plus many winds and special drums. Kammermusik No. 5, for viola, and Kammermusic No. 6, for the baroque viola d'amore, are less cheeky and arranged more for beauty than effect. Kammermusik No. 7 features an organ, 11 winds, some cellos, and a double bass. Truly excellent 2-CD recording with clever, refreshing performances.

LINK▶ *Paul Hindemith – Kammermusiken Nos. 1-7 –*
Ensemble Modern / Markus Stenz   *RCA 61730*
A decidedly different take on both performance and recording. The approach here is more revela-tory—as if the music is being played for the first time, delighting the players as much as the listener. The recording is also a bit cooler, thinner, and allows individual instruments to shine.

Mathis der Maler (Symphony) –
Israel Phil. Orch. / Leonard Bernstein   Deutsche Grammophon 429-404

Matthias Grünewald (1460–1528) was a German *maler*, or painter. His three-panel *Isenheim Altarpiece* provided Hindemith with a musical canvas for a struggle between an artist's desire for seclusion and his inevitable involvement in real-world conflict. Hindemith wrote a symphony and an opera based on these themes in the mid-1930s, as the Nazis were taking over. In the first movement, the artist seems self-contained and happy, but sometimes distracted. The second is a death march. The heart-throbbing third turns darkness into triumph. *Symphonic Variations on Themes of Weber*, from 1943, is melodic and robust.

LINK➤ *Paul Hindemith – Mathis der Mahler – Kölner Rundfunk Sym. Orch. / Gerd Albrecht*
Wergo 6255
Here on three CDs is the complete opera, sung in German and recorded in 1990. There are no English lyric translations, only some English liner notes. The music is especially fine during the many anguished passages. Try also the Fisher-Dieskau / Kubelik version (EMI 55237).

Sonatas for Brass Instruments & Piano –
Glenn Gould (piano), Philadelphia Brass
Ensemble members   SONY Classical 52671

Each of these five intriguing sonatas is a duet between pianist Gould and a brass soloist. Hindemith updates an old form with a great many imaginative ideas. In 1939's Trumpet Sonata, for example, Hindemith recalls Haydn's work but also presents music with a slightly military air and a very slight jazz flavor. The long-lost Trombone Sonata, written in 1941, came next; 1955's Bass Tuba Sonata was the last. Hindemith coaxed melodies from instruments more often associated with rhythm, while the piano served up some of his best work. The Horn Sonata, from 1939, and 1943's warmly melodic Alto Horn Sonata complete a recommended 2-CD set. Expertly recorded in 1975–76.

LINK➤ *10-Year Jubilee – Christian Lundberg (trombone)*   *BIS 638*
Seemingly a bunch of short pieces for trombone, this CD contains a surprising repertoire. Lundberg begins with Rimsky-Korsakov's Flight of the Bumblebee *and Saint-Saëns's* Camille, *but it's not long before he's working out on Iannis Xenakis, György Ligeti, Alfred Schnittke and Luciano Berio.*

Sinfonia serena, Die Harmonie der Welt –
BBC Philharmonic / Yan Pascal Tortelier   Chandos 9217
Four excellent 1990s CDs by Tortelier and the BBC Philharmonic feature remarkable pieces that are somewhat lesser known: Symphony in E flat and the *Nobilissima Visione Suite* (Chandos 9060); his Cello Concerto and *The Four Temperaments* (9124); and *Pittsburgh Symphony* and *Symphonic Dances* (9530). On this CD, 1946's Symphonia Serena, Hindemith's third symphony, is light, graceful, and apparently without an agenda. Hindemith returns to his typically zippy style in the fourth movement, however. Die Harmonie der Welt, from 1951, is derived from an opera about radical astronomer Johannes Kepler (1571–1630), who was excommunicated from the Lutheran Church after obsessing about the harmony of the spheres and their underlying mathematics.

LINK➤ *Walter Braunfels – Die Vögel (The Birds) –*
Hellen Kwon, Endrick Wottrich, Wolfgang Holzmair, others; Deutsches Symphonie-Orchester Berlin / Lothar Zagrosek
London 448-679
A remarkable man and a masterpiece of an opera. Braunfels fought the Nazis with all his power, then exiled himself near Lake Constance. He returned in 1946 to rebuild his country, beginning with the Köln's Academy of Music. This 1920 opera, modern and airy, is based on Aristophenes's comedy, The Birds. *Excellent performance.*

Vagn Holmboe

Distinguished Danish composer Vagn Holmboe was born in 1909 in Horsens, part of Denmark's East Jutland region. Music was a part of life at home; both of his parents played instruments. On the recommendation of Carl Nielsen, Holmboe enrolled in Copenhagen's Royal Danish Music Conservatory at age 17. Holmboe stayed for several years, then moved to Berlin, where he studed with Ernest Toch. While in Berlin, Holmboe met his future wife, Meta May Graf, a pianist from Roumania. During a trip to Roumania in 1933 and 1934, Holmboe began to understand the relevance of folk music in his own classical composition; it changed his approach to art. By the mid-1930s, the young family was settled in Aarhus, Denmark, and Holmboe gradually earned renown as a distinctly Danish voice. He became a major symphony composer, but also wrote a handsome catalog of chamber works. Holmboe died a national hero in 1996.

String Quartets Nos. 1, 3, 4 & 2, 5, 6 –
Kontra Quartet   dacapo 9203, 8.224026
Denmark's leading quartet presents an appealing, modern view of the string quartet. Holmboe provides textbook lessons in the use of variations and counterpoint, but these are only starting points. On the First Quartet, from 1949, Holmboe commences with a viola sonata, followed by a cello in counterpoint, the builds on an updated sonata form. The mood is a bit cold, yet somehow sentimental, analytical, and with heart. These subtle contrasts make for fascinating listening. The Third Quartet, also from 1949, experiments with ideas from Haydn and Bartók. Once again, the transformation of ideas, the intelligent combinations and juxtapositions of tonal color, time, and space are fine examples of Holmboe's creative gifts.

LINK▶ *Thomas Adès – Living Toys – London Sinfonietta / Markus Stenz*   *EMI 72271*
Composed by one of Britain's most promising young voices, the lead piece describes a boy at play—and works without melody, harmony, or other conventions. But the bunch of musical noise has unity. Arcadiana, performed by the Endellion Quartet, is relaxed, scattered, and frenetic, but more traditionally classical in style.

Complete Symphonies – Aarhus Sym. Orch. / Owain Hughes   BIS 843/846
Holmboe composed 13 numbered symphonies from 1935 until 1994, plus a memorial symphony. All are presented here in a 6-CD box. The performances and recordings are all fine; three symphonies debut on record here. The defiant Symphony No. 3, from 1941, strikes out against the Nazi occupation of Denmark. Symphony No. 5, completed in 1944, is built on a metamorphosis of themes; they're gradually modified toward a final coherent statement. The same technique is used to great effect throughout 1951's Symphony No. 7. Throughout the sequence, Holmboe does a superb job in combining the mathematics of musical composition with noble stature and vivid textures. It's music worth hearing.

LINK▶ *Allan Pettersson – Sym. No. 7 –*
State Phil. Orch. Hamburg / Gerd Albrecht   *cpo 999-190*
The Swedish Pettersson broke through with this 1967 symphony. It's a complicated work involving extreme stillness, effective motifs (a tuba and a trombone establishing an idea together), and a huge arc of development from the gloomy opening to the intense finish.

Gustav Holst

Gustav Holst was born in 1874 to a Swedish father and an English mother. The family lived in Cheltenham, Gloucestershire, England. Educated by his parents (an organist and a piano teacher), Holst enrolled in the Royal College of Music in 1893. At school he met Ralph Vaughn Williams, who became a lifelong friend. Holst's instrument was the trombone; in the early years of his career, he performed in theater and opera orchestras. In 1905, Holst started teaching at St. Paul's Girls School; he taught at Morley College beginning in 1907. These two London institutions provided both his income and his career until the early 1920s. Along the way, Holst became fascinated by Indian music; he composed an opera (*Savitri*) and several hymns based on Eastern ideas. Holst was also a collector of English folk songs. In 1923, his health was impaired by a fall, and he sank into a deep depression. Holst died in 1934.

The Cloud Messenger – Della Jones (mezzo-soprano); London Sym. Orch. & Chorus / Richard Hickox   Chandos 80038

After one of Holst's most earnest and resplendent orchestrations, the chorus surges onto center stage, celebrating, exalting, and soaring above the strings. This music positively glows; it is an exemplary sample of English choral music at its very best. Fortunately, the engineering supports the effort; it produces an enormous soundstage where individual voices and choral sections are well spaced and clearly delineated. Neglected for decades after its 1913 premiere (which was a disaster), *The Cloud Messenger* was inspired by the Indian poet Kalidasa (who lived two millenia ago). It's the story of a poet who places a message of love on a cloud passing toward the Himalaya. Underrated, fine, and sometimes stirring.

LINK➤ *Gustav Holst – Military Band Suites –*
Cleveland Symphonic Winds / Frederick Fennell   *Telarc 88038*
Holst's head-held-high brass arrangements are sublime and often heard. They're not notably tuneful, but themes emerge in handsome ways with fine arrangements involving deep-voiced brass instruments and flighty flutes. With Handel's Music for Royal Fireworks.

The Planets – Montreal Sym. Orch. / Charles Dutoit   London 417-553

After a bit of rumbling, Holst's theme for "Mars, the Bringer of War" blazes in full-scale military tumult; the "good parts" are dominated by brass and percussion. "Venus, the Bringer of Peace," has an entirely different idea in mind: a graceful, slightly rambling tranquility stated mostly by winds and strings. "Mercury, the Winged Messenger" prances like a ballerina. A bold idea and even bolder execution for 1916 (the likes of which England had not yet seen), the years have worn this work down to the status of a light classic. However, "Jupiter, the Bringer of Jollity," retains its depth and stature. Grand performance, but the horns are not perfectly recorded.

LINK➤ *Arnold Bax – Symphony No. 2 – London Phil. Orch. / Bryden Thomson*
Chandos 8493

Bax introduced Holst to astrology; the two British composers shared a talent for conjuring mysticism from the orchestra. The first movement of this 1926 symphony is only one of many examples in Bax's work. Magnificent symphonic writing, lovingly performed.

Honegger's parents were Swiss, and the rich blend of German and French influences had a significant effect on his compositions. Born in Le Havre, France, in 1892, Honegger spent the early years of his career in Paris. He was a somewhat incongruent figure in Les Six, a group of modernist French composers. Unlike Erik Satie, for example, Honegger was more interested in larger-scale Germanic symphonic expressions than in the rosy melodies of 1920s Paris. While appreciating a kinship with Francis Poulenc and Darius Milhaud, Honegger was sufficiently eclectic to embrace Stravinsky, Bach, and Debussy with equal vigor. By the 1930s, his interest in 20th-century Christianity led to a dramatic oratorio entitled *Jeanne d'Arc au Bucher* (Joan of Arc at the Stake). Honegger's interest in film led to a score for Abel Gance's *Napoleon*. A prolific and significant symphonist, Honegger died in Paris in 1955.

Pacific 231, Horace Victorieux – Orchestre du Capitole de Toulouse / Michael Plasson   Deutsche Grammophon 435-438

For better or worse, Honegger's most famous work is *Pacific 231*—a musical illustration of a locomotive building a head of steam, shuttling down a track, and slowing down to a stop. For Honegger, the 1923 composition was more than an aesthetic exercise; he was keenly interested in the mathematical power that informed the rhythm. Honneger called the piece a symphonic movement; it was a form he also used in 1928 to simulate the spontaneous field action of *Rugby*. The larger-scale *Horace Victorieux*, from 1921, was a ballet score set in legendary Roman times. Two suites from the soundtrack to 1934's *Mermoz* also address heroics, a key Honegger theme. Superb 1993 sound.

LINK▶ *Arthur Honegger – Symphonies – Czech Phil. Orch. / Serge Baudo*
                                                           Supraphon 1566

This 2-CD set, recorded with skill in the 1960s, presents not only Honegger's six symphonies, but also two symphonic movements, including Pacific 231, *and his* Tempest Prelude. *The interpretations are more lyrical, but not without the necessary tension and snap.*

Symphony No. 2 & 3 –
Berlin Phil. Orch. / Herbert von Karajan   Deutsche Grammophon 447-435

Karajan's renditions stand above all competitors. He treats these two symphonies as "musical documents of their time," focusing on the intense stress Honegger felt living in Nazi-occupied France. 1941's Symphony No. 2 is turbulent and depressing. A lone violin bravely steps out; an eye tears in witness to the surrounding destruction and oppression. Symphonic order creates a disciplined path through the chaos; it anxiously grasps the old order amidst larger forces. Symphony No. 3, from 1946, begins in battle, then meditates on man's condition, desperately reaches out for elusive hope, and prays. Building on religious imagery, Honegger grabs the heart. Performance and recording are suitable for these monumental works.

LINK▶ *On the 20th Century – Wynton Marsalis (trumpet); Judith Lynn Stillman (piano)*
                                                           SONY Classical 47193

Marsalis has proven himself to be as fine a classical trumpeter as he is a jazz man. This collection is representative of his interpretive power, energetic presentation, and perfect tone. It includes pieces by Honegger, Bernstein, Tomasi, Bozza, Hindemith, Ravel and Poulenc.

Alan Hovhaness

Alan Hovhaness Chakmakjian was born in Somerville, MA, in 1911, the son of Gornidas Varrabed, an Armenian priest and composer. His father was an important early influence on Hovhaness, as was the New Hampshire countryside, where the young composer developed a love of nature that would later inspire many of his works. Hovhaness also developed an appreciation for Eastern music and for the cultures of China, Japan, and India cultures. He studied Karnatic music in India in 1959, and Gagaku and Bunraku on trips to Japan in 1962. Supporting himself with grant money from a wide range of sources and composing with remarkable constancy, the prolific Hovhaness composed dozens of symphonies and other works. Despite this output, Hovanhess has suffered the plight of many twentieth-century composers: his music is infrequently performed in concert halls and not often heard on radio. As a result, his work and his name remain largely unknown, even in his home country.

And God Created Great Whales, Mysterious Mountain (Sym. 2) –
Seattle Sym. / Gerard Schwarz   Delos 3157
Composed to provide a pathway up the listener's philosophical mountain, Hovhaness points to a place where mundane and spiritual worlds meet. If this 1955 conception feels somewhat "new age," so be it. There are, in fact, hints of water dripping into pools, chimes, and other small moments amidst the orchestral grandeur. *And God Created Great Whales*, from 1970, may be Hovhaness's most famous piece of music. It is a joint venture between humans who begin in chaos, then provide a kind of fanfare for four humpback whale songs. Very cautiously, Hovhaness allows the orchestra to provide "free rhythmless vibrational passages" to accompany the whales. Somehow, it works.

LINK➤ *Christopher Rouse – Symphony No. 2 –*
Houston Sym. Orch. / Christoph Eschenbach   **Telarc 80452**
Born in 1949, Rouse brings elements of rock music's power to the symphony. With a well-honed sense of roller coaster drama, and a knack for incorporating seemingly unrelated sounds, Rouse is invigorating and sometimes challenging. Try also his Concerto for Trombone and Orchestra *(RCA 68410).*

Mount St. Helens Symphony; City of Light Symphony –
Seattle Sym. / Gerard Schwarz or Alan Hovhaness   Delos 3137
Hovanhess's report on Mount St. Helens is his fiftieth symphony. The music seems effortless, as if he took one look at the beautiful calm of the mountains and their surroundings, heard his inspiring first movement, and remembered simply to write it down. And if the first movement speaks of grandeur, the second suggests a spirituality, the threat of violence below the surface. Hovhaness lived nearby when Mount St. Helens erupted on May 18, 1980; he recapitulates earlier calm before the drums and brass become an explosion, frightfully engulfing the whole orchestra. And then there is a vital calm. In fact, there are some similarities with his urban portrait, Symphony No. 22 ("City of Light").

LINK➤ *David Diamond – Rounds for String Orchestra, other works –*
Seattle Sym. / Gerard Schwarz   *Delos 3189*
Volume 5 in a Delos / Schwarz excursion through the contemporary American composer's best music. Rounds is particularly engaging in a "happy work" composed for Mitropolous in 1944, when times were dark. Diamond is a modern romantic with enthusiasm and vigor. Fine recording, too.

Karel Husa

Husa is a 20th-century composer deserving of greater recognition. He was born in Prague in 1921, and as a teenager he wanted to become a civil engineer. The German occupation of Czechoslovakia from 1939 until 1945 forced Husa to pursue an alternative career. Always interested in music, he took private lessons and was accepted at the Prague Conservatory in 1941. Husa left his country in 1946; he lived in Paris until 1954 on a French government scholarship. There, he studied with Nadia Boulanger, Arthur Honneger, and others. During this time, he also started composing seriously. A three-year contract at Cornell University in the U.S. became a long-term committment. Husa became a U.S. citizen in 1959 and stayed at Cornell until his retirement in 1992. His distinguished career as a composer and conductor is marked by many awards, notably the 1969 Pulitzer Prize for his Third String Quartet.

String Quartet No. 1 – Suk Quartet   Panton (Supraphon) 90092

This Czech CD contains three pieces, each performed by a different chamber group. The Suk Quartet plays Husa's first string quartet, from 1948. The next few years deservedly brought numerous awards, noting Husa's ability to merge traditional Czech heart and soul with a fresh, modern approach. At first, 1994's *Five Poems for Wind Quintet* seems like a reminder of the 19th century, but it evolves into an edgier, wonderfully contemporary evocation of birds in flight. It was written in memory of Serge and Natalie Koussevitsky, who championed contemporary music. The final piece, *Variations*, considers various sounds of bells as spoken by stringed instruments. Husa's creativity makes one smile.

LINK➤ *Karel Husa – Violin Sonata; Piano Sonata 2 –*
Elmar Oliveira (violin), David Oei (piano); Peter Basquin (piano)   **New World 80493**
Two blisteringly difficult pieces, both emotionally charged master works. Husa's communicative abilities are extraordinary, particularly when the subject matter is anguish, pride, and his view of the cosmos. This CD is easy to find and provides a keen view of Husa's remarkable world.

Symphony No. 1 – Prague Sym. Orch. / Karel Husa; others   CRI 592

Composed in 1953 while Husa was studying in Paris, his First Symphony establishes a distinctive approach to orchestration. Husa operates in subtle ways, offering a quiet theme, widening its dynamic range, increasing its power to blasting proportions, and trailing off with a majestic afterthought. A study of contrasting weights, hues, and saturation, it's invigorating. His 1963 *Serenade for Woodwind Instruments* contains wonderfully conversational wind solos that are melodic and playful. Landscapes, completed in 1977 and performed here by the Western Brass Quintet, is more similar to a track by jazz's experimental World Saxophone Quartet than works in the classical canon. As with all of Husa's works, it's recommended listening.

LINK➤ *Czeslaw Marek – Suite for Orchestra, Serenade –*
Philharmonia Orch. / Dennis Brain   **Koch 6439**
Critically acclaimed Marek (1891-1996) was a romantic Czech composer with a slightly modern edge. Enormously gifted, this CD ought to be purchased with the follow-up, containing Capriccio *and other works (Koch-Schwann 364402).*

String Quartets Nos. 2 and 3 – Fine Arts Quartet   Phoenix 113

Rather than striking out in a wholly new direction, Husa is one of the few contemporary composers who makes intelligent use of chamber music's past. His String Quartet No. 2, from 1953, emits a slightly electronic feeling as each instrument speaks in an edgy, modern voice. Grounded in no-nonsense rhythms, the piece explores concepts rather than fully described melodies, but always with exuberance and a familiar strain. The Pulitzer-winning String Quartet No. 3, from 1968, is energetic and volatile, again emphasizing color and texture over thematic development. Husa pushes musicians to their limits; the extreme high notes and special effects of the third movement's violins are one of many examples.

LINK➤ (String Quartets) – Colorado Quartet   Albany TROY 259

Four fresh (female) faces present not only Husa's most challenging quartet (String Quartet No. 4 "Poems"), but also quartets from the noted (but largely unknown) Ezra Laderman and Mel Powell. Husa's 1990 quartet really pushes the edges of the sonority envelope.

Music for Prague 1968, Symphony No. 2 ("Reflections") – Slovak Radio Sym. Orch. / Barry Kolman   Marco Polo 8.223640

A cry for peace, *Music for Prague 1968* was composed after the Communists again seized power. Peace, initially expressed by the piccolo's bird call and other tranquil sounds, is interrupted by the army's advancing horns by subtle spirals of bombs in flight. Repeated distant bells represent a city desperate to survive. A Hussite battle song symbolizes noble Czech resistance, and it emerges as Husa's nationalistic climax. Husa completed Symphony No. 2 ("Reflections") in 1983, exploring unusual sonorities employing the same strained, mildly electronic sounds heard in the third string quartet. Constantly in motion, it's almost a cross between Stravinsky, Reich, and Carl Stallings (of Looney Tunes fame). This is intelligent, modern classical music.

LINK➤ K. Husa–Music for Prague 1968– Temple U. Wind Sym. / K. Husa   Albany TROY 271

Husa conducts the definitive version of Music for Prague *here, offering about 20 minutes of musical glory. Other works on this CD are good—three by Rimsky-Korsakov and one by Prokofiev—but they're not Husa's compositions.*

The Trojan Women, Fantasies for Orchestra, Divertimento – Orch. des Soloistes de Paris / K. Husa; Brno State Orch. / K.Husa   Phoenix 128

The Trojan Women is one of mankind's older literary works, but Husa found distinct parallels in the tragedy of a small Czech village decimated by the Nazis. This led to a ballet called *The Trojan Women*, which debuted in Louisville in 1981. Here, Husa conducts a suite that vibrates with tension; it's horrid in its comprehension of tragedy, but brilliant in its orchestrations. And although this is the CD's centerpiece, some similar feelings are evident in 1956's *Fantasies for Orchestra*, which Husa conducted in Paris. In fact, the darkness of the Aria contrasts with the Capriccio and Nocture sections of this fine work. A brass and percussion divertimento completes another outstanding Husa CD.

LINK➤ Poul Ruders – Violin Concerto No. 2 – Rebecca Hirsch (violin); Collegium Musicum / M.Schønwandt   da capo 9308

From 1991, an adventurous take on modern violin. Hirsch recalls the past for certain sequences and extends tones in a most contemporary way. Paired with Dramaphonia, *a 1987 exploration of moods, from "bleak" to "spiky," "frenzyish" to "sepulchral." (Titles from Ruders.)*

Charles Ives

Ives was probably the first important American composer, but his music was rarely heard before the late 1940s. Ives grew up in Danbury, CT, where his father worked part-time leading a marching band. (His father encouraged listening to the sound made by two bands simultaneously playing different songs, and other oddities.) As a Yale student, Ives told teachers he didn't think much of the "effeminate" music by Mozart and other supposed geniuses. Rather than pursuing a music career, Ives built an insurance company, Ives and Myrich, and developed term insurance. He composed in his spare time. Ives was a millionaire when he retired at age 56. He published his own music, and won a Pulitzer Prize in 1947 for a symphony he wrote in 1903. In fact, Ives's distinctly American compositions incorporated jazz, dissonance, atonality, polytones, and extremely unorthodox rhythms years before the Europeans caught on.

Symphonies Nos. 1, 4 – Chicago Sym. Orch. / Michael Tilson Thomas   SONY Classical 44939

This 1898 Yale graduation project is a world-class romantic symphony. Its first movement develops an appealing primary melody. The second movement is sometimes in storm, but more often in blazing sunshine. Solos clearly articulate the second movement's individual themes; the lively scherzo dances in a vaguely European way. The final movement ties up loose ends with handsome urgency. Ives's gargantuan Fourth Symphony, completed in 1916, employs dozens of extra musicians and singers. Multiple ensembles perform different music, at different tempos, simultaneously; a chorus is juxtaposed against discordant orchestral chaos. Hymns, patriotic songs, and folk songs are woven into fabulously complicated golden knots. The classical form is almost nonexistent; Ives prefers an all-American blend of anticipation and fireworks.

LINK➤ *Havergal Brian – Symphony No. 1 ("The Gothic") –*
CSR Sym. (Bratislava) & Slovak Phil. / Ondrej Lenard   *Marco Polo 8.223280*
Brian was an influential British composer in the first years of this century. He's best known for this enormous work, which requires most of two orchestras. It's ponderous, glorious, tedious, and in the choral section, thrilling. Nearly two hours long, it fills two CDs. Good performance and recording.

A Set of Pieces – Orpheus Chamber Orch.   Deutsche Grammophon 439-869

The first setting in 1914's *Three Places in New England* is "The Saint-Gaudens in Boston Common"; it's a somber Civil War memorial to steadfast black soldiers. The second, "Putnam's Camp," skews a patriotic march, which unravels because it's a childhood memory gone hazy. The third, "Houstatonic at Stockbridge," evokes a moment by a river. Ives's brief (27-minute) Third Symphony, known as "Ca mp Meeting," was completed in 1904. It, too, is a childhood memory. Instrumental simulations of Bach choruses and hymns recall a turn-of-the-century religious meeting. "The Unanswered Question" patiently considers the question of existence through several instrumental voices. There's much more on here, much of it extraordinary.

LINK➤ *The American Album–Itzhak Perlman (violin), Bos. Sym. Orch./Ozawa   EMI 55360*
The anchor here is Three American Pieces *by Lukas Foss, whose talent for unadorned, distinctively American songs has never been matched. Compare his simplicity and clarity with the intellectual complexity of Bernstein's* Serenade *or the formality of Barber's Violin Concerto, both included here.*

Symphony No. 2 – NY Phil. / L. Bernstein   Deutsche Grammophon 429-220

Folk and church tunes are the basis for all the themes of this 1909 symphony. There are lengthy quotations from Stephen Foster's "Massa's in de Cold Ground" and "Camptown Races," as well as the hymns "Bringing in the Sheaves," and "Beulah Land." The fiddle favorite "Turkey in the Straw" is also quoted at length. The symphony's climax is based on "Columbia, the Gem of the Ocean." Somehow, Ives adheres to a traditional 19th-century European format. He sneaks these well-known melodies into the arrangement before they're noticed, and alters each one so it perfectly suits the serious occasion. Bernstein's performance is thrilling, both on the symphony and on the five shorter pieces that complete this 1990 CD.

LINK► *American Contemporaries – Emerson String Qt.*   *Deutsche Grammophon 437-537*
The Emerson Quartet is one of classical music's most consistently excellent ensembles. Here, they explore three lesser-known American chamber works, the second quartet by Harbison, the third by Schuller and the fourth by Wernick. A worthwhile disc.

Holidays Symphony – Chicago Sym. Orch. /M. Tilson Thomas   SONY 42381

Ives's report on New England's four seasons is often dark, serious, and discordant. "Washington's Birthday" is a bleak winter landscape until the doors burst open for a barn dance. The music, complete with jaw harp, is sprinkled with quotes from "Turkey in the Straw," "College Horn-pipe," and other songs. "Decoration Day," a memory of honoring Civil War graves, combines hymns and marches. Representing summer, "The Fourth of July" is appropriately explosive; the music is intentionally written so the orchestra will sometimes miss a beat—just like a real marching band. It's an impossible piece, with musical quotes galore. A stern "Thanksgiving" represents autumn and dreads the weight of impending lifelessness. With several shorter works.

LINK► *The American Album – Anne Akiko Meyers (violin)*   *RCA 68114*
The main reason to buy this CD is Meyer's version of David Baker's jazzy-bluesy piece, Blues, *but she also fills the room with a magnetic rendition of Ives's Sonata No. 4 ("Children's Day at the Camp Meeting"). Also included are a Copland Nocturne and a Walter Piston Sonatina.*

Sonata No. 2 – Marc-André Hamelin (piano)   New World 378

Ives did not plan these well-known pieces for solo piano (subtitled "Concord, Mass., 1840-1860). His portrait of Emerson, for example, was originally intended as a piano concerto, with the piano representing Emerson's singular voice and the orchestra as his large audience. The "Thoreau" movement was to be performed by strings with a flute or horn (with similar plans for "The Alcotts" and "Hawthorne" movements). Ives's underlying theory was to move the music from complexity to simplicity—this construction was precisely the opposite of European sonatas. Ives's aggressive modernism and his meterless rhythms and polytonality may require some initial patience, but each piece eventually subsides into a lmore direct statement. Maurice Wright's Piano Sonata completes an important disc. Excellent performance by Hamelin.

LINK► *Charles Ives – American Originals –*
Emerson String Quartet   *Deutsche Grammophon 435-864*
Two quartets from Ives and one from Samuel Barber are here. Ives's first quartet, "From the Salvation Army," was composed in 1898. It was heavily influenced by hymns, but also shows signs of his future direction. The second quartet, completed in 1913, is a musical argument between four smart men.

Leos Janácek

Moravia is a region in Central Europe, roughly corresponding to the eastern half of the current Czech Republic. Janácek (pronounced yan-UHR-chehk) grew up and lived most of his life in Brno, the capital. He was born in the nearby mountain village of Hukvaldy in 1854 and moved to Brno at age 11. He went to school there and in Prague, then settled in Brno as a music teacher and occasional composer who enjoyed collecting rural folk tunes. Janácek was especially interested in Slavic culture and in Russia (he taught himself to speak Russian). At age 50, his opera *Jenufa* debuted in Brno; over a decade later, it opened in Prague. So began a decade or so of brilliant creativity, inspired by Czech independence from Germany, and a happy if one-directional infatuation with Kamila Stösslová, a married friend. Janácek died in 1928 after a cold grew into pneumonia.

Jenufa – Elisabeth Sönderström, Wieslav Ochman, others; Vienna Phil. Orch. / Sir Charles Mackarras   London 414-483

When this rather severe opera opens, a pregnant Jenufa is hoping her intended husband, her cousin Steva, will not be drafted. Meanwhile Laca, who wants her, approaches; when she turns him down, he slashes Jenufa's face. A lover's mess ensues, which Jenufa's stepmother solves by secretly drowning Jenufa's newborn in a nearby stream. The baby is discovered during Jenufa and Laca's wedding, but they decide to marry anyway. Janacek's knack for transforming the patterns of Czech speech into music, and his disinterest in arias and other outwardly musical approaches make this 1903 opera unique and surprisingly approachable. It's based on a play by Gabriela Preissová. Solid performances throughout.

LINK➤ *Andrew Lloyd Weber – Evita – Patti LuPone, Mandy Patinkin, others*   **MCA 11007**
The best of the epics written with lyricist Tim Rice, this story of Argentina's out-of-control political diety deflty combines rock and other forms to tell a complicated, charged story. The music is spectacular. LuPone is arguably the best Evita on record.

String Quartets Nos. 1, 2 ("Intimate Letters") –
Julliard String Quartet   SONY Classical 66840

Janácek's first quartet (1923) was inspired by Tolstoy's short story "The Kreutzer Sonata," which was in turn influenced by a Beethoven violin sonata. The story is about a battered wife. After a happy, if restless, first movement, strain is conveyed by the second movement's screechy strings. The third attempts reconciliation, but the reminder of horror is ever present. The fourth is devoid of hope. The Second String Quartet, from 1928, testifies to Janácek's love for Kamila Stösslová. Its skittish opening (their first meeting) leads to mutual happiness, her musical image, and finally, fear of the future. It's sparse, tentative, and modern. Alban Berg's twelve-tone *Lyric Suite* (1925), also a lover's statement, completes a well-engineered 1996 session.

LINK➤ *Bruce Adolphe – Turning, Returning –*
Maria Stroke (piano); Brentano String Quartet   **CRI 761**
Adolphe's work is gaining popularity. The various works on this 1997 CD are generally dark, but they're also clever, strange, colorful, and consistently interesting. Adolphe is also something of a minimalist, working with a very limited palette as if it's a kind of puzzle.

92

The Cunning Little Vixen –
Lucia Popp, others; Vienna Phil. / C. Mackerras   London 417-129

Janácek brings forest animals to life in a charming 1923 opera. He based the libretto and characters on a comic strip in a Brno newspaper. Adding some "circle of life" philosophy, he wrote the music after spending many happy days in the forest and listening to the sounds made by animals. Mackerras does a splendid job with Janácek's lush forest settings (mostly with the strings), and with the composer's unorthodox musical simulations of nature. As the Vixen, Lucia Popp rises to a difficult task; Janácek's score requires some vexing vocal tricks. Jedlicka skillfully sings the Gamekeeper. The 1982 recording is exquisite.

LINK➤ *Leos Janácek – Káta Kabanová –*
Sönderström, Dvorsky, other works; Vienna Phil. / Charles Mackerras   *London 421-852*
Janácek's infatuation with Kamila Stösslova inspired this 1921 opera and many of his later works. He's acting out: while husband Tichon is away, Kata has an affair. Overwhelmed with her guilt and her love for beau Boris, she tosses herself into the Volga River.

Sinfonietta, Lachian Dances, Taras Bulba –
Czech State Phil. / José Serebrier   Reference 65

Audiophile-quality engineering captures the golden glow of the horns that dominate 1926's *Sinfonietta*. Written at age 72, Janácek recreates with a youthful exuberance the feelings he experienced while listening to an outdoor band concert with Kamila Stösslová. Majestic fanfares give way to empassioned patriotic allegiance; Janácek is also writing of the newly independent Czechoslovakia and of places in Brno. After creating several Moravian-style folk dances for ballet, he reworked the music into a suite in 1925. It's imaginative, sometimes playful, and charming. *Taras Bulba*, finished in 1918 and based on Gogol's story of a Cossack leader and his sons, demonstrates Janácek's stunning skill as an arranger. Few composers so completely understood sonority. It's beautifully performmed.

LINK➤ *Leos Janácek – Sinfonietta, Lachian Dances, Taras Bulba –*
Slovak Radio Sym. Orch. / Ondrej Lenárd   *NAXOS 8.550411*
If it wasn't for the audiophile quality of Serebrier's recording, this wonderful 1988–90 rendition would win the game. By emphasizing the nobility of the Sinfonietta and the tensions inherent in Taras Bulba, *Lenárd delivers a masterful version of these popular works.*

Glagolitic Mass – Czech Phil. Orch. / C. Mackerras   Supraphon 3575

Janácek based his glorious choral work on the Old Church Slavonic Mass, connecting faith and nationalism. The music's character is based in the vernacular. Soprano Sönderström expresses pure and sacred joy in "Slava," but "Postludium," an organ solo, is rougher and not much like church music. Though it contains vocal solos and some duets, "Svet" is a surging chorale with country fiddling, fanfares, and substantial percussion. Few Masses are so wholly involving and entertaining. The melodies and arrangements are often thrilling, and the recording is whistle clean; with Mackerras in charge, these performances easily surpass any competitive version. The question remains: was this Janácek's fantasy wedding Mass for Stösslová?

LINK➤ *Pavel Haas – String Quartets Nos. 2 & 3 – Hawthorne Quartet*   *London 440-853*
Haas (1899-1944) was Janácek's student. He died at Auschwitz, as did Hans Krása, whose String Quartet shares this 2-CD set. Both make intelligent use of contemporary ideas, updating classical concepts taught by Janácek, while experimenting with tonality and jazz.

Jerome Kern

Kern was born in NYC in 1885 and studied in Europe as a young man. When he returned to NYC in 1905, he found work with various sheet music publishers, playing their songs on piano and selling their wares. He also reworked European operettas. Kern started contributing songs for musicals; 1912 marked the debut of *The Red Petticoat*, his first complete score. A series of hit shows followed, including 1915's *Very Good Eddie*, 1917's *Oh Boy!*, 1920's *Sally*, and the ground-breaking musical drama *Show Boat* in 1927, which may ultimately define American opera. Kern moved to Hollywood in 1933 and enjoyed a career as a film composer. He died in NYC in 1945. His life story was the basis of the 1946 MGM musical *Till the Clouds Roll By*.

Jerome Kern Treasury – London Sinfonietta / J. McGlinn   EMI 54883

Buoyed by the success of *Show Boat*, McGlinn and company fitted together 18 Kern songs from the composer's many Broadway shows. These are not art songs; rather they're full-scale stage songs designed for singing and dancing, big costumes and lavish scenery. From 1912, "Ragtime Restaurant" is vaudeville at its best and worst. Were it not for Schulyer Greene's tongue-in-cheek lyric ("Little lady, don't be depressed and blue. After all, we're in the same canoe"), 1915's "Babes in the Wood" might be taken more seriously. Then again, 1917's "Till the Clouds Roll By" is mighty pretty, as is "The Folks Who Live on the Hill."

LINK➤ *Jerome Kern – Sure Thing: The Jerome Kern Songbook – Sylvia McNair (vocals); André Previn (piano); David Finch (double-bass)*   *Philips 442-129*
Pop producer Phil Ramone expertly manages an audiophile recital with the simplest possible ingredients: superb songwriting ("I Won't Dance," "I'm Old Fashioned," "A Fine Romance," among others), a generous pianist, and a bassist to fill out the bottom end. A beautiful recording.

Show Boat – Frederica von Stade; Jerry Hadley, Teresa Stratas, others;
London Sinfonietta / John McGlinn   EMI 49108

Although it lacks some of the pedigree enjoyed by Gershwin's *Porgy and Bess*, this version of Kern's Broadway musical certainly suggests a close kinship with the opera form. That the music is sung mostly by opera voices makes the distinction even harder to draw. Well-known for American popular standards like "Ol' Man River," "Can't Help Loving Dat Man," and "Make Believe," *Show Boat* is a dark story of black oppression, life on the Mississippi River, and the fate of Julie, who is of mixed blood. McGlinn and his associates reconstituted Kern's original score—a major effort considering the cuts made for the Broadway stage and movie versions. The integration of individual themes is brilliant. Very special performances make for a demonstration-quality recording.

LINK➤ *Carlisle Floyd – Susannah – Cheryl Studer, Samuel Ramey, Jerry Hadley, others; Choer et Orchestre de l'Opera de Lyon / Kent Nagano*   *Virgin 45039*
Gossip surrounds Susannah (Studer), a pretty young woman in New Hope, TN. She loses her virginity to a traveling preacher named Blitch (Ramey), but refuses him the essential forgiveness that provides the entire opera with its theme. Composed in 1954, it's one of the few modern operas frequently performed.

Édouard Lalo

Lalo was born to a military family in Lille, France, in 1823. His father, who was decorated by Napolean, was against the idea of a musical career for his son. When Lalo left home in 1839 for Paris, he had virtually no money. Once in France, Lalo found a place in the Paris Conversatory, studying the violin. He earned his keep by playing the instrument and by teaching. Lalo slowly gained confidence and by the 1850s, he was playing viola in a string quartet. Getting noticed as a composer, however, was difficult. Lalo was 50 years old before his *Symphonie espagnole* brought his name before the public. A violin concerto rather than a symphony, the work was made famous by the highly regarded Pablo Sarasate in 1875. A cello concerto followed, and then an advanced ballet known as *Namouna* in 1882. Poor health, depression, and paralysis marred Lalo's later years. He died in Paris in 1892.

Cello Concerto – Sophie Rolland (cello); BBC Phil. / Gilbert Varga ASV 867

Served with Saint-Saëns's well-known Cello Concerto and Jules Massenet's lesser-known (but quite satisfying) *Fantasie for Cello and Orchestra*, it becomes clear that Lalo was the superior composer of works for strings. He draws wonderful colors from the cello during first movement, and as with *Symphonie espagnole*, he makes fine use of the full orchestra for emphasis and for background moods. It's as if virtuosity is a mere starting place; Lalo demands comprehension and communication. Listen to the small details: the way Rolland nimbly leaps from one beautifully played tone to the next, and the way she follows Lalo's unpredictable lines to their noble and dramatic conclusions. This is fine work, underappreciated, worth the investment.

LINK➤ *Reverie: Romantic Music for Quiet Times –*
Nathaniel Rosen (cello), Doris Stevenson (piano) **John Marks Records 10**
Although the title suggests background music, the selections and the performances inevitably turn the listener's attention to the loudspeakers and silence other activities. From Lalo to Chopin, Bach to Brahms, this is lovely, pensive work. Eighteen miniature masterpieces.

Symphonie espagnole, Violin Concerto – Sarah Chang (violin), Concertgebouw Orch. / C. Dutoit EMI 55292

Lalo was a distinguished arranger whose understanding of the orchestra's emotional palette was complete. In his most famous work, Lalo shows his range by combining two forms: a violin concerto and a symphony. And Sarah Chang demonstrates her interpretative ability with the very refined lines in the Andante section. The objective here is not pyrotechnics (although they are given a major league workout), but clear, unfettered communication. Lalo knows precisely when to bring in the full orchestra and how to rock the house. He's effective because he's so economical. Chang's replies are sweet and smart, and her ability to carry Lalo's intelligent development is impressive. Among the best recent violin discs.

LINK➤ *Miklós Rózsa–Complete Music for Solo Violin–Isabella Lippi (violin) Koch 7256*
The connection here is straightforward: violin playing from the heart. Rózsa was a famous Hollywood composer (Hitchcock's Spellbound, *among other films), but his compositions for violin are blazing with the passion and color of Hungary's peasant culture. This is bold, exciting music, lovingly performed.*

Franz Lehar

Forever known as the composer of the operetta *The Merry Widow*, Lehár was born in 1870 in Komárom, Hungary, which at that time was part of Austria-Hungary. Léhar's father led a military band, and so the aspiring musician received some encouragement from home. By age 12, Léhar was enrolled at the Prague Conservatory. He later followed in his father's military footsteps and led a band. Encouraged by Dvorák to concentrate on composition, Lehár worked on operettas in the mid-1890s and became a primary supplier to the Theater an de Wien in Vienna. A decade later, Léhar struck gold with *The Merry Widow*. He continued to work steadily until World War I; by then he was a wealthy man. During the late 1920s, Lehár revived his career with a series of operettas written for singer Richard Tauber. Happily married and comfortably housed in one villa and then another, Lehár died in 1948.

Paganini – Deborah Riedel, Jerry Hadley, others; English Chamber Orch./Richard Bonynge   Telarc 80435

Jerry Hadley performs the title role, originally written for tenor Robert Tauber, but the real star of this 1925 operetta is Paganini's nearly magical violin, played here by Paul Barritt. The opening sequence is less of an overture and more like a brief violin concerto. This biographical operetta, which takes considerable liberty with the Italian violinist's life, is performed in English and feels like a music-hall piece. Hadley has a delicious time with "Girls Were Made to Kiss" (lyrics: "Girls were made to love and kiss, and who am I to interfere with this?"). Sopranos Deborah Riedel and Naomi Itami are game, too. Bonynge adds a touch of class to a pleasant hour's entertainment. Fine engineering.

LINK➤ *Knudåge Riisager – Slaraffenland Suites I & II; other works – Håkan Hardenberger (trumpet); Helsingborg Sym. Orch. / Thomas Dausgaard   da capo (Marco Polo) 8.224082*
A lively burlesque-ballet combination with the same delicate attention to color and detail that dominate Tivoli, these suites are hugely entertaining with hummable melodies and glowing orchestral textures. The suites, whose title translates as "Fool's Paradise," come from 1936 and 1940.

Die Lustige Witwe – Cheryl Studer, Boje Skovhus, Barbara Bonney, Bryn Terfel; Vienna Phil. / John Eliot Gardiner   Deutsche Grammophon 439-911

This peppy 1905 operetta ("The Merry Widow") made Lehár famous, and Gardiner has a marvelous time with this lighthearted, warmly melodic material. The lavish Parisian setting— some of the best scenes are staged at Maxim's nightclub—is well upholstered by the Vienna Philharmonic's lush presentation and a crystal-clear sonic presentation. The story grows from misunderstandings between lovers, a ripe topic that lends itself to humor and good love songs. One of the best scenes features a duet between Valencienne (Barbara Bonney) and Camille (Rainer Trost). Cheryl Studer sings the part of the Widow, Hanna Glawari; her "Vilja Lied" is one of the best songs on an altogether spectacular CD.

LINK➤ *Franz Lehár – Die Lustige Witwe (The Merry Widow) – Elisabeth Schwarzkopf, Eberhard Wachter; Philharmonia led by Lovro von Matacic   EMI 47178*
For decades, this has been the preferred recording of Léhar's hit opera (only recently toppled by Gardiner's version). The 1963 sound is excellent, and the Schwarzkopf's instinct for the mysterious darkness of Hanna is unsurpassed. There's more dialogue here, too (it's on two CDs).

Franz Liszt

Liszt was born in Hungary in 1811. The son of a talented cellist, he was a child prodigy who dazzled audiences with his virtuosity. Taught by Antonio Salieri in Vienna and by private tutors in Paris, Liszt was a famous touring musician by 16, and began a series of well-publicized amorous affairs. In the early 1830s, he stopped touring and became obsessed with practice; he reemerged as a superstar. The touring and love affairs continued (one produced daughter Cosima, who married Richard Wagner) until the late 1840s, when Liszt took a job as music director for the grand duke of Weimar and settled down to live with a princess. Liszt transformed Weimar into a great European music center and frequently conducted radical new works. He was also a revered piano teacher. By 1860, Liszt was in Rome studying for the priesthood. After more years of composing, performing, and teaching, he died of pneumonia in England in 1886.

A Faust Symphony – Berlin Phil. / Sir Simon Rattle   EMI 55220

Although the Faust legend had been around since the 1500s, it was Goethe's telling of the tale in 1805 and 1832 that fired the imaginations of storytellers and composers. Berlioz introduced the story to Liszt, and after considering an opera, Liszt created this brilliant symphony in 1854. It's divided into three movements, each creating the emotional mood of a key character: Faust (whose soul is taken by the devil), Gretchen (Faust's sweetheart), and Mephistopheles (the devil). Rattle's articulation, helped by a supremely clear recording, crisply delivers the mystery and magic, eruptions of satanic will, impetuosity, and tenderness. This wondrous music is completely captivating. Gretchen's clarinet-violin conversation is especially lovely.

LINK➤ *Franz Liszt – A Faust Symphony –*
Boston Sym. Orch. / Leonard Bernstein   **Deutsche Grammophon 447-449**
This is the dark side—as menacing and sinister as the bleakest horror movie. Bernstein's threatening rendition of Liszt's work is ripe with dramatic purpose, and sometimes overcooked. For sheer theatrics, Bernstein would be first choice, but Rattle's characterizations possess added dimension.

Anneés de Pèlerinage, Books 1, 2– Jeno Jando (piano) NAXOS 8.55.548/9

This work consists of a series of piano impressions inspired by what Liszt saw and felt during trips to Switzerland (*Book 1*) and Italy (*Books 2 and 3*). (Pèlerimage, or "Pilgrimage," comes from Byron's *Childe Harold's Pilgrimage*.) *Book 2* is best (8.550549; composed mostly in 1839 and 1849, later revised), particularly "Après une lecture du Dante" (After a lecture by Dante) and "Sposalizio," written after seeing a Raphael painting of the Virgin Mary. *Book One* (8.550548) was originally composed around 1836. "Chapelle de Guillaume Tell" (Chapel of William Tell) is heroic, romantic, and befitting a national legend. Liszt's compositions are vivid and evocative; Jando brings them to life with nobility and a fine dramatic sense.

LINK➤ *Franz Liszt – Transcendental Studies (Complete Piano Music, Vol. 2) –*
Jeno Jando (piano)   **NAXOS 8.553119**
A significant step toward modern piano composition, well worth owning. This CD is one in an impressive series of Liszt piano recitals on Naxos. Other recommended titles are by Philip Thomson (Vol. 3, 8.553073), and Arnaldo Cohen (Vol. 1, 8.553852).

Hungarian Rhapsodies 1-6 – London Sym. Orch. / Antal Dorati
Mercury Living Presence 432-015

The first work on this vivid CD was composed by George Enescu. It's his First Roumanian Rhapsody, an ideal pairing with Liszt's *Hungarian Rhapsodies*. Many of the rhapsodies are based on popular songs and folk songs; one theme from the first of the *Hungarian Rhapsodies* was a drinking song, for example. The well-known second has a wonderfully robust, full-bodied feeling; it's also a popular concert piece. Children will recognize it as background music from a *Tom and Jerry* cartoon. All of Liszt's rhapsodies were originally composed for piano, but the orchestrations, with their gypsy-inspired instrumentation, are spectacular. This is a fun CD that's perfect for inspiring a child's interest in classical music.

LINK► *George Enescu–Sym. 1, 2–Monte-Carlo Phil. Orch. / Lawrence Foster*   **EMI 54763**
Enescu, who lived from 1881 until 1955, was Roumania's greatest composer. Although best-known for his Roumanian Rhapsody, *his two symphonies are his finest accomplishments. Combining the best aspects of R.Strauss, Mahler, and Rachmaninov, his talent for combining textures is admirable.*

Piano Concertos Nos. 1, 2 – Sviatoslav Richter (piano);
London Sym. Orch. / Kirill Kondrashin   Philips 446-200

This 1961 recording requires no apologies—it's rich, detailed, and pure. Liszt wrote these concertos as virtuoso turns for himself, and Richter is up to the task. Piano Concerto No. 1 is high drama; in a matter of minutes, the pianist is required to perform with lacelike delicacy and to emerge victorious from gladiatorial combat. The orchestra is fully integrated, far more than simple accompaniment, for it, too, constructs the theatrics. Piano Concerto No. 2 is entirely different: it's a small-scale symphony whose principal ideas are expressed by keyboard, winds, and strings. Moods ease from contemplative to impassive; time is taken to explore darkness and celebrate light. The Piano Sonata, recorded years later, completes the CD.

LINK► *Edward MacDowell – Piano Concertos Nos. 1 & 2 –*
Donna Amato (piano), London Phil. Orch. /Paul Freeman   **Olympia 353**
Liszt was a big supporter of MacDowell's music, and MacDowell's admiration was expressed by dedicating his first concerto to Liszt. There are apparent similarities in their compositional styles, with effective thematic development, virtuoso piano turns, vivid colors, and clever ideas.

Piano Sonata – Emil Gilels (piano)   RCA 61614

Many pianists have recorded this piece, but few find Gilels's balance of vitality, structure, and musicality. This 1961 "Living Stereo" recording sounds terrific. Although the piece requires tremendous skill (and stamina), it's not a virtuoso showpiece. Instead, it's a well-considered garden of themes that grow into fascinating forms, then make way for new life. Sometimes it's inelegant, angular, and challenging— forward-thinking for 1853; Gilels navigates this course brilliantly. The piece seems to be put together from sonic building blocks—some gossamer, some bronze, some solid rock. It's one of Liszt's best. Plus, an excellent Schubert Sonata in D (D.850).

LINK► *Franz Liszt – Nojima Plays Liszt – Minora Nojima (piano)*   **Reference 25**
Excellent 1987 rendition of Sonata in B minor, plus Mephisto Waltz No. 1 and three other pieces. Minoru Nojima is extremely impressive, and the liner notes are terrific. It's an audiophile recording, too. Try also Margaret Argerich's 1993 performance (Deutsche Grammophon 437-252).

Witold Lutoslawski

Lutoslawski was born in Warsaw in 1913 and died there 81 years later. His family was well-to-do, easing his path to life as a composer. Lutoslawski's early interest in mathematics is reflected in several of his compositions. He studied at the Warsaw Conservatory and joined the Polish army after his graduation in 1937; he spent part of WW II as a prisoner-of-war. Fortunately, Lutoslawski returned to Warsaw, where he earned a living by performing in clubs and cabarets. He started composing in the 1930s; his *Variations on a Theme of Paganini* reflects an early conservatism. Lutoslawski found his voice in the mid-1950s; over the next 30 years, his stature grew along with his willingness to innovate. As Poland gained its independence, Lutoslawski became a significant musical ambassador, a vivid reminder of Poland's artistic heritage, conducting his own works throughout the world.

Concerto for Orchestra, Symphony No. 3 –
Chicago Sym. Orch. / Daniel Barenboim   Erato 91711
Although confined to musical forms acceptable to the conservative Communist regime, Lutoslawski cleverly blended Polish folk music (which was acceptable) with the lively innovation of Bartók's *Concerto for Orchestra*. In Lutoslawski's 1954 concerto, the third movement is most significant. A passacaglia dance theme is put through 15 stinging variations before going silent. Then a powerful toccata is followed by a calming chorale, which is ultimately submerged by a big finish. Lutoslawski completed his radical Third Symphony in 1983. After a series of miniatures designed to whet the listener's appetite, Lutoslawski offers a few more isolated ideas, just minutes long, leaving the listener to connect the pieces as a symphonic whole.

LINK► *W. Lutoslawski – Concerto for Orchestra – BBC Phil. / Tortelier*   **Chandos 9421**
Several advantages here. Superior engineering is one, which is especially important during the gossamer celeste end of the first movement. The disc also includes Musique Funebre *("Funeral Music"), one of Lutoslawski's breakthroughs.* Symphony No. 3 *is not included.*

Symphony No. 2 – Dawn Upshaw (soprano), Paul
Crossley (piano), L.A. Phil. Orch. / Esa-Pekka Salonen
SONY Classical 67189

This is a very well-constucted investigation of Lutoslawski's work. *Fanfare for the Los Angeles Philharmonic* is righteous and victorious, but edgy and discordant. It lasts 53 seconds. An instant after its horns are silenced, quiet little wiggle-worms of winds and string sounds wend their way to Paul Crossley's piano call. They obey, behave, and pay attention as 1987's Concerto for Orchestra takes shape in its intricate way; it's an easy listen, both nostalgic and innovative. Then it's an adoring and somewhat mystical Dawn Upshaw on *Chantefleurs et Chantefables* ("Flower and Fable Songs"), a song cycle from 1990. Lutoslawski's remarkable Second Symphony (1967) follows. Very special performances, sonics.

LINK► *Witold Lutoslawski – Symphonies Nos. 2 & 4 –*
Rundfunk-Sinfonieorchester Saarbrücken / Roman Kofman   **cpo 999-386**
Happily, we're seeing more Lutoslawski being released by orchestras that seem to understand his vision. Try this CD and also Salonen's recordings of Symphonies Nos. 3 and 4, plus Les Espaces du Sommeil *("Realms of Sleep"), an unsual song cycle performed by baritone John Shirley-Quirk.*

Gustav Mahler

In 1860, Mahler was born in Kalist, Bohemia, a Jewish enclave south of Prague. Because of relaxed conditions in the Austro-Hungarian empire, he was permitted a fine musical education in Prague (previously an opportunity closed to Jews) and then in Vienna. In the 1880s, Mahler worked his way up through the opera industry, starting in a small city, gaining a reputation, and moving to a larger one. By 1897 (after converting to Catholicism), his conducting skills led Mahler to the Vienna Opera and the Vienna Philharmonic. A brilliant, hard-working, thick-skinned, harshly critical man, Mahler transformed Vienna's orchestra into one of the world's finest. He married in 1901, enjoyed his new family, and composed his best work. In 1907, Mahler moved to the United States to conduct the Metropolitan Opera and later the New York Philharmonic. He died in Paris of infections related to pneumonia at 50 years of age.

Symphony No. 1("Titan") –
Berlin Phil. Orch. / Claudio Abbado　　　　　　　**Deutsche Grammophon 431-769**
Technically his fifth symphony (the first four were lost), Mahler's official first symphony was completed at age 28. It begins slowly, quietly, and promises great things: for four minutes, the strings intone the A note in various octaves. Eventually, there's a fanfare, bird calls, and a melodic theme that evolves into a wild, head-spinning folk dance. The second movement carries this theme further, with formality and vibrant orchestration. With its bizarre funereal take on "Frères Jacques" and parody of dance-band music, the third movement is relentlessly strange. Somehow, Mahler brings it all together with a gargantuan burst of energy in the fourth movement. Customarily fine Abbado knows how to exercise the orchestra's muscle.

LINK➤ _Gustav Mahler – Symphony No. 1 –_
**Concertgebouw Orchestra / Riccardo Chailly**　　　　　　　_**London 448-813**_
A different interpretation with less emphasis on gusto and more on nuance. At first this seems a bit dull, but Chailly is a smart, capable conductor who finds much in this music that others have missed.

Symphony No. 2 (Resurrection) –
City of Birmingham Sym. Orch. / Simon Rattle　　　　　　　**EMI 47962**
Through 1894, Mahler continued composing his "Titan" legend. According to Mahler's own notes, he buries the hero in the troubled first movement, recalls the unforgettable image of time together (losing it in shadow) in the peaceful second, addresses memory's eerie ghosts in the third movement's spooky calm, explores spirituality in the fourth, and goes wild on Judgment Day in the spectacular fifth movement. Rattle's excellent 1987 recording conquers Mahler's schizoid music, which addresses life and afterlife, romanticism and the approach of 20th-century music, titanic swells of orchestral power, and the tiniest wind melodies. To this mix, Mahler adds songs, handsomely performed here by soprano Dame Janet Baker and soprano Arleen Augér. Extraordinary!

LINK➤ _G. Mahler – Das klagende Lied (Song of Lament) –_
**Soloists; San Francisco Sym. Orch. / Michael Tilson Thomas**　　　　　　　_**RCA 68599**_
Mahler's cantata requires a full symphony orchestra to provide the setting for four voices singing a fairy tale. The songwriting and orchestrations are marvelous, and MTT's balance results in a beautiful presentation. Mahler's songs are as intriguing as his symphonies.

Symphony No. 4 – Cleveland Orch. / George Szell   SONY Classical 46535

It's bracing to hear a fine 1965 recording by one of the century's great conductors. Mahler's most accessible symphony opens with a first movement that lavishly recreates an old-world Bohemian landscape: "a ray of light upon the meadow" and a "pearl of dew" in Mahler's description. The second movement is highlighted by fiddling "the gruesome dance of death," which is then tossed off as meaningless. Tranquility is imposed by the third movement. The fourth builds up to a big death scene, then relaxes for eternity. Frederica von Stade nicely sings "Songs of a Wayfarer"to complete the CD. That's from 1978.

LINK► *Gustav Mahler – Symphony No.3 –*
London Sym. Orch. / Jascha Horenstein   Unicorn (Harmonia-Mundi) 20006/7
A variety of well-organized ideas provides structure. One movement is about nature in general, others are about forest animals and the night. There's humor, humanity, a deeper philosophical context, and a generally lighter tone than Mahler's hero symphonies permitted. Fine performance, but the sound is only so-so.

Symphony No. 5 – Royal Concertgebouw Orch. / R. Chailly   London 458-860

A lone horn begins the first movement's funeral march. With gorgeous melodies and boundless orchestral fire, the second movement combines a storm and an elegy for the old ways. With his Fifth Symphony, Mahler proclaims himself a modernist. The third movement brings exaltation, dancing, and merriment, shaded by restraint. Of all the music Mahler composed, this symphony's fourth movement, the Adagietto, is the most satisfying. The conductor Mengelberg called it the "music of the spheres." Supernatural in feeling, soulful and not without new age characteristics, it's sublime. The final movement is about the future—striving, combining folk forms into new structures, improving on old fugues, stirring up trouble, capturing the light.

LINK► *G. Mahler – Symphony No. 5 – NY Phil. / L.Bernstein*   SONY Classical 63084
Mahler's symphonies were ideally suited to Bernstein's talent. This CD is part of the wonderous Bernstein Century *series, whose highlights also include Bizet's* Carmen *and* L'Arlésienne *suites (63081); Holst's* The Planets, *Elgar's marches (63087), and Beethoven's Symphonies 4 and 5 (63079).*

Symphony No. 6– Vienna Phil. / Pierre Boulez
Deutsche Grammophon 445-835

Star Wars composer John Williams must have found the heart of his sinister Empire music in the relentless evil of the first movement of Mahler's Sixth Symphony: high horns leading a grim procession of obedient destructors. This is the drudgery of a death foretold. Mahler's inextinguishable hero has departed for war. Despite the second movement's optimistic pomp and frenzied excitement, he will not return. (However, it's great fun to listen to the big drums, whistles, and other special effects along the way.) Mahler's showmanship is exquisite: the third movement abandons hope, and the fourth is simultaneously thrilling and cruel. Mahler's 1904 arrangements are brilliant, and the sonics on this 1995 recording are spectacular.

LINK► *G. Mahler – Symphonies 6-8 – London Phil. Orch. / Klaus Tennstedt*   EMI 64476
A discounted 4-CD set by a solid Mahler interpreter, with top singers like Felicity Lott. Tennstedt recorded these three symphonies with great intelligence and power in the early 1980s. Many consider these to be the best available. Very good digital recording, too.

Symphony No. 7 – Concertgebouw Orch. / Riccardo Chailly   London 444-446

Mahler's contemporaries disliked his erratic, disjointed jousting with good and evil, self-doubt, folk melodies, and death marches; this 1904-5 symphony is his most modern. The first movement is again funereal, and the second is a pastoral release. The third movement, a Scherzo, is at once a witchy cauldron and dreamlike in its lovely temperament. It's strenuously beautiful, but the thick portent of the drums almost never disappears completely. There's optimism in the final movement, heavy-duty tympani shots, victorious military drama, even some satire, a pastiche greeting the complicated 20th century. Chailly's 1995 performance is top-notch.

LINK➤ *Poul Ruders – Gong, Tundra, etc.–Danish Radio SO / L. Segerstam*   *Chandos 9179*
Modern Danish composer Ruders (born 1949) makes lavish use of a huge orchestra, exuberantly displaying its might and battling extremes of good and evil within a fabulously complex soundscape. A BBC commission, Symphony *is a fantastic modern view of the form.*

Symphony No. 8 (Symphony of 1000) –
Soloists, Phil. Orch. & Chorus / G. Sinopoli   Deutsche Grammophon 435-433

Completely unlike Mahler's other symphonies, this gigantic spectacle—originally performed with 1,000-plus singers—resembles a Haydn oratorio, a choral Mass, and a Mahler symphony. Its overwhelming presence is often badly captured on record, but Sinopoli's crew competently manages Mahler's extravaganza. The spiritual rapture of the opening "Veni Creator Spiritus" is developed into a devout affirmation, and an effective symphonic theme. A boys' choir sings a hymn. Symphonic fugues develop and resolve. Part Two is consumed with a new idea: Faust's safe delivery to heaven. The angelic voices of women and boys transport his soul, and the whole ensemble celebrates the finale. A complete religious entertainment experience.

LINK➤ *A. Zemlinsky – Lyric Symphony –Concertgebuow Orch./R. Chailly*   London 443-569
Released as part of London's Entartete series (music supressed by the Third Reich), Alexander Zemlinsky's Lyric Symphony *is a kin to Mahler, but his orchestrations are richer, deeper, more lustrous. And the vocal performances are magnificently sculpted. A major work.*

Symphony No. 9 – Berlin Phil. / Herbert von Karajan
Deutsche Grammophon 439-024

A supreme Karajan accomplishment, this live performance at the 1982 Berlin Festival approaches Mahler with blazing light and fresh optimism. Together they journey beyond the obvious. Certainly Mahler is saying good-bye to romanticism and to his personal frustrations and conflicts, but Karajan celebrates wonder and personal curiosity, as well as the nobility of the man and his original thinking. And so the second movement brings a smile, and the shadows of its folk dances cast wonderful inspiration into permanent relief, often with sharp and prickly edges. Karajan finds no regrets in the final movement's tranquil, heavenly strings and their hint of tension with the winds and cellos; no other symphony resolves so sweetly.

LINK➤ *G. Mahler – Das Lied von der Erde (The Songs of the Earth) –*
Peter Seiffert, Thomas Hampson, City of Birmingham Sym. Orch. / S.Rattle   EMI 56200
A beloved song cycle based on Chinese poetry, accompanied by a full orchestra. Mahler tried to pass it off as a replacement for his Ninth Symphony because he believed composers died after their Ninths. (In fact, he did.) Gorgeous music, an essential in any Mahler collection.

Bohuslav Martinu

Martinu was born in 1890 in a bell tower in Policka, a Bohemian highlands village. His family had an apartment at the top of the high church, and his father, a cobbler, earned extra money as a fire watch. A sickly child, Martinu spent many hours in that tiny apartment, contemplating a view he'd never forget (he carried a photograph for most of his life). A local tailor taught the boy violin; Martinu also tried composition. Community members funded an unsuccessful stint at Prague Conservatory. Martinu returned to Policka to teach, and joined the Czech Philharmonic Orchestra in 1918. His compositions gained notice among European conductors toward the late 1930s, when wartime chaos forced an exile, and Martinu moved to NYC. He taught at Princeton from 1948 until 1953, then left to live in Nice, France. He later taught at Philadelphia's Curtis Institute, and settled in Switzerland, where he died of cancer in 1959.

Nonet, La Revue de Cuisine (The Kitchen Revue) – Dartington Ensemble
Hyperion 66084

Pieces for nonet, sextet, and trio are capably handled by the Dartington Ensemble, capturing the Czech and Parisian blend characteristic in Martinu's life. The Nonet was written in 1959; it's spirited, smart, and multicolored. In Moravian and Bohemian influences, Martinu finds a sunny, affirmative attitude. *La Revue de Cuisine*, from 1930, is a suite taken a 1927 ballet; its offbeat plot concerns an interruption in the happy marriage between a pot and its lid, caused mainly by a stick and a washcloth. Martinu's Sextet maneuvers from march to tango, from jazz to Charleston, with a decidedly Parisian sense of style and humor. An appealing trio completes a fine CD.

LINK➤ *Arnold Bax – Nonet, Oboe Quintet, Elegiac Trio, other works – Nash Ensemble*
Hyperion 66807

The 1930 Nonet was originally conceived as a violin sonata and contains many ideas familiar from Bax's Third Symphony (Chandos 8454). But it's more relaxed, less challenging. Superb scoring for flute and harp. Harp Quintet, from 1919, is sweet, charming, and modern. Fine Nash workout.

Piano Concertos Nos. 2, 3, 4 –
Rudolf Firkusny (piano); Czech Phil. Orch. / Libor Pesek   RCA 61934

Firkusny debuted these three piano concertos (they were composed in 1934, 1948, and 1956), but he left Czechoslovkia in the mid-1940s. He returned 44 years later, and performed these wonderful pieces at Prague's Rudolfinum in 1993. The second concerto is lively, a fine balance between a lighthearted piano and the snap of an attentive orchestra. The more sophisticated Concerto No. 3 makes more use of contrasting orchestral flavors, adds some tension, and features a handsome arrangement. Concerto No. 4 seems to be a voyage through a theoretical jungle; its color palette is unique, unpredictable, and wholly satisfying. The CD offers a winning combination of virtuosity, fresh ideas, and fine engineering.

LINK➤ *Music for a Glass Bead Game –*
Arturo Delmoni (violin), Nathaniel Rosen (cello)   John Marks Records 15
Music that might accompany or be a part of the intellectual exercise described in Herman Hesse's book, this collection bounces between Bach and later pieces by Kodály, Giordani, Martinu, and finally, Handel. The performance is passionate, and the recording is spectacular.

Complete Symphonies –
Royal Scottish Nat. Orch. / Bryden Thomson — Chandos 9103-5

All of Martinu's six symphonies are worth owning, so it makes sense to invest in this convenient 3-CD set. The calm, lyrical First Symphony, from 1942, seems to glow in parts (the result of some clever horn arrangements). Light on its feet and perky in its syncopation, it's very enjoyable. Martinu's Second Symphony, from 1943, was inspired by his fascination with concerto grosso. Martinu finds a coherent, progressive voice in 1944's Third Symphony with its tension and dissonance, driving force and aggression; the music was no doubt a reflection of wartime fears and frustration. Symphony No. 6, completed in 1953, is more subtle in its dramatic scheme; at times, it sounds like improvisation.

LINK▶ *Bohuslav Martinu – String Quartets – Panocha Quartet* — ***Supraphon 994***
Don't think twice before investing in another Martinu 3-CD set. These seven quartets, well played and well recorded, are every bit as smart, optimistic, folksy, classical, complex, and modern as the rest of Martinu's remarkable catalog. A new experience each time you listen.

Cello Concertos Nos. 1 & 2 –
Raphael Wallfisch (cello), Czech Phil. Orch. / Jiri Belohlávek — Chandos 9015

Beginning with a brief but regal fanfare, the nobility of Concerto No. 1 slowly gives way to Wallfisch's searching conversation with the orchestration. His cello articulates so many emotions; in time, they're answered by the winds with eventual agreement from the fanfare's horns. This engaging interplay keeps the entire piece fresh, as Martinu demonstrates considerable skill with colorations, particularly through the slow movement that follows. The spritely third movement leaps from brass to a delightfully folksy cello. Originally composed in 1930, Martinu revised his concerto in 1939 and again in 1955. His second cello concerto, from 1945, is lush and lyrical, but deeply homesick for Czechoslovakia. It's a gentle, introspective work.

LINK▶ *Martinu–Cello Sonatas–Janos Starker (cello), Rudolf Firkusny (piano)* — **RCA 61220**
A deft integration of folk ideas into a broader, somewhat Romantic context. Sonata No. 1, from 1939, was composed as Martinu was leaving Paris and the sophisticated European culture to which he belonged. 1942's Second Sonata reflected Martinu's difficulty in establishing himself in the U.S.

The Epic of Gilgamesh –
Slovak Phil. Orch. / Zdenek Kosler — Marco Polo 8.223316

This very special recording gets the drama right. It's also engineered with sufficient skill to be recommended as an audiophile test CD. Completed in 1955, the piece begins with quiet warm-up sounds, then everything stops for a fanfare, a choral pronouncement of Gilgamesh's coming, and a bass singing his praises. The epic of this Babylonian hero who ruled Babylonia around 2700 B.C.E. is told through narrator's voice, soprano, tenor, baritone, and bass soloists. English lyrics are provided, and they're helpful, but the joy is mostly in Martinu's musical storytelling, the depth of the drama, and the ways in which the orchestra builds gargantuan moments with the bass singer.

LINK▶ *Carl Orff – Carmina Burana – Berlin Ch. & Orch. / E. Jochum* — ***Telarc 80056***
A huge choral and orchestral fete of love and sex, the dynamics and enthusiasm of Jochum's singers ace out any competition. This is supposed to be thrilling, heart-throbbing music, and despite the 1968 recording's occasional sonic strain, it delivers the goods. First performed in 1936.

Felix Mendelssohn

An astonishing child prodigy on the order of Mozart, Mendelssohn was raised in an upscale household (his father was a banker, his mother was an artist and musician, and his grandfather was a highly regarded philosopher). Ambitious for his son, Mendelssohn's father changed his family's religion from Jewish to Protestant so he would not be denied opportunities (hence the name change from Mendelssohn to Bartholdy). Mendelssohn's career flourished, first as a pianist, then as a composer and conductor. At age 20, he rekindled interest in Bach with his performance of *St. Matthew Passion*. Beginning at age 29, he transformed the Leipzig Gewandhaus into a top orchestra. Mendelssohn added teaching while in his 30s. He worked himself impossibly hard, married happily, and fathered five children, but the death of his (equally talented) sister Fanny cast the composer into a depression so dark that he died just six months later, at age 38. He was mourned throughout Europe.

Octet – Cleveland Quartet, Meliora Quartet   Telarc 80142

At age 16, Mendelssohn came up with the idea of composing an octet—a piece to be played by a pair of string quartets. Rather than staying within the bounds of the chamber world, he thought in terms of symphonic impact. More intellectually stimulating than emotionally satisfying, this work most resembles a big quartet piece, but with deeper hues. Those colors are painted with remarkable instruments: the Cleveland Quartet performs on centuries-old strings made by Stradivarius (and owned by Paganini!). The Quartet in A minor, composed two years later, is played exclusively on those glorious instruments; fortunately, Telarc's engineers have done their typically fine job in capturing everything.

LINK➤ *Felix Mendelssohn – String Quartets – Coull Quartet*   *Hyperion 44051/3*
The impeccable structure of Mendelssohn's chamber music, combined with his natural melodic sense, makes this 3-CD set an ideal follow-up to the Octet. The Coull Quartet is one of the U.K.'s finest, and the recording is extremely responsive to the cello and higher strings.

A Midsummer Night's Dream – London Sym. Orch. / A. Previn   EMI 47163

Shakespeare's play was so popular in the Mendelssohn household that Felix and sister Fanny took turns playing all the roles. By 17, Mendelssohn had composed an overture based on the play's moods and characters, and at 34, he satisfied a commission from the king of Prussia for incidental music by expanding ideas in his overture. In 1977, André Previn recorded a definitive performance of these works that beautifully portray Shakespeare's magical fantasy world. Beyond the famous "Wedding March," highlights include the wonderful overture and the Scherzo, which leads to the fairy world and Puck (note the meandering flute). Newer versions improve on sonics. The Finchley Children's Music Group enhances a charming performance.

LINK➤ *Mendelssohn – A Midsummer Night's Dream – C. Abbado*   *Sony Classical 62876*
A 50-minute performance deletes the funny "Bergomask" (a donkey dance), and other minor pieces, but allows enough open space to include a spectacular version of Symphony No. 4. Kenneth Branagh performs speaking parts on top of some music, playing all the roles himself.

Piano Concertos Nos. 1 & 2 –
Sinfonia da Camera / Ian Hobson — Arabesque 6688

Hobson leads the chamber orchestra and plays an impressive piano on this 1997 CD. The recording quality is very fine, but Hobson's fluidity on Piano Concerto No. 1 is what matters most here. Amidst often dainty keyboard figures, Hobson manages peaks of orchestral power, and amidst power-packed piano, he maintains proper orchestral balance. Inspired by a pretty pianist he met while traveling in 1831, Mendelssohn debuted the piece himself before the king of Bavaria. Piano Concerto No. 2 was written during his honeymoon in 1837; it's more dramatic, bigger, and makes more use of the full orchestra. Although popular, it isn't as satisfying as the first concerto. "Rondo Brilliant" and "Capriccio Brilliant" complete the 73-minute disc.

LINK➤ *Niels Gade – Echoes from Ossian, other works –*
Staatsphilharmonie Rheinland-Pfalz / Ole Schmidt — CPO 999-362

The influential Danish composer was Mendelssohn's contemporary and friend (Gade's first symphony was dedicated to Mendelssohn). The concert overture Echoes from Ossian, *energetic and romantic in its way, is probably Gade's best-known piece. Three others here provide a pleasant sampling.*

Symphonies Nos. 1, 5 – Bamberg Sym. Orch. / Claus Peter Flor — RCA

Composed when he was just 15, Mendelssohn's Symphony No. 1 is very entertaining. It launches into an optimistic juxtaposition of a pastoral melody tossed back and forth between the winds and strings, and the occasional blasts of energy, and manages to balance and interweave a series of intelligent, often urgent, themes through nearly a half-hour. Symphony No. 5, from 1830, is far more serious. Composed to commemorate a significant Lutheran event, it begins with a calling (played by horns) and proceeds through religious themes and motifs, often with passion but rarely with excessive force. More complex and earnest than his other symphonies, it sounds more like Mahler than Mozart.

LINK➤ *Encore – (Santa Fe Chamber Music Festival)* — Stereophile 11

The staff and associates of Stereophile *magazine take great care and pride in their own recordings. Brilliantly simple engineering yields a result very much like live performance. This is one of nine (so far). Good as the sound may be, fine performances are the reason to buy. This 1997 CD features chamber works by Brahms and Mendelssohn.*

Symphonies Nos. 3, 4 – Chi. Sym. Orch. / Sir Georg Solti — London 414-665

Both symphonies are well represented by fine recordings, but Solti's clarity of expression and relentless vigor make this a fine first choice. Symphony No. 3 (nicknamed the *Scottish* Symphony) was started during a visit to Britain in 1829 and completed in 1841. The hymnlike first movement recreates the uplifting mood of a chapel at Holyrood, where Mary Stuart lived. The second movement builds on a memorable melody, broad in its sweep and thunder, intriguing in its contrasting use of winds against strings. The third movement also establishes a singable theme on clarinet, then develops it among the breezy winds, collecting enough power to win over the orchestra. The fourth movement gathers all of these ideas into a tight bundle, then releases them with awesome force. In short, this is a fine model of a romantic symphony. Symphony No. 4 (the *Italian* Symphony) is better still. Started in 1831 after a trip to Italy, it was first performed less than two years later. The first movement jumps in with gusto and establishes a major theme; a secondary minor theme eventually combines with the first. It's truly ingenious and effective. The second movement is slower and based on a comfortable melody; the orchestra brings the music to a full boil before the notes fade off into the mist. Few composers make such good use of speeding violins or the contrasting lyrical tones produced by woodwinds. The third movement follows a similar form; it's graceful and quite athletic (and strongly melodic). The fourth movement is sheer exuberance (especially in Solti's hands).

LINK➤ *Franz Berwald – Symphonies Nos. 1-4 –*
Malmö Sym. Orch. / Sixten Ehrling   **BIS 795/6**
A contemporary of Schubert, Mendelssohn, and Chopin, this Swedish composer is best known for his Third Symphony. His Grand Septet has also remained popular. There's also a good performance by the Melos Ensemble on a collection with Spohr's Double Quartet (EMI 65995).

Violin Concerto –
Anne Akiko Meyers (violin), Philharmonia Orch. / Andrew Litton   RCA 61700
A delightful hour-long program of violin favorites, well played by one of the more interesting young violinists. Mendelssohn's Violin Concerto, which he wrote in 1844, is a pinnacle in any violinist's romantic repertoire. It's an opportunity to show off technique, with a wealth of opportunities for heartfelt expressiveness. Akiko Meyers does it well, finding and maintaining an appropriately sentimental tone without a hint of syrupy emotion. Also in this particular CD's favor is a intense, almost rapturous rendition of Ralph Vaughn Williams's *The Lark Ascending*, in which Litton provides especially effective and understated accompaniment. Pieces by Dvorák and Massenet piece complete the 1994 CD.

LINK➤ *Johannes Brahms – Rosen Plays Brahms –*
Nathaniel Rosen (cello), Doris Stevenson (piano)   **John Marks Records 5**
Soul-searching music, especially articulate on a high-quality stereo system (where the cello's nuances are clearly pronounced), this transcendent set contains two Brahms sonatas, Mendelssohn's Song without Words *(Op. 109), and several Schumann fantasy pieces.*

Elijah – Bryn Terfel, Renée Fleming, Patricia Barden,
Orch. of the Age of Enlightenment / Paul Daniel   London 455-688
Mendelssohn considered the possibilities of an oratorio about the fierce prophet Elijah in the late 1830s; an 1845 commission brought the necessary encouragement. Among English audiences, the work became nearly as popular as Handel's *Messiah*, although today's listeners may find the music somewhat stiff. Sung in English, the large-scale choral songs are most impressive, notably "Baal, we cry to thee," which builds on Mendelssohn's symphonic arranging skills. The small groups of angels in trio and quartet settings are breathtaking; their melodies heavenly. It's up to Terfel to deliver the fiercesome characterization of Elijah, and when he's not swallowing words or slightly off-mike, he's fine. Soprano Fleming and the contralto angel Patricia Bardon are superb.

LINK➤ *Felix Mendelssohn – Symphony No. 2 – Christoph Sperling*   **Opus 111 30-98**
An engaging, perhaps more immediately accessible entry into Mendelssohn's choral work, this "symphony-cantata" begins with several brief symphonic essays, then leads into songs with more emphasis on melody than those in Elijah. *Meticulous 1994 recording, fine period performance.*

Olivier Messiaen

An original thinker who embraced Eastern, medieval, and Peruvian music, as well as bird songs, Messiaen taught himself how to compose music. At his home in Avignon, France, he wrote his first pieces in 1915, at age seven. Messiaen enrolled at the Paris Conservatory following WW I; as a student there, he received many awards for his piano playing. Success as a composer followed several years later. A professorship at the École Normale de Paris paid Messiaen's way from 1936 until 1940. He was drafted during WW II and jailed as a war prisoner at Stalag VIII-A. Despite hunger, freezing temperatures, filth, and degradation—or maybe because of them—Messiaen composed his most important work, *Quartet for the End of Time*. He returned to Paris to teach after the war; during his three decades at the Paris Conservatory, he became a major force in 20th-century music. Nature, Japan, America, and God influenced his later work. Messiaen died in 1992.

Quartet for the End of Time – Chamber Music Northwest   Delos 3043

By design, this is not easy listening. A clarinet, still vital and intellectually curious, converses with two violins—one has a bit of energy remaining, but the other is weak, nearly lifeless. Its sound is similar to a theremin; it oscillates like an electronic signal, but it's barely audible. Then, a piano chimes in, and the clarinet is refreshed. The violin becomes upright and articulate. Bright moments of good fellowship follow. Then suddenly, there is the extreme sadness of life in the concentration camp. Another friend has died. Clarinet player David Shifrin flies over the devastation like a bird as he performs the sullen solo "Abime des Oiseaux" (Abyss of the Birds). With Bartók's *Contrasts*.

LINK➤ *George Benjamin – At First Light; A Mind of Winter; Ringed by the Flat Horizon – London Sinfonietta; BBC Sym. Orch.*   **Nimbus 5075**
Born in 1960, Benjamin was a long-time student of Messiaen. His Ringed by the Flat Horizon debuted at the 1980 London Promenade concerts (Proms); the other two works followed soon after. A genius in translating visual images and feelings to music, Benjamin's career holds great promise.

Turangalila Symphony – Jean-Yves Thibaudet (piano);
Concertgebuow Orch. / Riccardo Chailly   London 436-626

Although *Quartet for the End of Time* is Messiaen's best-known work, attention should also be paid to the spectacular demonstration of an organ's communicative power known as *Livre du Saint Sacrement*. (Jennifer Bate's recording is one of the best [Unicorn 9067/8].) The term "turangalila" comes from the Sanskrit words for time and love. Here too, Messiaen makes great use of music's phenomenal power—he plays it loudly, and outdoes Hollywood in terms of spectacle. Messiaen is well ahead of his time in his emphasis on rhythm, percussion ambience, and electronic keyboard (an instrument known as an "onde martenot"). Messiaen's walls and bridges and tunnels of sound aren't always user friendly.

LINK➤ *Olivier Messiaen –*
Angela Hewitt Plays Messiaen – Angela Hewitt (piano)   **Hyperion 67054**
Often, the purest distillation of a composer's ideas can be heard in piano solos. Hewitt, of course, is one of our best pianists. Here she performs Preludes, plus a few pieces from Quatre Études de Rhythme and Vingt Regards sur l'Enfant-Jésus. And she plays with true insight.

Darius Milhaud

Born in Aix-en-Provence, France, Milhaud made lavish use of his native region's atmosphere in his music. By age seven, in 1899, Milhaud was playing the viollin skillfully; this talent led not only to studies at the Paris Conservatory, but also to lessons from such masters as Paul Dukas and Charles-Marie Widor. In his twenties, Milhaud became involved with a group of creative intellectuals who called themselves Les Six; he also enjoyed some oddball adventures with Jean Cocteau, and was even secretary to a French diplomat to Brazil. By the 1920s, Milhaud was an established composer; he wrote film scores, traveled, and composed stage works. WW II forced him to leave France; he found a job at Mills College in Oakland, CA, and stayed until 1971. Milhaud also started a Paris Conservatory professorship in 1947. Frustrated by arthritis, he continued composing until 1973; he died a year later at age 82.

La Boeuf sur le Toit, La Création du Monde –
Orchestré de Lyon / Kent Nagano   Erato 45820
Entirely modern, *Le Boeuf sur le Toit* (The Bull on the Roof) is mostly French dance hall music and hot jazz, with tastes of the classical. Jean Cocteau created a fantasy scenario for a Prohibition-era bar in America, involving a policeman decapitated by a revolving fan, a cross-dressing Redheaded Woman who dances with the cop's head, a Boxer, a Black Dwarf, and so on. The recapitated cop must pay the bill. *Le Création du Monde* (The Creation of the World) is another 1920s Milhaud ballet based on jazz, and on African arts. This structure of this very original composition is based on abstract development and emphasizes colors in place of melodies.

LINK➤ *Darius Milhaud – Les Charmes de la Vie –*
Boaz Sharon (piano)   Unicorn-Kanchana 9155
A variety of piano pieces, including 1957's Les Chames de la Vie *and 1921's* Saudades do Brazil, *composed after several years in South America. Also try Alexandre Tharaud's recording of this piece, plus a complete* Madame Bovary *and* La Muse Ménagère *(NAXOS 8.553443).*

Symphonies Nos. 5, 6 –
Radio-Sinfonieochester Basel / Alun Francis   CPO 999-066
By the early 1950s, Milhaud's creative output was less bold and venturesome, more attentive to tradition. The fifth is bursting with energy and new ideas, and it's great fun to hear the flashes of orchestral fire in the midst of generally optimistic melodies. It was commissioned in 1953 for Italian Radio. The sixth, completed in 1955, begins with a lovely combination of high strings and winds, a comfortable spring day, and a happy one. Changes in color and harmony predominate; melodies tend to be simpler, with an emphasis on variations. This conception works most successfully in the third movement. This is very easy music to enjoy, nicely performed.

LINK➤ *Pierre Boulez – Pli selon pli – Phyllis Bryn-Julson (soprano);*
BBC Sym. Orch. / Pierre Boulez   Erato 45376
Best known today as a pianist and conductor, Boulez also deserves considerable recognition as an avant-garde composer. Created with consummate skill, Boulez masterfully manipulates color and pace, shape and feeling, and conducts the piece with a generous sense of open space.

Wolfgang Amadeus Mozart

Genius only begins to describe Mozart's incredible gifts; no other composer has created such a varied, perfect repertoire. Mozart was born in Salzburg, Austria, in 1756, and by age 6, the young prodigy and his talented sister were touring Europe (their father was a skillful promoter). By age 13, Mozart was composing works of lasting value. Touring paid some of the bills, but Mozart lacked a patron to support his composing career (he spent several unhappy years working for the archbishop of Salzburg). His most productive period was 1781–91, a time when he badly needed money; occasional employment as a music director and pianist did not provide the necessary funds. Still, through these trying times, Mozart composed several operas and many concertos, symphonies, sonatas, and chamber works of astonishing beauty. By 1791, Mozart was quite ill with several serious diseases; he is buried in an unmarked communal grave whose location is unknown.

Bassoon Concerto – Knut Sönstevold (bassoon); Swedish Radio Sym. Orch. / Sergui Comissiona   Caprice 21411

Among the many early Mozart works, including the violin/piano sonatas, here's an underappreciated gem. It's 1774, Mozart is 18 years old, composing without his father's help; he produces a work that is energetic and fun. It's pretty formal, but the darting and weaving of the wonderful bassoon between the buttoned-down strings keeps the first movement up. The second movement is impressive for its refined melodic development. The third movement is a rondo, similar to Mozart's later serenades and divertimentos. Sönstevold is highly communicative, setting him apart from most others who have recorded this piece. Excellent sound, too. Paired with Allan Pettersson's Symphony No. 7, a moody 20th-century piece—but don't let that stop you!

LINK▶ Allan Pettersson – Concertos for String Orchestra – Deutsche Kammerakademie Neuss / Johannes Goritzki   CPO 999-223

More accessible than Pettersson's symphonies, his three concertos are not often performed. They're difficult to play, but their cohesiveness is well ahead of the music of Penderecki and Ligeti, who worked in a similar medium in the 1950s. Best of all, unlike his symphonies, Pettersson's concertos are neither dark nor slow.

Serenade in B Flat (Gran Partita) – Academy of St. Martin-in-the-Fields / Sir Neville Marriner   Philips 412-726

Buy this work singly, or as *Vol. 5: Serenades & Divertimenti* (Philips 422-505) of the Complete Mozart Edition, a testament to the man's tremendous output of works. This particular serenade, from 1785—played by pairs of oboes, clarinets, basset (small bass) horns, bassoons, plus four horns and a double-bass—is Mozart's best work for wind instruments. Mozart brilliantly applies each instrument's unique tonal color, along with a variety of weights and tempos, to expand the very formal dance structures (minuets and such) into imaginative works of art. The recording brings out the fine points of each instrument's voice. Marriner is especially expert with Mozart.

LINK➤ *Eine Kleine Nachtmusik (plus others) – I Musici*   **Philips 410-606**
Mozart's famous serenade Eine Kleine Nachtmusik *(A Little Night Music) is beautifully recorded and gets a fine reading. It's placed alongside Pachelbel's* Canon *and formal dances by Beethoven, Haydn, Boccherini, and Albioni. Good starter disc.*

Les Six Quatuors Dédiés a Haydn (The Six Quartets Dedicated to Haydn) – Le Quatour Talich (The Talich Quartet)   Calliope (Qualiton) 9241/3

Mozart composed 23 string quartets, about half of them before 1773. He picked up on the format again in 1782, when he wrote a half-dozen more for his friend Haydn (who played violin while Mozart played viola in their original performances). This 3-CD set also includes two quartets and a violin/piano sonata composed by Haydn. Through 3 1/2 hours of chamber music, the Talich Quartet is polite, invigorating, careful, ambitious, and very accurately recorded (with instruments properly positioned and never made larger than they really are)—in other words, quite appropriate to the task of communicating Mozart's varied musical ideas. Quartet No. 15 in D minor (K.421) is anguished, confused, and disconnected; with its outbursts of viola madness and nervous violin, and darkly centered cello, it can be absolutely chilling. The well-known Quartet No. 17 in B Flat major (K.458), also known as the "Hunt Quartet" is bracing: trying emotions seem to be controlled by a newfound strength. The nuances of these feelings are particularly well expressed by the Talich Quartet and the refined recording; elsewhere, when overstated, their essence evaporates. In the opening section, Mozart effectively recreates the feeling of hunter's horns with stringed instruments, but with caution. By the third, it's agony once more as the cello tries desperately to calm things down; by the fourth movement, all seems well. The complex Quartet No. 19 (K. 465) is known as the "Dissonance"; it's spare and deeply sad, edgy with sparks of good humor. Follow the cello line—and be grateful for a recording engineer who understands subtlety.

LINK➤ *Franz Haydn – Erdody Quartets, Op. 76 – Tátri Quartet*   **Hungaraton 12812-13**
For purposes of comparison, try Haydn's final complete series of string quartets. They're considerably less emotional than Mozart's work, but Haydn's willingness to experiment results in a rapidly changing flow of original ideas. Spectacular musicianship brings these works to life.

Le Nozze di Figaro (The Marriage of Figaro) – Scottish Ch. Orch. / Mackerras   Telarc 80388

Although there are many fine versions of this 1786 opera, Mackerras wins the nod for an appropriately theatrical approach, enhanced by Telarc's superb recording. The libretto, written in Italian, is based on a story by Beaumarchais; it's a sequel to his popular *The Barber of Seville.* The plot is typically convoluted: Figaro is a servant to Count Almaviva, and he's going to marry another servant, Susanna, but not without the requisite attempted seduction, misunderstandings, trickery, mistrust, and so on. A fabulous overture and some of opera's finest arias highlight a comedy made light and entertaining with Mozart's consistently delightful music. This 3-CD set also includes 15 alternate scenes.

LINK➤ *Mozart – Idomeneo – Placido Domingo, Cecilia Bartoli; James Levine* **DG 447-737**
First played in 1781, Idomeneo *was Mozart's first successful opera. It features individual songs and few ensemble numbers, and while it's quite long (over 3 hours), these 1996 performances and a clear, strong recording should encourage a listen. John Eliot Gardiner's 1991 version, on period instruments, is also excellent (DG 431-674).*

Don Giovanni – Eberhard Wächter, Joan Sutherland, others; Philharmonia Orch. & Chorus / Carlo Maria Giulini   EMI 47260

This 1959 stereo recording stays on top for two reasons: terrific singing from (nearly) every cast member, and a coherent presentation by a conductor who gets the melodrama right. Other recordings are incrementally clearer, but lose out in song-by-song comparisons every time. Some key indicators: tenor Luigi Alva (Don Ottavio) singing "Il Mio Tesoro (My Treasure)," sopranos Joan Sutherland and Elisabeth (magnificent singing throughout), and Don Giovanni's (Eberhard Wächter) devishly seductive work on "La ci darem la mano (Give me your hand)." The story tells of the decline and fall of Don Giovanni (Don Juan), a nasty guy who gets what he deserves; Mozart wrote it quickly to follow up his hit *La Nozze di Figaro*.

LINK► *Mozart – Così fan tutte (Women Are Like That) – Renée Fleming, Annie Sofie von Ottter, others, Chamber Orch. of Europe / Sir Georg Solti*   London 44-174
The third of Mozart's Prague operas with librettist Lorenzo da Ponte, expertly handled by Solti in a fresh and joyful 1994 recording. Nice work from Renée Fleming on "Come Scoglio" (Like a Rock); the ensemble and orchestra explode on Mozart's big-blast finale (and the audience goes wild).

Die Zauberflöte (The Magic Flute) – Kiri Te Kanawa, Cheryl Studer, Samuel Ramey, others; Academy of St. Martin-in-the-Fields / Marriner   Philips 426-276

Mozart's final opera is an enormously complex work based on a fairy tale involving the recapture of a kidnapped princess, a horrifying queen, trials the hero must master, and good's triumph over evil (with magic's help). There are strong Masonic connections and plenty of opportunity for scholarly interpretation. Best of all, there are many extraordinary songs. Tenor Francisco Ariaza makes the most of "Dies Bildnis" (This Portrait), in which he falls in love with a painting of the abducted princess. Cheryl Studer, as the Queen of the Night, delivers the approriate "hellish vengence" on the impossible-to-sing "Der Hölle Rache" (My Heart Is Seething). Mozart's best opera, and the place to start.

LINK► *(Video) – Die Zauberflöte – Christiane Oelze, Cyndia Sieden, others; Monteverdi Choir; English Baroque Soloists / John Eliot Gardiner*   Archiv 072-447
Although an opera, like a movie, is best seen in a proper auditorium with a good stage, video is a convenient, collectible medium. Here, the visual emphasis is on relationships, and the scenery takes second slot. The result is a strong feeling of spontaneity, a definite strong suit for the video medium.

Piano Sonatas Nos. 1-18 – Mitsuko Uchida (piano)   Philips 422-517

Although the piano sonatas may not be considered the very finest of Mozart's creative works—he wrote them mostly for teaching—they are often charming, and frequently brilliant. Many of the themes have become famous. The exotic rhythm of "Rondo alla Turca" (Turkish Rondo), which is part of Sonata in A (KV. 331) became Dave Brubeck's "Blue Rondo a la Turk"; even around 1782, the feel was a bit jazzy. The opening allegro section of 1788's Sonata in C (KV. 545) contains a pretty dance sometimes heard in music boxes (and on cartoon soundtracks accompanying mischief). Uchida's work is just beautiful; superb sound, too. An essential 5-CD (discounted) box.

LINK► *Domenico Scarlatti – Keyboard Sonatas – Mikhail Pletnev (piano)*   *Virgin 45123*
Enthusiastically and precisely performed on high wire—Pletnev plays piano, not harpischord. He not only employs every tool available to a pianist, he also reveals endless surprises in Scarlatti's wonderful music. For a top harpischord version, try Andreas Staier on Deutsche Harmonia Mundi (77274).

Piano Concertos –
Mitsuko Uchida (piano), English Chamber Orch. / Jeffrey Tate   Philips 438-207

Mitsuko Uchida plays like an angel. And in conductor Jeffrey Tate, she has found an idyllic companion. Uchida caresses the piano, conjuring the most perfect resonances; the notes are so sublime that they seem to answer the question of whether Mozart was touched by God. Just listen to the delicacy of Uchida's masterwork on the second section of Piano Concerto No. 11, and the beautiful answers she receives from the English Chamber Orchestra's violins; few recordings capture music's glow so sweetly. The box contains 9 CDs, offering a roughly continuous series from Piano Concertos Nos. 5 to 27 (only 7 and 10 are missing); all are available individually. The recordings were all made in the mid-1980s, and the sound is wonderful. Mozart started composing piano concertos in the mid-1770s in Salzburg, but most of his best work was done in Vienna from 1784 through 1786 (that said, the remarkable Piano Concerto No. 27 was probably completed near the end of his life in 1791). The concertos numbered in the teens are generally uplifting entertainment, but Piano Concerto No. 20, Mozart's first in a minor key, is brooding and turbulent, peaking beneath the angst to explore a lighter side, only to be shoved back inside with greater force. Its second movement, a romance, is sad and resigned. And its third can be spritely, but never far from gloom. The second section of Piano Concerto 21 (a familiar theme because it was used in the film *Elvira Madigan*) is a slow, lush melody so perfectly played that the essential strain comes through the impressionist mist. (It's yet another testament to Tate's superb hand with this music.) Mozart's eloquence—and Uchida's special talent for expression—is perhaps most remarkable on another slow movement, the second part of Piano Concerto No. 23. As the music wells up, there's Uchida bravely continuing the sad story—it's one of instrumental music's finest moments (with a superb woodwind background). Compare this darkening music to the carefree light entertainment of Mozart's personal favorite, Piano Concerto No. 12—so full of life and hope, and written less than ten years before. More than any of Mozart's other works, the range of piano concertos provides insight into the changing patterns of his personality and, presumably, health and well-being. If you make only one purchase based on this book's recommendations, this would be the right choice.

LINK► *Wolfgang Amadeus Mozart – Piano Concertos Nos. 1-27 –*
Murray Perahia (piano); English Chamber Orch.   *CBS Masterworks 46441*
Evaluating musical performances always involves personal taste. For some, Perahia's recordings, made in the early 1980s, are the first choice. Certainly, this 12-CD box is masterful and often definitive. As with Uchida / Tate, each individual CD includes two concertos.

String Quintets – Grumiaux Trio   Philips 422-511

The term *masterpiece* fits comfortably here. Few CDs so completely demonstrate Mozart's ease, flow, and sheer comfort with a musical form. This 3-CD set contains 6 quintets composed mostly from 1787 to 1791; the recording brings out the music's excitement, and the musicianship is without equal. If any one of these extraordinary chamber works stands out, it's probably String Quartet No. 2 for its clever first movement conversations between lead violin, very attentive violas, and a cello periodically lost in its own thoughts. Also noteworthy is the romance of the second movement, in which all five partners dream together. String Quartet No. 1, written in 1793, is youthful, curious, and also a favorite.

LINK► *Johann Nepomuk Hummel – Piano Trios – Beaux Arts Trio*   **Philips 446-077**
Mozart's impact on his student ripples through much of his work. These piano trios are representative, and the performances are excellent. Try also Howard Shelley's version of Hummel's Piano Concerto (Chandos 9558).

Symphonies (Complete) –
Prague Sym. Orch. / Charles Mackerras   Telarc 80300

All of Mozart's later symphonies are essential, but this 10-CD box provides context and a deeper understanding of the composer's progress. Start with Symphony No. 1, which Mozart wrote when he was 8 (possibly with help from his father) while his father was sick in bed and he needed something to occupy his time. Only 12 minutes long, it's big on trumpets and drums, and repeats ideas often, but it's also coherent, dramatic, and serious, particularly in the second movement. Symphony No. 6 is considerably more sophisticated. The first movement begins with a whirling fanfare, a very dramatic buildup and release, and thrilling cascades. The second movement is pastoral; an undulating pattern of violas provides a landscape for an extended, formal flute melody. The added weight of oboes replaces the flutes for the rich and full-sounding third movement, and the final movement is a romp with a big dramatic finish. It was written in 1767; Mozart was 11 years old. Symphony No. 20, from 1772, is also a high point. The first movement sounds like the overture to an Italian opera. It's full of good humor, small constrasts, and informal dances with the full power of the orchestra brought to bear for brief blasts of impact. Compare these earlier works with the relentlessly optimistic crowd-dazzler, Symphony No. 31 (nicknamed "Paris") and the more mature Symphony No. 38 ("Prague"), composed in 1786 with gusto and an extremely strong sense of melodic development. As amazing as these symphonies may be, the best is yet to come. The whirlwind of anguish, desperation, and sheer exhaustion that begins Symphony No. 40 might be the result of the death of Mozart's six-month-old daughter in 1788; this is mighty music that attempts to probe the darkness, yet miraculously manages some childlike curiosity. The second movement, an elegy, is gorgeous. The story ends with Symphony No. 41 ("Jupiter"). Although it's sometimes similar to earlier works, this symphony feels like something completely new—almost as if Mozart is preparing for the next round of thinking. It's less formal, and more overtly emotional, more like a 19th-century work than one from the 18th. Thunderbolts crash about, but Mozart builds his finale on more intricate stuff: a collection of complicated fugues. As for Mackerras, whose output totals over 750 minutes, or more than 12 hours of music, he's phenomenally consistent, getting things right on the big dramatic climaxes and the smallest nuances. Superb work by Telarc's engineers, too.

LINK► *(Film) – Amadeus – Written by Peter Shaffer*   *Warner (ISBN: 0790734060)*
Amadeus *is not the film biography of Mozart, but a screen adaptation of Peter Shaffer's play. Antonio Salieri, jealous of Mozart's tremendous talent, tells the story of a brat who has been Chosen. Director Milos Forman is fabulously attentive to period details.*

Clarinet Concerto, Clarinet Quintet – Thea King (basset clarinet); English Chamber Orch. / Jeffrey Tate   Hyperion 66199

Thea King plays one of Mozart's finest concertos on the basset clarinet, whose lower ranges permit a particularly expressive performance. Sound quality is rich, but nicely focused on the tiniest sonic details. The concerto, written in late 1791 (two months before Mozart died), was composed for Anton Stadler, a brilliant clarinet player whose bad personal habits Mozart chose to overlook. The quintet, completed about two months before Mozart died, begins somewhat buttoned-down, but the strings quickly establish a very familiar theme, and the clarinet immediately follows in pursuit. The slow and lovely second movement is topped by the fourth, which turns the themes inside out with spirited variations. Absolutely wonderful!

LINK► *Carl Maria von Weber – Chamber Music –*
David Shifrin (clarinet; leader) / Chamber Music Society of Lincoln Center   *Delos 3194*
A crystal-clear recording of Weber's clarinet quintet begins a very special CD. Weber's genial way with melody, his striking conversations between the clarinet and strings, and his flights of fantasy are delightful. The Grand Duo Concertant *is better still, a showcase for clarinet and for Weber's piano virtuosity.*

Requiem Mass – Le Chappelle Royale, Collegium Vocale, Orchestré des Champs-Élysées / Philippe Herreweghe   Harmonia Mundi 901620

Spooked by a mysterious "man in black" who paid in advance for a requiem Mass, Mozart apparently convinced himself that this Mass was being written to commemorate his own death. At the time, Mozart was weak, nearly dying; in fact, he did not complete this composition (it was finished, per Mozart's instructions, by Franz Süssmayr). Herreweghe keeps the performance reverent, unfolding the adoration with tasteful respect and heartfelt grief. This 1997 recording is extraordinarily clear, giving prayerful voices space to breathe. The "Kyrie" vocal fugue, sung by the chorus, is uplifting. The combination of tenor voice, trombone, and paired basset horns is spare and chilling on "Tuba mirum." Nice orchestral balance, too.

LINK► *Mozart – Mass in C (Mass 18, The Great Mass) – Barbara Hendricks, Janet Perry, Peter Schreier; Berlin Phil. Orch. / Herbert von Karajan*   *Deutsche Grammophon 439-012*
Karajan goes for the gigantic, God-fearing, and theatrical—an approach that's the polar opposite of Herreweghe's. Karajan also has the singers to make it work. For a smaller period performance, try John Eliot Gardiner (Philips 420-210). The best of many Mozart Masses, it premiered in 1782.

Modest Mussorgsky

Mussorgsky's family had money, and he was brought up in a polite, well-mannered, fastidious way. These qualities served him well as a young officer in the Preobrajensky Regiment, where he learned to drink. In 1857, the 18-year-old Mussorgsky left his country's service for the alluring spell of Russian national music and the intellectual stimulation of the composer Balakirev. In 1861, the Russian serfs were freed, and Mussorgsky's family went bankrupt. He took a job as a clerk in the Ministry of Communications. Balakirev's group became known as "The Handful" (or "The Five"). They were five part-time composers who studied scores, generously taught one another about music, and became friends. The ultraserious Mussorgsky composed through a constant alcoholic haze and delirium tremens, living as a pauper with nothing but his friends and his music. He composed several important works, but died destitute at age 42.

Night on Bald Mountain, Pictures at an Exhibition — Cleveland Orch. / L. Maazel   Telarc 80042

Most people are introduced to Mussorgky's turbulent *Night on Bald Mountain* by watching Disney's *Fantasia*. He wrote it in 1867, and it was revised many times; the currently popular version was scored by Rimsky-Korsakov. Mussorgsky's thrill-ride animates a witches' coven, Satan's glorification, and a sacred witches' sabbath. Mussorgsky composed *Pictures at an Exhibition* in 1874 to memorialize Victor Hartmann, a talented painter and friend. Mussorgsky composed ten piano pieces; Ravel's gorgeous orchestrations are heard here (and on most other recordings). The "Promenade" theme is often heard, but the dank mossy stones of "The Old Castle" and lighthearted bounce of children in the "Tuileries" more effectively demonstrate Ravel and Mussorgsky's work.

LINK➤ *Pictures at an Exhibition – Emerson, Lake and Palmer*   **Rhino 72225**
The ultimate rock 'n' roll version of classical music. The star of this over-the-top extravaganza is keyboard wizard Keith Emerson, who raises electronic music-making well beyond symphonic levels. The group took a few liberties, but reached a huge audience.

Boris Godunov — Anatoly Kotcherga, Samuel Ramey, Sergei Larin, others; Berlin Phil. / Claudio Abbado   SONY Classical 58977

Russian opera has a reputation for density and turgid movement. This opera is probably the one that most supports the reputation. However, given the time and inclination to explore these three CDs, and with an ear for Russian language, the experience can be satisfying. Taken one song at a time, the work is extraordinary. Mussorgsky's economical scoring causes the vocalists to carry a severe story. In 1598, after murdering young tsar-to-be Dmitri, Boris takes his place. All is well until a monk finds him out; this brings on horrid visions of the dead Dmitri. Boris goes insane and dies. Abbado's selection of extraordinary voices greatly enlivens the presentation, as does an above-average recording.

LINK➤ *Alexander Borodin – Prince Igor – Mikhail Kit, Galina Gorchakova, others; Kirov Opera Chorus & Orch. / Valery Gergiev*   **Philips 442-537**
Famous for its "Polovtsian Dances," Prince Igor (1887) gets its first grand treatment on record here. It's one of Gergiev's finest achievements, a virile performance of a Russian treasure. The music's fine, but the convoluted story can be difficult to follow. Great sound.

Carl Nielsen

Danish classical music is a delight that periodically surfaces in the U.S., but doesn't seem to remain popular. It's hard to say why. Nielsen is a wonderful composer. He was born in 1865 in Nørre-Lyndelse, on the island of Fyn (also called Fünen). Nielsen learned the basics from his father, a fiddler; he then picked up trumpet and played in a military band in the nearby city of Odense. A promising young composer, Nielsen attended Copenhagen's Royal Conservatory. By age 24, he was a violinist in the Royal Theater Orchestra. Nielsen's big contribution was not as a musician, but as a composer. In 1894, the Royal Theater Orchestra debuted his First Symphony; this yielded an opportunity for him to create several operas. Nielsen left to compose and returned to lead the orchestra a few years later. In time, he became one of Scandinavia's leading musical figures, most famous for his symphonies. Nielsen died in Copenhagen in 1931.

Complete Symphonies–Royal Scottish Orch. / B. Thomson   Chandos 9163/5

Thomson's six Nielsen symphonies are available on three individual discs, or in this 3-CD box (Symphony No. 1 and Symphony No. 2: Chandos 8880; Symphony No. 3 and Symphony No. 5: 9067; Symphony No. 4 and Symphony No. 6: 9047). Nielsen's First Symphony, which debuted in 1894, pushes Brahms's romance to a more modern, exciting place. As is the case with many of Nielsen's works, the first movement is aggressive and relentless; it subsides only long enough to gather up another quiet theme established on winds or strings. The second movement is a model of reserve, a romantic panorama of the Nordic landscape. The key here—and probably the reason for Nielsen's instant fame—is the gracefully athletic final movement. A decade later, in 1902, Nielsen wrote his Second Symphony, *The Four Temperaments,* after a series of caricatures he saw in a village inn. Each is intepreted as a symphonic movement. The choleric first movement vehemently establishes a theme, then irritably shifts gears and finally ends up where it began. The phlegmatic second movement portrays a teenager who never amounted to much; a melanchoic and dark third movement is followed by an overconfident fourth. From 1911, Nielsen's Third Symphony, *Sinfonia Espansiva,* is a robust celebration of humanity, life, and all that is right with his world. There's a touch of Beethoven in the orchestral heaving and a beauty in its relief. Nielsen's wind melodies have become handsome, winsome, winning. Yet, how quickly things change. In 1916, no longer married, no longer at the center of Copenhagen's music scene, and no longer living in a peaceful world, Nielsen wrote his Fourth Symphony; he called it *The Inextinguishable.* The title refers to the inevitablity of natural regeneration. No matter what is destroyed, life cannot and will not be extinguished. Nielsen fans this flame into a monumental blaze; he also manages his use of the E major key as a goal that his music struggles to reach. It's a decidedly unorthodox approach that provides the piece with considerable power and resilience. This is Nielsen's finest work. From 1922, the substantial Fifth Symphony confronted his feelings about war by exploring powerful oppositions, with attempts at resolution often disturbed by chaos. Nielsen's Sixth Symphony, from 1925, is smoother and easier, but also somewhat satirical and puzzling as to its intent. Great symphonist, consistently good performances by Bryden Thomson.

LINK➤ *Carl Nielsen – Symphony 4 & 5 – SF Sym. / Herbert Blomstedt*   **London 421-524**
Thrilling performances of Nielsen's two best symphonies. These 1988 recordings are spectacular, and Blomstedt's ability to bring out the nuances, the attractive sweep of Nielsen's Nordic countryside, and its stormy thunder is without contemporary equal. Highly recommended.

Complete Concertos –
Danish National Radio Sym. Orch. / Michael Schønwandt   Chandos 8894

The schizophrenic Violin Concerto, from 1911, darts from light fairy tale optimism to fully charged orchestral blasts. Kim Sjøgren's violin sings happily, sometimes nearly alone. At times, it's swept away by a larger force. Neither lightweight nor elegant, 1926's flute concerto can be somewhat dark and combative; Toke Lund Christiansen's flute manages an optimistic temperament thoughout. In 1928, Nielsen pushed the clarinet's capabilities beyond accepted boundaries. Niels Thomsen's clarinet makes use of polyphony and twelve-tone music within a very modern structure, but the piece also follows some 19th-century guidelines. Against militaristic drums and deadly serious orchestrations, it honks and spirals furiously. But it also carries warm, wonderful melodies.

LINK➤ *Nicolai Miakovsky – Cello Concerto –*
Mischa Maisky, Russian Nat. Orch. / Mikhail Plentnev   *Deutsche Grammophon 449-821*
Miakovsky (1881–1950) was a composer whose emotions led his creative work. Here, Maisky finds considerable beauty by approaching his Cello Concerto with the reserve appropriate for an elegy. It's paired with Prokofiev's Sinfonia Concertante.

Wind Chamber Music – Bergen Wind Ensemble, others   BIS 428

Here's one of the best Nielsen recordings—and one of the many gems in the BIS catalog. It begins with a lighter-than-air *Fantasy for Clarinet and Piano* (fine Lars Kristian Holm Brynildsen on clarinet); it's formal and heart-warming. Two fantasies for oboe and a few more short pieces for horns follow. Turid Kniejski's harp and Gro Sandvik's flute gracefully state "The Fog Is Lifting," one of several selections from *Moderen* (The Mother). Best of all is the 26-minute Wind Quintet, from 1922, which is often heard in concert throughout the world. Nielsen's skill in weaving instrumental colors and fabrics is remarkable. This is a very special record.

LINK➤ *Various Composers – Oboe Concertos– John Anderson (oboe);*
Philharmonia Orch. / Simon Wright   *Marco Polo 8.223325*
The oboe's comely sound is not often heard in the concerto format, but these performances suggest that composers have missed a bet: Anderson's expressive treatment of Richard Strauss's concerto from 1945, is particularly stirring. Françaix's L'Horlage de Flore and Martinu's Oboe Concerto complete a fine, modern disc.

Per Nørgård

Twentieth-century classical music has thrived in Denmark, with Vagn Holmboe on the romantic side and Nørgård on the modern. Nørgård was born in 1932 and took lessons from Holmboe both privately, as a boy, and in the 1950s at the Royal Danish Academy of Music. He also studied in Paris with Nadia Boulanger. Nørgård's early work was derived from Scandinavian composers like Sibelius, but he broke away in 1960 with a theory based upon a fractal-like hierarchy; he called it an "infinity row." This approach, which occupied Nørgård through the 1970s, is heard to great effect on *Voyage into the Golden Screen*. He next found inspiration in the chaotic brilliance of Swiss poet Adolf Wölfi. Altogether, Nørgård's distinguished, varied compositional career includes five symphonies, operas (notably *Gilgamesh*), choral and chamber works, and more. Nørgård continues to compose; he also teaches in Denmark.

Luna, Symphony No. 3, Twilight – Tamás Vetö, Jan Latham-Koenig; Danish Nat. Radio Orch. / Herbert Blomstedt   da capo (Marco Polo) 8.224041

Here are three of Nørgård's most important works, all for orchestra. 1967's *Luna* is a visit to a floating world, where instrument sounds glisten and perform on their own or in small groups, then radiate toward one another for shades of melody and moments of harmony. It's not quite ambience; there is an infinite depth to the experience, as if glowing balls were suspended in midspace before dashing away into another dimension. Symphony No. 3, completed in 1975, adds layers of spectral development upon one another for an increasingly dramatic presentation. This fractal approach to musical composition is unique because it maintains orchestral sonorities, but moves to a far more modern place.

LINK▶ *Per Nørgård–Sym. 4, 5–Danish Nat. Radio Orch. / L. Segerstam*   *Chandos 9533*
With strong influence from the insane Swiss artist Adolf Wölfli, this view of smaller worlds within a larger one provides an ethereal basis for Symphony No. 4's first movement. The second is more rhythmic, but no less experimental. Symphony No. 5, from 1990, is more coherent.

Remembering Child – Pinchas Zukerman (viola); Danish Nat. Radio Sym. / Jorma Panula   da capo 9002

Samantha Smith was a 10-year-old American girl who wrote a letter of peace to Soviet leader Yuri Andropov. Three years after she visited his country, she died with her father in a plane crash. *Remembering Child*, from 1985, was composed in her memory and inspired by her strength. Zukerman charges forward on viola, pressing on against a background of swirling sounds (bombs?), tense overlays of uncomfortable instruments, and harsh struggles of nearly electronic sounds. That's the first movement. The second movement is an elegy; the same sounds are in the background, but they now behave and sometimes even fall apart. From the same period, *3 Movements for Cello and Orchestra* features Morten Zeuthen on cello.

LINK▶ *A Hilliard Songbook: New Music for New Voices*   *ECM New Series 21614*
Generally, the Hilliard Ensemble has been associated with early music. Here, the material is almost exclusively mid-20th century (although early music is reflected throughout the harmonies). Best is Ivan Moody's Endechas y Canciones, Piers Hellawell's True Beautie, and Veljo Tormis's Kullervo's Message. A 2-CD set.

Vitezslav Novák

A doctor's son who was initially resistant to music, Novák grew up in a small town in the south of Bohemia. Encouraged by the positive influence of a local music teacher, he became a promising young pianist and composer. Novák pursued two educational paths: law at Prague University and music at Prague's Conservatory. He had a tough time; his teacher, Antonin Dvorák, encouraged him, but a harmony teacher named Knittl was harshly critical. Novák continued his musical education after graduating in 1892 at age 22. He returned to the Conservatory in 1909 as a composition professor. Along the way, Novák collected and analyzed folk songs in Moravia and Slovakia; he used this knowledge to build programmatic music. Novák's 1910 composition for piano, Pan, made him famous in Central Europe. Although a flurry of wonderful creativity followed, Novák never became famous. He died in 1949, a respected teacher.

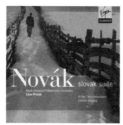

Slovak Suite – Royal Liverpool PO / Libor Pesek
Virgin 45251

The underrated Novák created a sweeping romantic landscape with this 1902 symphonic poem. His subject: an especially glorious region in the Carpathian Mountains. Novák holds nothing back as his gigantic orchestral climaxes soar over glacial peaks—and yet, he finds the gentility of local folk songs and dances. Strings gently trace a waterfall; winds embrace the mountain air; brass and drums trace a storm; and chimes make it all peaceful again. It's a fine piece of music, but center stage belongs to 1903's Slovak Suite (which titles the CD), a series of five settings defining church, children, love, dance, and the night. Novák's brushstrokes are so refined; emotional involvement is inevitable.

LINK➤ *Duke Ellington (& Billy Strayhorn) – Far East Suite*   **Bluebird (RCA) 66551**
Ellington and Strayhorn viewed the jazz orchestra as a singular instrument, and composed for its many variations. In that thinking, there are serious similarities to Novák's compositional approach. This is arguably the best of their original jazz suites.

Pan (Symphonic Poem) –
Slovak Phil. Orch. / Zdeneck Bílek   Marco Polo 8.223325

Novák first composed this musical poem for piano in five movements, but it's better suited to orchestra. His use of violins to capture the sweep of the mountainous landscape, his lush peaks and landscapes, and his free-spirited writing for the piccolo and flutes require the broad palette that only an orchestra can provide. Novák is invigorating, a romantic whose musical ideas are never obscure, always enthusiastically presented, and very easy to enjoy. His seascape, the basis for the third movement, contains few surprises, but it does successfully evoke the rolling waters of an ocean voyage. And so it goes, a smiling celebration of nature, orchestral color, and memorable melodies. Nicely structured, too.

LINK➤ *Uuno Klami – Kalevala Suite, Sea Pictures –*
Turku Phil. Orch. / Jorma Panula   **NAXOS 8.553757**
Klami was a Finnish composer, roughly 20 years Novák's junior. His approach is cooler, far more modern, a kin to Stravinsky as Novák might be to Dvorák. But there are similarities, particularly in their pictures of the sea. Certainly worth the investment.

Jacques Offenbach

Jakob Eberst Offenbacher was the son of a Jewish cantor and bookbinder. He was born in Cologne, Germany, in 1819, one of ten children. In 1833, the family, now known as Offenbach, moved to Paris. Jakob, now called Jacques, enrolled at the Paris Conservatory; he soon became a cellist at the Opéra Comique. Offenbach's career as a composer developed slowly; through the 1840s, his original compositions were performed infrequently, if at all. So Offenbach opened his own theater. After a few shaky years, the Bouffes-Parisiens began a ten-year run as one of the city's most popular entertainment venues. Offenbach excelled at creating satirical operettas— works that skewered every important institution and social grace. The fad ended with the Franco-Prussian War; by the 1870s, Offenbach was bankrupt and looking to the U.S. and England for adoration. After composing parts of his serious opera, *The Tales of Hoffman*, Offenbach died in Paris in 1880.

Gaîté Parisienne – Boston Pops / Arthur Fiedler   RCA 61847

Strictly speaking, Offenbach did not compose *Gaîté Parisienne*. Offenbach never heard it performed either, for it debuted in April 1938, a half-century after he died. The piece is a suite of a dozen dances and other brief episodes from his many works, orchestrated by Manuel Rosenthal for a performance by the Ballet Russe de Monte Carlo. From *The Tales of Hoffman*, there's a famous barcarolle. From *Orpheus in the Underworld*, there's the famous can-can (and vivo), and from *La Belle Hélène* and *La Vie Parisienne*, there are waltzes. Despite many competitive recordings, nothing has taken the place of Arthur Fiedler's 1954 version with his Boston Pops.

LINK► *Franz von Suppé – Overtures – Orchestre symphonique de Montréal / Charles Dutoit*
London 414-408
Light Cavalry is one of the great cartoon soundtrack themes. Other overtures are every bit as memorable and zippy. Suppé, who lived during the 19th century, worked as the musical director for comedic stage plays, which required overtures and incidental music.

Les Contes d'Hoffman (The Tales of Hoffman) – Joan Sutherland, Placido Domingo, others; L'Orchestre de la Suisse Romande / Richard Bonynge
London 417-363

Essentially, these are three *Twilght Zone* stories in an 1881 opera. The first involves Spalanzani, an inventor of human robots, one of whom Hoffman mistakes for the inventor's beautiful daughter, Olympia. She dances so quickly, she burns out. Hoffman's heartbroken when Coppelius, who made her eyes, shows up with them in his hand. The second story involves Giulietta, who steals souls. Antonia, in the third story, dies a little every time she sings. This is strange material, but it's irrepressibly popular. Hoffman (Domingo) sings "The Legend of Kleinzach." Sutherland, who plays each of the three loves, does Olympia's "Doll Song" and others. Best—and most deranged—is the third story's trio between Dr. Miracle, Antonia, and her mother.

LINK► *The Art of the Prima Donna – Joan Sutherland*   **London 452-298**
Australian coloratura soprano Sutherland was called "La Stupenda" by the press in Milan and became known by that apt nickname. A vocal acrobat of the highest order, she was best known for her work with Italian bel canto opera. Try also Grandi Voci *(London 440-404).*

Niccolo Paganini

By design Paganini's music is meant for showing off. Born in 1782, he was one of the great showmen of his time, a violin virtuoso who some said traded his soul to the devil for his skill. Paganini's father taught him to play; by age 11 he was performing for a fee. When he was 16, Paganini composed his Twenty-Four Caprices for a singular purpose: to dazzle audiences. Paganini moved from his native Genoa to Lucca in 1791; he remained there for eight years and gambled away his fortune. Paganini's reputation continued to grow, but because his approach favored show business over art, he resorted to trickery (he performed with only two strings on the violin, for example). Still, Paganini stunned audineces in Vienna in 1828 and conquered the rest of Europe. He retired to Parma in 1834, lost a fortune by investing in a Paris casino project, and died in Nice in 1840.

24 Caprices – Itzhak Perlman (violin)   EMI 47171

Published in 1820, this is a special effects and fireworks display for solo violin. Forget about emotion, and forget about the violin's depth of expression. This is high-class fiddling, fast and furious, demanding the likes of Perlman to issue sounds not often heard on the concert stage. The object of the game here is to present mastery in every significant violin technique: legato, tremelo, left-hand pizzicato, and so on. Still, these are not just technical exercises. Among many arguments in favor of Paganini's musicality, the often-heard theme and variations in Caprice No. 24 is haunting in its effectiveness. Brahms, Liszt, Rachmaninoff, and Schumann based original works upon Paganini's 24 caprices.

LINK► *Pietro Locatelli – L'Arte del Violino – Elizabeth Wallfisch (violin);*
Raglan Baroque Players / Nicholas Kraemer   **Hyperion 66721/3**
Locatelli worked around the same time as Vivaldi and Handel, about a half-century before Paganini wrote this set of difficult violin exercises. He's not much for melodies, but the ferocity of the fireworks is mighty satisfying. Good recording, too.

Violin Concerto No. 1 – Itzhak Perlman (violin);
Royal Phil. Orch. / Lawrence Foster   EMI 47101

With Haydnesque nobility and a pleasant, almost breezy approach to melody and arrangement, Paganini's first violin concerto debuted in Naples in 1819; it was composed earlier. Several light melodies emerge in the first movement, always with the violin as lead instrument; some are likely to resonate in memory (most likely, from cartoon soundtracks). As the piece progresses, the violinist is forced to extremes of speed, high notes that must be cleanly presented, and other pyrotechnics. It's not without emotion, especially in the hands of a wizard like Perlman, and after nearly two centuries, it's still zippy and entertaining. Pablo de Sarasate's *Carmen Fantasy*, another violin virtuoso showcase, completes the CD.

LINK► *Anne Sophie Mutter – Carmen-Fantasie –*
Anne Sophie Mutter (violin); Vienna Phil. / James Levine   Deutsche Grammophon 437-544
Sarasate's Carmen-Fantasie *is the centerpiece of this 1993 recital. Mutter generally chooses her pieces without visiting the warhorses, so we have Ravel's* Tzigane, *Tartini's* Teufelstriller Sonata, *and Henryk Wieniawski's* Légende en sol mineur *in place of the usual fare. A very solid workout.*

Arvo Pärt

Born in Paide, Estonia, in 1935, Pärt is one of several 20th-century composers whose work recalls ancient music . He studied at the conservatory in Talinn, focusing on atonal dissonance, perhaps as a statement against rigid Soviet thinking. For a decade beginning in 1958, Pärt was employed by Estonian Radio and composed film scores as well. By the late 1960s, his predominant influence became spiritual (this in a society that banned religion). Pärt's first sacred piece, Credo, was banned in his home country; his Third Symphony, which incorporated chant, was completed in 1971. Increasingly clear on his direction, Pärt paused for several years to meditate and study religion. By 1977, his course was set. That year, he composed *Tabula Rasa, Fratres,* and *Cantus in Memory of Benjamin Britten.* Pärt was granted permission to leave Estonia in 1978. He lived in Vienna until 1990 before moving to Berlin.

Tabula Rasa – Gidon Kremer (violin), Keith Jarrett (piano), Alfred Schnittke (prepared piano), others   ECM New Series 1275

Tabula Rasa, composed over the course of several months in 1977, presents Pärt at his most eloquent. Here, he stirs up beautiful silence associated with *Fratres* and adds a combination of frantically unraveling minimalism. Spots of intense violin playing by Kremer contrast with the oddball pounded sounds of Schnittke's prepared piano. There are cycles upon cycles, similar to the style of Glass or Adams, with dramatic dynamics not often heard Pärt's later work. *Fratres* is performed here with solemn progress by Kremer, Jarrett, and dozen Berlin Philharmonic cellists. *Cantus in Memory of Benjamin Britten* completes Pärt's first signficant recording (1984).

LINK➤ John Tavener – *The Last Sleep of the Virgin, The Hidden Treasure* – Chilingarian Quartet   Virgin 45023

The Hidden Treasure, from 1989, moves well beyond the stillness and subtlety associated with Pärt (whose Summa *and* Fratres *are included here), stabbing into the darkness with spine-chilling vigor. The Last Sleep, from 1991, is a somber veneration performed by quartet and handbells.*

ARBOS – Hilliard Ensemble, Brass Ensemble, Staatsochester Stuttgart, others   ECM New Series 1325

By presenting a series of mostly shorter pieces, ECM provides an opportunity to explore Pärt's work from several perspectives. Christopher Bowers, for example, presents *Pari Intervallo* as an organ solo. The Stuttgart State Orchestra's brass ensemble blares like gigantic church bells; it's a fanfare, to awaken the living and revive the dead. The real stars of this album are the Hilliard Ensemble, whose voices recall the distant past so beautifully on *De Profundis* and *Summa.* The one extended piece here is *Stabat Mater,* with three singers and three stringed instruments ever-so-gently working their way toward glowing passion. The voices are nourishing and uplifting, and the sonics are superb, too.

LINK➤ Arvo Pärt – *Te Deum* – Estonian Phil. / Tõnu Kaljuste   ECM New Series 1505

Pärt celebrates 1993's chant phenomenon. Justifiably popular, but there's more depth on 1988's PASSIO *(1370), and 1991's* Miserere *(1430), and on 1994's* Litany *(1592). Paul Hillier's Theatre of Voices'* De Profundis *(Harmonia Mundi 907182) is also superb.*

Walter Piston

One of America's foremost music educators, Piston was a composer generally known for a single work, *The Incredible Flutist*. A native of Rockland, ME, Piston was born in 1894 and taught himself several instruments, including the violin and piano. Interested in both architecture and music, he worked as a draftsman and also as a musician in dance bands, hotels, and theater orchestras around Boston. Piston graduated from Harvard in 1924 and went to Paris to study with Nadia Boulanger and Paul Dukas. He returned to the U.S. in 1926 and taught at Harvard until 1960. Along the way, Piston composed a great many pieces and taught Leonard Bernstein, Elliott Carter, and other notables. He also wrote two of music's most important textbooks, *Harmony and Orchestration*. Piston's vividly American music strongly contradicts the academic stereotype of a chess-playing professor who spent his spare hours gardening and reading. He died in 1976.

Incredible Flutist (Suite) – Seattle Sym. Orch. / Gerard Schwarz Delos 3126

A fabulous recording of an American classic—with room-shaking bass drums—the *Incredible Flutist* was a collaboration between Piston, conductor Arthur Fieldler, and Hans Weiner's ballet company. It debuted in 1938. Filled with smiling themes expertly arranged for a shimmering, often magical effect, it's the story of a traveling circus. At one point, the orchestra becomes a circus band, with unoccupied musicians cheering as a crowd. Piston musically photographs the rowdy circus vendors, the customers, the flutist's charming of a snake, the circus march, and so many other images. It's a terrific piece, but only 18 minutes long. More serious pieces, like a concerto and an orchestral suite, complete a recommended CD.

LINK▶ *Roger Sessions – Symphonies Nos. 6, 7, 9 –*
American Composers Orch. / Dennis Russell Davies Argo 44-519
Composed in 1966, 1967, and 1978, here's a third of Sessions's symphonic output. The Sixth Symphony celebrates New Jersey's 300th anniversary; typically, it's skittish, but adheres to themes whose intriguing, sophisticated variations demonstrate Sessions's all-American brilliance.

String Quartets Nos. 1-3, 4-5 – Portland Quartet   Northeastern 9001, 9002

A pair of fine CDs illustrate Piston's clear focus, energetic presentation, and perfectly balanced construction of 20th-century chamber music. His first three string quartets are included on Northeastern 9001, and his final two, along with a flute quintet, comprise Northeastern 9002. Start with the first quartet, from 1933. Piston instantly establishes a tense association between the cello and the violins, then carries a slightly discordant theme through some rapid variations before exposing the second theme hidden within the first. This airtight construction and constant flow of new ideas keeps the listener wide-eyed and alert through all of Piston's chamber works. Even in his slow movements, there is a feeling of perpetual motion.

LINK▶ *Walter Piston – Sonata for Piano, Quintet for Pianoforte and String Quartet –*
Leonard Hokanson (piano), Portland String Quartet Northeastern 232
More fine recordings in the Portland's chamber music series. The 1926 sonata is Piston's only large work for keyboard. Mostly, it's a compositional exercise whose fruits would be born by later efforts. Piston's 1949 quintet is deeply classical, with a jazzy finale.

Francis Poulenc

Poulenc was born into money. His father operated a top pharmacy in Paris. His mother adored music and provided her son with his first lessons. In 1916, at the age of 17, Poulenc studied under Ricard Viñes, one of the top piano teachers in Paris. Encouraged by Eric Satie, Poulenc started composing, but was clearly the weakest of Les Six, a Paris clan of young, outspoken, and sometimes outrageous composers. Poulenc studied, learned his craft, and became quite competent and original. He also embraced music outside France and spent some time studying new Viennese music in the early 1920s. After living the high life of 1920s Paris and establishing himself as a wit, Poulenc found himself fascinated with Catholicism, often to the exclusion of secular music. Many of his religious pieces remain popular, but for general audiences, Poulenc's light touch in the chamber repertoire has kept his name alive. He died in 1963.

Chamber Music –
Pascal Rogé (piano), Patrick Gallois (flute), Maurice Bourgue (oboe), Michel Portal (clarinet), Amaury Wallez (bassoon), André Cazalet (horn)   London 421-581
More than most composers, Poulenc developed a particular expertise in composing chamber music for wind instruments. He takes full advantage of their loose, spontaneous bearing, and their potential for humor. *Sextour for Piano and Wind Quintet*, from 1932, isn't all merriment; its varied offerings include some hearty introspections that are much enriched by the acid warmth of the woodwind duets' interaction with the piano's brighter countenance. Three sonatas, for flute (1956), clarinet (1962), and oboe (also 1962) explore both formal classicism and jazzlike possibilities. These unusual sonorities are best presented in 1926's *Trio for Oboe and Bassoon*, where Mozart-style melodies and arrangements meet swing jazz. Full of surprises.

LINK➤ *Charles Koechlin – Le livre de la jungle (The Jungle Book) –*
Rheinland-Pflaz Phil. / Leif Segerstam   **Marco Polo 8.223484**
Koechlin was Poulenc's teacher, and a very talented man who never became famous, despite more than 200 compositions. This vivid symphonic poem is charming, easy on the ears, and a good place to start. Try also his Works for Bassoon *(cpo 999-434). There's much to discover in Koechlin's catalog.*

Piano and Organ Concertos – Pascal Rogé (piano), Peter Hurford (organ);
Philharmonia Orch. / Charles Dutoit   London 436-546
The organ's rumble is suggestive of a horror movie, and the urgency of the strings confirms the 1938 Organ Concerto's theatrical intentions. While this interpretation is hard to resist, Poulenc considered the work reverential, even sacred. In fact, the piece does progress in a less vaudevillian direction, but the finale sure sounds like a chase scene around a carousel. The Piano Concerto, from 1949, is serene and subdued, with pretty melodies carried off by springtime violins and echoed by gleaming brass. Bits of gamelan and moments of movie-style melodrama keep things interesting. Concerto for Two Pianos, from 1932, is a showcase with endless quirks; it's the CD's most popular work.

LINK➤ *Francis Poulenc – Dialogue des Carmélites – Catherine Dubose, others;*
Lyon Opéra Orch. / Kent Nagano   **Virgin 59227**
Completed in 1955, this opera tends toward the minimalist and celebrates the abstract concept of graceful behavior. In its way, Dialogue des Carmélites *is also a sophistication of the classical songwriting that Poulenc had pursued for decades.*

Sergei Prokofiev

An talented child quite taken with his own worth, Prokofiev was nothing but trouble at the St. Petersburg Conservatory. He graduated at age 22, in 1914. Prokofiev stayed in London for a while and visited Siberia, Japan, and the U.S. before settling in Paris for a few years in the 1920s. During this period, Prokofiev composed several important works, including three ballets by Diaghilev and one by Koussevitsky. He returned to Russia in 1927, left again for Paris, and landed back in Russia in 1936 with high hopes for preferred treatment because of his status as a famous composer. Stalin's regime treated him horribly, publicly humiliating him and disparaging his work. Despite political persecution, a failed marriage, and health problems, Prokofiev composed prolifically during the 1940s. Over time, however, the Communists beat the creative spark until it was extinguished. He died in Moscow in 1953.

Violin Concertos 1 & 2 – Cho-Liang Lin (violin),
L.A. Phil. Orch. / Esa-Pekka Salonen   SONY Classical 53969

Seventeen years separate Prokofiev's violin concertos, but they are more similar than one might expect. Violin Concerto No. 1, from 1917, cautiously probes Russian folk styles and doesn't travel far. The peppier second movement dances; blasts of orchestral power never wilt the violin's zesty enthusiam. The third movement is secure and affecting, a handsome composition, dashed with controlled theatrics. Violin Concerto No. 2, written in 1934, finds an original lyrical path from the start and remains on that course through the second movement. Chao-Ling Lin's articulation of Prokofiev's intelligent, heartfelt ideas is impressive. Amid its twisted dances, the third movement is angry, with much symphonic chest pounding. Excellent fidelity. Stravinsky's Violin Concerto completes the CD.

LINK➤ *In the Shadow of World War II –*
Joel Krosnick (cello), Gilbert Kalish (piano)   *Arabesque 6682*
Three distinctive cello sonatas, each composed a few years after the WW II, each one expressing deep-seated emotions. Krosnick and Kalish are brilliant in their varied portrayals of sonata statements by Sergei Prokofiev, Francis Poulenc, and Elliott Carter. A superb find.

Symphonies No. 1 (Classical) & 5 –
Berlin Phil. / Herbert von Karajan   Deutsche Grammophon 437-253

Smiling is appropriate when listening to Prokofiev's First Symphony. The 26-year-old composer mimics the likes of Mozart, Haydn, and Brahms, getting everything nearly right, and then shifts a note here or a harmony there to parody an older style. Coincidentally, it's a brilliant neoclassical symphony. The Fifth Symphony, from 1944, unfolds several lyrical themes in a slow first movement, then races to life with percussive rhythms in the second, and grows intense in the third. Prokofiev brilliantly pulls all of these ideas together in a very exciting final movement. This is studied, serious symphonic music. Both Karajan performances (1981 and 1968, respectively) are excellent, as is this budget-priced recording.

LINK➤ *Gavriil Popov – Symphonies Nos. 1 & 2 – Moscow State Sym, Orch.,*
USSR TV and Radio Sym. Orch. / Gennadi Provatorov   *Olympia 576*
Popov lived from 1904 until 1972. His first symphony debuted in 1932, and became somewhat popular among Western conductors. The invigorating Russian patriotism of his Second Symphony (early 1940s) demonstrates a keen talent for exciting, emotive orchestrations.

Piano Concertos Nos. 1–5 – Boris Berman or Horacio Gutiérrez (piano); Royal Concertgebouw Orch. / Neeme Järvi   Chandos 8938

The extremely negative reactions received in 1912 by Prokofiev's Piano Concerto No. 1 only strengthened his resolve; he started work on Piano Concerto No. 2 in a similarly aggressive style. The piano pounds away in a percussive strike, then diminishes into pretty little figures against gossamer strings and winds. Inquisitive, but never vague, even his exploratory sequences are sharply defined in a forward-thinking, 20th-century-progress way. It's easy to understand how the third movement of Piano Concerto No. 1 would have confused and disturbed critics; this is the music of change, with only smatterings of 19th-century romance. Berman makes this tricky music look easy. Gutiérrez is the pianist for Piano Concerto No. 2, which is somewhat smoother and sophisticated because of a 1923 revision. (The 1913 original was lost in a fire.) He also performs Prokofiev's best-known and accessible Piano Concerto No. 3, which received positive reviews when the composer debuted it with the Chicago Symphony in 1923. Here Prokofiev's use of the whole orchestra has become more skillful. He changes moods often, but the edges are smoothed. The music breathes; there is now time for full development of interesting themes. And there's a fine finale. Piano Concerto No. 4 is a tough piece written for one hand, but Berman aces it. Berman also performs Piano Concerto No. 5 from 1932. Showy in the style of Liszt, it's also jazzy, reminiscent of Bernstein. It's also Prokofiev's best concerto.

LINK► *Aram Khachaturian – Piano Concerto – Dora Serviarian-Kuhn (piano), Armenian Phil. Orch. / Loris Tjeknavorian*   *ASV 964*
Influenced by not only Prokofiev, but also Borodin and Liszt (and other composers), this percussion-heavy piece has its exciting moments. This version rules; competitors lack the sparkling fantasy. Not a great work, but an engaging performance.

Symphonies Nos. 1–7 – Scottish Nat. Orch. / Neeme Järvi   Chandos 8931/4

An extremely worthy addition to any classical library, these smashing performances were engineered with the utmost skill and care. The result is one of the finest boxes of classical music available anywhere. Järvi's versions of Prokofiev's First and Fifth Symphonies are among the best on record, but there's more to explore here. (Do so gradually, however, for one serving of Prokofiev can be quite filling.) The hardening of molten steel informs the tough-minded Symphony No. 2; its industrial anguish outweighs traditional classicism. Symphony No. 3, from 1929, was based on Prokofiev's opera *The Fiery Angel*, and although it's more of a suite of excerpts and adaptations, there are many intriguing passages. Symphony No. 4 is drawn from Prokofiev's ballet *The Prodigal Son*. Two versions are included: a 1930 original and a 1947 revision. The best part, the rowdy "allegro eroico," accompanied the fleecing of the Prodigal Son by false friends. By the time he wrote the Sixth and Seventh Symphonies, Prokofiev was badly beaten by poor health and political troubles, and so, they lack the vigor and bold new ideas that made his earlier creations so appealing. A somber tone surrounds the Sixth, particularly in the confused first movement. The final movement musters whimsy and enthusiasm, counterweighted by depressing reflection. It represents not only the dreary war years, but victory and its sad aftermath. 1952's Seventh is more relaxed, and closer to Prokofiev's First Symphony: uplifting with intriguing bits of melody and instrumentation, and a happy bearing.

LINK► *Sergei Prokofiev – The Fiery Angel – Kirov / Valery Gergiev*   *Philips 446-078*
A blistering statement of raw emotion (akin to Berg's Lulu*), this surge for salvation is complicated by demons and evil spirits, physical pain, and witchery. Gergiev drives a harsh, eerie, sometimes bloocurdling performance. He's relentless, perhaps better than the opera itself.*

Romeo and Juliet (Op. 64) – Montreal Sym. Orch. / Dutoit   London 430-279

Prokofiev had a tough time getting his 1930s ballet performed, so he did the next best thing: he composed orchestral suites based on the music. Over time, the suites (with various additions from the original score) became very popular. Dutoit's version runs 75 minutes and includes about 50 percent more music than the suite itself. The music tells the story of the star-crossed lovers, scene by scene. "Folk Dance" introduces Romeo and Juliet to each other; the heartfelt "Balcony Scene" (performed as a pas de deux on stage) is dreamy and wonderfully romantic; "Romeo at Juliet's Tomb" is confused, frenzied, angry, deeply sad, and an emotional nightmare. Dutoit and his engineers excel.

LINK► *Sergei Prokofiev – Cinderella –*
Russian Nat. Orch. / Mikhail Pletnev   *Deutsche Grammophon 445-030*
Highly regarded 1995 recording of Prokofiev's popular ballet. Precisely played and engineered, it's also stiff. Ashkenazy's 1983 session with the Cleveland Orchestra (London 410-162) captures the ballet's magic; so does Previn's with the London Symphony Orchestra (EMI 68064).

Peter and the Wolf –
Sir John Gielgud (narrator); Academy of London / Richard Stamp   Virgin Classics 61137

Children (and childlike adults) warm to Prokofiev's introduction to the instruments through storytelling. And the moment John Gielgud opens his mouth, it's obvious that this 1988 performance is the definitive version for the current generation. Prokofiev keeps his musical story simple, allowing ample space for the clarinet (the cat) to establish its comely theme before sneaking up on the flute (the bird). The splashes of drama ("Look out!" shouted Peter) acquaint children with the orchestra's dynamics. Prokofiev's scoring keeps the principal instruments in front while providing a thorough symphonic experience. As is typical on modern discs, another composer's work shares the CD, in this case Saint-Saëns's *Carnival of the Animals*. Essential!

LINK► *Sergei Prokofiev – Peter and the Wolf –*
NY Phil. / Leonard Bernstein   *Columbia 37765*
The definitive baby boomer version. The recording isn't as crisp, but Bernstein's unabashed love of teaching and his talent for entertaining any crowd make this recording special (Gielgud's the better actor, but Bernstein is more deeply involved). Fine work from the New York Philharmonic, too.

Alexander Nevsky Cantata, Lieutenant Kije Suite –
Los Angeles Phil. Orch. / André Previn   Telarc 80143

Lieutenant Kije never existed; the czar made a mistake reading a report, and his courtiers did not want to correct him. In time, Kije's life is manufactured; he falls in love, marries, and (to the relief of the courtiers), he also dies. Prokofiev repackaged his film music into a 1934 suite; the famous "Kije's Wedding" and "Troika Song" are highlights. The melodies and tongue-in-cheek pomp are among Prokofiev's best work. Prokofiev's cantata recreates the most dramatic moments in Eisenstadt's landmark battle epic; like his original score, the cantata is ponderous, and fervently Russian. Previn's mastery of these dark colors brings the saga to life. Telarc's digital recording is spectacular.

LINK➤ *(Film) – Alexander Nevsky – Sergei Eisenstein (director)*   **Kubicek & Assoc**
ISBN: 6301816218

Directed with D.I. Vassiliev, this 13th-century tale of Teutonic knights is a masterpiece of the Russian (and world) cinema. It's available on VHS from Movies Unlimited (800-4-MOVIES) and also on DVD from Image Entertainment. Prokofiev's score is integral to the storytelling. Try also ISBN 1-57299-127-5.

Complete Piano Music (Vol. 1-9) –
Boris Berman (piano)   Chandos (various numbers)

Most people think of Prokofiev as an orchestral lion, but in his own time, he was equally famous as a pianist—one who challenged conventions with irrepressibly modern, often difficult music. This series is great fun, in part because so many themes are familiar, including the tunes from Love of Three Oranges and the many pieces from *Romeo & Juliet* on *Vol. 1* (8851), as well as the ten pieces from *Cinderella* on *Vol. 5* (9017). *Vol. 2* (8881) features the intriguing miniatures from 1915-17 known as *Visiones Fugitives*, but the individual sonatas, scattered throughout the series, present Prokofiev's finest piano work, certainly his most inventive alterations of a very old form.

LINK➤ *Sergei Prokofiev – Violin Sonatas Nos. 1 & 2 –*
Vadim Repin (violin), Boris Berezovsky (piano)   ***Erato 10698***

The jewel is Sonata No. 2, transcribed from a flute sonata for David Oistrakh; it's lighter than air, spirited, elegant and heart filling. It's also beautifully performed here. Sonata No. 1 is more traditional, but very dreary and gray. Two opposing views of Russian music.

War and Peace – Orchestra National de France /
Mstislav Rostropovich   Erato 45331

Russian opera's impenetrable reputation does not apply here. Given time to explore four hours of music (on a 4-CD set), most listeners will discover one of Russian literature's great epics majestically scored by a master. In fact, the first half of the story is told in peacetime, a network of love stories set in 1810, just before Napoleon marches into Russia. The second half depicts war in its blood-drenched ugliness—battles, drudgery, heartbreak, and death. This version's pluses include a wide-open recording, a real sense of place, and a sensitive touch that brings out the characters. Although some of the casting is imperfect, this is still the preferred version.

LINK➤ *Sergei Prokofiev – War and Peace –*
Kirov Chorus & Orch. / Valery Gergiev   ***Philips 434-097***

This 1992 version is more rugged, often brisker, and benefits from generally finer voices. But the atmosphere and ease in storytelling are sacrified, and in many cases, the Rostropovich version simply sounds better. Still, this 3-CD version is a very strong contender.

Giacomo Puccini

If Puccini had followed the custom of four previous generations, he would have remained a church musician for his entire career. At age 18, in 1876, the teen from Lucca saw Verdi's *Aida* and decided he wanted to write operas. He entered a Milan music publisher's contest—and won. This led to a commission, for which he wrote the unsuccessful *Edgar*. Puccini persevered; in 1891, he succeeded with the hit *Manon Lescaut*. Next came *La Bohème* (which was first conducted by a young Arturo Toscanini) and then *Tosca*. By 1900, Puccini was rich, famous, and the owner of a new villa outside Florence. Four years later, he married his longtime lover Elvira Gemignani; she became sufficiently jealous of her husband's philandering to cause the death of an innocent servant girl. Puccini continued to compose and enjoy the good life until his death from a heart attack in 1924.

Manon Lescaut – Mirella Freni, Luciano Pavarotti, others; Met. Opera Orch. & Chorus / James Levine   London 440-200

Levine's experience with stage performances brings a lively and energetic approach to a solid score. *Manon Lescaut* was Puccini's first successful opera; it debuted in 1893. He chose the story because he was sure that audiences would feel for its heroine, Manon Lescaut (Freni). She's on her way to the convent when Des Grieux (Pavarotti) falls in love with her at first sight; soon they elope to Paris, but her affections wander to Géronte, and when she tries to steal his jewels, she's deported. Manon and Des Grieux end up in Louisiana, where she dies in his arms from thirst and exhaustion. Hit tune: Manon's "In quelle trine morbide" (In this guilded cage).

LINK► *Pietro Mascagni – Cavalleria Rusticana (Rustic Chivalry) – Renata Scotto, Placido Domingo, others; Nat. Phil. Orch. / James Levine*   **RCA 3091**
From 1979, the best among modern recordings of Mascagni's exciting 1889 one-act opera. Big performances, a pot-boiler plot, and violence set a new course for Italian opera. It's frequently performed with Pagliacci, *which is also brief and deals with somewhat similar themes.*

La Bohème (The Bohemians) –
Victoria de los Angeles, Jussi Björling, others; RCA Orch. & Chorus / Sir Thomas Beecham   EMI 47235

The half-century-old mono recording always wins best in class. The sound is surprisingly alive, and the tragic sincerity of Björling's Rodolfo still sends shivers down the spine. In Paris's Latin Quarter, several starving artists begin the story by burning manuscripts to keep warm; still, they manage to enjoy one another's company. When Mimi (de los Angeles) knocks at the door, they fall in love, and spend the rest of the play worrying about her tuberculosis. Mimi dies in one of opera's saddest scenes. The music is lavish and heartfelt throughout; several arias, especially "Che galida manina" and "Si chiamano Mimi" are drenched in melodramatic emotion. Simply gorgeous and absolutely essential.

LINK► *RENT – Original Cast*   **DreamWorks 50003**
Very loosely based on La Bohéme, *this musical drama about life in Manhattan's Alphabet City proved that rock music and Broadway could coexist in the 1990s. The devastation of AIDS is at the center of this colorful story. Hits include "Seasons of Love."*

Tosca — Maria Callas, Giuseppppe di Stefano, Tito Gobbi, others; Orchestra del Teatro alla Scala / Victor de Sabata   EMI 47174

In marked contrast with the weak Mimi, Tosca (Callas) is a clever, manipulative, wily woman. And she's certainly no victim. Tosca deals sharply with the local police chief, Scarpia (Tito Gobbi) to save her lover, Cavaradossi (Giuseppe di Stefano). In the end both men die, and she escapes. The keys to this 1900 opera are the soaring arias; one astonishing performance follows another: Cavaradossi's "Recondita armonia" (Hidden harmony) and Tosca's "Vissi d'arte" (I have lived for art), in which she wiggles her way out of trouble with Scarpia. (Callas is phenomenal.) This truly spectacular performance of a wonderful opera was recorded in 1953 and is still the definitive version. Good mono sound, too.

LINK➤ *In Concert – José Carreras, Placido Domingo, Luciano Pavarotti*   **London 433-433**
From 1990, the original "three tenors" concert. This is all about tenors as heroic singers, and two songs from Tosca *fit the bill: Pavarotti's "Recondita Armonia" (Mysterious Harmony) and Domingo's "E Lucevan le Stelle" (And the Stars Were Shining). Often thrilling.*

Madama Butterfly — Mirella Freni, José Carreras, others; Philharmonia Orch. / G. Sinopoli   DG 423-567

After a dismal premiere and a rewrite a few months later, London playwright David Belasco's story of a U.S. naval officer and his Japanese bride became Puccini's 1904 hit. While stationed in Japan, Lieutenant Pinkerton marries Cio-Cio San (she's 15), then leaves for home. While Cio-Cio San ("Butterfly") waits with his child, Pinkerton marries Kate, an American woman, whom he brings to visit Japan. When Butterfly finds out about Kate, she kills herself. The score is gorgeous, with magical arias, including Butterfly's justly famous "Un bel di vidremo" (One fine day we'll see). Puccini's flirtations with faux-Oriental music can be interpreted as either charm or kitsch. Very pleasant 1987 performance.

LINK➤ *Puccini – La Fanciulla del West – Covert Garden Orch. / Z. Mehta*   **DG 419-640**
Puccini bought the rights from Belasco for this love story, set in 1850 in the romantic heart of California's Gold Rush. The Western trappings—a saloon, a sheriff, gunfights between grimy miners—are an odd fit for Puccini's Italian lyrics and style. Some good arias, but not his best work.

Turandot — Joan Sutherland, Luciano Pavarotti, Montserrat Cabellé, others; London Phil. Orch. / Zubin Mehta   London 414-274

Puccini died before he completed Turandot, so his family hired lesser light Franco Alfano to finish the score from his notes. In 1926, Puccini's evil princess tale was staged to great acclaim. The setting is Peking (Beijing). Princess Turandot promises to marry the man who can answer her riddles and to kill any suitor who fails. Calaf rises to the occassion, solves her puzzles, turns the tables on Turandot, teaching her love's true nature. *Turandot* contains a stunning number of spectacular arias: Pavarotti (Calaf) singing "Nessun Dorma" (No Man Shall Sleep) and Sutherland (Turandot) and Pavarotti giving their all in "In questa Reggia" (Within this palace).

LINK➤ *Roberto Gerhard – La Dueña – Opera North / Antoní Ros Marbá*   **Chandos 9520**
Based in part on a 1775 opera, Gerhard reworked the Seville soap opera with a score that evokes 18th-century Spain and makes very effective use of twelve-tone ideas (he was a student of Schoenberg) to fine dramatic effect. Remarkable pinpoint placement of singing voices.

Henry Purcell

The highly regarded baroque composer Purcell was born in London in 1659, and died there just 36 years later, in 1695. After a few years of smaller jobs (including a stint as the composer for the King's violins), Purcell became Westminster Abbey's organist at age 20 and worked feverishly until his early death. He wrote all sorts of music, and plenty of it, from operas to pub songs, neatly combining the art music of continental Europe with the folk and religious traditions of his own country. Purcell was central to the music of royalty; he composed coronation music for James II, and several years later for Mary (daughter of James II) and her spouse, William III. He was also called upon for considerable amounts of church music, as was common in the era (Bach, whose career overlapped for a decade, also composed a great deal of music for religious ceremonies), and for funeral work.

Dido & Aeneas – Les Arts Florissants / William Christie — Erato 98477

Although 1689's *Dido & Aeneas* wasn't the first opera, it's one of the few pre-1700 operas whose music, story, and structure can be enjoyed as entertainment, not history. Purcell skillfully combines voices and baroque instrumentation to tell Nahum Tate's version of Virgil's love story. Briefly: Dido (Queen of Carthage) and Aeneas (a Trojan prince) fall in love. Meddlesome witches destroy Carthage and mess with Aeneas's head; Dido kills herself. The overture is inspiring and full of life; Dido's funereal "Thy hand, Belinda" (sung by soprano Véronique Gens) is deeply sad as only opera can be. Energetic, exciting, and delightfully delicate, it's far more interesting than Vivaldi or other baroque music.

LINK► *Claudio Monteverdi – Orfeo – Ainsley, Gooding, Bott, New London Consort / Pickett*
L'Oiseau Lyre 433-545
First performed in 1607, this is an interesting excursion into the early roots of opera. Arias were still to be developed, but the music is occasionally melodious, and parts are quite pleasant. From 1676, Jean-Baptiste Lully's ATYS (Harmonia Mundi 1257) is prettier and more satisfying.

The Fairy Queen – Soloists; The Monteverdi Choir, English Baroque Soloists / John Eliot Gardiner — Deutsche Grammophon 419-221

Here's an especially good example of a semi-opera, a Restoration-era variety show combining a dramatic play with incidental vocal music and end-of-scene musical numbers (only the musical numbers are included on this 2-CD set). Based on Shakespeare's *A Midsummer Night's Dream*, and first performed about a hundred years later in 1691, Gardiner finds "an authentic musical equivalent to the poetic and enchanted world of Titania, Puck, and Oberon." Gardiner's detailed liner notes guide a tour through the music, pointing out the remarkable sites. One is a dance suite that opens the presentation. Another is the goofiness of "Song of the Drunken Poet," an early attempt at musical comedy.

LINK► *Henry Purcell – The Indian Queen – Deller Consort* Harmonia Mundi 90243
Another semi-opera, from 1695, presented with emphasis on the dramatic. Although this is less famous than The Fairy Queen, *it's tighter and more satisfying. Try also the 1691 semi-opera* King Arthur *(Erato 8535) by Christie and the Florissants.*

Sergei Rachmaninov

When his father squandered the family fortune, Rachmaninov's mother left her husband and the family home in Novogrod, Russia. She moved the children to St. Petersburg. Rachmaninov later studied at the Moscow Conservatory; he became an excellent pianist. At age 23, in 1896, his first symphony debuted to dreadful criticism (the conductor was probably drunk); as a result, Rachmaninov became seriously depressed. He valiantly traveled to England and continued writing, but the depression returned. Rachmaninov couldn't even think about a new symphony until hypnotic therapy improved his outlook. He did become a well-known composer and conductor, but that all ended with the Bolshevik Revolution in 1917. Rachmaninov reinvented himself as a concert pianist, toured Scandinavia, and eventually moved to Los Angeles, where he lived in a home that was a precise duplicate of his Moscow home. He died in Beverly Hills in 1943 from cancer.

Sonata for Cello & Piano –
Yo-Yo Ma (cello), Emanuel Ax (piano)   SONY Classical 46486

When wandering around a classical record department, this CD is an easy decision. Ma and Ax are a winning combination. Rachmaninov is sentimental and romantic here, very much on the conservative, classical side of the emerging Russian culture. The piece also provides students with a textbook example of structure; it is a beautiful piece of work. All of this is brought into very sharp focus when Rachmaninov's piece is compared with the CD's opener, Prokofiev's Sonata for Cello and Violin. Although his ideas begin in a romantic realm, Prokofiev's grotesque, ironic handling of classicism comes from 1949, a decidedly different era in Russian history.

LINK▶ *The Rostropovich Edition – Mstislav Rostropovich (cello); others*   *EMI 65701*
A fine (budget-priced) 3-CD survey of concertos for cello, performed by one of this century's finest musicians. Most of this work comes from the 1970s (some earlier). There's an especially good Miaskovsky concerto, plus good work on Bloch's Schelomo, *and in Strauss's* Don Quixote.

The Four Piano Concertos & Rhapsody on a Theme of Paganini –
Earl Wild (piano); Royal Phil. Orch. / Jascha Horenstein   Chandos 8521/2

Start with the second disc in this set because it contains two of Rachmaninov's towering compositions: Piano Concerto No. 2 and Piano Concerto No. 3. Sit back and enjoy the absolute technical precision of Rachmaninov's compositions. An expert pianist whose prowess is duplicated by the remarkable playing of Earl Wild, Rachmaninov utilizes the piano's piercing presence as his principal instrument, allowing the substantial strings of the orchestra to comment and contrast. The sentimental draw of the strings is pure romance, but he always returns to that piano for thematic clarity and for filigree. The second movement is extremely touching; it is carried mostly by the piano and winds (one theme will be familiar as Barry Manilow's "Never Gonna Fall in Love Again"). The crash of Russian dancing is the key to the third movement, as the orchestra swells to interrupt the pianist's long, rather complicated virtuoso turns. It's fast, dramatic, and suddenly releases into the string section's version of one of classical music's great romantic themes. When the energy gathers again, the result is a huge finale. Piano Concerto No. 3, written in 1909, is one of the most difficult in the repertoire, but it is also sophisticated and beautifully constructed. Gone are the competitions between piano and orchestra that dominated Piano Concerto No. 2 from eight years before. The contrasting textures of the piano's absolutely defined notes and chords and the strings' blends are complementary and coherent, especially in the first movement. One magnificent theme follows another, and they're brilliantly woven into a constantly inspiring presentation. The second movement lifts the listener to a quieter place, a relaxed spot where the music effortlessly drifts along. True to form, the third movement snaps the listener to attention, builds on past ideas, and shapes everything into a series of heart-pounding climaxes. Piano Concerto 1 is certainly worth a listen; it's a popular work Rachmaninov composed as a teenager and later reworked. Somehow, whatever magic Rachmaninov had in the two middle concertos, he lost when he composed his fourth. *Rhapsody on a Theme of Paganini*, written in 1934, is a snappy series of variations for piano and orchestra; it's very clever and enormously popular. Highest possible recommendation to this 2-CD set, in part for its spectacular sonics. From 1965.

LINK➤ *Sergei Rachmaninov – Piano Concerto No. 3 –*
Martha Argerich (piano); RSO Berlin / Riccardo Chailly   *Philips 446-673*
Amazing interpretation of Rachmaninov's most difficult work, supported by a splendid and attentive orchestra. Paired with the equally awesome Piano Concerto No. 1 by Tchaikovsky. Extraordinary sound supports two of the better contemporary performances of these works.

24 Preludes – Vladimir Ashkenazy (piano)   London 443-841

The roots of many of Rachmaninov's ideas can be traced to Prelude in C-sharp minor, Op. 3, No. 2, composed in 1892. It leads off a bargain-priced 2-CD virtuoso spectacular. Ashkenazy energizes these famous piano pieces in some of his finest performances (circa 1974–75). Following Chopin's example, Rachmaninov wrote miniatures for each of the major and minor keys (hence 24 preludes). His Op. 23, No. 5 in G minor, from 1904, possesses the same style of romance he'd often work into the string section in a symphony. The set also includes the popular Op. 32, No. 5, written in 1910, as well as Piano Sonata No. 2. Dignified, uplifting, consistently intriguing work.

LINK➤ *Alexander Scriabin – Piano Concerto, Prometheus, other works –*
Vladimir Ashkenazy (piano); London Phil. Orch. / Lorin Maazel   *London 417-252*
Scriabin started out as a Russian pianist, but by 1898, his interest in mysticism and music were inexorably linked. Both pieces are large scale and somewhat maniacal. Prometheus *is a conflict between man (the piano) and the cosmos (the orchestra). In time, unity is achieved.*

Symphonies Nos. 1-3 –
Concertgebouw Orch. / Vladimir Ashkenazy   London 448-116

Rachmaninov's First Symphony, composed at age 22, was not well received. It's not bad, but it's not great either. Ashkenazy approaches Symphony No. 2 with an expansive, serious attitude; he is supported by skillful engineering that brings out the lower registers and the timbre of the winds. Rachmaninov builds on this depth with sweeping themes that develop slowly, principally through the strings. Patience is rewarded with the full exposition of two themes and a momentous, festive finale. His Third Symphony, completed in 1936, jumps between old-fashioned romantic sentimentality and concise popular melody styles, sometimes suggesting American jazz or movie music. Fine sonics, excellent performances, and a bargain two-for-one price make this worth adding to your music collection.

LINK➤ *Sergei Rachmaninov – Symphony No. 3 – St. Petersburg Phil. Orch. / Mariss Jansons*
EMI 54877

Jansons's 1993 rendition emphasizes the handsome polish of Rachmaninov's formal farewell to Russian romanticism. The sophisticated ease and the attention to nuance make this quite different from Ashkenazy's interpretation. Symphonic Dances *completes the disc.*

Symphonic Dances – The Philharmonia / Neeme Järvi   Chandos 9081

Rachmaninov truly understood how to compose and arrange for the orchestra's singular voice. His talent for building drama over long periods makes his work an ideal intellectual dream for those who pay attention in concert halls (and a snooze for those who don't). There is no better example of Rachmaninov's resplendent communication than the subtle integration of folk tunes into the tranquil landscape of his *Symphonic Dances*. Written in the U.S. in 1940, this late work suggests a ballet, but lacks the stagey dynamics required for that form. Even his gypsy-inspired "Dances from Alekois" sounds mostly reserved, with only occasional zest. Superb Chandos recording matches the excellent performance of the Philharmonia.

LINK➤ *Leonard Bernstein– Dybbuk – NYC Ballet Orch. / Leonard Bernstein*
SONY Classical 63090

Just 34 years after Rachmaninov composed his Symphonic Dances, *Bernstein joined forces with Jerome Robbins and the NYC Ballet to create a 1974 ballet based on Jewish mythology. Bernstein is unafraid of the new, but here he's more centered in older styles and traditional ideas.*

Vespers –
Croydon Singers / Matthew Best   Hyperion 66460

Vsenoshchnoe Bdenie, the All-Night Vigil, contains three services, all included here. Vespers begins at sunset. Matins and the First Hour are sung next in anticipation of the new day. This is sacred music composed by a man whose own relationship with the Russian Orthodox Church was intermittent. That said, Rachmaninov instills a reverential tone and connection with unadorned chant and quiet beauty. The a cappella Croydon Singers are blended into a singular choral voice, an approach Rachmaninov often employed in symphonic orchestrations. "Nyne Otpushchaeshi" is especially fulfilling, and "Bogoroditse Devo" contains one of the few passages where voices are raised. Recorded in 1990 at St. Alban's Church in London.

LINK➤ *Sergei Rachmaninov – Vespers of 1610 –*
Croydon Singers / Matthew Best   **Telarc 80453**

An opulent Mass, performed by a very large chorus, seven solo singers, and an enormous array of instruments. Pearlman superbly commands all these forces, and Telarc's engineers do some of their best work here, too. A 2-CD set released in 1997.

Einojuhani Rautavaara

Born in Helsinki, Finland, in 1928, Rautavaara was the son of an opera singer and cantor, and a doctor. He studied piano in Turku, then continued studies at Helsinki University and the Sibelius Academy, and received private instruction from Aarre Merikanto until the early 1950s. His career took shape with an award from the 90-year-old Jean Sibelius, who selected a promising young Finnish composer to study in the U.S. on scholarship. Rautavaara spent 1955 and 1956 in NYC at the Julliard School, with summers at Tanglewood, learning from Aaron Copland and Roger Sessions. Studies continued in Europe through the 1950s. After years of preparation, Rautavaara's work as a composer gained some recognition in the 1960s and 1970s, but it wasn't until several 1990s recordings that his name and his music became well known outside of Finland. He has written in every major form, including symphonies, operas, and choral works.

Cantus Arcticus, Symphony No. 5 – Leipzig Radio Sym. Orch. / Max Pommer
Catalyst 62671

The 1972 *Cantus Arcticus* is subtitled *Concerto for Birds and Orchestra*; throughout, Rautavaara presents various types and groupings of birds as principal elements. This musical tribute to the awe-inspiring calm of the Arctic forests proceeds through three movements: "The Bog," "Melancholy," and "Swans Migrating." Rautavaara's understanding of an orchestra's capabilities is complete: his arrangements are lush, but development is gradual and within a narrow dynamic range, careful not to disturb nature's balance. The repeated cycling and gradual changes are likely to appeal to New Age listeners. The CD continues with Rautavaara's Symphony No. 5, a 1986 composition that applies considerably greater force to crashing eruptions. The meditative String Quartet No. 4, from 1975, completes the CD.

LINK▶ *Jouni Kaipainen – Symphony No. 2 – Helén Jahren (oboe);*
Finnish Radio Sym. Orch. / Sakari Oramo   *Ondine 855*
Kaipainen is a modern Finnish composer well outside the influence of Sibelius. Three works from 1994 are featured here: a lush, meandering, sometimes ardent Second Symphony; a very fine modernist take on the oboe's sonic palette (with some nods to Bach); and Sisyphus Dreams, *with its mythical accretions of tension and release.*

Angel of Light (Symphony 7) – Helsinki SO / L. Segerstam   Ondine 869

The zenith of Rautavaara's creative output was inspired by a personal fascination with angels. His reading was not the gift store variety, but the archetypal angel who has guided human behavior and creative endeavors through the millennia. Rautavaara's tendency toward blending traditional and postmodern styles is well suited to this material. The first movement of this 1994 symphony floats on warm currents of optimistic air; earnest horns and strings carry Rautavaara's message with minimal strife and are overcome by a flowing arrangement. The second movement introduces angry eruptions, but these are reduced to a dream in the third. The fourth movement rises to the ultimate light and climactically reaches toward heaven.

LINK▶ *E. Rautavaara – Angels & Visitations –*
Elmar Oliveira (violin); Helsinki Phil. Orch. / Leif Segerstam   *Ondine 881*
A 1997 Grammy nominee, here's the first of Rautavaara's explorations into the world of angels. The CD also contains a dark violin concerto. For more on Rautavaara's angels, try Angel of Dusk (BIS 910), *featuring bassist Esko Laine and conducted by Jean-Jacques Kantorow.*

Maurice Ravel

Ravel was born near Saint-Jean-de Luz, France, to a Swiss father and a Basque mother. A talented youngster, he began his studies at the Paris Conservatory in 1889 at the age of 14, and remained there until 1905. One reason for Ravel's lengthy stay was his ongoing attempt to win the Conservatory's prestigious composition prize—the Prix de Rome. Ravel never did win, and his early-round elimination in 1905 caused a scandal that toppled the Paris Conservatory's director. By then, however, Ravel was already famous, partly due to the scandal, but more largely on the merits of his originality. For nearly three decades, Ravel was one of France's finest artists, creating ballets with Diaghelev, an opera with Colette, and significant piano literature. Ravel was never a strong man. He lived quietly in a meticulously kept villa with his beloved Siamese cats. After a five-year struggle with a debilitating brain disease, Ravel died in 1937.

Ravel Orchestral Works –
Montréal Sym. Orch. / Charles Dutoit   London 421-458

For many listeners, this one set may represent a complete Ravel library. In the early 1980s, Charles Dutoit recorded most of Ravel's important orchestral works on four digital CDs. They've been re-released on this budget 4-CD set. The sound is uniformly excellent, and the performances are among the best on record. Start with the inevitable *Boléro*, based on two themes that repeat themselves over and over and over again. In time, as the sexual temperature rises, more and different instruments add thurst. There's an orgasm, and a release (the piece originally scored an erotic ballet in 1928). Originally composed within a set of five Spanish piano pieces, 1905's *Alborada del gracioso* (Jester's Morning Serenade) portrays a fool who assists musicians as they perform a musical wake-up call. Ravel's skillful instrumentation results in a vivid vignette. *Rapsodie Espagnole*, from 1907, is similar, and is also derived from the piano set. Both feel like sketches rendered with magical colors. Two waltzes, 1911's *Valses nobles et sentimentales* and 1920's *La Valse*, develop into large-scale Viennese-style dances distinguished for their superb taste and evocations of a sumptuous culture. Ravel, however, goes beyond frivolous nostalgia. *La Valse* is a razor-sharp comment on the artificialty of that past world, viewed through a postwar lens. Written in 1908, *Ma Mère l'Oye* (Mother Goose) is a loving tribute to childhood, told through miniatures like "Hop o' My Thumb" (inspired by Perrault's Tom Thumb fairy tale). The music is intentionally simple—Ravel hoped children could perform the work. It's delightful. *Pavane pour une infante défunte* (Dance for a dead princess) was a 1910 creation, originally composed for piano (this was true of many of Ravel's best pieces). His mastery of orchestral nuance, his sparkling palette, and his gift for lustrous melodies are on display here; 90 years later, the music is still awesome. *Le Tombeau de Couperin* (The Tomb of Couperin) is an elegy for 18th-century French music. Theodore Baskin's oboe solo provides baroque flashes, but the sweep of the strings develops the themes further in soft, interesting, unexpected ways. The set proceeds through the famed Piano Concerto in G major, and also through the complete ballet score of *Daphis et Chloé*. Both are superb performances.

LINK▶ Maurice Ravel – (Various orchestral pieces) –
Orch. of the Opéra National de Lyon / Kent Nagano   Erato 14331

A smaller sampler that includes Le Tombeau de Couperin, Pavane pour une infante défunte, Ma Mère l'Oye, *and* Alborada del Gracioso *(plus* Une Barque sur l'Océan*). Handsome 1996 recordings, polished performances.*

Piano Works – Pascal Rogé (piano)   London 440-836

When Ravel composed, the piano was his principal tool; orchestral arrangements came later. *Miroirs*, a five-part piano solo, alternates fast and slow patches to suggest Europe's Atlantic seacoast. Two of its sections, "Alborado del gracioso" and "Rapsodie espagnole" grew into popular orchestral works. Additionally, there are keyboard versions of *Le Tombeau de Couperin, Pavane pour une infante défunte, Ma Mère l'Oye*, and others. Technical excellence and strong wrist muscles are demanded by the angry Russian-style masterwork *Gaspard de la Nuit*, Ravel's most challenging—and interesting—composition. Filled with essential, groundbreaking, highly influential creative work, this 2-CD set presents spectacular Rogé performances with superb sonics.

LINK➤ *Henri Dutilleux – Violin Concerto –Pierre Amoyal (violin), Lynn Harrell (cello); French Nat. Orch. / Charles Dutoit*   London 444-398
With enormous imagination, a palette and style related to Ravel and Debussy, and perhaps a finer sense of textures and economical communication, Dutilleux created this wonderful pair of concertos. Try also Symphonies Nos. 1 and 2 by the BBC Philharmonic led by Tortelier (Chandos 9194).

Piano Trio – String Quartet in F   Deutsche Grammophon 437-836

A resolutely optimistic tune becomes engulfed in the darker colors of the viola and cello, and then another noble melody emerges, sturdier but less optimistic. In time, the concept of melody is lost in the struggle. Instead of resolving the situation peacefully, Ravel grinds a harsher reality before allowing the initial melody to surface again. The first movement is the strongest of the three, and the most original. The second movement is romantic, and the third movement tries too hard. Ravel's first movement is a close kin to start of the Debussy String Quartet that begins this CD, and points the way for Webern's 1905 experimental quartet. Exemplary Hagen performance benefits from warm and honest fidelity.

LINK➤ *Erik Satie – 3 Gymnopédies, other works – Pascal Rogé (piano)*   London 410-220
Irresistible bonbons of a fairly sophisticated flavor, nicely played and recorded. Satie's advanced poetry can also be heard on London 421-713. Also try the orchestrated versions by the New London Orchestra led by Ronald Corp (Hyperion 66365).

Daphnis et Chloé (Complete) –
Boston Sym. Orch. / Charles Munch   RCA 61846

RCA's unique Living Stereo approach allows a 1955 recording to compete quite successfully and without apology against a top-notch Dutoit from the early 1980s and a 1993 disc by Kent Nagano (see link). There's a slightly overcooked charm about this recording, particularly the way the wordless chorus led by Robert Shaw performs. This ballet score, commissioned by Diaghilev and completed in 1912, is more like an enormous symphony, complete with large chorus. Munch matches the required subtlety with hammerlike flashes; it's a robust approach that brings out the best in Ravel's multicolored masterpiece. Highlights include the opening sunrise, the many advanced uses of tonal color, and the finale's no-holds-barred lovefest.

LINK➤ *Maurice Ravel – Daphnis et Chloé – London Sym. Orch. / Kent Nagano*   Erato 91712
A finer recording, sweeter and better suited to the cinematic nuances emphasized by Nagano's smooth approach. Less bombast, positively glowing tones. Good as Living Stereo may be, a superior 1993 engineer possesses greater control through better tools.

L'Enfant et les sortileges (The Child and the Sorcerers) –
Françoise Ogéas, Jeanine Collard, Jane Berbié, others;
Orchestre National de la R.T.F. / Lorin Maazel   Deutsche Grammophon 423-718

Ravel's enchanting lyrical fantasy, a sort of operetta, may remind listeners of Sondheim's best Broadway scores. A fairy tale by Colette insists upon surreal punishment for a child whose earsplitting tantrum causes his room's furnishings to come to life. Among other things, a china cup dances with a Wedgewood teapot. As this bizarre cacophony grows, the cup sings with what sounds like a Chinese voice and backyard animals attack the child's past cruelties through a nasty ballet. Somehow all of this translates into the first truly modern opera—certainly a landmark in 20th-century eccentricity. The cast's energy and stagey operatic vocals match Ravel's frenzy, and the 1960 sonics are pleasing.

LINK➤ *Cecilia Bartoli – Chant d'Amour – Myung-Whun Chung (piano)*   London 452-667
Although she's mostly associated with Rossini (Rossini Heroines [London 436-075]) and with Mozart (A Portrait [London 448-300]), Bartoli is especially effective on the various Ravel songs that complete a disc filled with Bizet, Delibes, Berlioz, and Pauline Viardot. From 1996.

Piano Concerto in G – Alicia De Larrocha (piano);
Saint Louis Sym. Orch. / Leonard Slatkin   RCA 60985

Slatkin, an American specialist, brings out the jaunty, jazzlike quality of the 1931 Piano Concerto in G. The first movement is sassy, quick-witted, and clever; the second is measured and slightly reminiscent of Bach, but its ethereal flute solo could only be a Ravel creation. The concerto's third movement returns to jazz and to Gershwin's apparent influence (it's nearly an answer to 1928's *An American in Paris*). The splendid *Piano Concerto for the Left Hand* was written in 1929 for a pianist who lost his right hand in the First World War. *Valses nobles et sentimentales* and *Sonatine* complete a terrific disc. Excellent, attentive, fun-loving De Larrocha throughout. (Don't be misled by her matronly cover photo.)

LINK➤ *Augusta Holmès – Orchestral Works –*
Rheinland-Pfalz Phil. / Samuel Friedman   *Marco Polo 8.223449*
Marco Polo's quest for obscure, deserving composers uncovers another jewel in a female composer from France who worked in the late 19th century. Boldly dramatic (most unladylike for her time) with a good sense of structure, these pieces should be heard. Very accessible.

Max Reger

The son of a Bavarian schoolteacher, Reger was born in the small town of Kenmath in 1873. As a child, he demonstrated promising musical talent, inherited partly from his father, who had near-perfect pitch. By age 11, Reger was able to re-create music he'd heard in a military band concert, note for note. He supported himself as a fairly traditional teacher of German classical music, first in Wiesbaden and Munich, and ultimately in Leipzig. Reger's strength grew from a fantastic preoccupation with the music of Bach and Beethoven, and to a somewhat lesser extent, Brahms. He had the poor fortune to focus on this work at precisely the moment when those composers were out of favor. As a result, his various works have never quite found their audience. Still, they do present an interesting transition from older forms of classical music to the new ideas of the 20th century.

String Quartets – Berner Streichquartett   cpo 999-069
A delightful 3-CD set recorded in 1994, here's the finest demonstration of Reger's considerable creative gifts. His first quartet is a Mozart kin. Opus 54 in G minor introduces some discord. Composed in 1990, it points the way back toward Bartók. The master work here is Opus 74 in D minor; it fills CD2 with 53 minutes of music. Unbalanced from the start, it was outrageously modern in 1903. The creative approach presages Schoenberg, the structure is loose with emotional outbursts, and often, dissonance outweighs tonal beauty. Opus 109 in E flat major, from 1909, starts with a nod to Haydn and Beethoven; it then proceeds to show modernists the way to the future.

LINK▶ *Max Reger – Cellos Sonatas Nos. 1 & 4 –*
Reimund Korupp (cello), Rudolf Meister   *cpo 9990394*
The German label cpo has done a fine job keeping Reger's name alive with distinguished performances and recordings. The gem here is 1910's Opus 116 in A minor—a perfect blend of romance and modernism. Try also Piano Works by David Levine (cpo 999-074).

Böcklin Suite, Hiller Variations –
Royal Concertgebouw Orch. / Neeme Järvi   Chandos 8794
Art lovers may know Böcklin's painting *The Isle of the Dead* (which inspired a Mendelssohn symphonic poem). Reger created a suite of four tone poems based upon four Böcklin paintings, the best of which is *Der geigende Erremit* (Hermit Playing the Violin). That piece seems to expand and contract, from sweeping chorale to a sad little fiddle, then back again. It's quite winning. Johann Adam Hiller was an 18th-century German composer notable for his invention of the singspiel; in 1907, Reger composed 14 variations and fugues based upon a rococo theme from Hiller's 1772 singspiel, Der Aerndtekranz. It is the very model of variation writing. A very fine performance, too.

LINK▶ *Various Composers – Romances for Saxophone – Branford Marsalis (soprano*
saxophone); English Chamber Orch. / Andrew Litton   *CBS Masterworks 42122*

An encouraging "light classical" debut for a fine jazz saxophone player. This is a survey of brief passages from well-known classical works, from Fauré's Pavane to Villa-Lobos's Bachianas Brasileiras. The engineering and musical support are world-class. So is Marsalis's tone and interpretative feeling.

Steve Reich

Contemporary music of a serious nature embraces many cultures and styles. New Yorker Steve Reich employs electronics, jazz, found sounds, and traditional music from other countries in his compositions. Born in 1936, Reich, like so many of his peers, attended NYC's Julliard School. In San Francisco, he learned from minimalist Terry Riley, who encouraged experimentation with tape loops of repeated spoken words. Reich collaborated with Philip Glass in the late 1960s, then lived with the Ewe people in Ghana; he returned to create 1971's *Drumming* and several more works that gained critical acclaim from modern music and rock critics. Later in the 1970s, Reich studied Indonesian music and Hebrew chant. Orchestral and chamber music occupied him in the 1980s. Visualizing ideas was the next step. Reich's 1993 work, *The Cave*, is an audiovisual history of Israeli-Arab relations and was the result of a four-year collaboration with his wife, video artist Beryl Korot.

Music for 18 Musicians –
Steve Reich (and others)   ECM New Series 1129

The oscillating patterns of repeated sounds suggest a pulse; they're generated by acoustic instruments (mostly winds) and some chirping human voices. A second rhythm is articulated by pianos, marimbas, and xylophones. The effect is not unlike rapid breathing. It's also related to electronics but without any circuitry beyond microphones. Although the music breathes quickly, concepts develop slowly, almost as a musical mosiac generated, pixel by pixel, before the ears and eyes. It's an abstract hour, but also entrancing for the open-minded, patient listener. A pivotal piece of modern music from 1978, the music theory is carefully explained by the composer in the liner notes. Excellent ECM recording quality, too.

LINK► *Steve Reich – Octet, Music for a Large Ensemble, Violin Phase –*
Steve Reich and others   *ECM New Series 1168*
Music for a Large Ensemble *(1978)* and Octet *(1979) are further explorations of similar ideas. Violin Phase, from 1967, is a variation on the concept of rounds—the solo violinist plays patterns against two identical out-of-phase recordings. Recommended modern listening.*

City Life, Proverb – The Steve Reich Ensemble, others   Nonesuch 79430

Nearly two decades later, Reich continues to favor repeated patterns, but he's found considerable flexibility in his approach. *Proverb*, completed in 1995, is mostly a vocal piece for three sopranos and two tenors. The sopranos are doubled by an organ, and vibraphones are heard in the background. The effect suggests early music, but seems rhythmically free, while in fact, it's quite structured. The other significant piece here is 1995's *City Life*, scored for pairs of winds, pianos, and samplers, plus percussion, bass, and string quartet. An appealing fabric is woven from these instruments, musiclike repeats of spoken words from city people, and sound effects, such as the slamming of car doors.

LINK► *New York Variations – Stephen Hough (piano)*   *Hyperion 67005*
Pianist Hough performs four pieces by NYC composers. The best is George Tsontakis's Ghost Variations, from 1991. As the title suggests, there's a struggle here between the spirit world and the "real" world. Fine pieces by Corigliano, Copland, and lesser-known Ben Weber complete a fantastic CD.

Ottorino Respighi

The Italian composer Ottorino Respighi was born in Bologna in 1879. He studied at the Liceo of Bologna from 1891 until 1899 and moved to St. Petersburgh, Russia, where he took composition lessons from Rimsky-Korsakov until 1903. Back in Italy, Respighi earned a living as a violinist and wrote several popular comic operas. This led to an appointment as Professor of Composition at Rome's Santa Cecilia Conservatory in 1913 and a job as its director in 1924. Two years later, Respighi resigned to devote all of his attention to composing. Several popular pieces followed, notably the last of his Roman portraits (inspired by the sensual decadence of the poet D'Annunzio). Also well received was "The Birds" (inspired by 18th-century composers like Pasquini) and a Botticelli triptych. Respighi died in Rome in 1926. Today he is mostly remembered for vivid, emotional presentations and not so much for serious compositions.

The Fountains of Rome, The Pines of Rome, Roman Festivals –
Phila. Orch. / Riccardo Muti   EMI 47316

One key moment in these musical picture postcards is the Triton fountain gushing to life; it's the moment by which all recordings should be measured. Not only does Muti get it right, EMI's engineers do, too. The moment typifies the overall excellence of this 1985 CD. Respighi's tour begins amidst unimaginable splendor at the Villa Borghese; children play in the pine groves. Then the scene switches to the pines outside a catacomb, and the mood abruptly changes. The walk continues to the imagined soldiers pounding along the Appian Way. Other notable stops include the end-of-day shimmering of the Villa Medici fountain and the huge theatening crowd of the Circenses. From 1916–24.

LINK➤ *Classical Zoo–Itzhak Perlman (violin); Atlanta Sym. Orch./Yoel Levi   Telarc 80443*
Bruce Adolphe, a remarkably talented composer and honestly funny music educator based at Lincoln Center, wrote new contemporary kid-friendly poetry for Saint-Saëns's Carnival of the Animals, the heart of this entertaining CD. Also included are some works by Rossini, Respighi, and others.

Ancient Airs and Dances –
Orpheus Chamber Orch.   Deutsche Grammophon 437-533

Although he lived centuries after the fact, Respighi was a gifted interpreter and composer of Baroque music. This is demonstrated not only in the reworkings of lute and guitar music found in the suites of Baroque dances, but throughout much of this beautifully performed album. The Airs and Dances flow smoothly; the dignity and embroidery of an earlier age are evoked with pure love and absolute precision. Better still is "The Birds," a series of bird portraits from 1927 based on music from the same era. "Three Botticelli Pictures," also from 1927, are original works inspired by period music. Predictably, "The Birth of Venus" is the centerpiece. Sounds real good, too.

LINK➤ *Ottorino Respighi – Sinfonia Drammatica –*
BBC Philharmonic / Sir Edward Downes   *Chandos 9213*
Completed in 1914, Respighi's only symphony never quite finds its dramatic zenith, but contains a great many colorful passages. The performance here is very persuasive and recorded with typical Chandos care. It is, therefore, worth a listen.

Nikolai Rimsky-Korsakov

Nikolai Rimsky-Korsakov wanted to be like his older brother; he dreamed of life in the Russian navy. At age 12, in 1856, the wealthy, aristocratic St. Petersburg youth enrolled in naval school. He took piano lessons on the side, but his heart was with the navy. He also met the great conductor and composer Balakirev, who encouraged him to compose. They kept in close contact, and in 1865, Balakirev introduced Rimsky-Korsakov's first symphony. This encouraged the composer to study music very seriously, but his surprise appointment as a composition professor forced Rimsky-Korsakov to admit how little he actually knew about the technical details of composing. He intensely studied harmony, counterpoint, and other aspects of music theory, becoming an expert teacher and an influential composer with an extraordinary understanding of orchestration. With other important St. Petersburg composers, he was one of a social and intellectual group called "The Five." He died in 1908.

Sym. Nos. 1 & 2 ("Antar") – Bergen PO / Dmitri Kitajenko   Chandos 9178

Although a drunken conductor destroyed the First Symphony's premiere in 1865 (causing Rimsky-Korsakov a nervous breakdown), it's noble, well constructed, and handsome. Ideas are more sharply focused a dozen years later as Rimsky-Korsakov looks to Arabian legends and authentic Arabian songs for inspiration. The paired bassoons nicely shape a world-weary character; solo flute arabesques suggest a gazelle and set the scene for fantasy. Excitement comes in the form of "pleasures": vengeance and power, then a love scene causing the mythical hero's death. A textbook lesson in orchestral color and sonority, Rimsky-Korsakov's Second Symphony is a major accomplishment in arrangement. With *Capriccio Espagnol*. A fine recording benefits from the best possible stereo system.

LINK➤ *Alexander Borodin – Sym. 1 & 2 – Royal Phil. Orch. / Ashkenazy   London 436-651*
After a vivid depiction of a caravan making its way in a brief symphonic poem entitled In Central Asia, *Ashkenazy uncovers the heroic romanticism in Borodin's 1867 debut symphony. The second is better-known. Very impressive, too often forgotten. Terrific performances, fine engineering.*

Schéhérazade, Capriccio Espagnol –
London Sym. Orch. / Charles Mackerras   Telarc 80208

Based on various characters and scenes from *The 1001 Arabian Nights*, this 1889 symphonic suite contains some of classical music's best-known themes and arrangements. Several familiar horn blasts introduce "The Sea and Sinbad's Ship," and this becomes the Sultan's theme; Schéhérazade's haunting, sensual theme is expressed by solo violin and harp. Using vivid orchestral colors, Rimsky-Korsakov renders the undulating sea with its endless dark blue vista and its power and calm. As the piece progresses through other stories of princes, festivals, warriors, and storms at sea, the mood is more familiar than the individual musical sequences. *Capriccio Espagnole* is another model of exemplary orchestral arranging. Spectacular engineering.

LINK➤ *Rimsky-Korsakov – Scheherazade – Chi.Sym. Orch. / Fritz Reiner   RCA 60875*
Once again, nobody does it like Reiner. His colors are brighter, his quiet moments are more sensual, and his individual string instruments sound more like violins. In short, Reiner brings this music to life like no other. This 1960 recording is equally good on Debussy's La Mer.

Gioacchino Rossini

Rossini defined and then largely dominated opera for a half-century. His father was a trumpet player in their small town of Pesaro, Italy, where he also inspected the slaughterhouses. Born in 1792, young Rossini easily learned to play several instruments and became a locally popular boy soprano. He composed an opera at age 16; by 21, his *L'Italiana in Algeri* (An Italian in Algiers) was a sensation. Rossini became a reliable machine; he wrote 40 operas in less than two decades. Then, around 1830, he stopped. Nobody knows why. He never wrote another opera; he just about stopped composing altogether. Already married, he took a mistress and eventually married her. He moved from Paris to Italy then back to Paris again, where food became a passion (both eating and devising new dishes). Rossini also became known as a wit, the life of any party. He died a hero in 1868.

Overtures – Chi. Sym. Orch. / Fritz Reiner   RCA 60387

Once you've heard Reiner on these six overtures, there's not much point in listening to anyone else. Reiner lights up the sky with life-affirming fireworks on this 1958 recording. Everything is handled with the relentlessly positive energy of a Sousa march (particularly *La gazza ladra* [The theiving magpie]), but even the slower passages seem to glow with appropriate incadesence. Listen, for example, to the early stages of *Gugielmo Tell* (William Tell), which are thick with cellos and sad strings; Reiner's approach (and a rich recording) rivets attention and emotion on every note; the well-known second part of this overture is a phenomenon. *Il barbiere di Siviglia* (The Barber of Seville) is also revelatory.

LINK➤ *Gioacchino Rossini – Complete Overtures –*
Sir Neville Marriner, Academy of St. Martin-in-the-Fields   ***Philips 434-016***
Reiner's stupendous achievement should lead to an even wider selection of Rossini's overtures. This 3-CD set contains all 26 of them (Rossini wrote almost 40 operas, but not all were preceded by an overture). The performances are a bit polite and pale by comparison with Reiner.

L'italiana in Algeri (The Italian Girl in Algiers) – Agnes Baltsa, Ruggero Raimondi, others; Vienna Phil. / C. Abbado   Deutsche Grammophon 427-331

Even at age 21, Rossini knew how to work fast and how to please a crowd. He jumped into this assignment when another composer failed to deliver, wrote over two hours of entertaining music in less than a month, and came up with a hit. The overture only hints at the Marx Brothers–type antics in this "opera buffa" (comic opera)—a quintet of sneezers, physical complaints compared to silly instrument sounds (so carefully worked into the score that you might miss the comedy), and various Italian street performers' tricks onstage. "Pensa alla Patria" (Think of Your Country) was a longtime popular song in Italy. Terrific singing, ideal orchestral accompaniment, fine recording.

LINK➤ *Gioacchino Rossini – Stabat Mater –*
Soloists, London Sym. Chorus, City of London Sinfonia / Richard Hickox   ***Chandos 8780***
More than a decade after his last opera, Rossini approaches the liturgy with ascendent results. The opening choral quartet is chilling, and the tenor aria "Cujus Animam Gementem" (Her Weeping Heart) is very reminiscent of lyric opera. Extremely clear recording, fine performance.

Il barbiere di Siviglia (The Barber of Seville) –
Failoni Ch. Orch. of Budapest / Will Humburg
NAXOS 8.660027/9

Within the first few minutes, town barber Figaro brags about himself in Rossini's most famous song. This is followed by another handsome duet by Figaro and (the disgused) Count Almaviva. So begins the amiable nonsense outside of old fool Doctor Bartolo's house. Inside is Bartolo's beautiful ward, Rosino, the object of the count's desire. Amidst a story that grows crazier by the minute, there are some sweet moments, like Rosino's aria "Contro un cor" (Against a heart). Bravo to Humburg for performing a stage comedy—and not holding out for a work of pristine art! (A 3-CD set, but why no English libretto?) Rossini's biggest hit, first performed in 1816.

LINK▶ *Rossini – String Sonatas 1-6 – Orch. of the Age of Enlightenment Hyperion 66595*
Rossini was 12 years old when he wrote these sonatas for two violins, cello, and bass. More fun than Mozart's youthful work, these sonatas sometimes sound like student pieces while showing glimmers of Rossini's future humor. It's also fun to hear a boy's fascination with the big bass sound.

La Cenerentola (Cinderella) – Cecilia Bartoli, others; Orch. & Chorus of the
Bologna Teatro Comunale / Riccardo Chailly   London 436-902
This 1817 Cinderella story isn't quite the Disney version (here, Cinderella has a nasty father, bracelets instead of glass slippers, and the prince's friend in place of her fairy godmother). The story's arc still moves Cinderella from poverty to princess, but in Rossini's hands, Cinderella is outspoken and not so helpless. Cecilia Bartoli submits one of her finest performances here, particularly on the closer, "Non più mesta" (No longer sad), her song of forgiving. Tenor William Matteuzzi (the prince) takes full advantage of Rossini's show-off writing on "Sì ritrovarla io giuro" (Yes, I swear I'll find her again). Amazing Chailly; incredible recording.

LINK▶ *Gioacchino Rossini – Semiramide –*
Joan Sutherland, Marilyn Horne, others; London SO / Richard Bonynge   London 425-481
It's 1823. Rossini gets serious with Voltaire's political potboiler in Babylon. Lots of dazzling arias, including Sutherland's famous version of "Bel raggio lusinghier." Recorded in 1965, and still champ.

Guglielmo Tell (William Tell) – Luciano Pavarotti, Mirella Freni, others, ,
National Phil. Orch. / Riccardo Chailly   London 417-154
Enormous scale makes this 1829 saga nearly unstageable—a 4 1/2 hour performance, painfully expensive scenery, and absurd demands on the voice of Arnold (Tell's cohort). On record, the music's under three hours (4 CDs), there's no scenery, and tenor Pavarotti gives the performance of his life. The story's good, too: heroic adventurers fight for their Swiss homeland. Find a comfortable seat for the slow-ish Act 1; stay tuned for Act 2 to enjoy Pavarotti's "Quand l'Helvetie" and Freni's "Sombre forêt." Act 3 snoozes, but Pavarotti's room-bursting aria, "Asile hereditère" (homeland tribute) opens the action-packed fourth. Loving 1978–79 performance.

LINK▶ *Rossini – Guillaume Tell –*
Nicolai Gedda, Montserrate Cabellé, ;Royal Phil. Orch. / Lamberto Gardelli   EMI 69951
Sung in the original French (Chailly's is in Italian), this version is equally spectacular. Gedda is a phenomenal Arnold, and Caballé sings beautifully. This 1973 recording is room-shaking, with turbulent orchestral energy, but also grace, and ease. Monumental.

Camille Saint-Saëns

Born in Paris in 1835, Saint-Saëns was a child prodigy, a pianist whose premiere professional recital was held at age 11. Music came easily; he was composing by age 6 and became a stunning sight-reader who amazed Wagner with his instincts. By the time he was 22, Saint-Saëns was the organist of Paris's Church of the Madaleine. There he developed a reputation as the world's finest organist and a talented improviser. He stayed with the Madeleine for two decades, but also toured as a concert pianist. Saint-Saëns taught piano at École Niedermeyer and founded the Société Nationale to promote French music. Everything changed in 1878 with the death of his two children. Saint-Saëns abandoned his wife in 1881; by 1890, he was a sour old man who criticized the newer French music and traveled extensively to other remote places in order to escape his misery. Saint-Saëns died in Algiers in 1921.

Cello Concerto No. 1, others – Yo-Yo Ma (cello),
Orchestre National de France / Lorin Maazel and others   SONY Classical 66395
From 1980, here is one of Yo-Yo Ma's most famous performances. Ma's nobility and grace, and the extraordinary emotion he draws from the simplest, most perfect sounds are wholly absorbing and transcend the composition itself. That said, Saint-Saëns provides a refined, stylish basis for Ma's musical conversation with the equally effective Maazel; few concertos are so ideally balanced. In its most recent incarnation, Ma's workout is paired with violinist Cho-Liang Lin's equally astonishing Violin Concerto No. 3 (with Michael Tilson-Thomas and the Philharmonia Orchestra). This piece begins as a gypsy theme and builds into a workout where alarming technical skill is essential. A less stellar Piano Concerto No. 2 completes the CD.

LINK➤ *The Great Guitar Concertos – John Williams*   *CBS 44791*
The emphasis is on early Italian works by Vivaldi and Giuliani and on early 20th-century Spanish compositions by Rodrigo (his Concierto de Aranjuez, *for example) and Castelnuovo-Tedesco. Easily overlooked, it's a very good 2-CD collection.*

Danse macabre (and other short pieces) –
Kyung Wha Chung (violin), various orchestras / Charles Dutoit   London 425-021
Saint-Saëns's expressive tone poems were painted with broad strokes that communicated with great effect. One of the scariest series during radio's golden age had a Saint-Saëns theme song, *Le rouet d'Omphale* (Omphale's Spinning Wheel). This tone poem tells the story of the Lydian Queen, Omphale, who imprisoned Hercules. Another myth is the basis of *Phaéton*. When the sun god's chariot went out of control, falling toward Earth, Zeus's thunderbolt saved the planet. A younger Hercules returns for *Le jeunesse d' Hercule*, a study of contrasting themes involving the choices offered to a hero on his way to immortality. *Introduction et Rondo capriccioso* is one of two challenging violin pieces in which Chung excels.

LINK➤ *A Tribute to Jascha Heifetz –*
Itzhak Perlman (violin), Samuel Sanders (piano)   *EMI 49604*
With 19 short pieces (including Le Cygne *by Saint-Saëns), Perlman re-creates the decidedly schmaltzy approach to classical fiddling that made Heifitz so popular. This is pure cinematic romance, a soft touch to melt the heart. Best is Manuel Ponce's "Estrellita" (Little Star).*

Piano Concertos Nos. 1-5 –
Pascal Rogé (piano), various orchestras / Charles Dutoit   London 443-865

Saint-Saëns's five piano concertos are the works of a serious composer in constant pursuit of style, grace, and beauty. They are captivating because the creator was at the top of his form and because Rogé and Dutoit are so completely comfortable with this repertoire. Written in 1868, Piano Concerto No. 2 floats from one musical idea to the next. These smooth transitions, an orchestral accompaniment reduced to its essence, and the fluid path to and from dramatic climaxes, are the characteristics of Saint-Saëns's music that few composers have ever matched. Even the concerto's finale is very polished and refined. Saint-Saëns set up 1875's Piano Concerto No. 4 in two movements, each with submovements. The first movement looks back to the days of Chopin and the salon culture; it is frilly and nostalgic with virtuosity on display. There's also an edge provided mainly by the orchestra, a longing satisfied by a music-hall novelty song, and a swirling close. The second movement is entirely different; it transforms themes from one style to another and is an active rather than weary participant in the unfolding events of the world. These two concertos are Saint-Saëns's most popular, but the other three are excellent as well. Unfortunately, there isn't much emotional depth here, except perhaps in the youthful fun of Piano Concerto No. 1, which embodies a playful joy in music making. The others, for all of their grandeur and keyboard pyrotechnics, offer little more than colorful facades.

LINK▶ *Music for Flute & Harp – Jean-Pierre Rampal (flute), Marielle Nordmann (harp)*
SONY Classical 44552

Salon music at its most delicate. The style is French on Saint-Saëns's Fantasie *and several pieces by Fauré, but there's also some Beethoven, Donizetti, and Rossini to liven things up. The recording and musicianship are precise and refined.*

A Hi-Fi Spectacular!
Symphony No. 3 (Organ Symphony), more –
Berj Zamkochian (organ); Boston Sym. Orch. /
Charles Munch   RCA 61500

An orchestral spectacle from 1886 (the end of an era) and a colossal advertisement for Living Stereo's astonishing sonics. Exciting sections and ideas galore—including some evil ones—make the first movement of Symphony No. 3 an adventurous thrill ride. Saint-Saëns brings the depth of the organ into the second movement's background. (You'll need a subwoofer to feel the room shake.) The third movement collects various classical styles and scatters them about. The gargantuan fourth movement with its bellowing organ, crashing cymbals, blaring horns, and heroic strings became the theme for *Babe*, the 1995 Oscar-nominated movie about a pig. While Munch's performance is huge, it somehow is also suitable for Debussy's La Mer and Ibert's *Escales*.

LINK▶ *A Celebration – Marie-Claire Alain (organ)*   *Erato 15343*
An organ recital of spectacular dimension, this 5-CD set surveys just about the whole organ repertoire, from Vivaldi and Handel to contemporary works composed by Alain's family members. Alain's performances are often definitive, and the sonics are generally favorable.

Alfred Schnittke

The eclectic, iconoclastic composer Alfred Schnittke was born in 1934 in the Volga Republic, then an autonomous region for Germans within the Soviet Union. Without a radio, his childhood exposure to music was extremely limited. Schnittke studied in Vienna, where his family lived after WW II, and then at the Moscow Conservatory, where he later became a teacher. He began composing in earnest by 1961, and continued in a most prolific fashion for more than three decades. Schnittke wrote over 60 film scores, mostly in a popular style unlike his classical endeavors. His work began its unique, original course with 1968's Second Violin Concerto; by the time his first symphony debuted in 1972, Schnittke was branded as undesirably radical by the influential Soviet Composers Union. As a result, his music was rarely performed at home. Fortunately, a wide range of admiring musicians assured a regular flow of commissions. Schnittke died after a series of strokes in 1998.

Concerto Grosso No. 1 –
Chamber Orch. of Europe / Heinrich Schiff   Deutsche Grammophon 429-413
This up-to-date version of a concerto grosso (completed in 1977) introduced listeners to Schnittke's unique "polystylistic" voice. It's a moody piece, with many of the Schnittke hallmarks: dynamic shifts that are seductive and ultimately jarring; classical structure embellished or altered with modernist language; and unusual tonal colors. Violinist Gidon Kremer popularized the work (and many other Schnittke compositions). The idea of combining musical genres was very much a part of Schnittke's outlook. The shorter piece, *Moz-Art a la Haydn*, explores a structure reminiscent of Mozart and a melodic approach that recalls Haydn; somehow the whole project is unquestionably a Schnittke creation. *Quasi Una Sonata*, which explores the Italian sonata form, completes an intriguing CD.

LINK➤ *Peter Maxwell-Davies – Renaissance and Baroque Realisations –*
Fires of London / Peter Maxwell-Davies   Unicorn 2044
Here another modern composer with similar interests presents a more literal version of the same idea—working older forms and embellishing them with a highly sophisticated musical sensibility.

The Complete String Quartets – Kronos Quartet   Nonesuch 79500
On this 1998 release, the Kronos Quartet emphasizes the drama and intensity of Schnittke's Four Quartets. (The Third Quartet was previously released a decade ago on *Winter Was Hard* [Nonesuch 79181]). The First Quartet, composed in 1966, seems shy and frail. More a series of scratchy sketches than a coherent conception, it tries ideas without the bold confidence that would come with 1980's Second Quartet. The Agitato section of the Second Quartet is Schinttke at his motorized best, with scattered ideas that take shape to form a fascinating whole. Better still is 1983's Third Quartet—an accretion of old ideas presented with heart. A fine 2-CD set.

LINK➤ *Erich Wolfgang Korngold – The Sea Hawk, Symphony in F sharp –*
Oregon Sym. / James DePreist   Delos 3234
Korngold's soundtracks—especially his Academy Award winning The Adventures of Robin Hood— *are legendary. Presented here is a fine-sounding version of* The Sea Hawk. *Korngold's classical side is even more satisfying. His 1919 Symphony in F sharp has cinematic scope and snap, plus an intelligent structure and well-executed modern ideas. Stunning engineering.*

Arnold Schoenberg

Arnold Schoenberg was born in Vienna in 1874. He had learned to play several instruments by age 20 and as a young musician was deeply influenced by Wagner. Around 1907, Schoenberg was struggling to conceive a new approach to music. By 1909, he had left the traditional world of tonality, key signatures, and harmony and developed his own atonal approach. The music sounded strange and made many people so uncomfortable that they aggressively hated his work. Schoenberg persisted and found adherents in two younger composers, Anton Webern and Alban Berg. In 1924, he further sophisticated the atonal system with a structure called twelve-tone serialism. Schoenberg left his base in Berlin for the U.S. in 1933 and after teaching music in Boston, made his way to L.A. There, he settled into a teaching position at UCLA. Schoenberg died in L.A. in 1951.

Verklärte Nacht (Transfigured Night) – Hollywood Qt.   Testament 1031

The original string sextet version of Schoenberg's 1899 setting of a poem by Hamburg's Richard Dehmel is among the Hollywood Quartet's finest recordings (a cello and a viola were added for the 1951 sextet). Schoenberg stays close to Dehmel's approach: "Two people walk through a bare, cold grove. A woman's voice speaks, "I am carrying a child but not by you. I walk beside you in a state of sin." When he forgives her, the bleak night is transformed: "May the child you've conceived not burden your soul. See how brightly the universe shines!" Schoenberg's effectiveness lies in tonal choices, contrasting colors, and constancy of tempo. Fine mono sound.

LINK➤ *Arnold Schoenberg – Verklärte Nacht (Transfigured Night) –*
Chamber Orchestra of Europe / Heinz Holliger   *Teldec 77314*
This more commonly heard string orchestra version of Verklärte Nacht *was arranged in 1917, and it's nicely done here. The disc also includes Schoenberg's second chamber symphony, completed in its original form in 1916. Good 1994 digital recording.*

Five Pieces for Orchestra, Serenade –
BBC Sym. Orch., Members of Ensemble Intercontemporain/
Pierre Boulez   SONY Classical 48463

A leading proponent of 20th-century music, Boulez communicates Schoenberg's unorthodox ideas here with intelligence and artistry. Just 15 minutes long, Schoenberg's Five Pieces for Orchestra, from 1909, is one of the century's most influential works. To gain some insight into Schoenberg's experimentation with colors and timbres, listen carefully to the third movement, then experience the slightly off-kilter feeling caused by Schoenberg's choice of sounds in the fourth movement. *Serenade*, written in 1923, deconstructs not only tonality but also some aspects of rhythm and form, employing Schoenberg's "note-row" method. Offering unique solo instruments, such as the mandolin, and very original instrumentation, *Serenade* mimics burlesque, march, and other musical forms in a frequently satisfying way. Excellent sound.

LINK➤ *Anton Webern – Complete Works, Op. 1 to 31 –*
Julliard String Quartet; London Sym. Orch. / Pierre Boulez; others   *SONY 45845*
A very comprehensive survey of Webern's surprising versatility and emotional value as interpreted by one of the few conductors who understands his work. Contains songs (leider), chamber works, cantatas, and many miniatures.

Classical CD Listener's Guide   *149*

Gurrelieder — Susan Dunn, Brigitte Fassbaender, others; Berlin Radio Sym. Orch. / Riccardo Chailly   London 430-231

Gurrelieder is an enormous undertaking, a gigantic cantata. Schoenberg's line from Wagner is direct, romantic, and wholly unrelated to atonality or serialism. It is the musical story of King Waldemar and Tove, who live in 14th-century Gurre. (Translated from German, the title of this choral work is "Songs of Gurre.") After Tove is murdered, Waldemar strongly questions God, a situation that resolves itself in pantheistic glory through the final movement. Completed in 1911, this 20-minute, 2-CD extravaganza is notoriously difficult to perform and record; with a double chorus, extra instruments, and Schoenberg's boundless enthusiasm for orchestral color, this 1991 rendition gets the singing and instrumentation right.

LINK► *Harry Partch – The Harry Partch Collection (Various Artists)*   CRI 751-754

Partch (1901–1974) was raised by missionary parents, came of age among hoboes on society's sidelines, and developed "just intonation," a microscopic approach to pitch, and necessarily developed his own instruments. These four CDs show Partch's enormous effect on modern music.

Pierrot Lunaire — Jane Manning, Nash Ensemble / S. Rattle   Chandos 6534

Abrasive and challenging to this day, Schoenberg's neo-musical nightmare is the best place to absorb his dramatic departure from music's accepted structure. Schoenberg wrote it in 21 smaller pieces—he was not yet capable of applying his complex ideas to a single, large work—mostly for four or five instruments (whose combinations vary), plus the human voice. Jane Manning speaks and sings, dragging and clustering her phrasing so she seems like a human instrument. Schoenberg wrote this music to accompany Albert Giraud's morbid expressions of an artist's visions, including a bloody Eucharist, hanging, and decapitation, among other horrors. At the time, these poems were popular in Germany.

LINK► *Arnold Schoenberg – Moses und Aron / Pierre Boulez*   DG 449-174

Schoenberg had a tough time writing serialist opera, and even though he couldn't figure out how to complete this piece, it's well worth hearing (especially on this excellent 1996 recording). Difficult to perform, it makes huge demands on the listener's patience.

Variations for Orchestra, Erwartung, Chamber Symphony No. 1 — City of Birmingham Sym. Orch. / Simon Rattle   EMI 55212

For those who doubted—and continue to doubt—the communicative powers of Schoenberg's twelve-tone system, 1928's *Variations for Orchestra* offers persuasive evidence of its effectiveness. These miniatures explore particular instrument sounds, or a rhythm, or a musical style such as jazz. It's easy to get past the edgy character of Schoenberg's palette. From 1909, *Erwartung* is a one-woman opera; the main character is horrified because she may have killed her lover. It's also a coherent demonstration of atonality, demanding unusual skills from soprano Bryn-Johnson. 1906's Chamber Symphony No. 1 salutes Richard Strauss's tone poems and Mahler's symphonies, but maintains originality through thick textures and extraordinary thematic development. Try also Karajan's version (DG 415-326).

LINK► *Frank Zappa – Vols. I & II – Lon. Sym. Orch. / Kent Nagano*   Rykodisc 10540/1

Don't dismiss Zappa as a weird outspoken rock musician. Bob in Dacron is a modernist ballet about a guy looking for sex in a singles bar, and Mo 'n Herb's Vacation is a striking, complicated piece that questions rules about tonality, structure, and the distinction between rock and classical music. A worthwhile 2-CD set.

Franz Schubert

Schubert was a short, chubby schoolteacher's son who never figured out how to make money with the music he wrote day in and day out. He grew up outside Vienna; by age 11, in 1808, he was expertly playing several instruments and singing in the imperial court's chapel choir. Schubert left the mainstream to compose at home and to teach at his father's school. He later returned to Vienna, where he became a central figure in a community of young artsy intellectuals; on some nights, his friends hosted a Schubertiad, a party featuring his music. Sadly, Schubert's music was not often heard in public; critics considered him insignificant and esoteric. Depressed and poor, Schubert kept composing, even while hospitalized with the venereal disease that later took his life. Schubert idolized Beethoven, and in 1888, 60 years after Schubert's death, the two bodies were moved to adjacent gravesites. Schubert's vast store of manuscripts laid forgotten until the mid-1800s.

Piano Quintet in A (Trout) – John O'Conor (piano); Cleveland Quartet
Telarc 80225

One of Schubert's happiest pieces, the "Trout Quintet" is also one of the world's most popular chamber works. The name comes from an original Schubert song about fishing; Schubert based the 1819 quintet on that song. The key sound is the shimmering piano (probably the trout stream) working into and out of the springtime melodies of the strings. Good spirits abound. The third movement is peppy and bracing, and very often heard as a student example of chamber music. The Cleveland Quartet's performance is attentive and flowing; O'Conor is wonderful (as always), and the sound quality is fine. Quartet No. 13 in A minor completes the package; it's a darker, more introspective work.

LINK▶ George Walker – The Music of George Walker –
George Walker (piano), Gregory Walker (violin), Phyllis Bryn Julson (soprano)   CRI 719
Former chair of the Rutgers University music department, Walker parallels Schubert in his versatility and his gift for piano pieces, chamber works, and songs. As a 20th-century composer, he dabbles in atonality and jazz, but the foundation is boldly classical. Don't miss this one.

Fantasia in C (Wanderer) – Artur Rubinstein (piano)   RCA 6257

By 1822, Schubert's experience composing leider and his keen admiration of Beethoven seemed to coalesce into an advanced piano sonata form he called a "Fantasia." While the structure of the piece resembles Beethoven's sonatas, the four movements are more like Schubert's songs than formal dances. In Rubenstein's 1965 interpretation, emotions seem to well up from beneath the surface, and are then swept along through a style that seems wholly spontaneous. The "Wanderer" in the title refers to a theme in the second movement, whose variations were inspired by "Der Wanderer," a song from *Die Schöne Müllerin*. Rubenstein is, of course, excellent on the two impromptus and sonata that complete the disc.

LINK▶ Nikolai Medtner – The Complete Piano Sonatas – Marc-André Hamelin (piano)
Hyperion 67221/4
A 4-CD survey of a fabulous Russian piano composer, one whose name is not well known. His sonatas are thoughtful, dramatic, and wholly involving. Hamelin plays beautifully. Excellent!

Impromptus – Murray Perahia (piano) SONY Classical 37291

As with Mozart's piano work, the choice between Mitsuko Uchida (Philips 456-245) and Perahia makes for a very close call. Both artists approach these pieces as miniatures, precious and picturesque, yet somehow grand and memorable. And both retain the improvisational quality inherent in Schubert's piano work. This is Schubert at his best, experimenting with harmonies to evoke multiple emotional responses; effortlessly shaping melodies he deconstructs and rebuilds. Of the two sets of four Impromptus, the nobility and passion of Opus 90, No. 2 make it a particular favorite. Heaven is nearby. These pieces were composed in 1827, a year before Schubert died, but the anxiety present elsewhere is rare here.

LINK► *Franz Schubert – Moments Musicaux – Maria João Pires (piano)* *DG 427-769*
Schubert's most beautiful colors rendered with complete understanding by a remarkable contemporary pianist. Very highly recommended. The remainder of the disc contains 2 scherzos and a sonata.

Symphony 5, 8 (Unfinished) – SF Sym. / Herbert Blomstedt DG 445-514

Schubert wrote seven complete symphonies, sketched out another (Symphony No. 7), and finished at least two of four movements for the "Unfinished" Symphony No. 8 (the remaining two were either lost or never realized to Schubert's satisfaction). Even in its incomplete form, these two movements are spectacular: the cellos carry a winsome melody to the strings, who repeat its sweetly lyrical song before the full orchestra's report; still the brave melody emerges, grows hearty, and eventually overwhelms. This is majestic writing, and Blomstedt masters the procedings, aided by crystalline sound. The slower second movement is remarkable for its violin scoring. The companion pieces, Symphony No. 5 and the "Rosamunde" Overture, are among Schubert's best.

LINK► *Hans Pfitzner – Orchestral Works; Concertos –*
Soloists; Bamberg Sym. Orch. ; others / Werner Andreas Albert *CPO 999-259*
A 5-CD set exploring most of the romantic German composer's important music, except the 1917 opera Palestrina *(Deutsche Grammophon 427-417). Pfitzner's skill with subtle colorations and easy melodies makes for very easy listening.*

Die Schöne Müllerin (The Fair Maid of the Mill)
Ian Bostridge (tenor), Graham Johnson (piano)
with Dietrich Fischer-Dieskau Hyperion 33025

The simplicity of Bostridge's golden tenor voice and Johnson's piano work is charming, entirely suitable for Wilhelm Müller's poetry and Schubert's pretty melodies. Close your eyes, listen to the singer's innocent agony, imagine young love; "Der Neugierige" (The Inquisitive One) is sung by a boy stung by curiosity about whether a girl loves him as he adores her. The creative partnership between Bostridge and Johnson is sublime on "Pause," where Johnson's piano insinuates the miller's lute (which hangs on a wall) as Bostridge sings. His heart has been broken; he can no longer make music. Fischer-Dieskau reads several more Müller poems to complete the story. Highest recommendation.

LINK► *Schubert–Lieder–Barbara Bonney (sop.), Geoffrey Parsons (piano)* *Teldec 90873*
An extremely well-sung version of Schubert's "Ave Maria" begins the disc, which is an appealing recital accompanied only by piano (and in one case, clarinet). Highlights include "Gretchen am Spinnrade," "Ganymed," and several songs known as the Mignon-Lieder.

Octet – Academy of St. Martin-in-the-Fields Chamber Ens.   Chandos 8585

Chandos's delicious recording draws the listener into the heart of this ensemble; the clarinet and bassoon are especially appealing. Schubert wrote this commissioned piece in February 1824 for an amateur clarinet player, on the condition that it sound "exactly like Beethoven's Septet." Schubert adhered to a more formal structure than usual, wrote some danceable movements, satisfied his patron, and remained true to himself (he also added a second violin, hence the octet). With extraordinarily intelligent use of each instrument's strengths, Schubert brilliantly highlights the clarinet's lines, warms to the horn, and uses the strings as a small orchestra for statements of substance. Delicate melodies and near-symphonic romance combine nicely.

LINK➤ *Ludwig van Beethoven – Septet – Gaudier Ensemble*   Hyperion 66513
A fresh reading of Beethoven's youthful chamber piece, nicely recorded with the necessary clarity to bring out the winds. It's coupled with the not-often-heard Wind Sextet. Or try the Vienna Octet's famous version (London 448-232).

The Last Quartets – Melos Quartett   Harmonia Mundi 901408 /9

Although the nickname of Quartet No. 14 ("Death and the Maiden") suggests a dramatic storyline, it's merely a reference to a song Schubert wrote in 1817 (the song becomes the basis for some second movement variations). And while this work does muster heroic happiness, it's often taken with the drudgery of daily existence, and some seemingly endless spirals into deep wells of hopelessness (a reflection of Schubert's financial and physical condition). And that's just the Allegro (the part that's supposed to be happy and upbeat!). Quartet No. 13 and Quartet No. 15, plus the snippet known as "Quartettsatz," complete a handsome 2-CD recording.

LINK➤ *(Book) – Illustrated Lives of the Great Composers: Schubert – Peggy Woodford*
Omnibus Press ISBN 0-7119-0255-0
Roughly four dozen well-known composers are memorialized in this extraordinary book series. Highly readable text is combined with carefully selected photographs, graphics, paintings, and performance programs to create a kind of portable museum visit. This one is representative.

Winterreise (Winter Journey) – Wolfgang Holzmair (baritone), Imogen Cooper (piano)   Philips 446-407

Schubert turns again to Wilhelm Müller's wonderful poems for this bracing walk through the depths of cold depression. Among many fine recordings of this famous song cycle, few singers project the young ex-lover's despair as directly as the baritone Holzmair. It's spectacularly dark work, composed by a despondent Schubert in 1827. It's also beautiful, majestic, soulful, and melodic. The first song, "Gute Nacht" (Good Night), demonstrates the close relationship between voice and piano in establishing mood; it's their best work. "Der Linderbaum" (The Lime Tree), where he carved words of love in happier times, is on the edge of tears (the next song is "Wasserflut [Flood]"). "Frühlingstraum" (Dream of Spring) is also bracing.

LINK➤ *Franz Schubert – Schwanengesang (Swan Song) –*
Peter Schreier (tenor), András Schiff (piano)   London 425-612
Just as tenor Schreier and pianist Schiff deserve serious consideration for their Winterreise *(London 436-122), they capture the essence of this collection of Schubert's last songs. Warning: Schubert's songs can lead to serious addiction.*

Piano Sonatas – András Schiff (piano)   London 440-310

Start with Schubert's last piano work, Sonata in B Flat major (D.960), arguably his finest sonata, which shares *Vol. 6* in this series with two lesser-knowns. At first it feels distant, expansive, difficult to grasp; then rigidly upright it proudly approaches, communicating delicate themes with increasing power. It then backs off to a pretty restatement. The variety is staggering; the music pulls the listener into an unreal world. Schiff's intepretations are wholly inviting, not only here but throughout this 6-volume series. Try also *Vol. 2* (440-306) for 1817's peppy Sonata in E minor (D566) and the precision of 1825's D Major Sonata (D850). The whole series is fine.

LINK➤ *Ludwig van Beethoven – Piano Sonatas – Garrick Ohlsson (piano)*
Arabesque 6677

Up-and-coming pianist Ohlsson is especially dramatic on Beethoven's top three sonatas: "Pathetique," "Moonlight," and "Waldstein." The quality of the 1996 recording is impressive. A very different touch from Schiff. Compare with Alfred Brendel's classicist reading on Philips (438-730).

Complete Trios – The Beaux Arts; The Grumiaux Trio   Philips 438-700

The youthful String Trio in B Flat was composed in 1817, probably for performance at home; that's the Grumiaux Trio's contribution to this 2-CD set. The Beaux Arts Trio does the heavy lifting on two chamber masterpieces: Piano Trio in B Flat, and Piano Trio in E Flat. Both are performed by violin, cello, and piano—with the cello providing both soul and humor. Schubert interweaves various melodies and variations through these works, and apart from some dark patches, they're clever, optimistic, intricate, and very entertaining. Schubert is especially facile in his blending of tonal colors, particularly in his writing for violin. This is very special music.

LINK➤ *Songs My Mother Taught Me* – Alberto Delmoni (violin)   *John Marks 1*

What makes these fifteen short romantic pieces for violin and piano so appealing? Two simple answers: sincere performances and fine engineering. Nice range of material, too, from Gluck, Smetana, Valdez, D'Ambrosio, plus standard violin fare from Brahms, Sarasate, Kreisler, and more.

Symphony No. 9 ("The Great") – Vienna Phil. / George Solti
London 430-747

Yes, the "great" in the title seems justified. Nowhere has Schubert so successfully maneuvered melodic concepts so engagingly into a single work, working in theatrics for maximum impact, attending to the tonal variations available from each instrument and section. The lyricism of the second movement, pierced by the advancing strings, is magnificent. The third movement envelopes small sounds from the winds within the massive orchestral force, then calls both parties to conversation, while brilliantly suggesting yet another theme. Contrasting weights have never been ideally balanced. The finale, which builds for 15 minutes, is best of all. Excellent performance and sonics, but Blomstedt's hard-to-find 1992 London recording with the San Francisco Symphony is better still.

LINK➤ *Franz Schubert – Symphonies Nos. 1-6, 8, 9 – Dresden Orch. / Sir Colin Davis*
RCA 62673

In addition to the superb Symphony No. 8 and Symphony No. 9, Davis masters the entire cycle. His 1994 workout competes with another extraordinary 4-CD set by Nikolaus Harnoncourt and Concertgebouw from 1992 (Teldec 91184) and Claudio Abbado's groundbreaking 1989 5-CD package (DG 423-651).

Robert Schumann

Schumann, the son of a successful, well-educated Saxony bookseller, was born in 1810. The bookseller died in 1826, and his none-too-stable son became deeply depressed. Still, he attended the University at Leipzig, toured Europe, and beginning in 1829, studied music with Friedrich Wieck, whose young daughter Clara was a talented pianist. Over the next few years, Schumann started composing, stopped playing piano (due to physical problems with his right hand), suffered from hallucinations, fell in love with teen-aged Clara Wieck, and invoked the wrath of her father. He also became a leading music critic. In 1840, after a legal battle, he won Clara's hand, and composed some of his best music. Clara became a renowned pianist, and later a revered teacher. By the mid-1840s, Schumann's physical and mental problems were affecting his work. An 1854 suicide attempt led to an asylum, where he grew weak and died in 1856.

Carnaval – Artur Rubenstein (piano)   RCA 61264

Carnaval is one of Schumann's earlier piano pieces (from 1835) and easily his most spontaneous. It's a series of 21 brief (1–2 minute) glimpses of carnival time. Bear in mind that all effects are created by a single piano, and that the pianist is the singularly talented Artur Rubenstein. The series begins by trumpeting a fanfare; Pierrot stumbles in, tries to hide his giggling, and stumbles some more. He's followed by the brilliantly colored Harlequin, and then by a waltz. In time we meet Papillons (butterflies), the energetic young men who dance so badly, the co-quette, and others. *Fantasiestücke* and two other pieces complete an excellent early 1960s recording.

LINK► *Robert Schumann – Kreisleriana, Fantasia – Artur Rubenstein (piano)*   **RCA 61264**
Rubenstein was one of the century's greatest Schumann interpreters. Besides this CD, get his 1982 Royal Festival Hall appearance for Kinderszenen *(Scenes from Childhood) (RCA 61414). Murray Perahia's* Kreisleriana, *paired with Sonata No. 1, is also recommended (Sony 62786).*

Davidsbündlertänze, Fantasiestücke – Murray Perahia (piano)
CBS Masterworks 32299

Here are two favorite Schumann piano works, both enthusiastically performed in 1973 by a youthful Murray Perahia. The title of the first work, from 1837, comes from Schumann's fantasy world. As a music critic, Schumann often employed two imaginary characters, Florestan and Eusebius, to argue his points; they were members of the Davidbund (David's League), whose literary ball Schumann celebrates here. Schumann dissects and embroiders the offhanded tribute to Chopin in *Davidsbündlertänze.* Florestan and Eusebius return in *Fantasiestücke* to argue, or contrast, the dreamy versus aggressive sides of Schumann's personality. Or, dispense with the background and simply enjoy a gorgeous performance of romantic piano music.

LINK► *Carnegie Hall Debut Concert (Highlights) – Evgeny Kissin (piano)*   **RCA 61202**
The key work here for purposes of understanding and enjoying Schumann, is the half-hour long Symphonic Etudes, *composed in 1834. Among the finest romantic piano pieces, they were also once the state of the art in keyboard experimentation. Kissin was only 20 at the time of this performance.*

Dictherliebe, Liederkreis –
Matthias Goerne (baritone), Vladimir Ashkenazy (piano)   London 458-265

Although Goerne lacks the acidity of Fischer-Dieskau (Philips 416-352), the young baritone manages at least some of the angst inherent in Heinrich Heine's poetry. The songs in Schumann's popular *Dichterliebe* (1840) are based upon Heine's *Buch der Leider*, published in 1827, as are the songs in his earlier cycle, *Leiderkreis*. Clear, strong, and confident, Goerne is an apt partner for pianist Ashkenazy, whose role is equal to the vocalist in Schumann's songs. There are many hard-core mood swings here, from sentimentality and melancholy to stoicism and masochism. References to love's unremitting sadness and images of death abound. Crystal clear 1997 sound.

LINK➤ *Hugo Wolf – Italienisches Liederbuch –*
Dawn Upshaw (soprano), Olaf Bär (baritone), Helmut Deutsch (piano)   EMI 55618
A hardcore romantic whose personal life was a shambles, Wolf's Italian songbook is his best work. Accompanied by a very talented pianist, these two singers seem to communicate effortlessly. The Barbara Bonney / Häkan Hagegård version on Teldec is also excellent (72301).

Symphony No. 1 ("Spring") – Seattle Sym. / Gerard Schwarz   Delos 3084

Completed in 1833 with the encouragement of Clara, Schumann's First Symphony is appropriately nicknamed "Spring." Mostly, brass is the reason why. Each time the symphony eases into a pastoral string sequence, the brass section leaps in and wakes up the landscape with glorious sunshine. The fanfare in the first movement—one whose theme has become quite famous—leads to clarinets and a festival of lyricism that continues throught the second movement. A similar transition eases the flow to the third movement and its disarming pair of lighthearted dances. Recalling the first movement's freshness and power, the finale presses these ideas to a giant climax. Two equally bracing Schumann pieces complete the CD.

LINK➤ *Robert Schumann – Symphony No. 1 –*
Radio-Sinfonie-Orchester Frankfurt / Eliahu Inbal   Denon 18005
In fact, all four discs in this series are among the finest Schumann symphonic recordings in the catalog. The performances are focused and committed, and the recorded sound is excellent. The others are Symphony No. 2 (Denon 78843); Symphony No. 3 (78822); and Symphony No. 4 (18014).

Cello Concerto – Janos Starker (cello); London Sym. Orch. /
Stanislaw Skrowaczewski   Mercury Living Presence 432-010

One of the all-time great cello records, this 1962 session also yielded Lalo's concerto; the CD is filled out with a 1964 reading of a Saint-Saëns's concerto, with Dorati now conducting the same orchestra. Schumann was supposedly attracted to the cello in the 1850s because his health was poor and his ears could no longer tolerate higher instrument sounds. While the cello seems to carry a certain sadness, Schumann has lost nothing of his lyricism or sentimentality. The result is a generally optimistic, tuneful, emotional composition with outstanding nobility. The second movement is quite sad, but a ray of hope is always present in the distant higher instruments. A spectacular Mercury recording.

LINK➤ *Ernest Bloch – Suite for Cello & Piano – Adolph Baller (piano), Gabor Rejto (cello),*
Michael Davis (violin), Nelson Harper (piano)   Orion (NAXOS) 7813
The award-winning 1919 cello suite visits the depths of despair, and although it resonates with Jewish tradition, the vision here is Indonesia. This is smart, innovative music, very well played; it should be heard. Also excellent is Baal Shem Suite, which is Jewish in origin.

Piano Concerto – Murray Perahia (piano); London Sym. Orch./ Sir Colin Davis   SONY Classical 44899

When Schumann completed this concerto in 1845, he did not follow convention. For example, there was no obvious virtuoso outburst for the pianist. And there was no conflict between piano and orchestra. For these reasons, the work was dismissed as a rhapsody. Ironically, it has become one of Schumann's most popular pieces. Lyricism and graceful balance are this romantic concerto's strong suits; Schumann's clever integration of formal chamber-style orchestration and coherence within variations on a singular idea provide a resilient structure. Within these boundaries, Schumann explores natural influences. With Grieg's Piano Concerto.

LINK➤ *25th Anniversary Edition – Murray Perahia (piano)*   **SONY Classical 63380**
Four logically arranged CDs highlight an exquisite catalog. CD1 presents traditional fare: Scarlatti sonatas, a Schubert impromptu, a Chopin ballad. The adventurous CD2 contains solo work by Bartók, Berg, and Tippet. CD3 features chamber music, and CD4 , Mozart and Chopin concertos.

Piano Quintet, Piano Quartet – Beaux Arts Trio with Samuel Rhodes (violin), Bernard Greenhouse (cello)   Philips 420-791

In a fit of creativity, Schumann conceived and completed the popular Piano Quintet in less than three weeks in 1842. The first movement contains one of Schumann's best melodies, which he states on piano and strings, and then uses as the basis of a conversation between cello and violin. The second movement seems to be an exercise in funereal writing; the playful third movement toys with scales; it's a venture made more intriguing by rapid speed. The virile fourth movement pounds the depths, but also manages delicacy. The Piano Quartet, also from 1842, emphasizes the cello (it was commissioned by an aristocrat who played that instrument). Pleasantly romantic with a slightly dark edge that keeps things interesting.

LINK➤ *Robin Holloway – Fantasy-Pieces on the Heine Liederkreis of Schumann; Serenade in C – Nash Ensemble*   **Hyperion 66930**
Holloway is a leading British composer who was once rescued from a compositional dry patch by obsessing about Schumann. In the midst of Holloway's piece is a song cycle by Schumann (performed by tenor Toby Spence and pianist Ian Brown). Also includes a modern octet called Serenade in C.

Symphony No. 3 ("Rhenisch") – L.A. Phil. Orch. / Giulini   DG 445-502

Paired with a fine recording of Beethoven's Fifth Symphony, Schumann's tribute to Germany's Rhine River more than holds its own. Schumann's unabashed enthusiasm for the region inspired his boldest music—large-scale climaxes celebrating the landscape. Many dances, adaptations of what he saw and heard around the Rhine; musical versions of legends are also presented. Since this symphony wasn't composed to a particular program, it's up to the listener to interpret Schumann's ideas. The one exception occurs with the trombones in the fourth movement that suggest the Renaissance; it's one of several devices used to illustrate the Cologne Cathedral. This fanfare and its aftermath are among Schumann's best-known themes. Composed in 1850.

LINK➤ *R. Schumann – Symphonies Nos. 1-4 – Hanover Band / Roy Goodman*   **RCA 61931**
A 2-CD set filled with period instrument versions of Schumann's symphonies, plus the Overture, Scherzo, and Finale (Op. 52). The combination of scholarship, a vital group of musicians, and a substantial recording, and unexpected instrument sounds and combinations is revelatory.

Dmitri Shostakovich

After years of piano lessons from a talented mother who played professionally, the 13-year-old Shostakovich attended the St. Petersburg Conservatory in 1919. By then, Communists controlled Russia; Shostakovich spent his entire professional life creating under their rule. It was his role, his job, and his duty to serve the state by creating art. Shostakovich's progressive First Symphony made him famous; 14 symphonies followed, along with more than 100 other works, including opera, ballets, and string quartets. Often, his cutting-edge tendencies and creative liberties annoyed Soviet leaders, whose definitions of boundaries were blurry at best. By 1941, Shostakovich was teaching at Moscow's conservatory, but he was made an example in 1948 and lost his job. Film scores kept him busy through the early 1950s. The death of Soviet leader Josef Stalin allowed considerably more freedom within certain political realities. The next two decades were especially productive for Shostakovich. He died in Moscow in 1975.

Symphony Nos. 1 & 7 "Leningrad" –
Chicago Sym. Orch. / Leonard Bernstein
Deutsche Grammophon 427-632

Written when he was 20, Shostakovich's first symphony magnificently contrasts small songs with eruptions of orchestral power. It's a complex work, with ideas that knit together brilliantly , and climaxing in a huge finale. The Seventh Symphony, composed by Shostakovich shortly after his voluntary service as a firefighter during 1941's German siege of Leningrad opens as the city's happiness is wrecked by a vivid depiction of war: crashing percussion, endless military marches, a xylophone punctuating the horror, a lone bassoon eulogizing heroes. The second movement filters happiness though melancholy; the third fills the heart with nature and wonder, perhaps looking for reason before leading to the final movement's anger, sorrow, and look toward the future.

LINK▶ *Dmitri Shostakovich – Symphonies Nos. 1 & 6 –*
Royal Phil. Orch. / Vladimir Ashkenazy   *London 425-609*
Superb performance of the First Symphony, emphasizing the youthful exuberance and creative flow. The Sixth Symphony is one of Shostakovich's most imaginative, with unusual and unexpected touches (though the brooding can become a bit much) Ashkenazy's entire series is spectacular.

Lady Macbeth of Mtsensk –
Galina Vishnevskaya, Nicolai Gedda, others;
London Phil. Orch. / M. Rostropovich   EMI 49925

Plenty of themes reside under the surface of this unforgiving love story, and careful listening uncovers themes that mock individual characters' weaknesses and circumstances. The despondent center of this saga is Katerina, an unfaithful wife who poisons her father-in-law and murders her husband. Her new love, Sergei, marches with her to a Siberian prison; along the way, Katerina kills herself and Sergei's new lover, Sonyetka. Shostakovich's frenetic, edgy score oozes with sex (one magazine called it "pornophony") and violence brought about by sheer boredom, personal frustration, and police corruption. Completed in 1934, the opera was an instant hit, but Stalin's negative reaction ultimately resulted in the work's 27-year disappearance.

LINK➤ *Mikhail Glinka – Ruslan and Lyudmila –*
Soloists; Kirov Theater Orch. **& Chorus / Valery Gergiev** **Philips 446-746**
Another in the exciting series of lesser-known Russian operas revived by Gergiev. His treatment of the overture—not too fast but vivid and exhilirating—sets the course for an opera that's at once distinctly Russian and yet draws heavily on Italian influences. A tad rigid, but well sung.

Symphony No. 5 – Scottish Nat. Orch. / Neeme Järvi   Chandos 8650

Among many outstanding recordings, Järvi's spirited 1988 rendition of Shostakovich's Fifth Symphony is recommended for its balanced attentiveness to beauty and tension and for its engineering excellence. In his popular 1937 symphony, Shostakovich builds early themes mainly with strings, adding a throbbing sensation for emphasis. Sometimes, he'll wax lyrically; inevitably, prettiness yields to nervous winds, growling horns, or a megalomaniacal march. Then peace is presented by muted strings. The monoliths hover over the folk dancers in the second movement: Soviet machinery surrounds a shadow's suggestion of old-style normality. Strings carry the third movement's cloudlike drift. The fourth movement's struggle resolves in celebratory triumph, but for whom? The creative Shostakovich, or the Soviet system?

LINK➤ *Mikis Theodorakis – Sinfonie No. 3 –*
Orchester der Komischen Oper Berlin / Heinz Rögner **Berlin Classics 1128**
An absolutely stunning emotional release from one of the century's finest composers. This gargantuan symphony, from 1981, combines present and past, drums and chimes and stabbing choral energy, and ultimately studies the meaning of death. The performance and recording are world class. His Liturgie No. 2 completes the 2-CD set.

Complete String Quartets (1-15) – Shostakovich Quartet   Olympia 5009

Available in a 5-CD box or as individual CDs (531 through 535), these string quartets are among the finest music in Shostakovich's extensive catalog. Stately, expressive, and extremely personal, they're masterfully performed by one of Russia's top chamber ensembles. String Quartet No. 1, from 1938, is plucky and optimistic, a springtime work that pleasantly meanders as the composer learns a new form. String Quartet No. 2, from 1944, is entirely different— dissonant, confident, and weighty. Lower ranges are pressurized, higher ones dance as if to escape. By the third movement, the effect is one of bewilderment; by the fourth, it's difficult not to be completely entranced by the Russian sorrow so plainly stated by these eloquent musicians. The slow draw of cello and the thin, high sound of a single violin, the development of a nostalgic melody with the slighest remnant of lifeblood remaining—these are musical images for the ages. It's no wonder Shostakovich came to love this musical format. Moving ahead some years, he completed String Quartet No. 8 in three days in 1960 after immersion in the wartime devastation of Dresden's art treasures. Shostakovich dedicated the composition "to the memory of the victims of fascism and war," and quotes from his own First Symphony before a slashing attack against oppressors. Later in the 1960s, Shostakovich's quartets signified death and despair, but 1968's Quartet No. 12 bravely applies a twelve-tone system, ignores melodic development, and embraces heroics, not gloom. Extraordinary music!

LINK➤ *Dmitri Kabalevsky – Cello Concertos Nos. 1, 2 –*
Alexander Rudin (cello); Moscow Sym. Orch. / Igor Golovschin **NAXOS 8.553788**
Composed in 1948 and 1964, there's an sadness about this pair of works; imagination is trying to emerge from under impossible circumstances. Even the happy moments are subdued. Kabalevsky was Shostakovich's very talented contemporary. This disc provides a glimpse of what might have been.

Classical CD Listener's Guide

Violin Concerto No. 1 – Maxim Vengerov (violin); London Sym. Orch. / Mstislav Rostropovich — Teldec 922256

With the threat of horrifying retribution, the ruthless Communist leader Andrei Zhdanov publicly demanded apologies from Shostakovich and others for "crimes" they commited against the Soviet people by composing modern music. Shostakovich responded with this subversive concerto, which he held back for seven years, until 1955. The first movement is dangerous because it expresses individual emotions (as opposed to music for the masses); it's a nocturne, music of a dark time. It also includes some encoded musical messages. The second movement's urban dance is on the cynical side; the third's despondent violin solo centers the work. The fourth movement burlesques Zhadnov and all he represents. Prokofiev's 1917 Violin Concerto, from a simpler time, completes the disc.

LINK➤ *Dmitri Shostakovich – Violin Concertos Nos. 1 & 2 –*
Lydia Mordkovitch (violin); Scottish Nat. Orch. / Neeme Järvi — *Chandos 8820*
Shostakovich wrote the concerto for David Oistrakh, who taught his student Lydia Mordkovitch much of what she knows. Her intensity is phenomenal, and she pulls the listener in. Also, don't miss Shostakovich's cello concertos; Truls Mørk's version sounds fine (Virgin 45145).

24 Preludes and Fugues – Tatiana Nikolayeva (piano) — Hyperion 664441/3

After studying and admiring Bach's *The Well-Tempered Clavier*, Shostakovich composed a prelude and a fugue in each key. This 3-CD set, from 1991, is performed by the Russian pianist Tatiana Nikolayeva; Shostakovich wrote these pieces for her during the winter of 1950–51. With this modern music, key decisions are just a launchpad. The liner notes provide ample analysis of each prelude-fugue pair. Fugue No. 12, associated with G sharp minor, for example, fills the head with complicated ideas, then soothes the intellect in a few closing phrases. Sixteenth-notes (semiquavers) flood Prelude 21 in B flat major, setting up a pairing that sometimes drifts from tonality and regular rhythms. Stinging, intellectual music.

LINK➤ *The Piano Album – Stephen Hough (piano)* — *Virgin 59509*
Hough is one of the finest pianists of his generation, adventurous, but grounded. There's no shortage of keyboard pyrotechnics here (notably on pieces by Rosenthal and Moszkowski), but the real joy is in discovering works by MacDowell, Quilter, Woodforde-Finden, and Levitzki.

Symphony No. 10 – Helsinki Phil. / James DePreist — Delos 3089

Completed in 1953 just after Stalin's death, Shostakovich painted the Soviet ruler's musical portrait. Officials fretted over issues of optimism and pessimism. The first movement gradually accumulates power, beginning with dreadful seriousness, nurturing darkness. A lone clarinet, soon joined by a few violins, defines a hollow version of beauty. Disturbing, yet heroic in its own way, the movement gains power and climaxes, and then settles in for the long haul with a more reflective (and no less devastating) mood. Coarse fury, angry edges, and horrifying colors define the anxious second movement; death's dance dominates the third, and themes collide in the fourth. Stalin's force loses. Shostakovich is ecstatic. A fabulous 1990 recording.

LINK➤ *Dmitri Shostakovich – Symphony No. 11 (The Year 1905) –*
Helsinki Phil. / James DePreist — *Delos 3080*
Contrary to the title, Shostakovich probably didn't write this 1957 symphony to celebrate the October Revolution's 40th birthday. Instead, he subversively portrayed contemporary Russia's crushing blows to smother Hungary. The eerie quiet of the entire first movement is terrifying.

Jean Sibelius

Johan Sibelius was the son of an army doctor who died about two years after the composer's birth in 1865. He later changed his name to the French-sounding Jean. The family lived in Hämeenlina, in southern Finland; Sibelius was raised by his mother and grandmother. After considering a law career, Sibelius opted to study music in Helsinki, Berlin, and Vienna with progressively more impressive teachers. His 1891 return to Finland was soon followed by the crowd-pleasing *Kullervo* Symphony; the piece stirred nationalist pride in a country recently freed from Russian rule. Sibelius studied Finnish mythology and produced works for his countrymen through the support of a government grant. Still, there were money problems and health problems, too (not helped by Sibelius's love of alcohol and cigars). World War I and a Finnish civil war complicated his life, but Sibelius continued composing until 1929, when he retired. He died in 1951 of a cerebral hemorrhage.

Finlandia, The Swan of Tuonela, Valse Triste, Tapiola –
Berlin Phil. / Herbert von Karajan   **Deutsche Grammophon 413-755**
Breathing life and energy into 1893's *The Swan of Tuonela*, Karajan shines up the black swan and Gerhard Stempnik's cor anglais (English horn) solo fairly glows with mythological magic. This 1984 recording also captures Sibelius's unintended anthem in its patriotic splendor; it is among the best renditions of 1900's *Finlandia* on record. Extremely popular for a century, *Finlandia* shows Sibelius's awesome power to whip up emotions through orchestral color. The fantasy world also provides raw material for the composer's final work, 1926's *Tapiola*, a dank, gloomy setting for sprites and other forest legends who obey the composer's desire for moderation. Engineering brings out the best.

LINK► *Sibelius–Lemminkäinen Legends, Tapiola–Helsinki PO/ L. Segerstam*   **Ondine 852**
The Swan of Tuonela *was one of four movements in a symphonic poem presented here in its complete form. It's slow going. Focus on Sibelius's gorgeous palette of hues and subtle shadings. This material is, of course, standard repertoire for a leading Finnish orchestra.*

Symphonies Nos. 2 & 6 –
London Sym. Orch. / Sir Colin Davis   **RCA 68183**

Sibelius's greatest impact has been through his symphonies. The Second Symphony, from 1902, establishes its themes in fragments. It seems restless. A wind rarely expresses a phrase without the violins vibrating in the background, anxiously zigging into the spotlight. Hope, perhaps represented by the horns, stands bravely against the gusts of violin chaos. Independence emerges as the finale's central idea, expressed through a wonderfully patriotic song. Sibelius fills the heart with nobility and bravery. The Sixth Symphony, from 1923, differs. It's serene, patient, and filled with pretty melodies and wonder. Sibelius's orchestrations can be subtle, but Davis is extremely attentive to details; a fine stereo system can really bring them to life.

LINK► *Jean Sibelius – Sym. Nos. 1 & 4 – London Sym. Orch. / Sir Colin Davis*   **RCA 68163**
Sibelius's First Symphony, from 1899, establishes and broadens its themes in refreshing ways, a sort of post-Tchaikovsky approach to composition. The Fourth is a dark struggle that reflects the recurrence of Sibelius's cancer; it's a fear-struck psychological study. Start with the others, then buy this one.

Violin Concerto –
Leonidas Kavakos (violin), Lahti Sym. Orch. / Osmo Vänskä   BIS 500 & 581

Most recordings of this 1905 virtuoso piece are stately and boring; they get the notes right, but they're clueless about its soul. Kavakos carries the weight of the Finnish world on each of those tiny strings and coaxes the spirit out of Sibelius's lyrical first movement. And when Vänskä's orchestra comes in for emphasis, it's pure thunder—nothing is held back. The cystal-clear recording becomes an enormous asset in the second movement when those lower strains sound and Kavakos draws his lines just a little longer to create a dreamland. The third movement's counterweighted fiddling and dark orchestration are breathtaking. An earlier version, plus *The Tempest*, complete this low-priced 2-CD set.

LINK➤ *Karl Goldmark – Violin Concerto No. 1 –*
Nai-Yuan Hu (violin); Seattle Sym. Orch. / Gerard Schwarz   _Delos 3156_
Paired with Bruch's Violin Concerto No. 2, and sold under the title Romantic Violin Concertos, *the Austro-Hungarian's first violin concerto is a beautiful, lyrical work; it's one of many pieces that Schwarz has unearthed and displayed with great heart.*

Symphonies Nos. 3 & 5 – London Sym. Orch. / Sir Colin Davis   RCA 61963

The form and substance of Sibelius's creativity reach a peak with the 1919 revamped version of his Fifth Symphony. Sibelius erased traditional lines between movements, stated and developed his themes very clearly, and weaned himself away from icy Russian music and Finnish flag waving to create something exciting and new. The best part of Symphony No. 5 is the finale, which is marked by frenzied strings, earnest winds and horns, breezy orchestration, and a knockout use of pauses that end the affair in most unexpected way. The often-forgotten Third Symphony, from 1907, is majestic. The strings carry several handsome themes, and the winds provide piquant accents. Realistic sonics and a spirited performance throughout.

LINK➤ *Sibelius – Symphony No. 5, En Saga – Lahti Sym. Orch. / Osmo Vänskä   BIS 800*
An earlier (1915) version of the famous Fifth Symphony provides insight into Sibelius's formative ideas. En Saga is also exposed through an earlier (1892) version. Thanks to a superlative performance and a recording to match, neither work feels unsatisfying.

Symphony No. 7, Kullervo Symphony, other works –
London Sym. Orch. / Sir Colin Davis   RCA 68312

A trombone pierces through a lush orchestra, not once but several times, carrying the only melodic theme in this one-movement symphony. These moments are chilling and heroic; mostly, this 1924 work is built on motives, variations, and broadly painted orchestral ideas that blend without thematic delineation. Yet, this is a bracing, intriguing sonic landscape. It bears comparison with the several earlier works included on this 2-CD set, certainly 1905's revision of *En Saga*, a classic Sibelius tone poem, and the *Kullervo* Symphony, which pulled the nationalistic heartstrings of an 1892 Helsinki audience by reflecting Finland's struggle for identity. For a satisfying experience, patient listening and a good stereo system make the difference.

LINK➤ *Allan Pettersson – Symphonies Nos. 3 & 4 –*
Rundfunk-Sinfonieorchester Saarbrücken / Alun Francis   _CPO 999-223_
Petterson was a relentlessly angry Swedish composer whose dark, aggressive (and longish) symphonic psychotherapy sessions may not be for everyone. At his best, Pettersson communicates very effectively through an updated version of romantic composition.

Bedrich Smetana

From the time of his birth in 1824 until 1861, Smetana's Bohemian homeland was part of an oppressive Austrian empire. A brewer's son, he showed an early aptitude for music, but his subsequent progress was slow. He took lessons in Prague, but acting on the advice of Franz Liszt, in 1856, he moved to Götheberg, Sweden, where he became a popular teacher and found the time and inspiration to compose his first symphony. By 1861, Prague was under the control of Austria, so Smetana returned; he soon became involved in a growing arts community. By 1863, he was musical director of the new Prague Provisional Theater and the author of the first opera to make use of Bohemian heritage and culture. Nationalistic music became Smetana's strong suit, and his impact grew through the 1870s. Sadly, the effects of syphilis ravaged his mind and body; Smetana died in a Prague asylum in 1884.

Má Vlast – Czech Phil. Orch. / Rafael Kubelík   Supraphon 1208

Recorded in celebration of Czech independence in 1990, this spirited rendition of a beloved national work also represents the return of Kubelík to his home country. The music is sophisticated and brilliant—a cycle of symphonic poems dedicated to the life and history of Bohemia. The first, "Vysehrad," recalls a glorious old kingdom and castle; harps set the elegiac scene, horns and thick strings suggest nobility. "Vltava," also known as "Die Moldau," uses the Bohemian river as a path through the nation's culture; its programmatic structure is ideal for music students. The other four poems depict battle successes and the warm feeling of the homeland. Recording is adequate.

LINK▶ *Zdenék Fibich – Symphony No. 1 – Detroit Sym. Orch. / Neeme Järvi   Chandos 9230*
Paired with a good performance of two Má Vlast excerpts, the quality of Järvi's conducting brings Fibich's symphony to life. Fibich's strong reliance upon Bohemian ideas makes his music distinctly Czech in character. Try also Symphonies Nos. 2 and 3, also by Järvi (Chandos 9328).

The Bartered Bride – Gabriela Benacková, Peter Dvorsky, Richard Novák; Czech Phil. Chorus & Orch. / Zednek Kosler   Supraphon 3511

After adjusting the original structure of his second opera, Smetana found the proper format for this lighthearted opera in 1870, and it's been popular ever since. This 3-CD set, recorded in late 1980 and early 1981, is an entertaining, well-performed version by an attentive conductor and orchestra. As the story goes, Marenka and Jenik love one another, but Marenka's father insists that she marry Vasek instead. Complications include the interference of a marriage broker and a circus performer who convinces Vasek to dress in a bear's costume. Smetana's music is consistently cheerful and easy to enjoy, the voices are good, and the melodies are winning. A very pleasant time.

LINK▶ *Sigmund Romberg – The Student Prince –*
Norman Bailey, Marilyn Hill Smith, others; Phil. Orch. / John Own Edwards   TER 1172
Completed in 1924, Romberg's operetta became one of the most popular Broadway shows of the decade. Based on an 1860s operetta called Alt Heidelberg, *it's the story of prince who falls love in his younger days, then assumes the crown and searches for past glory.*

William Grant Still

One of America's finest classical composers, Still was born in Woodville, Mississippi in 1895. He was a son of mixed blood: black, Spanish, Cherokee, Scottish, and Irish. Still grew up in Little Rock, AR, listening to his grandmother sing and his stepfather play operas on the phonograph. He started violin lessons, took music seriously, and attended Wilberforce University, where he studied medicine, conducted the college band, and performed in a string quartet. After a stint in Memphis with W.C. Handy, Still studied at Oberlin Conservatory. By 1921, at age 26, Still was in NYC, playing oboe in the pit band for Noble Sissle and Eubie Blake's *Shuffle Along*. He then studied with George Chadwick and Edgar Varèse, wrote arrangements for Paul Whiteman, counseled George Gershwin, and supervised music for the new CBS and NBC radio networks. Still later composed for movies and television. He died in 1978.

Sym. No. 1 ("Afro-American") – Detroit SO / Neeme Järvi   Chandos 9154

Congratulations to Chandos for its elegant full-scale treatment of Still's First Symphony. Completed in 1930, it's a grand combination of traditional European romance and distinctively American sounds, complete with banjo, folk tunes, and a jazzy brass and winds. Still deftly works the street-smart jazz themes into a series of variations, which he develops in a typically classical way. His elegant touch and knack for transforming American life into music leave Ives and Gershwin in the dust. This was also the first symphony composed by a black American to be performed by a major orchestra (kudos to leader Howard Hanson and the Rochester Philharmonic). A pleasant Duke Ellington classical suite completes the CD.

LINK▶ *American Voices: The African-American Composer's Project –*
Carmen Lundy (vocals); Akron Sym. Orch. / Alan Balter   **Telarc 80409**
A wonderful CD filled with music that should be better known. Billy Childs opens with a song cycle about being an African-American. David Baker's Jazz Suite explores three African-American dances; William C. Banfield salutes Miles Davis, Duke Ellington, and Sarah Vaughan. A personal favorite.

Symphony No. 2 ("Song of a New Race") –
Detroit Sym. Orch. / Neeme Järvi   Chandos 9226

Sadly, Chandos stopped after just two Still symphonies. (He wrote three more that remain unrecorded.) Leopold Stokowski debuted this symphony in 1937 with the Philadelphia Orchestra. Still's Second Symphony is considerably more sophisticated than his first, without the gimmickry of the vernacular (except in one movement, and even then it's mild). Still gracefully develops his musical concepts into some beautiful extended themes, portrays each one with drama suitable for a movie soundtrack, and keeps moving so that the audience is never waiting long for something special. The distinguished Tuskegee Institute choirmaster William Levi Dawson contributes *Negro Folk Symphony* (1930), built from spirituals. It's excellent. The CD ends with Ellington's evocative *Harlem*.

LINK▶ *Virgil Thompson – Four Saints in Three Acts –*
Betty Allen, Gwendolyn Bradley, others; Orch. of Our Time / Joel Thome   Nonesuch 79035
The first collaboration between U.S. composer (and noted music critic) Thompson and writer Gertrude Stein compares the creative process to saintliness, with younger talents guided by the old. It's surprisingly effective, with a score that blends sacred feelings with an emerging American classical voice. Composed in 1928.

Get on Board – Sierra Winds   Cambria 1083

These pieces were mostly composed in the 1960s for a series of museum concerts. This magnificent disc begins with five miniatures for oboe, flute, and piano. All are refined, but careful listening reveals connections to Mexican ballads, Negro spirituals, and even Inca music. Several of Still's folk suites were based entirely on Indian music from both American continents. "Quit dat Fool'nish" is a conversation between Still (represented by his piano) and his dog Shep (a honking alto sax); the pair drove across the U.S. together in 1934. "Summerland," Still's lighter-than-air flute and piano piece, exquisitely synthesizes—and sanitizes—America's melting pot. "Get on Board" represents both the Underground Railroad and the heavenly road.

LINK➤ *William Grant Still – Summerland –*
Alexa Still (flute), Susan DeWitt Smith (piano); New Zealand String Quartet   Koch 7192
Alexa Still (no relation) does an even better job with "Summerland," and the quality of this recording is marginally better than the Cambria release. There's no reason to choose: with one complete Folk Suite and more fine chamber music, both releases belong in every library.

Works by W.G. Still – Videmus   New World 80399

Boston's Videmus chamber ensemble promotes minority composers, including women. They bring an earnest seriousness to Still's chamber music. *Suite for Violin and Piano* is given a suitably formal setting, yet the music retains its heart and energy. Similarly, baritone Robert Honeysucker performs Still's songs (settings of Black poetry) so they compare favorably to works by Barber and Copland; inevitably, Still selects one humorous poem and composes an appropriately snappy melody for Paul Laurence Dunbar's "Parted." 1956's *Ennaga* is a smiling celebration inspired by what little Still knew of African music. A piano and strings simulate an African harp.

LINK➤ *Aaron Copland – Old American Songs, other works –*
Willard White (vocals); Graeme McNaught (piano)   Chandos 8960
Bass vocalist White presents Copland's songs with the authority they require in order to be effective. Best is "Simple Gifts," which appears as part of Appalachian Spring. *Ten American spirituals and three Caribbean folk songs illustrate Copland's influences. Very good work.*

Africa: Piano Music of William Grant Still – D. Oldham   Koch 7084

On this 1991 CD and on his 1995 *Piano Music* album (Altarus 9013), pianist Denver Oldham carries the torch for Still's impressive—and sadly obscure—keyboard compositions. *Blues from "Lenox Avenue"* comes from a 1936 ballet score (Still's collaboration with Verna Arvey, who became his wife). Still combines a certain mysticism (long an aspect of his spirituality) with love for Arvey on 1939's *Seven Traceries*, whose individual titles describe their musical qualities: "Cloud Cradles," "Mystic Pool," "Woven Silver," and so on. Africa, from 1928, was one of Still's first serious works to gain notice; it was originally scored for orchestra. *Summerland* and a setting of Stephen Foster's "Swanee River" are also highlights.

LINK➤ *Charles Tomlinson Griffes – Collected Works for Piano –*
Denver Oldham (piano)   New World 80310
Although it comes last on the CD, Griffes's Sonata is probably his finest piece, a serious composition with roots somewhere between Liszt, Chopin, and the U.S. circa 1917. Includes many carefully crafted miniatures often evoking nature, such as "The Lake at Evening," and "Nightfall."

Johann Strauss II

Johann Strauss, who lived from 1804 until 1849, learned about music from traveling musicians who visited his father's inn outside Vienna, Austria. He learned to play the violin and found a job with a local orchestra as a viola player; there he befriended violinist Josef Lanier. Together, the pair formed their own orchestra, which became two successful orchestras. Johann had 11 children: 6 were with his wife, Anna, and 5 others were with a mistress. Strauss's son Johann II started his own orchestra in 1844 and competed directly with his father and Lanier. After the elder Strauss died of scarlet fever, his son took over the orchestra; Johann Strauss II then ran a European dynasty consisting of six orchestras. Dubbed the "Waltz King," he earned a fortune from them and through touring. By 1871, Johann II focused on composing and became interested in the operetta form. For many, "Johann the Younger" represented a glorious, carefree age.

Die Fledermaus (The Bat) — Hermann Prey, Julia Varady, Lucia Popp, others; Bayesrisches Staatsorchester / Carlos Kleiber　Deutsche Grammophon 415-646

With its lighthearted melodies, sparkling waltzes, and sharp humor, *Die Fledermaus* is an operetta, blending opera and musical comedy. Strauss is so skillful that the structure and quality of his operetta outshines most operas. Deutsche Grammophon's engineers did some of their best work on this 1975 session. The 2-CD set is talky, with a surprising amount of spoken dialogue (and lots of laughing). The plot wickedly satirizes the aristocracy; Prince Orlovsky is one of several cleverly drawn characters. There are plenty of good songs, including the "Donner and Blitzen" (Thunder and Lighting) polka, and the champagne toast "Im Feuerstrom der Reben" (In the Grape's Fiery Stream). A silly, robust good time.

LINK► *Vienna–Jerry Hadley (tenor); Munich Radio Orch. / Richard Bonynge　RCA 68258*
Hadley gets the spirit of Vienna right on this engaging recital. He spends about a third following the lead of Richard Tauber (famous for his leads in Lehár's operettas), but the most fun is in discovering lesser knowns, like Kálmán and Fall.

Vienna — Chicago Sym. Orch. / Fritz Reiner　RCA 68160

For today's generation, a waltz might be more closely associated with a carousel than a formal Viennese dance. Certainly, there's a feeling of spinning, horses pumping up and down, and elaborate color schemes deep inside this music. And there are smiles. As many times as you've heard "On the Beautiful Blue Danube" or tunes in works you might not know by name, such as "Emperor Waltz," "Roses from the South," or "Vienna Blood," it's a sunshine day with lilting string sections, and the tightest and loudest drums you've ever heard—all presented for maximum visceral impact. Strauss's touches are often brilliant. And his father's use of bird sounds in "Village Swallows" is also splendid.

LINK► *Johann Strauss II – Overtures, Waltzes and Polkas –*
Vienna Phil. / Herbert von Karajan　　　　　　　　　　　　　　　EMI 66395
With the similar EMI 66396, a collection of old recordings (1946–49) with thin sound and elegant performances. Where Reiner goes for the gusto, Karajan applies a thinner, more artful approach. For even more fun, try Arthur Fiedler's Strauss Family Waltzes *(RCA 61688).*

Richard Strauss

A perversely difficult man, Richard Strauss was the son of Franz Strauss, Munich's finest horn player. (His father performed solos in many of Wagner's operas, but hated the German composer.) The younger Strauss was born in 1864, quickly learned several instruments, and became a prolific composer while a teenager. By 1885, he had established himself as a conductor in Meiningen, and within a short time became the Munich Opera's leader. Through the 1890s, Strauss was one of Germany's most powerful musical personalities; he aggressively experimented with newer musical forms, furthering ideas ignited by Wagner. Strauss became rich and built a villa outside Munich; still, he scrambled for money. Despite his polished veneer, many considered Strauss mean and petty. During WW II, Strauss served the Nazi cause through his music; he forced Jewish music out and substituted for other conductors who refused to work for the Nazis. Strauss did it for the money. Death came in 1949.

Kempe Conducts Richard Strauss 1 –
Staatskapelle Dresden / Rudolf Kempe   EMI 64342

Probably the best way to experience Richard Strauss is by investing in EMI's trio of 3-CD boxed sets performed by Rudolf Kempe and the Staatskapelle Dresden. The performances are uniformly excellent, and they sound terrific. Any doubts should be erased by 1976's Horn Concerto No. 1, dominated by Peter Damm's French horn, with a very spirited orchestral partner. It's quite straightforward, joyful, uncluttered, youthful work— Strauss was 19 when he wrote it. Compare it to the weary and subtle Horn Concerto No. 2 (composed when Strauss was 78) with its occasional pleasures and beautiful sonorities. The *Duet Concertino*, created five years later in a chamber format, exploits Strauss's ear, his gift for contrasting colors. Clarinet and bassoon offer an engaging fairy-tale view of a princess and a bear (inspired by a Hans Christian Andersen story). The circuslike show business panache of *Burleske* is an attitude that fully blossoms in *Till Eulenspiegel's Merry Pranks*, which became Mickey Mouse's centerpiece, with brooms and a whole lot of water, in Disney's *Fantasia*. Three years later, the self-absorbed Strauss completed *Ein Heldenleben* (The Hero's Life), an egomaniacal work that requires an enormous orchestra to express its boundless romance. And in fact, it is glorious. For over 40 minutes, Strauss tells the philosophical story of his own importance, but he also fully develops uplifting themes, battles against the awkward woodwind squawking of the critics, fights every conceivable enemy, and recaps his best works as an ultimate expression of peace.

LINK▶ *Richard Strauss – The Two Horn Concertos –*
Dennis Brain (horn), Philharmonia Sym. Orch. / Wolfgang Sawallisch   *EMI 47834*
A classic 1956 recording, brought to life through digital technology, offers a very intriguing view of the 1942 concerto. It's mono, but that doesn't matter here. What does matter is Brain's rather brilliant illumination of Strauss's ideas and his politely careful ease of expression.

Kempe Conducts Richard Strauss 2 –
Staatskapelle Dresden / Rudolf Kempe   EMI 64346

The bombastic *Sinfonia Domestica* was intended to illustrate the relative calm of life at the Strauss home. The overall impression: it's warm and cozy, but nobody sits still for very long. There are plenty of handsome melodies, dramatic writing, and interesting themes, but ultimately it feels like incidental music, not a symphony. It's unlikely that anyone but serious collectors would go out of their way to purchase Strauss's Violin Concerto (written when Strauss was a teenager). One of the best available versions of *Also Sprach Zarathustra* begins CD2 (presented without track breaks). It's followed by 1889's *Tod und Verklärung* (Death and Transfiguration), which is probably Strauss's most remarkable accomplishment because it was created entirely from his own head and heart and not from a poem or other existing work. Strauss portrays a dying man, first through an erratic heartbeat, then with the warmer colors of life's last few breaths, followed by the stabbing seriousness of death itself, the rush of childhood memories, the fight to hang on, and the ultimate peace and beauty available only in the afterlife. The sweep of orchestral emotion, the grandeur of the forces brought to bear on the poor invalid, Strauss's stunning manipulation of ordinary instruments to create a most extraordinary feeling—these are the marks of genius. The recording is absolutely fantastic. After this, the presentation of several waltzes from *Der Rosenkavalier* is an enormous relief, and the "Dance of the Seven Veils" from *Salome* is a familiar friend. Lesser-known works fill CD3.

LINK▶ *Richard Strauss – Also Sprach Zarathustra, Tod und Verklärung –*
Vienna Phil. / André Previn   **Telarc 80167**

World-class recording, room-shaking sonics, and very sensitive playing from one of the best orchestras on the planet. If you're out for just one Strauss, this would be the ideal choice. Quickly, you'll realize that the sonics matter less than the excellent interpretive details.

Kempe Conducts Richard Strauss 3 –
Staatskapelle Dresden / Rudolf Kempe   EMI 64350

Contemporary thinking cannot reconcile the reasons behind *Metamorphosen*, a piece Strauss composed to soothe his upset over such World War II casualties as the Munich Court Theater, where *Die Meistersinger* debuted and his father used to play horn. Strauss cooperated with and tolerated the Nazis, then expressed despair over the destruction they left behind. If you can bear *Metamorphosen*, you'll find an articulate, heartfelt elegy, quite well played here. The *Alpine Symphony* is a musical travelogue of the Alps that uses the voluptous measure of a symphony orchestra to describe the majestic heights, the tiny villages, the sunshine and clouds, the frigid temperatures, and the wonder. Kempe is at his celebratory best here. It's quite a workout for any stereo system and really exposes the quality of woofers and sub-woofers in the best systems. *Aus Italien*, which is not as well known, comes from 24 years earlier, and also uses the orchestra to narrate a travel essay. Strauss is quite expansive, but it all comes together with the folksy Neapolitan frenzy of "funiculi-funicula" in the fourth movement. Paul Tortelier is the cellist on an outstanding rendition of *Don Quixote*. Most of Strauss requires careful listening—he does not play well as background music—and here, the attentive listener is rewarded with striking characterizations artfully drawn by individual and paired instrumentalists. The warmth and coherence of this particular recording is without equal. Several other pieces complete this 3-CD set, including *Dance Suite* from pieces by François Couperin and a Macbeth tone poem.

LINK➤ *Richard Strauss – Ein Alpensinfonie –*
Berlin Phil. / Herbert von Karajan   **Deutsche Grammophon 439-017**
One of Karajan's great orchestral showpieces, captured in 1981 and now considered a classic in Deutsche Grammophon's catalog. Plenty of ominous darkness, blazing sunlight, big thinking, and execution. This is about power, with the occasional nod to the graces.

Also Sprach Zarathustra, Don Juan –
Staatskapelle Dresden / Herbert Blomstedt   Denon 2259
Also Sprach Zarathustra is an intelligent exploration of themes expressed by the philosopher Nietzsche, based upon Zoroaster's centuries-old religious teachings. After the famous dawning, which became a quest for knowledge in *2001: A Space Odyssey*, Strauss explores the great longing to become self-reliant, free from superstition; other passages consider science's power, the connection between passion and virtue, and free will. It's cutting-edge thinking about mankind and progress, circa 1896. *Don Juan*, from 1888, Strauss's first tone poem, is essentially a one-movement romantic symphony. A proud fanfare introduces the legendary lover, and his theme periodically returns; it's one of several recurring melodies suggesting sexual climaxes, female loveliness, and courtship.

LINK➤ *Richard Strauss in High Fidelity: Also Sprach Zarathustra, Ein Heldenleben –*
Chicago Sym. Orch. / Fritz Reiner   **RCA 61494**
Definitive proof that Also Sprach Zarathustra *was not composed for a 1960s science fiction movie. And a mighty, heroic, well-considered version this is, too. A magnificent Living Stereo recording from 1954, frequently superior to current digital work. Excellent Heldenleben, also.*

Don Quixote –
Jacqueline duPré (cello) with New Phil. Orch. / Sir Adrian Boult   EMI 55528
Cellist DuPre's 1969 rendition of our hero's cello theme fits into Boult's well-told musical story. Ten variations describe the various adventures of Don Quixote, Sancho Panza, Dulcinea, and other souls in Cervantes's tale. (The music makes more sense with detailed notes, available from any public library.) Quixote's evil "giant" provides the orchestra with a tongue-in-cheek drama in "The Adventure with Windmills." Quixote's theme incorporates Dulcinea's music in "The Knight's Vigil," as he dreams of rescuing his fair maiden. In "The Meeting with Dulcinea," Quixote's constant theme is strained, for he is annoyed at Panza. The frightened stable girl identified as Dulcinea comes to life as an oboe theme. With Lalo's Cello Concerto.

LINK➤ *Alexander Zemlinsky – Die Seejungfrau (The Little Mermaid) –*
Cologne Gürzenich Orch./ James Conlon   **EMI 5515**
Based on Hans Christian Andersen's heroine, Die Seejungfrau *is a lovely example of Zemlinsky's fine handiwork. It's a tone poem that may recall some aspects of Mahler, but the gorgeous sounds made by the woodwinds are all his own. Zemlinsky escaped the Nazis, but died in the U.S. in 1942.*

Salome – Cheryl Studer, others, Orchester der Deutschen Oper Berlin /
Giuseppe Sinopoli   Deutsche Grammophon 431-810
Decadent, erotic, and shocking even by modern standards, Strauss's 1905 reworking of Oscar Wilde's story provides soprano Studer with her finest showcase. John the Baptist is arrested by King Herod, who lusts for the 16-year-old Salome, the daughter of his brother's wife. Salome is attracted to John the Baptist, who is imprisoned (Herod's not wild about John's promise of

salvation and talk of the Messiah). Lust wins out: when Salome agrees to do the "Dance of the Seven Veils," Herod promises her whatever she wants. She asks for John's head—on a platter. Salome's big number has to do with making love to the bloody head and kissing it on the lips. Thrilling, large-scale, dangerous music.

LINK➤ *Richard Strauss – Elektra –*
Birgit Nilsson, others, Vienna Phil. Orch. / Sir Georg Solti   **London 417-345**
Don't miss the Nilsson / Solti version of Salome *(London 414-414), but be sure to sample Strauss's 1908 nightmare of mother hatred, murder, and delirium. The atonality of music associated with a mother (Clytemnestra) is intentionally annoying. Brilliantly insane Nilsson.*

Der Rosenkavalier (The Knight of the Rose) –
Kiri Te Kanawa, Anne Sofie von Otter, others;
Staatskapelle Dresden / Bernard Haitink   EMI 49354

And now for something completely different. After a two bizarre operatic bloodbaths, Strauss suddenly becomes a master of romance and courtly comedy. The key to a successful performance of this opera is the casting of the three sopranos, and all three talented women sing beautifully. This comedy of manners is light-hearted, but musically intricate: a network of connected leitmotifs reveals character and relationships. Hugo von Hoffmannstahls's libretto is set in 1740 Vienna, and he does a marvelous job shaping period characters. In reality, however, he's addressing the end of the 19th century, often with a satirical point of view. The subtleties are likely to be missed unless the liner notes are read carefully.

LINK➤ *Richard Strauss – Der Rosenkavalier –*
Elizabeth Schwartzkopf, others, Phil. Orch. & Chorus / Herbert von Karajan   **EMI 49354**
Undoubtedly the best available performance. The recording is 50 years old, yet it still sounds fine. For better or worse, times have changed, and the affected fussiness of Schwartzkopf's soprano is difficult for modern listeners to take seriously.

Four Last Songs –
Jessye Norman, Gewandhausorchester Leipzig / Kurt Masur   Philips 411-052

At first, an acquired, perhaps even rarefied taste. The first song features soprano Jessye Norman at full throttle, which may shock and irritate some listeners. "September," based on lyrics by Herman Hesse, is a pleasant elegy, a soaring voice calmed to autumnal measure with sweeping orchestral accompaniment (Hesse supplied lyrics for the first three songs). "Im Abendrot" (At Sunset) begins with a lengthy, engaging instrumental section, and it's followed by a warm, absorbing vocal. By now, it's difficult not to be captivated—even if you don't generally enjoy classical songs. Moods and lyrics are philosophical and wistful, but willing to face death. Six earlier songs complete the set. Appealing 1982 recording.

LINK➤ *Montserrat Caballe: Casta Diva*   **RCA 23675**
What a voice! Cabelle's crystalline articulation, emotive power, and sheer wiles send tingles down the spine. She sings several Strauss songs here, along with more by Mompou, Schubert, Falla, Verdi, Bellini, and Puccini. This is a stunning CD and a handsome recording, too. Don't hesitate.

Igor Stravinsky

Stravinsky's father, a Russian opera singer, wanted his son to become a lawyer. Stravinsky dutifully attended law school in St. Petersburg, where he befriended Rimsky-Korsakov's sons. Stravinsky became Nikolai Rimsky-Korsakov's private student, and started composing. Ballet impressario Diaghilev attended a Stravinsky concert and surprised him with a commission. In 1910, Diaghilev's Ballets Russes debuted *The Rite of Spring* at the Paris Opera. The work made the 28-year-old Stravinsky famous. More successful Stravinsky-Diaghilev collaborations followed. During WW I, Stravinsky lived in Switzerland, then moved to Paris in 1917—political conditions in Russia discouraged his return. The threat of war in the 1930s, combined with the death of his wife and daughter (from tuberculosis), brought change. After time at Harvard, Stravinsky moved to Hollywood in 1940, joining an erudite classical community. He toured extensively. By the 1960s, he was as celebrated as Picasso. Stravinsky died in 1971 in NYC.

The Firebird – London Sym. Orch. / Antal Dorati
Mercury Living Presence 432-012

Ballet Russe director Serge Diaghilev heard Stravinsky's Fireworks, which begins this CD, and asked him to write a dance score based on Russian fairy tales related to the firebird legend. In 1910, Stravinsky submitted his delighfully original score. Like few composers before him, Stravinsky lifted the orchestra to a new interpretative level. Listen to the clarity of expression: the glow of morning light on "Daybreak"; the feeling of falling in love during "Khorovod"; or the calming interaction of strings and winds on "Lullabye." A work of genius, magnificently performed and recorded. *The Song of the Nightingale*, *Scherzo á la Russe*, and *Tango* complete this essential disc, recorded in 1959.

LINK➤ *Mutter Modern – Anne Sophie Mutter (violin)*   **Deutsche Grammophon 445-487**
A 3-CD collection of modern classical music. The music does not seem challenging, although it might have been considered so when it was introduced. Witold Lutoslawski and Wolfgang Rihm take their places next to Bartók and Stravinsky. An intelligent, thought-provoking set.

Petrushka, Pulcinella –
Royal Concertgebouw Orch. / Riccardo Chailly   London 443-774

Stravinsky's best ballet score, engineering that reveals every detail, and a world-class orchestra make this CD irresistible. Composed in 1911 and revised in 1947, *Petrushka* is the story of a tragic Russian puppet hero with a soul. He loves the heartless ballerina puppet, and he's abused, then killed, by the Black Moor puppet. The score overflows with captivating themes, swirling combinations of straightforward melodies, repetitions, rapid variations, and melodies that bring the story and its characters to life. The dramatic tension is so refined that every moment shimmers. *Pulcinella*, from 1920, is a ballet whose story is gracefully sung by several vocalists; the commedia dell'arte story and accompanying baroque musical experience is expertly handled.

LINK➤ *Frank Martin – Concerto for 7 Wind Instruments, other works – London Phil. /*
Matthias Bamert   *Chandos 9283*
The Swiss-born Martin sometimes composes work reminiscent of Stravinsky, as in 1949's Concerto for 7 Wind Instruments, Percussion and Strings. *The careful construction of the organ-based* Erasmi momentum *recalls Ravel and Fauré, as it weaves organ and orchestra.*

La Sacre du printemps – London Phil. / Kent Nagano Virgin-EMI 61249

After an inviting bassoon solo, Stravinsky topples conventional orchestral thinking with *The Rite of Spring*. He devises a musical fantasy world by maneuvering rhythmic length and intensity; harmony and melody are present, but he doesn't rely upon them to advance his argument. At times, the result is a pandemonium that was shocking to 1913 audiences (it caused a riot); it's still invigorating decades later. The orchestra racks the senses with noisy repeated phrases and submerges into a mythological epic that contains delicate evocations of wisdom, springtime, young girls, and later, a sacrificial dance. Contrast this with the set's second CD containing *Perséphone*, a sung-and-spoken stage work that also addresses spring and rebirth.

LINK➤ *Richard Danielpour –*
Concerto for Orchestra – Pittsburgh Sym. Orch. / David Zinman SONY Classical 62822
Like many contemporary composers, Danielpour (born 1956) claims Stravinsky among his influences. And like others of his generation, Danielpour brings many styles to bear: romantic classicism, humor, quotations from other composers and pop culture, and high drama.

Histoire du soldat – Carole Bouquet (narrator), Gérard Depardieu (devil), Gulliaume Depardieu (soldier); Shlomo Mintz (violln, conductor) Auvidis 4705

Unlike most of Stravinsky's works, this 1918 effort was intended to be small in scale. The ensemble consists of a clarinet, a bassoon, a cornet, a trombone, a double bass, a jazz drummer, and leader/violinist Shlomo Mintz. The acting is wonderful, but the story is told in the original French, without an English translation. Voices and instruments are magnificently recorded, so the resonances of the few instruments are richly presented. In this tale, a hapless soldier trades his violin to the devil for the promise of riches and success. The story is told through a series of vignettes, mostly spoken word, with music deftly woven to support story and enhance mood.

LINK➤ *Igor Stravinsky – The Soldier's Tale –*
Christopher Lee (narrator); Scottish Chamber Orch. / Lionel Friend Nimbus 5063
The story in English, acted in a distinguished, conspiratorial tone by Christopher Lee, who plays all three roles. For the instrumental suite, try Neeme Järvi's version (Chandos 9291), which includes Petrushka, Octet, *and* Ragtime.

Symphony in C, Symphony in 3 Movements –
Royal Scottish Orch. / Sir Alexander Gibson Chandos 6577

1940's Symphony in C suggests a chamber symphony, smaller in scale and somewhat traditional in structure. With Stravinsky, older forms offer a launchpad for more sophisticated thinking. The piece puts an appealingly simple melody through rhythmic changes. The second movement passes a theme from one section to the next, eventually building some modern-sounding harmonies. The final movement overlaps one idea onto the next in a language that only Stravinsky could speak. Symphony in 3 Movements, from 1945, starts by mimicking wartime newsreels, but finds its own jazzy expression. The taste of European formal dance in the second movement is updated by edgy sonorities that continue through an imaginative third movement.

LINK➤ *Igor Stravinsky – The Composer: Volume VIII: In New Directions –*
Orch. of St. Lukes / Robert Craft MusicMasters Classics 67158
Six ambitious pieces, mostly from the 1950s, not often heard. Craft worked directly with Stravinsky, and this extensive series presents the composer's best-known material, plus many other pieces. The recordings are quite good, and the liner notes by Craft are excellent.

172

Oedipus Rex – Anne Sofie von Otter, Vinson Cole, Simon Estes, others; Swedish Radio Sym. Orch. / Esa-Pekka Salonen   SONY Classical 48057

With the skillful voices of Vinson Cole as Oedipus and Anne Sofie von Otter as his mother, Jocasta, Salonen's odds of succeeding with the underappreciated opera increased considerably. Sophocles supplied the basic storyline, Jean Cocteau wrote the libretto, and Stravinsky composed an intentionally formal score (magnificent here, but dull in the wrong hands). Stravinsky starts with relatively simple music and straightforward choruses and arias, like Oedipus's "Individia fortunam odit" (Envy hates the fortunate). When Jocasta arrives to start the second act, the chorus's tones are upsetting and urgent; her aria "Nonn' erubescite, reges" (Aren't you princes ashamed?) is centered, commanding, yet elegant. Sung in Latin. Beautifully recorded.

LINK➤ *Virgil Thomson – The Mother of Us All – Santa Fe Opera Co. / Raymond Leppard*
New World 288/9
Here's the exalted story of Susan B. Anthony, women's rights activist and model of the emerging modern woman. Lyrics by Gertrude Stein. An abstraction with John Adams, Ulysses S. Grant, and Thaddeus Stevens, with Thomson and Stein included as characters, it debuted in 1947.

Apollon Musagète – Sinfonietta de Montreal / C. Dutoit   London 440-327

By choice of subject matter (Apollo inspiring the Muses) and Stravinsky's respect for earlier musical forms, this ballet score fits into a period some call neoclassicist. Formal and allegorical, the music traces Apollo's influence on Calliope (the goddess of poetry and rhythm), Polyhymnia (mime and rhetoric), and Terpsichore (movement and dance). The music tends toward the relaxed and thoughtful, but always with a slightly out-of-place strain that separates it from its ancestry. Among several other pieces here, 1938's Concerto in E flat (called "Dumbarton Oaks" for the Washington, D.C., home of the couple who commissioned it) recalls Bach's fugues, but its clarinets or bassoons always seem askew.

LINK➤ *George Antheil – Printemps, Ballet mécanique, other works*   *RCA 68066*
Darling of the 1920s Parisian art scene, Antheil's shattering art intentionally drew attention to itself. Milder by today's measure, his "Jazz" Symphony, Fighting the Waves, and Ballet mécanique should be a part of every modern collection. Stravinsky was a significant influence.

The Rake's Progress – Dawn Upshaw, Jerry Hadley, Samuel Ramey, others; Choer et Orchestre de l'Opera de Lyon / Kent Nagano   Erato 12715

Poet W.H. Auden wrote the libretto for a supremely enjoyable rendition of Hogarth's eight satirical paintings of 18th-century England. Initially, the recording's clarity is striking, and so are the voices: Dawn Upshaw and Jerry Hadley have rarely sounded better on an opera recording. Stravinsky's modern (1951) view of Mozart-era opera is fascinating and fun (a harpsichord here, bel canto singing there, with Stravinsky's distinctive voice throughout). Sung in English, the lyrics are intelligent. The plot turns on the fate of Tom Rakewell, who inherits money, marries a bearded lady, goes mad, and dies in Bedlam, presumably due to his own weaknesses and the influence of his devilish sidekick, Nick Shadow.

LINK➤ *Sir Harrison Birtwhistle – The Triumph of Time, Gawain's Journey – Philharmonia Orch. / Elgar Howarth*   *Collins Classics 1387*
Far more forceful than Stravinsky, but grown from similar roots, The Triumph of Time is based on a Bruegel painting. Gawain's Journey is adapted from Birtwhistle's opera. Birtwhistle's music is rough, sparse, and something frightening in its emotional coolness. Two important modern works.

Karol Szymanowski

Born in the Ukraine to a wealthy family in 1882, Szymanowksi often performed original works at his parents' elaborate parties. He attended the Warsaw Conservatory. The distractions of travel (mostly Mediterranean, to explore ancient cultures), a World War (which resulted in the destruction of his family home in 1917), and an unpublished novel (*Efebos*, about his homosexuality and desperation) delayed a dedicated composing career. The independence of Poland after World War I inspired him. Szymanowski became a leading Polish intellectual and an active composer in search of Poland's new musical identity. In the 1920s, he explored bold new 20th-century music. Over time, the folk traditions of Poland's Tatra Mountains became raw material for his work. By the early 1930s, Szymanowski had taken charge of the Warsaw Conservatory and spent less time composing. Suffering from tuberculosis, he died in a Laussane, Switzerland, sanatorium in 1937. A state funeral honored him as a national hero.

Three Mythes—L. Mordkovitch (violin), M. Gusak-Grin (piano)   Chandos 8747

Composed in 1915, Szymanowski's *Three Mythes* are high points in the literature of violin-piano duets. "The Fountain of Arethusa" shimmers with the reflection of moonlight. Clear and refreshing, it's a mood piece with the gentlest possible theme. In "Narcissus," the violin and piano reflect one another's melodies, just as the title character was fascinating with his own reflection. A feeling of water pervades both pieces. "Dryads and Pan" is wholly different—a balletic dance caused by a breeze through a unmoving forest. It's a fantasy (or more accurately, a scherzo fantastique) with endless special effects. Szymanowski's youthful Violin Sonata, a nocturne, and a tarantella complete a lovely CD.

LINK➤ *White Moon: Songs to Morpheus – Dawn Upshaw (soprano),*
Margo Garrett (piano), members of the Orpheus Chamber Orch., others   Nonesuch 79364
Music associated with night, sleep, and the silvery moon. Shimmering music centered by a Handel song called "Gentle Morpheus," and as diverse as songs by George Crumb (born 1929) and John Dowland (born 1563). A delightful exploration.

Stabat Mater, Litany to Virgin Mary, Sym. 3 – City of Birmingham Sym. Orch. / Simon Rattle   EMI 55121

Soprano Elzbieta Szmytka does a marvelous job in setting the exhalted mood for 1924's *Stabat Mater*, a work of considerable subtlety and reverence. Rattle maintains a decidedly understated presentation, allowing solo and choral voices a clear path to the heavens. The second movement's funeral march, the a capella angel voices of the fourth movement, and the exciting, climactic fifth movement are each thrilling in their special ways. Symphony No. 3, from 1916, is arguably his best in the genre (for the others, try Karol Stryja's recordings on NAXOS [8.553683-4]). Subtitled "Song of the Night," it's a choral symphnony based on 13th-century Persian poetry.

LINK➤ *Karol Szymanowski – Violin Concertos, other works –*
Thomas Zehetmair (violin), City of Birmingham Sym. Orch. / Sir Simon Rattle   EMI 55607
Two vastly different violin concertos. The first feels lighter, more impressionistic, with understated influences from the East. The second grows from folk music influences, but doesn't shy from deep impact. Also includes a few other pieces with pianist Silke Avenhaus.

Piotr Ilyich Tchaikovsky

One of Russia's greatest composers, Tchaikovsky somehow managed to create exquisite works despite a difficult emotional life. He was born in 1840 in Votkinsk, Russia, and lost his beloved mother to cholera at age 14. Tchaikovsky started composing and studied at St. Petersburg's new music conservatory, all the while following a parallel path from law school to an unhappy stint as a law clerk. By 1865, Tchaikovsky had settled into a more appealing job as a music professor, although he unfortunately married a woman who proved herself to be a suicidal nymphomaniac. He composed prolifically during the 1860s and 1870s, working himself into two nervous breakdowns. In 1876, Tchaikovsky began a letters-only relationship with Nadhenza Von Meck, who supported him until 1890, then added to his emotion instability by abruptly cutting him off. Despite endless awards, successful tours, and accolades for his compositions, Tchaikovsky's struggle with personal issues, including his homosexuality, made him miserable. He died in 1893, probably by suicide.

String Quartets Nos. 1-3 – Borodin Quartet   Teldec 90422

The big news here is String Quartet No. 1, composed in 1871, with its accordionlike first movement (the strings seem to simulate a squeeze box), and the extraordinary Andante Cantible. This second movement is stunning in its graceful melancholy, its noble melody, and its nod to Russian folk music (it was based on a folk song). The joyful fourth movement, with its sudden pauses and oddball timing, is Tchaikovsky at his playful best. "Souvenir de Florence," from 1890, is a grand sextet; here, it's by Yuri Yurov on viola and Mikhail Milman on cello. String Quartet No. 2 is moody, serious, and discomforting; No. 3 is richer, but also introspective. Terrific Borodin; decent recording.

LINK➤ *Zoltán Kodály – Starker Plays Kodály – Janos Starker (cello)*   *Delos 1015*
Extremely accurate recording whose centerpiece is the half-hour unaccompanied cello sonata. Starker unearths every conceivable color and mood, casting a fantastic spell. Duo for Violin and Cello, with Josef Gingold (violin) is also admirable.

Concerto for Piano and Orchestra – Martha Argerich (piano),
Berlin Phil. / Claudio Abbado   Deutsche Grammophon 449-816

The first movement is one of classical music's great themes; it's the sort of weighty romance that plays behind commercials with 800-numbers. It's tough to get past that contemporary reality. One way is simply to follow Argerich's very capable keyboard work and the inspired ways in which Tchaikovsky counterbalanced the sound of the piano with the sounds of, for example, the winds. After those overwrought first few minutes, the piece dances with its own spritely delicacy, in a style not unlike *The Nutcracker*'s best moments. In fact, a two-piano arrangement of *The Nutcracker Suite* (Nicholas Economou plays the second piano) completes this fine CD. Very good recording.

LINK➤ *Franz Scharwenka – Piano Concerto No. 4 –*
Stephen Hough (piano), City of Birmingham Sym. Orch./Lawrence Foster   Hyperion 66790
Gramophone's Record of the Year for 1996 recognized the talent of a man who in his time (1908) was as popular as Tchaikovsky or Liszt—and as well respected. This is a world-class piano concerto, romantic and noble, dramatic and unerring; it should be heard.

Swan Lake – Montreal Sym. Orch. / Charles Dutoit   London 436-212

Tchaikovsky's first attempt at ballet music was considered a flop, but this music has endured as one of ballet's most popular scores for over 120 years (it debuted in 1877). Besides offering a gorgeous range of dance music, Tchaikovsky's music very effectively explores themes, moods, and ideas suitable for audio-only listening. There are many melodies that will instantly sound familiar. One is the peasant's waltz, the first fully choreographed scene in the ballet. The swan's theme, performed on oboe and with orchestra, is one of Tchaikovsky's tenderest and most enduring. As in *Nutcracker*, the composer presents music from different cultures, including a Hungarian csárdas, a Spanish bolero, and a Polish mazurka.

LINK➤ *Piotr Ilyich Tchaikovsky – Swan Lake –*
Saint Louis Sym. Orch. / Leonard Slatkin   *RCA 62557*
Special gift-box edition is suitable for children (particularly young ballet students). It includes card-board cutout figures, a reasonably clear scenario, and nice color illustrations. The music is also well played and well recorded.

Symphony No. 4 – Oslo Phil. Orch. / Mariss Jansons   Chandos 8361

All of Jansons's mid-1980s recordings in this symphony cycle are extraordinary. They sound wonderful, and the performances draw out Tchaikovsky's deepest emotions (he finished it in 1877 after a horrible divorce and a nervous breakdown). A bold and bracing start drowns in a deep vortex of depression. The second movement shows the composer's astonishing control of orchestral tone in a lovely, quiet introspection (it's subtitled "in a mocking mood"). The plucked balalaikas (violins) weave into a fabric of Russian folk melody as the third movement unfolds. The fourth movement is huge—soaring in its high spirits and life affirming. A thrilling 41-minute ride through an emotional theme park.

LINK➤ *Piotr Ilyich Tchaikovsky – Complete Symphonies –*
Oslo Phil. Orch. / Mariss Jansons   *Chandos 8672/8*
Jansons is arguably this generation's finest conductor of Tchaikovsky symphonies. Before buying just one of the Chandos discs, give very serious consideration to the entire set. Also includes the Manfred Symphony and "Capriccio Italien."

Violin Concerto in D –
Maxim Vengerov (violin), Berlin Phil. / Claudio Abbado   Teldec 90881

Violinist Vengerov delicately walks the line between the syrupy sweetness that this piece some-times requires and the honest melodies that glide through one of Tchaikovsky's most satisfying works. It's easy enough to enjoy: Vengerov takes advantage of deeply emotional patches, and the attentive Abbado is always on the spot with just the right verve. The second movement, or Canzonetta, can disintegrate into emotional slop, but Vengerov understands how to express sadness. Excellent control and a wonderful break into the dancelike melody begin the finale. Glazunov's Violin Concerto in A minor was favored by a similar muse, and has a similar social outlook. It's all very nicely recorded, too.

LINK➤ *Alexander Glazunov – The Seasons –*
Minnesota Orch. / Edo de Waart   *Telarc 80347*
Glazunov really came into his own with this 1899 ballet. As the title suggests, each section evokes the mood of a season. Frequently conservative, Glazunov allowed himself creative freedom here, and the result is original, fresh, and enormously engaging.

Eugene Onegin – Covent Garden Orch. / Sir Georg Solti   London 417-413

In marked contrast with the stereotypically turgid Russian opera, Tchaikovsky transforms Puskin's poem into gently lyrical music. One significant highlight is the love letter that the lovesick Tatyana (Teresa Kubiak) writes, in the dark of night, trying to determine how the new man, Eugene Onegin, might fit into her life. As she considers the possibilities, she performs Tchaikovsky's famous "Letter Scene." The warmth of "Ya lyublyu vas" (I love you), sung by Vladimir Lensky (Stuart Burrows), and the various arias of Onegin (Weikl) are stirring, but Solti's consistently heartfelt conducting and creative decisions provide the real soul of this 2-CD set. Skillful 1974 engineering really captures the special qualities of the various voices.

LINK➤ *Tchaikovsky–Pique Dame–Kirov Opera & Orch./Valery Gergiev   Philips 438-141*
Wholly different from Onegin, *but also based on Pushkin, this blustery 1890 opera pushes characters and situations toward their fateful end. It cleverly intertwines leitmotifs and generally holds together as a strong, coherent work. Very lively Gergiev, too. A 3-CD set.*

1812 Overture – Minneapolis Sym. Orch. / Antal Dorati   Mercury Living Presence 434-360

This 1958 performance and recording blows away every one of its digital-age competitors. Expertly engineered with just three microphones by Robert C. Fine, Dorati gets the speeds and enthusiasm right. Those bold cannon blasts come from a 1775 gun that predates the composition by a century. The "cereal that's shot from guns" part is just the finale; the rest is a battle of the French and Russian themes and anthems ("La Marseillaise," "God Preserve the Czar," and so on) recalling a bloody 1812 battle. Deems Taylor offers an interesting backstage view, and he's followed by Tchaikovsky's "Capriccio Italien" and another noisy piece, Beethoven's "Victory" (featuring a 12-pound howitzer and other musical artillery).

LINK➤ *Tchaikovsky – Overtures & Fantasies – SO of Russia / V. Dudarova   Olympia 512*
Tchaikovsky wrote many smaller pieces for orchestra, the best of which are very well played on this 2-CD set. Contents include "Festive Overture," "The Tempest," "Francesa da Rimini," "Fantasy Overture: Hamlet," "Capriccio Italien," and the best gunless "1812 Overture." From 1992.

Symphony No. 5 – Oslo Phil. Orch. / Mariss Jansons   Chandos 8351

Wow! This 1888 symphony goes for the jugular in the first few minutes and never lets go. A somber "fate" motif is a reliable presence. The first movement struggles through frequent outbursts and patches of calm—a spectrum of brief melodic ideas and varied orchestrations. The second movement takes a deep breath, calms down, and allows time for the proper establishment of three handsome instrumental themes (once again, Tchaikovsky's use of the winds and strings sets him apart). The third movement recalls his ballets. The fourth addresses fate directly, and, after a false surrender, a theme associated with Tchaikovsky's spirit wins out.

LINK➤ *The Moscow Sessions – Moscow Phil. Orch. / Lawrence Leighton Smith or Dmitri Kitayenko   Sheffield Lab 25, 26, 27*
A great idea, flawlessly executed. Smith conducts Tchaikovsky's Fifth Symphony, Shostakovich's First, plus pieces by Glinka, Mussorgsky, and Glazunov. Kitayenko visits the U.S. with Copland's Appalachian Spring, *Piston's* Incredible Flutist, *and works by Barber, Gershwin, and Ives. An essential 3-CD set with spectacular sound.*

The Sleeping Beauty –
Czecho-Slovak State Phil. Orch. / Andrew Mongrelia   NAXOS 8.550490/2

Whenever Naxos aces a major work, it's a big win for consumers. That's what happened here with an absurdly inexpensive 3-CD version of Tchaikovsky's best ballet. Mongrelia charges up "Entrance of King Florestan and His Court," then goes warm and intimate for "Entrance of the Good Fairies"—very attentive conducting. Act 1's waltz is so dreamy, romantic, refreshing, and fulfilling—it's another Tchaikovsky miracle. Tchaikovsky's genius, evident in all three of his ballets, is in his manipulation of tonal colors. The fairy dances—gold, silver, sapphire, and diamond—are among several exquisite examples. Excellent sonics, too. Very highly recommended—even for those who don't think much of ballet.

LINK► *Adolphe Adam–Giselle–Slovak Radio SO/Andrew Mogrelia   NAXOS 8.550755/6*
A romantic ballet served up in grand style, Giselle *debuted in Paris in 1841. The story is based on a folk tale of unfulfilled love. The melodies are familiar and winning, and the two-hour performance is consistently engaging. A complete delight.*

The Nutcracker – London Sym. Orch. /
Sir Charles Mackerras   Telarc 80137

Among a crowded field of fine recordings of the complete 1892 ballet score, this Telarc CD stands out. Mackerras fills the room with enchanting, often thrilling sound. Tchaikovsky beautifully rendered the world of a child and her dolls. His ravishing musical portraits of soldiers, snowflakes, flowers, and sugar plums are presented through a cleverly manipulation of pace, rhythm, tone, instrumentation, time and space. Truly, this is a creative masterwork. And if this music is performed a little too often, or too closely associated with an annual ballet fund raiser—get over it! Just let yourself dream in Tchaikovsky's magnificent world of imagination. (And just once, explore E.T.A. Hoffman's sometimes grotesque, sometimes erotic original story.)

LINK► *Tchaikovsky – The Nutcracker –St. Louis SO / Leonard Slatkin   RCA 61704*
Here's a wonderful gift box for the child who adores this ballet. The package also includes three scenic backdrops, five cardboard cutout characters, and a storybook. The 1985 recording is energetic and pleasant, but Mackerras (and Ashkenazy on London 433-000) sound better.

Symphony No. 6 – Oslo Phil. Orch. / Mariss Jansons   Chandos 8446

Gloomy bassoons and basses begin this 1893 symphony, a sequence more clearly presented on the Pletnev version (unavailable as a single CD). Sentiments brighten when violins and higher winds come in, but Tchaikovsky is caught by an unforgiving force. In time, the breezy dream of a beautiful melody recalls all that was well with life, closer in feeling to Russian "patetichesky," which inadequately translates as "Pathétique" and, worse, "Pathetic." This romantic theme is followed by the second movement waltz's somewhat lopsided timing, and an oddly disorganized third movement march. The fourth movement carries a heavy burden, manages some hopeful flourishes, then submerges into bass and bassoon gloom. (Tchaikovsky says good-bye.)

LINK► *Tchaikovsky–Sym.Nos. 1-6 –Russian Nat. Orch./Michael Pletnev   DG 449-967*
Deutche Grammophon's 4D recording technology proves itself on this 5-CD demonstration of contemporary engineering excellence. Jansons brings a bit more emotion to these works, but Pletnev's pinpoint accuracy is also very appealing. Jansons is the definite first choice.

Michael Tippett

An iconoclastic British composer, Tippett was born in London in 1905, but didn't take up music in any serious way until age 18—and then he did so with tremendous passion and focus. From 1923 until 1928, Tippett studied at the Royal College of Music and continued with two more years of private instruction. He was also a music professor through the 1940s. Tippett's first work was publicly performed in 1934. Just five years later, his best-known work, and one of the century's finest oratorios, *A Child of Our Time*, was completed. A pacifist jailed for his convictions during WW II, Tippett became well known as a BBC commentator and as a conductor in the years that followed. His many works include four symphonies, several operas, and numerous chamber works. Still, Tippett's works were not often performed until the 1960s in Europe and the 1970s in the U.S. Knighted in 1966, Sir Michael Kemp Tippett died in 1998.

A Child of Our Time – Cynthia Haymon, Cynthia Clarey, Damon Evans, Willard White; London Sym. Orch. / Richard Hickox   Chandos 9123

What begins as a somber report on Nazi genocide, a sad oratorio presented by elegiac horns and respectful chorus, turns out to be just that and considerably more. Tippett assigns one theme the role of scapegoat; this is "A Child of Our Time." Then Tippett proceeds with an unexpected series of choral quotations from spirituals, so that "Steal Away," "Nobody Knows the Trouble I See," and related literature become central to his argument. These elements are sung by the all-black soloists and arranged so that they blend into the overall presentation. At first, this is disconcerting, but patience proves Tippett's approach remarkably effective. The recording is excellent.

LINK➤ *The Music Survives!*   *London 452-664*
The subtitle of this CD is "Degenerate Music Suppressed by the Third Reich." It's a sampler that begins to explain what happened to this century's great classical voices: they were silenced. Here is Pavel Haas, Erich Wolfgang Korngold, Walter Braunfels, and seven others. Striking and excellent.

Fantasia Concertante on a Theme of Corelli, Symphony No. 4 – Bournemouth Sym. Orch. / Richard Hickox   Chandos 9233

Hickox recorded a series of Tippett symphonies for Chandos, each accompanied by a second work. Composed in 1953, *Fantasia Concertante* was based upon the work of Arcangelo Corelli—a man who helped to define the sonata and concerto grosso over 250 years earlier. Tippett begins with a formal statement of Corelli's idea, then pits darkness against light. The fugues build to a climax, before the music returns to a pastorale finale. Symphony No. 4, from 1977, follows a birth-to-death conception, a journey through a life cycle. It's a struggle, a constant fight for peace that's marked by mysteries, realizations, warmth, and frigid cold.

LINK➤ *Charles Wuorinen – American Masters*   *CRI 744*
Each CD in CRI's American Masters series collects about four works by a significant 20th-century U.S. composer. Wuorinen's Chamber Concerto for Tuba (1970), scored for 12 winds and 12 drums, is a difficult, challenging, seemingly scattered work. His 1966 Piano Concerto is more accessible.

Ralph Vaughan Williams

For much of this century, Vaughan Williams (whose first name is pronounced "rayf") was one of England's most popular composers. His success is rooted in an honest appreciation for the English folk music tradition; with his friend Gustav Holst, Vaughan Williams collected and catalogued traditional English songs. He was born in Down Ampney, a Cotswolds village in Gloucestershire. He attended the Royal College of Music, Trinity College, and subsequently studied with Bruch and Ravel. Vaughan Williams started composing seriously in the early years of this century and continued working until the late 1950s. His contributions to English music include eight symphonies, plus a great many vocal works, frequently inspired by poetry. In 1951, after his wife died, he moved to London and was frequently seen at concert halls and special events, the grand spirit of British music. Vaughn Williams died at age 85 in 1958.

Symphony No. 2 (A London Symphony) –
London Phil. Orch. / Sir Adrian Boult   EMI 47213

Vaughan Williams's Second Symphony debuted in 1914; Boult performed the first of many revisions in 1918. A half-century later, in 1971, Boult recorded the magic that illuminates this symphony from within—the glow of its violin solos and the swirls of lush arrangements. The first two movements are slow explorations of London's gray nooks and ancient crannies. Development is gradual, rendered with pastel and watercolor, dignified but not without surprises. London's Westminster Embankment and the distant Strand inspired the third movement's snap and crackle. The fourth movement more aggressively presses a theme. Memories are then dimly recalled, a clock tolls, and the Thames carries on. With *Fantasia on a Theme by Thomas Tallis*.

LINK➤ *Ralph Vaughan Williams – Works for String Orchestra –*
English String Orch. / William Boughton   *Nimbus 5019*
The effortless flow of V-W's, aided by the unadorned simplicity of this setting, result in one of the finest versions of Fantasia on Greensleeves *on record. The Oboe Concerto is enchanting, and the* Tallis Variations *are more effective than on full-scale symphonic recordings.*

Symphony No. 5 – Royal Phil. Orch. / André Previn   Telarc 80158

Inspired Telarc engineering embues this peace-loving symphony with inviting resonance. Composed in 1943 and revised 1951, it's based on themes developed for an opera, *The Pilgrim's Progress*. Amid many tranquil passages, there's feverish passion. In the first movement, horns reach out, drums shout with passionate thunder, and strings and winds are ecstatic. In the second movement, there's joyous, sometimes devilish, dancing. Darker patches are subsequently brightened by what often sounds like English choral music set for orchestra. The third movement is smooth and transcendent; it is the symphony's heart. The formal fourth movement closes by incorporating ideas from the first. In addition, the *Tallis Variations*, based on a 16th-century theme, are beautifully presented here.

LINK➤ *R. Vaughan Williams–The Pilgrim's Progress–London PO/ Boult*   *EMI 64212*
Vaughan Williams's symphonies are most easily understood after exposure to this decidedly British musical milestone. Quite overblown in its combination of opera and choral music, it's sung in English. On a rainy Sunday afternoon, it's worth the 2-CD excursion.

Giuseppe Verdi

Verdi's parents ran an inn in Parma, Italy. He grew up with only a modest education, but nurtured a dream to compose music. Turned down by the Milan Conservatory, he took a local music job near home, got married, and started composing. In 1839, at age 29, Verdi moved to Milan, where a year later, La Scala produced *Oberto*, his first opera—an astonishing accomplishment for a novice and newcomer. Sadly, his wife died the same year. Still, Verdi kept working and his third opera, *Nabucco*, made him famous. For the next three decades, Verdi wrote more than a dozen popular operas. He stopped after 1871's *Aida*, but started again 15 years later, at age 75, and produced several more hits. He also founded Casa di Riposa, a musician's retirement home; his royalties continue to support this. Verdi died in 1901; his funeral attracted a quarter-million people.

Nabucco (Nebuchadnezzar) – Piero Cappuccilli, Ghena Dimitrova, others; Chorus and Opera of the German Opera, Berlin / Giuseppe Sinopoli   DG 410-512

Composed in 1842, this early Verdi opera made him famous, mostly because of the popularity of a choral anthem, "Va, pensiero" (Fly, thought), performed by the enslaved Hebrews on the banks of the Euphates. In this story of the Babylonian captivity of the Jews, Nabucco goes insane, then regains himself in time to save the life of his daughter and to revere the Hebrew God. There's some intrigue with Abigaille, a power-hungry warrior and pretender to the throne whose low birth proves her downfall. Although arias share the limelight with choruses, Cappuccelli's Nabucco is rock-solid on "Tremin gl'insani" (Let the Madmen Tremble), and Dimitrova gets several arias to burnish her evil.

LINK➤ *(Book) – Verdi : A Biography – Mary Jane Phillips-Matz, Andrew Porter*
Oxford U. Press   *ISBN 0-198166001*
This definitive 1993 scholarly work focuses on Giuseppe Verdi as a man of his times: an era when Italian unification and anticlericism were paramount concerns. Those with only a passing interest should try the Verdi volume in the Illustrated Lives of the Great Composers *series (Omnibus Press).*

Rigoletto – Renato Bruson, Edita Gruberova, others; Coro e Orch. dell'Accaemdia Nazionale di Santa Cecilia / Giuseppe Sinopoli   Philips 412-592

A treasure—majestically performed and perfectly recorded. It's based on Victor Hugo's play *Le Roi s'amuse*, whose lead character is the lecherous duke of Mantua. Verdi recenters his 1851 story on a hapless court jester, Rigoletto, providing one of opera's few great baritone roles. Rigoletto is a miserable fool, one who pokes fun at the duke's victims; in the end, he bears the saddest joke of all, causing the death of his beloved daughter Gilda (in one of opera's best tearjerker finales). The duke sings two great arias: "La donna e mobile" (Wayward Woman) and "Questo o quella" (This woman or that)—just two of at least six famous numbers.

LINK➤ *Caruso Sings Verdi – Enrico Caruso*   *RCA 61242*
The accompaniment is soft, but Caruso's huge, expressive voice comes through loud and clear. The masterful performances from Rigoletto, Aida, Il Trovatore, *and other Verdi favorites were recorded between 1906 and 1916, yet there's very little objectionable in the sound.*

Classical CD Listener's Guide   *181*

Il Trovatore (The Troubador) – Leontyne Price, Placido Domingo, Sherrill Milnes, others
New Philharmonia Orch. / Zubin Mehta   RCA 6194

Based on a Spanish play, this 1853 opera is a bel canto throwback, a crowd-pleaser demanding huge voices. The convoluted story involves infanticide (presumably caused by a gypsy), dueling, abduction, spying, poison, and fratricide. Who cares? It's the music that matters. Price is amazing on "Tacea la notte placida" (The silent, peaceful night), baritone Milnes conquers "Il balen del suo sorriso" (The light of her smile), and Domingo, at his smoothest, delivers a championship "Ah, sì, ben mio" (Ah yes, my love)—one of Verdi's most challenging songs. Mehta provides the proper tone and atmosphere, and the 1969 recording is impressive. The only thing missing is the audience's cheering bravos!

LINK► *Giuseppe Verdi – Simon Boccanegra – Piero Cappuccilli, Mirella Freni, Jose Carerras, others; La Scala Orch. & Chorus   Deutsche Grammophon 449-752*
In an effort to duplicate the success of Il Trovatore, *Verdi composed a comparatively sad score that hasn't been as popular. Still, there is much to recommend the score and this particular performance, notably Abbado's work and Freni's rendition of Amelia.*

La Traviata (The Fallen Woman) – Angela Gheorghiu, Frank Lopardo,
Leo Nucci, others; Covent Garden Orch. / Sir Georg Solti   London 448-119

Dumas's *La dame aux camélias* provided the basic plot, but this 1853 opera was reduced to the story of a classy prostitute (Violetta) who gives up a true love (Alfredo) on the insistence of his father (Germont). Predictably, she dies at the end in an emotional death scene. The raucous "Brindisi" (Drinking Song) provides the opera's best-known melody. Tenor Frank Lopardo (Alfredo) gets a big solo number, and baritone Leo Nucci (Germont) gets another, but their best work is in songs featuring Angela Gheorghiu (Violetta), who sings beautifully. Her grace and power is magnificent. Solti's performance is fresh (he was 82!). Excellent 1994 live sound.

LINK► *My World – Angela Gheorghiu (soprano)   London 458-360*
Most of this world tour takes place in Europe, where songs from Italy, Spain, France, and Germany predominate. The most interesting material is a modern Greek pop tune, a classical song from Korea and a 1960s hit from Japan. Gheorghiu also sings four songs from her native Roumania.

Un Ballo in Maschera (A Masked Ball) – Luciano Pavarotti, Margaret
Price, Renato Bruson, others; Nat. Phil. Orch. / Sir Georg Solti   RCA 1864

Although they're often obscured by the shadow of his most famous works, these Verdi operas also deserve attention: *Macbeth* (Sinopoli; Philips 412-133), *La forza del destino* (The Force of Destiny) (Levine; RCA 81864), *Don Carlos* (Pappano; EMI 56152), and *Falstaff* (Giulini; Deutsche Grammophon 410-503). In 1859, Verdi completed this conspiratory tale; the governor of Boston, Massachusetts, is to be killed at the masked ball. (Boston's "governor" was a last-minute replacement for a Swedish king, whose story was Verdi's model). Among Verdi's many fine works, this opera is particularly stylish, with a near constant flow of splendid music and an altogether delightful demeanor. The voices and the recording are excellent.

LINK► *Verdi – Preludes, Overtures & Ballet Music – BBC Phil. / Downes   Chandos 9510*
The strength and musicality of Verdi's composition is presented with great verve. An invigorating addition to any Verdi collection. Typically fine Chandos sonics, too.

Aida – Leontyne Price, Jon Vickers, Robert Merrill;
Orch. e Coro del Teatro dell'Opera di Roma / Sir Georg Solti   London 417-416

Onstage, *Aida* is over the top, with its huge marching parades, elephants, and enormous arias for gigantic voices. There are several fine musical numbers, notably "Celeste Aida" (Heavenly Aida), and "Gloria all'Egitto" (Glory to Egypt), both fine demonstrations of Grand Opera circa 1887. Among a surprisingly small selection of *Aida* recordings, Solti's 1962 session with Leontyne Price as the Ethiopian slave Aida and Jon Vickers as captain of the guards Radames is best (good, but not spectacular sound). Radames brought Aida back from a battle triumph and loves her. The king's daughter gets involved, and the triangle resolves itself with Radames and Aida buried in a pyramid. A 3-CD set.

LINK➤ *Ruggiero Leoncavallo – Pagliacci – Carlo Bergonzi, Giuseppe Taddei, others;*
Coro e Orch. del Teatro alla Scala / Herbert von Karajan   **Deutsche Grammophon 449-727**
As over-the-top as Aida, *this death-of-a-clown story is opera at its best. Karajan makes the most of a lush score, and Bergonzi gets every bit of blood out of the big tenor scene, "Vesti la gubbia" (Put on Your Costume) with the famous "Ridi, Pagliaccio" (Laugh, Clown).*

Requiem Mass – Susan Dunn, Diane Currey, Jerry Hadley;
Atlanta Sym. & Chorus / Robert Shaw   Telarc 80152

When Telarc was a young record label, its engineers chose Verdi's *Requiem* to show off digital technology. Sure, this is a Mass, but it was written by Giuseppe Verdi, who treated the liturgy as if it was a dramatic opera. With its big bass drum and its whirlwind orchestration, "Dires irae" is competitive with Tchaikovsky's 1812 Overture as a thrilling demo piece. The voices are aggressive—more like a Broadway chorus than a chapel full of monks—and Verdi's use of horns furthers the energetic agenda. This 2-CD set also includes several songs from other Verdi operas. The 1987 recording isn't perfect, but exciting moments more than compensate.

LINK➤ *Charles Stanford – 3 Motets, Beati quorum via, other works –*
Stephen Cleobury (organ), John Mark Ainsley (vocals); King's College, Cambridge Chorus
EMI 55535
Stanford was one of England's choral masters, and this magnificent collection of his sacred compositions are thrilling. Best is 1918's Magnificat for Double Choir, *and 1908's* Postlude in D minor. *For more, try CRD 3497 with the Oxford Chorus.*

Otello – Placido Domingo, Cheryl Studer, others;
Opera Bastille / Myung-Whun Chung   Deutsche Grammophon 439-805

One of two Shakespeare plays adapted by Verdi in his later years (he finished *Falstaff* in 1893), both adapted by Arrigo Boito (who was known for his own opera, *Mephistofele*). By combining the best styles of Italian and German opera, the 74-year-old Verdi created his finest work, with unified music and dramatic action. As a result, this opera is not especially concerned with crowd-pleasing arias. It is, however, filled with exciting music: the opening storm, Iago's "Credo," and the trio by Otello with Cassio and Iago are among many outstanding songs. Domingo is extraordinary, here and in the earlier 1977 James Levine set (RCA 2951). Don't miss this!

LINK➤ *Heroes – Placido Domingo*   **EMI 666532**
Filled with recordings from the 1970s, here's Domingo in some wonderful performances. Notables include Verdi and Puccini warhorses ("Celeste Aida," and "Recondita armonia," respectively), but also work from Gounod's Faust, Boito's Mephistopheles, *and others.*

Heitor Villa-Lobos

After learning cello from his father, an amateur musician, Villa-Lobos taught himself to play every instrument in the orchestra. Contradicting his parents' hopes for a medical career, the teenaged Villa-Lobos headed for Rio de Janiero and its street life. Around 1907, at age 20, Villa-Lobos traveled throughout Brazil, studying and absorbing a wide range of traditional music. He returned to Rio with high hopes for studying at the National Music Institute, but left school because it wasn't his style. Villa-Lobos continued his home-brewed education; by 1915 he was a very popular concert performer whose presentation combined European classical music with Brazilian folk music. Artur Rubenstein brought Villa-Lobos to the attention of European patrons, and the composer debuted in Paris in 1923 to great acclaim. By 1930, he was director of the National Music Institute; it was the beginning of two decades of work as the leading figure in Brazilian music education. Villa-Lobos died in 1959.

Bachianas Brasieiras 2, 4, 8 –
Cincinnati Sym. Orch. / Jesús López-Cobos   Telarc 80393
Skillful engineering captures the magic of Villa-Lobos's tone poems. Inspired by Bach and European romance, this graceful Brazilian music employs color and texture. From 1933, No. 2's final movement, "O Tremzinho do Caipira" (The Little Train of Caipira), is a symphonic railroad journey; the obligatory choo-choo rhythm is present, but so are noble strings and horns, jazzy influences, and moderated splashes of energy. From 1944, No. 4's "Canto do Sertão" (Song of the Jungle) finds majesty in the hues of its winds and luminiscent strings, while a single xylophone note is endlessly repeated to suggest the araponga bird's call. Very special.

LINK➤ *Heitor Villa-Lobos – Bachianas Brasilieras Nos. 1, 5, 7 –*
Barbara Hendricks (soprano); Royal Phil. Orch. / Enrique Bátiz   *EMI 47433*
The perfect mate. It begins with Hendricks's wordless reverie—1938's often-performed No. 5, scored for eight cellos. In time, Hendricks sings the central nocturne, a lovely dream set to beautiful music. In No. 7, the interpretation of a Quadrille is painted with bolder tones.

The Discovery of Brazil (Suites 1-4) –
Slovak Radio SO / Roberto Duarte   Marco Polo 8.223551
Marco Polo's distinguished Latin-American Classics series includes 15 Villa-Lobos CDs; many, such as the String Quartets, are particularly fine. The origin of these four suites is a 1936 educational film soundtrack. Reworked for orchestra, it is a revelation—comparable to Copland or Dvorák's best. The First Suite follows ships from Portugal; it travels from dances to calm sea, from stormy sea to throbbing anticipation. The Second Suite is the landing; one of its highlights is a musical simulation of a rattlesnake. This remarkable composition culminates in "Primeira Missa no Brasil" (First Mass in Brazil), a juxtaposition of Portuguese and Indian voices in Latin chant and native song.

LINK➤ *Joaquin Rodrigo – Concierto de Aranjuez –*
Norbert Kraft (guitar); Northern Chamber Orch. / Nicholas Ward   *NAXOS 8.550729*
Villa-Lobos wrote 1951's Guitar Concerto for Andrew Segovia. The Italian Mario Castelnuovo-Tedesco contributes a 1939 Guitar Concerto as well, but the most famous work is Joaquin Rodrigo's Concierto de Aranjuez, notable for its glorious combination of brass and guitar.

Antonio Vivaldi

Vivaldi grew up in the sunny culture of Venice, Italy. He was born in 1678, and learned music from his father, a violinist at St. Mark's church. In his early 20s, Vivaldi was ordained a priest (a job he rarely took seriously) and became a teacher at the Conservatorio della Pietà, an orphan girls' school noted for music education. In 1704, he started seriously composing music and wrote hundreds of vocal and instrumental works for the school's student instrumentalists and choir, as well as for visiting professionals. A decade later, Vivaldi began a prolific run as an opera composer (he wrote nearly 50). In 1718, he left Venice to work for the Governor of Mantua, and met La Giró, an opera singer who traveled with him (bad idea for a priest). He lived the life of a successful composer until the early 1730s, when his music lost its popularity, the Church came down hard, and he lost his Pietà commission. The downward spiral resulted in poverty, illness, and death in Vienna, where he was trying to arrange a final commission, in 1741.

The Four Seasons (Violin Concertos Nos. 1-4) –
Tafelmusik with Jeanne Lamon   SONY Classical 48251
Violinist and Tafelmusik group leader Jeanne Lamon brings a fresh voice to a familiar and make it new again. With meticulous scholarship, plus an inspired sense of time and space, each of Vivaldi's portraits of the natural world is transformed into a delightful miniature. Each is explained in the liner notes: the springtime breezes that lead into a thunderstorm with lightning (all simulated by solo violin—Vivaldi's own instrument), the suffocating August heat that engulfs even a birdsong (this time on bass), the winter's frozen landscape, complete with a violin's suggestion of chattering teeth. Excellent recorded weight and dimension. Ton Koopman's version is equally fine (Erato 94811).

LINK➤ *Tomaso Albioni – Complete Oboe Concertos –*
Anthony Robson (oboe); Collegium Musicum 90 / Simon Standage   *Chandos 0579*
CD featuring eight tidy concertos from the early 1700s performed on period instruments. Robson does a magnificent job in exploring Albioni's long lines, allowing this formal music to sound fresh and even improvisational. Albioni's gift for melodic development is captivating, too.

Flute Concertos – Patrick Gallois (flute);
Orpheus Chamber Orch. Deutsche Grammophon 437-839

Vivaldi wrote concertos for violin, cello, oboe, flute, guitar, bassoon, and many other instruments. All are pleasant, and most are similar. These performances stand out because the Orpheus Chamber Orchestra plays with such gusto. The feeling is cheery. Gallois's flute fits the mood nicely. The inevitable imitation of a birdsong is the basis for Concerto No. 3, "Ilgardelino" (The Goldfinch). Concerto No. 1, "La tempesta di mare" (The Storm at Sea) recalls *The Four Seasons*—more of a pleasant afternoon rainfall than a tempest. Some of Vivaldi's favorite opera themes are the basis of Concerto No. 5; he often drew upon previous works to patch together new ones. Excellent sound.

LINK➤ *Antonio Vivaldi – Oboe Concerti, Vols. 1 & 2 – Stefan Schilli, Deithelm Jonas (oboes),*
others; Failoni Chamber Orch. / Béla Nagy   *NAXOS 8.550859, 60*
Choose the concertos based on your favorite instrument sound. And be sure to explore the many options available on Naxos; the Cello Concertos (8.550907, 08, 09) are also recommended.

Richard Wagner

Few artists in any field have been so consumed by the importance of themselves and their art as Richard Wagner. Born in 1813, he grew up in Leipzig, Germany, an illegimate child who enjoyed creating his own stories. Through the 1830s, he composed operas while struggling with a failing opera company; he was twice jailed for gambling debts. In the 1840s, Wagner became well known as an opera composer, and built the Dresden Opera into a respected company. By 1849, he left Germany to escape arrest (for political reasons). Safely in Switzerland, Wagner survived due to the patronage of a silk merchant (and enjoyed an affair with the merchant's wife). He moved on to father three children with Cosima von Bülow (Liszt's daughter) before convincing her husband to give up his wife. Adventures with "Mad" King Ludwig followed; together they ransacked the Bavarian treasury to build a Bayreuth concert hall devoted to Wagner's music. He died in 1882.

Der fliegende Holländer (The Flying Dutchman) – Simon Estes, soloists; Bayreuther Festspiele / Woldemar Nelsson   Philips 434-599

Wagner's first important opera is the story of a Dutch sea captain condemned to eternal wandering—unless he can secure an "ideal woman" (who represents redemption). He finds her in Senta, the daughter of another sea captain, but falsely accuses Senta of infidelity. Senta kills herself, and because she dies untainted, the Dutchman is redeemed. They travel to heaven together in the finale. This 1986 Bayreuth performance, starring an impeccably noble Simon Estes as Der Holländer is both exciting and appropriately melodramatic. Lisbeth Balslev carries the right tone for Senta's innocence, loveliness, and ultimate madness. The recording is clear on voices, but the huge sea swells of Wagner's orchestrations are sometimes congested.

LINK▶ *Richard Wagner – Der fliegende Holländer – Alfred Muff, Ingrid Haubold, others; Austrian Radio Sym. Orch. / Pinchas Steinberg*   **NAXOS 8.660026-6**
Buying low-priced operas performed by unfamiliar names is often risky, but the NAXOS name frequently assures not only quality, but a world-class performance. That's certainly the case here; Muff's Dutchman is, in many ways, superior to Estes's. A very solid choice.

Tannhäuser – P. Domingo, C. Studer; Phil. Orch. / G. Sinopoli   DG 427-625

After spending a year in the fantasy world of Venusberg, the knight Tannhäuser returns home to Wartburg, where he rejoins his friends and makes life miserable for Elizabeth, who loves him. He sings a nasty song about pleasures of the flesh; the Pope turns down his plea for redemption. Elizabeth only wants her misery to end. It does, and in the midst of her funeral, Tannhäuser dies (and drops onto her dead body), only to be forgiven by the Pope (in the original version, he simply returned to fantasyland). Domingo's unrepentant knight and Studer's suffering Elizabeth are among the best on record. Sinopoli's sensitivity lovingly enhances the storytelling.

LINK▶ *Richard Wagner – Tannhäuser –*
René Kollo, Helga Dernesch, others, Vienna PO / Sir Georg Solti   **London 414-581**
Another fine recording of the 1861 Paris version (with the first ending), well sung and well recorded in 1971. For the original version (Tannhäuser returns to Venusberg), try Wolfgang Sawallisch's 1962 recording (Philips 434-599). All three Tannhäusers are 3-CD sets.

Lohengrin – Placido Domingo, Jessye Norman, others; Vienna Phil. / Sir Georg Solti London 421-053

Our hero, an anonymous knight, shows up on a swan boat when princess Elsa is accused of murdering her brother. He defeats the evil Count Telarud. Forced to reveal his secret identity, Lohengrin says he's a knight of the Holy Grail, the son of Parsifal. The dead brother returns (he was the swan on Lohengrin's boat), Elsa dies, and Lohengrin vanishes, assisted by a dove associated with the Grail. Attentive listeners will note Wagner's increased use of motifs to establish character and situation, as well as his deepened integration of orchestra and singers in a singular creation. Domingo's Lohengrin is heroic and clear-headed. Solti's leadership is superb.

LINK➤ *Jules Massenet – Manon – Ileana Cotrubas, Alfredo Kraus, others; Toulouse Capitol Orch. / Michael Plasson* **EMI 49610**
The French Massenet employs leitmotifs as an essential storytelling element in this 1884 opera. Puccini told the same story, but Massenet's is more gripping. As expected, Plasson delivers a top-flight performance. Plasson's version of Massenet's Don Quichotte *(EMI 54767) is also excellent.*

Der Ring des Nibelungen (The Ring of the Nibelung) – Vienna Phil. Orch. / Sir Georg Solti London 455-555

For some, these four operas represent a supreme artistic achievement. Wagner studied Teutonic and Norse mythology and created a world of his own, one inhabited by remarkable creatures and monumental combinations of orchestration and song. For others, this is fairly silly, often boring stuff. Wagner frequently got his myths and legends wrong; Brünhilde comes off as comic icon of all that's ridiculous about German opera, and the stories themselves are not particularly well told. Yet Wagner's mighty force is indisputable, and his imagination is stunning. Solti's 1959 recordings are the standard; slight misgivings about stiffness are dismissed in view of the precise, often perfect creative choices (notably casting). Remastered in 1998.

LINK➤ *Johan de Meij – The Lord of the Rings (Symphony No. 1) – Ensemble Vents et Percussion de Québec / René Joly* **ATMA 2139**
In search of modern mythology, de Meij brilliantly latched on to J.R.R. Tolkien's epic adventure. It's a symphony whose movements are devoted to the wizard Gandalf, the Hobbits, and so on. Renderings of Tolkien's ideas are good, but not as clearly sketched as one might hope. (ATMA is in Québec.)

Das Rheingold (The Gold Ring) – Günter von Kannen, John Tomlinson, otheres, Orchester der Bayreuther Festspiele / Daniel Barenboim Teldec 91185

A very complicated story told through recitatives (essentially, scripted words put to music) and lacking in arias, *Das Rheingold* requires patience and suspension of critical thought. In broad strokes, the story is about gold: the Rhinemaidens guard it, Alberich (a subterranean dwarf) steals it, Wotan (king of the gods) steals it from the dwarfs, and Alberich places a curse on the gold (Wotan loses it). Along the way, Wotan builds a big new home called Valhalla (introduced by a very famous thunderbolt). A superior recording allows Barenboim's dramatic sense and Wagner's close integration of voices and orchestra to be presented very effectively. It's live, and not without stage and audience noise.

LINK➤ *Wagner – Der Ring des Nibelungen – Met. Opera / James Levine* **DG 072-522-3**
At 937 minutes in length, this VHS series captures the legendary 1990 James Levine performance for the Metropolitan Opera. The potent combination of excellent staging, superior production design, fine sound, and fine performances sets the standard. It's better still on laserdisc.

Die Walküre (The Valkyrie) — John Tomlinson, Anne Evans, others, Bayreuther Festspiele Orch. / Daniel Barenboim   Teldec 91186

Once again, fine sound and vital performances make Barenboim's recording special. Wagner's vision of a unified German theater encompassing music, acting, staging, and pyrotechnics vividly takes shape on the cycle's best opera. Valkyries are Wotan's attendants—beautiful maidens who bring slain warriors to Valhalla. The story reunites Wotan's human offspring, Siegfried (who discovers his own identity after pulling his father's magical sword from a tree) and Sieglinde, with whom he falls in love. Wotan's wife sends Brünnhilde, a valkyrie, to intervene. Siegfried dies, Sieglinde has his baby, and Brünnhilde is put to sleep. Listen for "Winterstürme" (Wintry Storms), one of Wagner's best songs, and the famous "Ride of the Valkyries."

LINK▶ *Operatic Arias – Bryn Terfel*   *Deutsche Grammophon 455-866*

You've got to respect a young singer who puts together a disc of arias he'd like to perform onstage someday. His voice is so clear and strong, and so consistently communicative and attractive, he breathes new life into oldies by Mozart, Wagner, Donizietti, Rossini, and Offenbach.

Siegfried — Wolfgang Windgassen, Birgit Nilsson, others; Vienna Phil. Orch. / Sir Georg Solti   London 414-110

Siegfried is Siegmund and Sieglinde's son. He was raised by Alberich's brother, a dwarf named Mime, for one purpose: to get the golden ring and helmet. After a long setup (this opera is also on 4 CDs, and nothing happens quickly), Siegfried slays a dragon, tastes a drop of the dragon's blood, and suddenly understands (with the help of a bird's song) that he must take the gold. He also discovers the sleeping Brünnhilde, doesn't know she's a woman (he's never seen one before), and wakes her; the two wander off to make love in a cave to end the opera. Lots of godlike thunder and quiet recitative. Fine Solti.

LINK▶ *Carl Maria von Weber – Die Freischütz (The Marksman) – Luba Orgonasova, Christine Schäfer, Erich Wottrich, others; Berlin Phil. Orch. / Nikolas Harnoncourt*
Deutsche Grammophon 415-432

A significant landmark on the road to Wagner, this 1821 work helped to establish German opera. The story of a marksman who makes a pact with dark forces to win a contest (and the maiden), it makes good use of German folk music, particularly in the choral sequences.

Götterdämmerung (Twilight of the Gods) — Wolfgang Windgassen, Brigid Nilsson, others; Bayreuther Festspiele Orch. / Karl Böhm   Philips 414-115

The happy pair leaves the cave. Brünnhilde sings a love song, and Siegfried heads off in search of adventure. Unfortunately, he finds Gibichungs and a nasty plot to nab the gold ring; Siegfried, drugged, steals it from Brünnhilde. A lot happens: Siegfried is murdered, but his corpse raises an angry hand (with the ring on a finger); Brünnhilde commits suicide in an impressive "Immolation" scene; Valhalla goes up in blazes; the Rhine floods; and the Rhinemaidens get the ring back. The best of Wagner is found in the incidental music and in two songs associated with Siegfried, "Rhine Journey" and "Funeral March." Boehm's entire 1966–67 series is equally fine.

LINK▶ *Engelbert Humperdinck – Hansel und Gretel –*
Anne Sophie von Otter, Barbara Bonney, Bavarian Radio SO / Jeffrey Tate   *EMI 54022*

A friend of Wagner's (they prepared Parsifal *for publication together) and the supplier of a name for the 1960s pop star, Humperdinck wrote just one hit opera. His sister crafted the libretto from a popular fairy tale by the brothers Grimm. It's far lighter than anything by Wagner.*

Tristan und Isolde – Wolfgang Windgassen, Birgit Nilsson;
Bayreuther Festspiele Orch. / Karl Böhm   Deutsche Grammophon 419-889

Two great voices make all the difference on this live 1966 Bayreuth Festival recording. Wagner rewrote this Irish legend very skillfully, creating a passionate love story and one of his most complete works. It's here that students study Wagner's use of motifs to express character and heart. This is probably Wagner's finest work. It's certainly his richest, with dozens of themes anticipating resolution, hot with desire, and fascinating in their beautiful interweaving and loving themes. Dramatic musical highlights on this 4-CD set (and there are many) include the simmering, then near-orgasmic Tristan-Isolde duet—left unconsummated because her intended husband shows up. The magnificent sadness and longing of the orchestral finale is genius.

LINK► *The Last Recording – Vladimir Horowitz (piano)*   **Sony Classical 45818**
Horowitz mastered both ends of the spectrum from gentility to fire, from Chopin to Liszt—and everything in-between. His spine-chilling climb toward transcendency takes place in this CD's climax: Liszt's reworking of Isolde's Liebestod from Wagner's Tristan und Isolde.

Die Meistersinger von Nürnberg (The Mastersingers of Nurenberg)–
**Ben Heppner, Cheryl Studer, others, Bayersiches Staatsorchester /
Wolfgang Sawallisch**   **EMI 55142**

Without the pretense of the Ring, this light story of Germany's Mastersinger societies goes down easy. The central figure is Hans Sachs (1494–1576), who wrote thousands of very German songs and poems. Wagner finished this piece in 1867. The story is good: the knight Walther enters a singing contest so he can win Eva's hand. He doesn't win, but he does impress Sachs, who eventually (after various plot twists and turns) teaches Walther about the Meistersinger tradition and mission (to keep German songs alive) and invites him to join his Meistersinger society. Heppner and Studer are wonderful, and the 4-CD set's 1994 digital sound is very good.

LINK► *Richard Wagner – Die Meistersinger von Nürnberg –*
Ben Heppner, Karita Mattila, others; Chi. Sym. Orch. / Sir Georg Solti   **London 452-606**
Extraordinary sound (considerably better than Sawallisch, which itself is quite good), a very fine 1995 performance (Heppner singers Walther here, too), and one of Solti's last on record. A very close call, but the intangible flow and musicality of Sawallisch's set wins by a nose.

Parsifal – Peter Hoffman, Dunja Vejzovic, others;
Berlin Phil. Orch. / Herbert von Karajan   **Deutsche Grammophon 413-347**

Just years before his death, Wagner continues his interest in the Holy Grail story. Musically, however, he moves in a new direction. This is primarily a mood piece, one that moves rather slowly unless the listener is very much on Wagner's wavelength. Its effect is cumulative, based not upon gargantuan orchestral moments and fine songs, but on chants, choral themes, and a religious feeling that ultimately results (as the Grail is raised for all to admire) in the golden glory of redemption. Wagner's reinvention of Christ as a non-Jew (perhaps the most pronounced of his Aryan fixations) is among several odd subtexts worth exploring. One of Karajan's best operas on record.

LINK► *Richard Wagner – Parsifal / Hans Knappertsbusch*   **Philips 416-390**
No conductor has so successfully captured Wagner's spiritual intent; he's supported by a splendid cast starring Jess Thomas and a good recording. Audience noises can be disruptive. Try also Barenboim's superb digital version with Siegfried Jerusalem (Teldec 74448).

William Walton

Although he was born in Oldham, England, William Walton grew up in Oxford, where, at age 10, he became a member of the Christ Church chorus. His parents both had musical backgrounds: his mother sang, and his father was a chorus master and organist. At Oxford, the young Walton became friendly with the upper-class Sitwell family. The Sitwells funded his education, and Walton lived with them periodically over the next decade at their homes in Italy and London. Walton started composing; by age 21, in 1923, he'd completed *Façade*, a clever cluster of pieces involving music and spoken word; it has remained popular through the decades. More serious accomplishment came with concertos and symphonies, film soundtracks, and *Belshazzar's Feast*, a major British choral work. After WW II, Walton married and moved to Ischia, an island near Naples. He continued composing through the early 1960s and died in 1983.

Belshazzar's Feast – Bryn Terfel, others;
Bournemouth Sym. Orch. / Andrew Litton   London 448-134
Several horn blasts give way to a small male chorus, and then a larger one with mixed voices. Economical arrangements highlight very specific sounds, generating an impressive stage for baritone Terfel; the extraordinary clarity of this recording allows a beautiful chorus and orchestra to shine. Walton completed this exhilirating biblical chorus in 1931. "Praise ye the god of gold" is one of many examples of the work's uniqueness: sections of the chorus soar while a brassy band and odd percussion suggest the golden riches. The constant rhythm that underscores the chorale finale is joyful noise, indeed. Two additional works fill the1995 recording: Suite from *Henry V* and *Crown Imperial* ("Coronation March").

LINK▶ *(Cello works)–Raphael Wallfisch (cello), Peter Wallfisch (piano)   Chandos 8499*
Four British pieces for cellos, from various times over the past century; ultimately, this father-son performance (Raphael is the son) is a study of how Walton, Delius, Arnold Bax, Frank Bridge composed for the most fundamental of instruments. Wonderful sound.

Violin Concerto, Symphony No. 2 –
Tasmin Little (violin), Bournemouth Sym. Orch. / Andrew Litton   London 444-114
Walton created his 1939 Violin Concerto for virtuoso Jascha Heifetz. Ms. Little generates precisely the right dreamlike mood for its opening sections. She gazes, perhaps nostalgically, with the refined accompaniment of a lovely orchestra. Walton requires a more athletic workout for soloist and symphonists in an ultimately delicate second movement that periodically dances formally and blasts furiously. The third movement relies on pretty lyricism and also shows off some bravura. Walton's Second Symphony, from 1960 (he worked slowly, and missed a deadline by three years) is energetic and bombastic, but with rich hues and romantic, cunning melodies worked out by small groups of strings or winds. State-of-the-art 1994 engineering.

LINK▶ *William Walton – Cello Concerto, Symphony No. 1 –*
Robert Cohen (cello), Bournemouth Sym. Orch. / Andrew Litton   *London 443-450*
The companion CD. The Cello Concerto, written for Piatigorsky in 1956, is sparsely accompanied, allowing the soloist's delicious colors to shine through. Walton's First Symphony, completed in 1935, nods to Sibelius (an influence), but combines British majesty with bombast.

Kurt Weill

Weill is one of very few composers whose work has been successful in the concert hall, opera house, Broadway stage, and jukebox. Born a cantor's son in 1900, Weill received the very best musical training; his teachers included Busoni and Humperdinck. Early on, he was heavily influenced by Wagner, Mahler, and Schoenberg, and became known as an opera composer. Playwright Berthold Brecht became a collaborator; together, they created operas and stage plays, notably 1928's *Die Dreigroschenoper* (The Threepenny Opera). In 1933, after the Nazis had discouraged his audiences with propanda and staged rioting, Weill fled Germany with his wife, Lotte Lenya. The couple first went to Paris, and then came to the U.S. While working in NYC, Weill became one of Broadway's top composers. His collaborators included Moss Hart, Langston Hughes, Alan Jay Lerner, and Ira Gershwin. Despite a high-end reputation, many projects were produced, notably 1949's anti-apartheid *Lost in the Stars*.

Die Dreigoschenoper (The Threepenny Opera) –
René Kollo, Ute Lemper; Berlin RAIS Orch. / John Mauceri   London 430-015

Composed between the wars, when many Germans were satisfied with what appeared to be an acceptable status quo, Weill, with partners Berthold Brecht and Elisabeth Hauptman, shined a cabaret's glaring footlights on the seedier side of life. It is the story of Macheath, a theiving murderer who marries Polly Peachum. Her mother bribes Jenny, a prostitute, to turn him in. The police chief's daughter, Lucy Brown, helps Macheath escape; he's caught and killed. Mack emerges as a national hero. The music is spectacular, stylish, spirited, and often familiar. "Mack the Knife" has been popular for 70 years, but don't miss "Ballad of the Good Life" and others.

LINK➤ *Ernst Krenek – Jonny spielt auf (Jonny Plays On) – Heinz Kruse, Alessandra Marc, Krister St. Hill, others; Leipzig Opera Chorus & Orch. / Lother Zagrosek   London 436-631
Krenek's 1926 opera was among the first to employ jazz, but overall, the work lacks the impact and immediacy of Weill's opera. Still, it's worth the investment to hear the committed performances of Alessandra Marc and Krister St. Hill, whose instincts for Krenek's ideas are excellent.*

The Seven Deadly Sins (Die Sieben Todsünden) –
Lotte Lenya   SONY Classical 63222

The grotesque cover art is more severe than the vocal treatments. In fact, Lenya is smoother and more refined in the details of her acting, providing a crystal passage to Weill's intent. The first nine tracks come from a 1956 performance of *Seven Deadly Sins* (with four other voices); Lenya plays the two sides of Anna's personality as she struggles with Sloth, Pride, Anger, and so on. Next are three songs from *Die Dreigroschenoper*, sung by one of its finest interpreters. And then, three more from *Aufsteig und Fall der Stadt Mahagonny*, including "Alabama-song." (Lenya's performance is a revelation.) Other stunning highlights include "Surabaya Johnny" and songs from *Berlin Requiem* and *Der Silbersee*.

LINK➤ *Ute Lemper – Berlin Cabaret Songs – Matrix Ensemble   London 452-849
"Fall in love but after kissing, check your purse to see what's missing" is typical of the cynicism of these smart (and cheeky) songs from the 1920s and 1930s. Composers include Berthold Goldschmidt, Mischa Spoliansky, and other lesser knowns. Lemper's absolutely devasting style sells it all.*

Stratas Sings Weill   SONY Classical 44529

Somewhere between opera, art song, cabaret, and Broadway lives the Weill song. And among contemporary vocalists, no one gets under the skin of Weill's seedy-side view with more snake-like effectiveness than Teresa Stratas. She establishes her attitude early with the first cut, "I'm a Stranger Here Myself," but finds perfection on "Surabaya Johnny," Weill's famous story of a ne'er-do-well seaman loved by a desperate woman who can't help herself. It's sung in German; other songs are sung in English or French. "Lonely House," from *Street Scene*, is one of the finest loneliness songs ever written. With the Y Chamber Orchestra led by Gerard Schwarz.

LINK➤ *Hanns Eisler – Songs – Dietrich Fischer-Dieskau*   Teldec 43676
Early in his career, Eisler was Schoenberg's student, but developed his own ideas about bringing music to the people. Political songs, with lyrics by Bertholt Brecht, became his medium. Also worth tracking down is "Tank Battles," sung by Dagmar Krause (Antilles 8739).

Lost in the Stars: The Music of Kurt Weill   A&M 5104

As the writer of music like "Alabama Song," ("Oh, show us the way to the next whisky bar; oh, don't ask why . . ."), Weill has been popular with rock stars and other cultural troublemakers for decades. This quintessential tribute album, produced by Hal Willner in 1985, presents Weill's opera music in a most accessible, frequently beautiful way. Jazz musicians Carla Bley and Phil Woods are featured in an instrumental "Lost in the Stars"; Sting and Dominic Muldowney do "The Ballad of Mac the Knife"; Marianne Faithfull and Chris Spedding are surprisingly effective and decadent on "Ballad of the Soldier's Wife." Other contributors include John Zorn, Henry Threadgill, Van Dyke Parks, Todd Rundgren, Aaron Neville, and Tom Waits.

LINK➤ *Kurt Weill – September Songs – Various Artists*   SONY Classical 63046
The 1997 sequel, a soundtrack to a television film. Lou Reed returns for a performance of "September Song." Older recordings brought back to life include Lotte Lenya's "Pirate Jenny." Betty Carter does "Lonely House." Many fine moments, but the A&M original is far superior.

Street Scene – Kristine Ciesinski, Janis Kelly, others;
Orch. & Chorus of English Nat.Opera / Carl Davis   Jay 21185

A complete recording of the 1996 London Cast (146 minutes on two CDs), this production gets to the heart of immigrant life in NYC during a very hot summer earlier in the century. With lyrics by Langston Hughes and a book by Elmer Rice, this is outstanding theater. There's no libretto, but the story is easy to follow because the spoken dialogue is included. Accents are essential to the characters; European accents are fine, but English actors trying to sound "New Yawk" are sometimes slightly off. No matter. The songs are splendid, from stagey tunes like to "Wouldn't You Like to Be on Broadway," and "Moon-Faced, Starry-Eyed" to more serious numbers like "Lonely Town."

LINK➤ *The World So Wide –*
Dawn Upshaw; Orchestra of St. Luke's / David Zinman   Nonesuch 79458
Every Upshaw recital CD is a surprise package. This one, from 1998, includes "Lonely House" from Street Scene, and also "Ain't It a Pretty Night" from Carlisle Floyd's opera, Susannah. Samuel Barber, Leonard Bernstein, and John Adams are represented, as is Tania León.

Anonymous 4

The Anonymous 4 are Johanna Maria Rose, Susan Hellauer, Ruth Cunningham, and Marsha Genensky. The NYC-based a capella quartet was formed in 1986, at first as an experiment. The woman were curious about the effect of higher female voices on medieval chant and polyphonic music. Clearly, the formula worked, first at St. Michael's Church in NYC (which continues to be their home base), then on record, then in concerts worldwide; aided by a general public receptivity to medieval chants, the Anonymous 4 became one of the best-selling classical groups the 1990s. Prior to forming the group, Rose worked in visual arts and theater; Genensky was a folk singer; Cunningham performed on baroque flute and recorder; and Hellauer played antique brass instruments. The group gets its name from a name assigned by scholars to a thirteenth-century British journalist who described the innovative music being made in Paris around 1270.

An English Ladymass   Harmonia Mundi 907080

This 1992 release secured the a capella group"s future in the classical record business. It featuares 13th- and 14th-century chant performed with enthusiasm, insight, and inspiring beauty. Only a trained ear will recognize the stylish distinctions between polyphonic songs, sequences, and song (and other related forms); each seems a rich, dark, medieval harmonic experience, presented by voices possessing otherworldy magic. A Ladymass, incidentally, was said daily at the Lady Chapel of the Salisbury Cathedral. It was dedicated, as most Ladymasses were, to the Virgin Mary. The liner notes explain the various types of songs, and their role in the Mass.

LINK➤ *Carlo Gesualdo – Tenebrae – The Hilliard Ensemble*   **ECM New Series 21422**
Flawless recording of six male a cappella voices singing 400-year-old sacred music. At first, this 2-CD set sounds like the same idea over and over again (the liner notes provide lyrics, but the commentary is obtuse). Very fine performance.

Hildegard von Bingen: 11,000 Virgins   Harmonia Mundi 907200

This story probably begins before the fifth century, when a British princess led a pilgrimage of 11,000 devout Virgins to Rome. Ursala was martyred when she refused the Huns, near present-day Cologne, Germany. Hildegard von Bingen was a talented 12th-century nun who was a mystic, healer, herbalist, writer, poet, and composer of sacred songs for her convent. Here, seven of Von Bingen's works are part of a medieval Mass by Karlsruhe LX, Arweil Antiphoner, and others. The program simulates a liturgy that might have been performed with the utmost solemnity at Von Bingen's convent near Cologne. The scholarship is very impressive. Recorded in 1997.

LINK➤ *Jewish Masterworks of the Synagogue Liturgy –*
Hazzan Steven C. Burke, Cantor Elizabeth S. Berke; Madrigalchor der Hochschule
für Musik in München   **Deutsche Harmonia Mundi (BMG) 77388**
Recorded to celebrate the re-establishment of Liberal Judaism in Germany, this collection of Jewish songs of celebration and ritual, heard mostly (but not exclusively) during temple services, provides an essential view on the history of religious music. Gcod 1996 recording.

Maria Callas

Cecilia Sofia Anna Maria Kalogeropoulous was born in NYC in 1923. At age 14, she moved to Greece with her sister and mother. In 1942, Callas made her professional debut at the Athens Opera as Tosca. She returned to the U.S. in 1944, but finding work was difficult. After many disappointments, she finally attracted some attention in a 1947 Verona, Italy, performance of *La Gioconda*. The conductor was Tullio Serafin, who became a great friend and supporter. Over the next five years, Callas emerged as one of the busiest and finest singers in the opera world. By the early 1960s, however, she was slowing down. Callas's personal life began overtaking her art; she entered into an unhappy marriage with G.B. Meneghini in 1949 and next joined the world-class jet-set. Callas left her husband in 1959 for Aristotle Onassis, who years later unceremoniously dumped her for the former Jacqueline Kennedy. Callas died alone in Paris in 1977.

La Divina
EMI 65746

This 4-CD boxed set offers two advantages over the three *La Divina* single CDs (EMI 54702, 55016, 55216). First, there's more music. Second, there's a glamorous book that details Callas's extraordinary life. Make the investment; Callas was a magical figure. In a collection such as this, nearly every selection is a highlight. Many are pinnacles of twentieth-century opera. For marvelous vocal calisthenics, several stunning examples of soprano song will amaze even those who are reluctant to spend time listening to opera; one of many examples is "Una voce pop fa" from Rossini's *The Barber of Seville*, which Callas recorded with Tuilio Serafin in 1955. Callas was much more than a voice; she was a splendid interpreter. And when she casts her spell on "Un bel di, vedremo" from Puccini's *Madame Butterfly*, or "Donde lieta uscì" from *La Boheme*, everything else in the room seems to disappear from view. Callas is captivating. Romance is her strong suit, but she reflects her real-life steel (in legendary arguments with opera directors, for example) on "O don fatale" from Verdi's *Don Carlos*. Callas also performed the mad scenes well, as the 1959 excerpt from Donizetti's *Lucia di Lammermoor* demonstrates. For Bizet, she was also a bold Carmen. In fact, one of the best features of this set is the diversity of characters Callas successfully portrayed, and the range of composers whose work she performed. There's an abundance of Puccini here and some Verdi, but also work by Gluck, Saint-Saëns, and Bellini. CD4 contains 1967 and 1968 interviews with Edward Downs.

LINK➤ *The Essential Leontyne Price – Leontyne Price (soprano)*   **RCA 68153**
Price sailed smoothly into the high Cs, acted nearly as well as she sang, and set the standard for Verdi roles, for Carmen, and for a long list of others. One of the top sopranos of the 1960s, this 11-CD set is decidedly not overdoing it. Shy? Try RCA 68883 (which collectors nicknamed "the blue album") or any of the 2-CD excerpts from this box.

Vladimir Horowitz

One of the century's greatest pianists, Horowitz grew up in Kiev, Russia. Born in 1903, he began his studies with his mother, a musician. Serious professional studies began at age 15 with Felix Blumenfeld; performances began two years later in Kiev, Moscow, and Leningrad. By age 21, Horowitz was a star. He performed in Berlin, Hamburg, and Paris. He made his Carnegie Hall debut in 1928. Horowitz first performed with Arturo Toscanini in 1933; during rehearsals, he met Toscanini's daughter, Wanda, who later became his wife. Horowitz became a U.S. citizen in 1942; a short time later, he raised $11 million for war bonds in a single performance. By 1953, Horowitz had slowed down, taking time for himself and his own studies. After returning to public life in 1965, he selectively recorded and performed, often for television. The 1985 film, *The Last Romantic*, reawakened public interest in Horowitz's long career and special gifts. He died quietly in NYC in 1989.

Live at Carnegie Hall   CBS Masterworks 44681
A historical return to live performances after a 12-year absence, the first of these concerts was a landmark event in 20th-century music history. Horowitz delivers with intelligence, passion, maturity, and gentility; his performance of Bach's Toccata in C Major, which begins the May 9, 1965, concert, is worth the price of this 3-CD set. (Horowitz had opened his 1928 U.S. debut concert at Carnegie Hall with this piece.) The other two concerts, from 1966 and 1968, measure the heart of the piano repertoire. Chopin plays a significant role; also included are two noble Scriabin etudes, two versions of Schumann's *Träumerei*, and a smattering of Liszt, Mozart, and Scarlatti. Simply beautiful work.

LINK▶ *Vladimir Horowitz – The Private Collection, Vols. 1 & 2*   **RCA 62643, 62644**
It's easy to ignore the slight surface noise on these 1945-1950 Carnegie Hall performances, for these may be Horowitz's finest hours: works by Chopin, Liszt, Clementi, and Poulenc make for a wider variety than on later recordings. Very carefully restored by a top RCA producer.

The Studio Recordings: New York 1985   Deutsche Grammophon 419-217
Horowitz continues to mine the work of his favorite composers—Schumann, Scarlatti, Liszt, Scriabin, and Schubert share his billing on the front cover—but the stature and ease of his interpretations have transformed the music into his own. Horowitz's mastery is complete. He is 82 years old. By his own reckoning, he no longer plays Schumann's *Kreislerana* too quickly; Horowitz now appreciates colors that can be observed only with a milder pace. He recaptures the romance of Vienna in Schubert's *Impromptu*. Scarlatti is a particular favorite; one can feel Horowitz smiling as he dances through a pair of the composer's sonatas. With Schubert's *Military March*, Horowitz musters a powerful finale, too.

LINK▶ *Vladimir Horowitz – Horowitz in Moscow*   **Deutsche Grammophon 419-499**
A promising young pianist, Horowitz left his home in Kiev in 1925; this 1986 concert at the Moscow Conservatory was the first time he had played in Russia in 60 years. The performances are fabulous, and the emotions are palpable.

Kronos Quartet

One of the most important groups of the twentieth century, the Kronos Quartet consistently commissions new works and breaks down perceived barriers among such artists as Shostakovich, Howlin' Wolf, and Hamza El Din. Violinist David Harrington founded the group in Seattle in 1973; after a two-year residency at SUNY Geneseo, the quartet settled in San Francisco. By 1978, the ensemble featured Hank Dutt on viola, John Sherba and Harrington on violin, and Joan Jeanrenaud on cello. By the early 1980s, the Kronos Quartet was a fixture in the Bay Area; the group signed with Nonesuch in 1985. Extensive touring, multimedia stage shows, radio programs, and the start of a long relationship with producer Judith Sherman (who shared the quartet's Grammy nomination for *White Man Sleeps*) established the quartet's worldwide reputation for excellence and imagination. The group's enormous list of collaborators includes Dawn Upshaw, Foday Musa Suso, Wu Man, and the Throat Singers of Tuva.

25 Years   Nonesuch 79394

The versatility of the Kronos Quartet is stunning: here's a classical quartet at home with Ken Benshoef's hardcore klezmer, and Astor Piazzolla's street-smart tango, and with the widest possible range of 20th-century composers (whose works aren't often performed by other chamber groups). The emphasis here is on those composers, and not on the eclectic or international. This ten-CD set is generally organized by composer, so that Morton Feldman, Philip Glass, Henryk Górecki, Arvo Pärt, Terry Riley, and Alfred Schnittke each get their own CDs; another is shared by Steve Reich and George Crumb, and another is dominated by Kevin Volans. To hear Morton Feldman's 70-minute Piano and String Quartet elegantly and sensitively performed—and perfectly recorded—is the kind of extraordinary experience that only the Kronos Quartet seems to provide. It must have been difficult to whittle down the repertoire to just ten CDs; every performance leaves the listener wanting more. This is certainly true of Philip Glass and his four string quartets on CD4. The texture and depth of Osvaldo Golijov's *The Dreams and Prayers of Isaac the Blind* is revelatory: it's a smear of tango, klezmer clarinet, tragedy, and ancient drama. With eight of the ten CDs occupied by "serious" modern composers, this panorama obscures as much as it displays. For a clearer view of the Kronos Quartet's offerings, this 10-CD set should be supplemented by the 2-CD collection *Kronos Released 1985-1995* (79394) also recommended here.

LINK➤ *Otto Luening – American Masters – Sinnhoffer Quartet, others*   **CRI 716**
Luening's development spans three-quarters of the 20th century. The CD begins with a fairly traditional, albeit slightly atonal, quartet from 1928, but 1962's Trio for Flute, Cello and Piano *seems to derive humor from overtly modern tendencies. The engineering is exquisite.*

Kronos Released: 1985-1995

Nonesuch 79394

Although each of the Kronos Quartet's dozen or so releases is unique and should be heard in full, this 1995 set is a useful table of contents for a spectacular catalog. Among CD1's highlights is "Mai Nozipo," a string quartet beautifully interwoven with African percussion (from 1992's *Pieces of Africa* [Nonesuch 79275]). "Asleep" is a tango played with Astor Piazzolla playing his bandoneon (from 1991's *Five Tango Sensations* [Nonesuch 79254]). In 1994, the Kronos Quartet released *Night Prayers* (Nonesuch 79346), a world music celebration filled with interesting collaborations; "A Cool Wind Is Blowing," with Armenian dudek virtuoso Djivan Gasparian, hints at the complete album's dreamy-eyed delights. The Kronos Quartet is one of the few popular classical groups with modern works in its repertoire: George Crumb, Terry Riley, Phillip Glass, and Steve Reich are represented here. There's also a heartfelt rendition of Samuel Barber's "Adagio," a more traditionally classical piece from 1988's *Winter Was Hard* (Nonesuch 79181). The second CD contains just four tracks, all previously unreleased. "Dinner Music for a Pack of Hungry Cannibals," by Raymond Scott, seems to combine swing music, wacky cartoon soundtrack styles, and chamber music. Michael Daugherty's "Elvis Everywhere" is an entertaining pop culture pastiche. The jewel on CD2, however, is the Kronos Quartet's highly regarded chamber version of Jimi Hendrix's "Purple Haze." The piece is done not as a gimmick, but rather as serious, modern, rocking chamber music complete with violins simulating electric guitar distortions and similar effects.

LINK➤ *Muzsikás – Máramaros: The Lost Jewish Music of Transylvania – Hannibal 1373*
Outstanding folk quartet music performed by a meticulous Hungarian quartet. The roots of the quartet are here; music like this inspired Bartók in his innovations. The group's enthusiasm is infectious, and their performances are spectacular. Terrific sound quality, too.

Black Angels

Nonesuch 79242

With a shattering shriek of electric insects at its start, George Crumb's *Black Angels* is likely to frighten away most casual listeners. This is "Threnody I," the start of a modern, terrifying report inspired by the Vietnam War. Threatening, dark, curious, sometimes Asian sounds blast color onto a rusty canvas. Even the most conservative listeners will find genius in "God-music," which recalls 19th-century music, and "Ancient Voices," which follows. This is music worth exploring, with patience and without expectation. It's intelligently supported by Thomas Tallis's *Spem in Alium* (Sing and Glorify) from the 16th century, Shostakovich's Eighth Quartet, and a positive, uplifting, somewhat patriotic piece by Charles Ives. From 1990, this is arguably the best Kronos CD.

LINK➤ *Kronos Quartet – White Man Sleeps*   **Nonesuch 79613**
The music here is quite varied in style and includes South African Kevin Volans's White Man Sleeps #1, a scherzo by Charles Ives, Ornette Coleman's "Lonely Woman," a Bartók quartet, and the group's stylized version of "Amazing Grace."

Yo-Yo Ma

Cellist Yo-Yo Ma was born in Paris in 1955. He began his studies with his father at age 4, but his time with Leonard Rose at NYC's Juilliard School set the course for his professional life. Ma's relationship with Juilliard began in 1962, but his scholastic experience was broadened by a Harvard major in humanities. By 1978 Ma was a respected young musician and winner of the Avery Fisher Prize. When he was awarded the Edison Prize in 1986, the jury's analysis of his talent was wholly accurate: "this ability to give the listener the feeling that he has always underestimated the merits of the work in question." Ma has brought enthusiasm to all sorts of music and performance formats, from Bach's cello sonatas (visualized in various settings for television) to the music of Appalachia; from Tanglewood to *Sesame Street*. His exploration of new material and his proficiency with the old makes him an inspiring role model for modern musicians.

Made in America   SONY Classical 53126

Four distinctively American composers are represented on the best of Ma's excursions into twentieth-century repertoire. Leonard Bernstein's Clarinet Sonata is rescored for lead cello (Bernstein introduced the 7-year-old Ma to American television audiences). The sonata was a student composition, but in Ma's hands, its meandering lines and jazz tinge are transformed into a piece worth hearing. The piece is played as a duet with pianist Jeffrey Kahane. Leon Kirchner's *Triptych* comes from 1988; it's fun to listen to Ma and violinist Lynn Chang coax a challenging range of unusual colors and textures from their instruments. Three Gershwin Preludes are also a complete delight. A lively Ives trio completes one of Ma's best CDs. From 1993.

LINK➤ *Appalachia Waltz – Yo-Yo Ma (cello), Edgar Meyer (bass), Mark O'Connor (fiddle)*
SONY Classical 68460
This piece is neither classical, nor bluegrass, but rather something in between. Fine performances by two classical musicians (Ma and bassist Edgar Meyer) and the versatile fiddler Mark O'Connor. It's a lot of fun. For a more seriously classical view of Ma's talents, try Portrait of Yo-Yo Ma *(44796).*

The New York Album
(with Baltimore Sym. Orch. / David Zinman)
SONY Classical 57961

Not quite as modern and considerably more serious than the *Made in America* CD, this 1994 release features Ma as soloist in front of a very attentive orchestra. He performs three difficult pieces. The program begins with Concerto for Cello and Orchestra, composed by Stephen Albert (1941–1992). It's a triumphant merging of three cello themes. The work seems to struggle with emotional challenges, intelligently considers alternatives, and finds its way to resolutions. Béla Bartók's Concerto for Viola and Orchestra was not originally written for cello, but Ma makes this reality seem dubious. It's very skillfully played. Ernest Bloch's *Schelomo: A Hebrew Rhapsody for Cello and Orchestra* closes the CD.

LINK➤ *Stephen Albert – River Run – Nat. Sym. Orch. / Mstislav Rostropovich*   **Delos 1016**
Winner of the 1985 Pulitzer Prize, this symphony is representative of Albert's talent for emotionally charged contemporary music communicated with the elegance of 19th-century orchestral styles. Also try Intro Eclipse *(New World 381) and watch for new recordings.*

Luciano Pavarotti

The greatest Italian tenor of our times was born in Modena, Italy, in 1935. With the encouragement of a father who often sang in the chorus of a local opera house, young Pavarotti considered a career in music education, before deciding to become a professional opera singer. At age 23, Pavarotti debuted as Rodolfo in *La Bohème*; six years later, he sang at Covent Garden as a replacement for an ailing Giuseppe di Stefano. Appearances at the Glyndeborne Festival followed. Pavarotti's reputation grew during the 1960s; by the 1970s, a series of Italian opera recordings with Joan Sutherland had solidified his place as one of opera's finest voices. During this time Pavarotti became known as the "King of the High C's." Deeper roles, like Pagliacci, have come with maturity. In the 1980s and 1990s, Pavarotti has used his fame to encourage music education on a worldwide scale. He's also been a central figure in many high-visibility charity ventures.

Tutto Pavarotti   London 425-681

The best of a great many opera collections starring Pavarotti, this 2-CD set from 1989 gets the balance right. It's also budget priced. Although the program encompasses the years from 1968 to 1988, most of the tracks come from the 1970s, when Pavarotti's voice was graced with the best possible combination of vigor, expressiveness, and experience. Pavarotti is absolutely marvelous singing Ernesto's "Com'è gentil" on 1970's *Don Pasquale*, and commanding as Radamès on "Celeste Aida" from 1972. When he sings quietly and sadly, the world spins a little more slowly; Pavarotti's "Una furtiva lagrima" from Donizetti's *L'elisir d'amore* demonstrates the expanse of his vocal range and power. Just about every opera favorite by Pavarotti is included here, from 1971's "La donna è mobile" from *Rigoletto* to 1972's "Vesti la giubba" from Leoncavallo's *Pagliacci* (one of Pavarotti's finest roles). His rendition of "Nessun dorma" from *Turandot* is also a defining moment in modern opera. And while opera arias predominate, the collection begins with eight beloved songs. Pavarotti does a fine job with "'O sole mio" and "'A vuccella." And he's not shy about dabbling in Italian show-biz songs, like the sentimental "Mamma" (arranged by Henry Mancini) and "Caruso," a moody recreation of this century's early years, composed for a motion picture. Still, opera is the heart and soul of this collection. When Pavarotti unleashes "Dai campi, dai prati" from Boito's *Mephistofele*, or of "Addio alla madre" from Mascagni's *Cavalleria Rusticana*, he demands undivided attention. A beautiful set.

LINK➤ *Pavarotti in Hyde Park – Luciano Pavarotti*   London 436-320

By the 1990s, Pavarotti had become a major figure in the "opera as show business" domain; he was one of the Three Tenors; this large-scale outdoor concert was also a television special and a successful home video. It's good, but Pavarotti is better on Tutto Pavarotti.

Itzhak Perlman

Violist Itzhak Perlman was born in Tel Aviv, Israel, in 1945. He learned quickly and steadily as a child, and by age 10 was performing regularly in public. An apperance on the *Ed Sullivan Show* in 1958 led to study at New York's Juilliard School. Perlman debuted in Carnegie Hall in 1963. Honors followed, and have continued throughout his career. Perlman became a popular soloist throughout the classical world. In chamber settings, Perlman did some of his best work with Pinchas Zukerman (viola), Lynn Harrell (cello), and Vladimir Ashkenazy (piano). Travels behind the Iron Curtain resulted in the documentary *Perlman in Russia*, which won a 1992 Emmy Award. Perlman has given his time generously to causes related to the handicapped; he has also participated in many children's educational efforts (notably *Sesame Street*) and Jewish goodwill efforts. In recent years, Perlman has become quite fond of klezmer music; his fame has focused attention on this Eastern European form of jazz.

The Art of Itzhak Perlman   EMI 64617

This 4-CD set covers much of Perlman's finest work. It covers roughly twenty-five years, from the early 1970s to the early 1990s (the set was released in 1993). The discs are organized, more or less, by styles of music. CD1 presents Perlman doing the standard violin repertoire with an emphasis on the Romantic. He's astonishing in terms of both technique and expressiveness on Bach's Partita 3. And in combination with chamber players Ray Still (oboe), Pinchas Zukerman (violin), and Lynn Harrell (cello), he's lighter than air on Mozart's Oboe Quartet in F. His duet with pianist Vladimir Ashkenazy on Brahms's Violin Sonata No. 3 showcases extraordinary technique (from both musicians), and a warm, tender love of the music. CD2 and CD3 are about concertos—the perfect balance between Perlman the soloist and a symphony orchestra. Christian Sinding's Suite for Violin and Orchestra was performed by Jascha Heifitz when Perlman was a child; Perlman never forgot it. And Perlman performed Wieniaski's Concerto No. 1 at his Carnegie Hall debut. CD2 is completed by a Sibelius concerto. CD3 concentrates on the modern: Khachaturian, Korngold (a particularly good Violin Concerto in D), and Stravinsky. The many shorter pieces on CD4 show Perlman's wide-ranging interests, and his lighter side. He plays "My Yiddishe Momma," Stephen Foster's "The Old Folks at Home," Scott Joplin's "The Rag-Time Dance," Fritz Kreisler's "Liebefreud" and "Liebesleid," and then ties it all up with a virtuoso showcase: Pablo Sarasate's "Carmen Fantasy." A wonderful collection.

LINK➤ *Ernest Bloch – Schelomo – Ofra Harnoy (cello);*
London Phil. Orch. / Sir Charles Mackerras   **RCA 60757**
Based on music heard in Jewish temple services, Bloch's Schelemo *(1916) is paired with another great work in the Hebrew classical repertoire, Max Bruch's 1881* Kol Nidrei, *as well as four other Bruch selections (including* Ave Maria). *Beautiful heartfelt performances.*

Photo & Graphic Credits

Thanks to these record companies for the use of CD cover art. Page numbers follow each credit.

Arabesque Recordings: 106
BMG Classics:(RCA) 14, 17, 36, 45, 50, 64, 72, 76, 98, 138, 141, 144, 147, 161, 166, 182
©Deutsche Grammophon Gesellschaft mbH: 15, 21, 57, 77, 101, 102, 131, 158, 185
EMI Classics: 2, 9, 25, 29, 40, 55, 62, 66, 94, 95, 112, 122, 130, 142, 158,167, 170, 174, 180, 194
Erato: 33, 129
Harmonia Mundi usa: 135, 152
Naxos of America: 35, 63, 79, 84, 104, 119, 145, 184
New World: 165
Nonesuch Records: 196
Philips Music Group: 53, 153, 171, 177
Courtesy of Sony Classical: 12, 31, 32, 37, 44, 47, 48, 49, 58, 60, 78, 81, 83, 90, 99, 149, 157, 198
Telarc: 3, 9, 61, 67, 68, 96, 111, 114, 116, 143, 178
Virgin Classics: 39, 120, 128

We also thank the following photographers, artists, composers, and organizations who supplied photographs for use in this book.

David Tägtström, Svensk Musik/Swedish Music Information Center: 4
Sir Malcolm Arnold, CBE; the Malcolm Arnold Society: 6
Karel Husa: 88
Weill-Lenya Research Center, New York: 191
Christian Steiner/Harmonia Mundi usa: 193

Index of Linked Artists

More books in this series:

The JAZZ CD Listener's Guide
(ISBN 0-8230-7662-8)
The WORLD MUSIC CD Listener's Guide
(ISBN 0-8230-7663-6)
The BLUES CD Listener's Guide
(ISBN 08230-7675-X)
Each is written by Howard J. Blumenthal, published by Billboard Books, and available at your local bookseller.